Presidential Government
in Gaullist France

Presidential Government in Gaullist France

A STUDY OF EXECUTIVE–LEGISLATIVE RELATIONS
1958–1974

WILLIAM G. ANDREWS

State University of New York
College at Brockport

State University of New York Press ALBANY

To Scott, my severest critic

Published by
State University of New York Press, Albany

Printed in the United States of America

For information, address State University of New York
Press, State University Plaza, Albany, N.Y., 12246

Contents

Preface

This book comes neither to bury de Gaulle nor to praise him. It neither attacks nor defends the governmental system he founded. Rather, it seeks to understand and explain.

Understanding is sought by presenting a substantial amount of information on the original design of the regime, its practice in law making, and the personnel and structure of its political executive. Much of the material has been rendered into statistical form to increase precision. It focuses on the executive–legislative relationship in the formulation of legislation. Its general import is to correct the exaggerated perception of overwhelming executive dominance that has marked so much of the literature on that topic since 1958.

Explanation is offered through interpretation of the intentions of the framers of the 1958 constitution, practice in the regime and changes in French society, and by comparison with selected Western democratic political systems. The constitution is shown to have been solidly parliamentary in design. Practice appears to have moved toward presidentialism. French society is described as having evolved very significantly from fragmentation toward cohesion between 1946 and 1962. Comparison of democratic regimes in Great Britain, Germany, and France suggests that more cohesive societies have more presidential governmental systems, tending to confirm that explanation for the French case.

This study began in 1973–74 with the aid of a sabbatical leave from Brockport and a National Endowment for the Humanities senior fellowship. It has accumulated many debts as it lumbered slowly along. The research and writing for the first draft were done at the libraries of the *Institut d'études politiques*, the *Documentation française*, and the National Assembly in Paris and the Assembly's statistical services, with much help from their hospitable staffs. Two of the chapters were completed during three-week stays in Paris in the summers of 1975 and 1977 with the assistance of grants-in-aid from the SUNY Research Foundation's University Awards Program. Another chapter was written and the final revisions on the book were made during a Spring 1981 sabbatic. The other chapters were completed during time snatched away from administrative and teaching responsibilities with the benevolent acquiescence of Brockport's former president, Albert W. Brown; its academic vice presidents, especially Ralph Gennarino and Vera King Farris; and my department chairman, Harold Rakov.

Earlier versions of four chapters were presented as papers at annual meetings of the American Political Science Association, the International Studies Association, a triennial congress of the International Political Science Association, and at the 1978 Brockport Conference on the Fifth French Republic. They benefited greatly from the comments of the other panelists. Also very helpful were the reviews by readers for the SUNY Press. In particular, I want to thank Nicholas A. Wahl, Gerhard Loewenberg, John Ambler, Ezra Suleiman, Stanley Hoffmann, and my colleague, Henry L. Bretton.

So many typists' fingers helped prepare the manuscript that I have lost track. The most substantial contributions were made by Shirley Schuff, Barbara Duffy, Chris Charge, and Gladys Preston. Especially, I want to thank my dear friend, Bonnie Kennedy, for pitching in with volunteer help when a deadline was hard at hand. On the other hand, I had no research assistance on this project at all.

William G. Andrews

Brockport, N.Y.

Key to Abbreviations

AN   *Assemblée nationale*, National Assembly.

CC   *Conseil constitutionnel*, Constitutional Council, nine-member body with limited authority to adjudicate certain disputes over constitutional and parliamentary procedures and electoral regularity and to decide some matters of presidential succession.

CCC   *Comité Constitutionnel Consultatif*, Consultative Constitutional Commission. The group, composed mainly of members of the 1956 parliament, that reviewed the initial draft of the 1958 Constitution.

CDU   *Christlich demokratische union*, Christian Democratic Union (of West Germany).

CE   *Conseil d'Etat*, Council of State, the highest body in the professional civil service, including a tribunal for the adjudication of complaints against governmental action.

CE   *Recueil des décisions du Conseil d'Etat, Collected decisions of the Council of State*, the official publication of the findings and opinions of that tribunal.

CFTC   *Confédération française des travailleurs chrêtiens*, French Confederation of Christian Workers, the Catholic trade union confederation of the Fourth and early Fifth Republic. It split in 1964, the majority becoming the CFDT, the minority continuing under the old name.

CGC	*Confédération générale des cadres*, General Confederation of White Collar Workers, the largest trade union federation for office workers.
CGPME	See PME.
CGT	*Confédération générale du travail*, General Confederation of Labor, the largest French labor union federation, dominated by the PCF.
CGT-FO or FO	*Confédération générale du travail-force ouvrière*, General Confederation of Labor-Worker's Force, a trade union federation formed by predominantly Socialist dissidents from the CGT.
CNPF	*Conseil national du patronat français*, National Council of French Management, the leading organization of large businesses.
D.	*Décrêt*, decree, initial character in coding system for identifying executive orders (decrees) in the *Journal officiel*.
DC	*Décision constitutionnelle*, constitutional decision, a Constitutional Council ruling on a complaint or query regarding a possible violation of the constitution.
diss. Rad.	Dissident Radicals, a political party formed by Radical-Socialists who defected at the time Pierre Mendès-France led the party late in the Fourth Republic.
ECSC	European Coal and Steel Community.
EEC	European Economic Community.
ENA	*Ecole nationale d'administration*, National School of Administration, government school for in-service training of civil servants for executive careers.
FGDS	*Federation de la gauche democrate et socialiste*, Federation of the Democratic and Socialist Left, coalition of non-Communist leftwing parties in the 1960s.
FNR	*Fin de non-recevoir*, dismissal, Constitutional Council order rejecting a complaint.
FNSEA	*Fédération nationale des syndicats d'exploitants agricoles*, National Federation of Farmers' Unions, the largest association of farm owners.
FO	See CGT-FO.
GD	*Gauche démocratique*, Democratic Left, the Radical-Socialists and allies in the upper chamber of parliament.

IMC	Interministerial Committee, especially the cabinet committee that supervised the drafting of the 1958 Constitution.
Indep. or Ind.	*Indépendants*, Independents, members of the IPAS.
IPAS	*Indépendants et paysans d'action sociale*, Independents and Peasants of Social Action, a conservative party of the Fourth and early Fifth Republics.
JCC	Joint Conference Committee (of parliament).
JO	*Journal officiel. Official Gazette*, the official publication series of the French government for the proceedings of parliament, laws, decrees, etc. All dates refer to sittings, not publication. The series includes:
JO. AN.	*Journal officiel. Débats parlementaires. Assemblée nationale*. The proceedings of the National Assembly in plenary session.
JO. AN. Documents	*Journal officiel. Assemblée nationale. Documents parlementaires*. Supplementary parliamentary materials of the National Assembly, mostly its committee reports and supporting materials.
JO. ANC.	*Journal officiel. Assemblée nationale constituante*. The proceedings of the Constituent Assembly of 1945–46.
JO. CD.	*Journal officiel. Débats parlementaires. Chambre de députés*. The proceedings of the Third Republic Chamber of Deputies in plenary session.
JO. CD. Documents	*Journal officiel. Chambre de députés. Documents parlementaires*. Supplementary parliamentary materials for the Third Republic Chamber of Deputies.
JO. CR.	*Journal officiel. Débats parlementaires. Conseil de la république*. The proceedings of the upper chamber of the Fourth Republic in plenary session.
JO. LD.	*Journal officiel. Lois et décrêts*. The official texts of statutes and executive orders.
JO. S.	*Journal officiel. Débats parlementaires. Sénat*. The proceedings of the Senate in plenary session.
JO. S. Documents	*Journal officiel. Sénat. Documents parlementaires*. Supplementary parliamentary materials for the upper chamber of the Third and Fifth Republics.
JO. Tables	*Journal officiel Tables*. The index to the entire series.
L.	*Loi*, law, initial character in coding system for identifying statutes in the *Journal officiel*.
LGDJ	*Librairie générale de droit et de jurisprudence*. General Library of Law and Jurisprudence, a book publisher.

LO	*Loi d'orientation*, orientation law, a statute of general scope intended to organize an entire policy area, such as agriculture or education.
MP	Member of Parliament.
MRG	*Mouvement des radicaux de gauche*, Movement of Left Radicals, a party formed by defectors from the Radical-Socialist Party. It formed an alliance with the PSF and PCF.
MRP	*Mouvement Républicain Populaire*, Popular Republican Movement, the Christian democratic political party of the Fourth and early Fifth Republics.
Ord.	*Ordonnance*, ordinance, initial characters in coding system for identifying executive orders of statutory content in the *Journal officiel.*
ORTF	*Office de la radio-télévision française*, French Radio-Television Agency.
PCF	*Parti communiste français*, French Communist Party.
PME or CGPME	*Confédération générale des petites et moyennes entreprises*, General Confederation of Small and Medium-Sized Enterprises, the principal association of small and medium-sized businesses.
PRA	*Parti du regroupement africain*, African Rally Party.
Prog.	*Progressistes*, Progressives, small Fourth Republic party allied closely to the PCF.
PSF of PS	*Parti socialiste français*, French Socialist Party.
PUF	*Presses universitaires de France*, University Presses of France.
Rad. or Rad.-Soc.	Radical, member of the *Parti républicain et radical-socialiste*, center-left, anti-clerical party that was important in the Third and Fourth Republics, but barely survives in the Fifth, usually called the Radical-Socialist Party.
RFSP	*Revue française de science politique, French Review of Political Science*, journal of the French Political Science Association.
RGR	*Rassemblement de la gauche républicaine*, Rally of the Republican Left, federation of minor parties and the Radical-Socialist Party in the Fourth Republic that became a political party after 1955.
RPF	*Rassemblement du peuple français*, Rally of the French People, the Gaullist political party, 1947–53.

SFIO	*Section française de l'international ouvrier*, French Section of the Workers International, the name of the principal democratic socialist party, 1905–1969. It changed its name to French Socialist Party in 1969.
Social Rep.	Social Republicans, the Gaullist party of the Fourth Republic.
SPD	*Sozial demokratische partei deutschlands*, the Social Democratic Party of Germany.
UDR	*Union des démocrates pour la république*, Union of Democrats for the Republic, the successor to the UNR.
UDSR-RDA	*Union démocratique et socialiste de la résistance, Rassemblement démocratique africain*, Democratic and Socialist Union of the Resistance-African Democratic Rally, center-left party of the Fourth Republic and its African affiliate.
UNR	*Union de la nouvelle république*, Union of the New Republic, the Gaullist party in the early Fifth Republic.

I

STRUCTURE

1

The 1958 Constitution

"Gentlemen, you are preparing France's last experiment in parliamentary government." [1]

Thus, Prime Minister de Gaulle began the Cabinet deliberations on the constitution being framed under his leadership in June 1958.

"This constitutional reform is the last chance given to the men and parties who believe that France can remain both one of the powerful nations of the world and a democracy." [2]

So spoke Michel Debré, the principal author of that constitution, in presenting the draft to the French Council of State in August 1958.

This "last chance of the Republic" will determine whether "the French nation will flourish again or will perish," warned de Gaulle in making public the final text.[3]

Those voices had cried in the wilderness of 1938, of 1940, of 1946, of 1951. Now, in 1958, they sounded a final clarion call for salvation. The apocalyptic atmosphere of that frenetic summer gave their tocsin special resonance. De Gaulle summarized the situation vividly in June: [4]

> The degradation of the State which is being precipitated. French unity in imminent danger. Algeria plunged into a tempest of trials and emotions. Corsica subjected to a feverish contagion. In the motherland contradictory movements with passions and actions rising hour by hour. The army long-tired by bloody and worthy tasks, but scandalized by the instability of the authorities. Our international position battered to the breaking point even within our alliances . . . France . . . finds herself menaced by . . . possible civil war.

That grim diagnosis suggested drastic remedies, perhaps including the installation of a presidential regime. Such dramatic rhetoric implied that parliamentary government, the traditional form of the French Republic, had proven to be inadequate.

Three other factors heightened the impression that presidential government was in the wings. One was de Gaulle's reputation as a presidentialist. Many statements by him and his associates since World War II had been given that construction, rightly or wrongly. The second was a non-Gaullist press campaign for presidential government that had attracted much attention during the preceding two years.[5] Finally, some of de Gaulle's critics and opponents expressed loud concern that he would introduce presidential government as a vehicle for "personal power." So much activity, excitement, and fear obscured reality. The strident hysteria of drastic upheaval drowned out the measured deliberations of negotiated reform.

This chapter takes a fresh look at the constitutional events of that turbulent summer with a view toward dissipating the obscurity. It examines the drafting of the new constitution in order to establish a baseline for understanding the evolution of the French political system since then. Its focus is the executive–legislative relationship, but that nexus is not always clearly separable from the rest of the constitutional fabric.

The thesis of this chapter has two interwoven parts. First, it argues that the drafting process was very complex, allowing many people of all political orientations to influence its product significantly. Time and polemic have fostered the impression that the 1958 constitution was a closet document turned out by de Gaulle, Debré, and a few ardent Gaullist (presidentialist?) associates. These pages attempt to correct that misperception. The other part of the thesis holds that those numerous constituents were predominantly committed to the retention of a parliamentary system of government and that their will prevailed. Almost all of the men (no women had significant roles) and institutions involved in the drafting process were steeped in the parliamentary tradition. There lay their experience, interests, commitments, and habits of mind. Thence flowed the force of their influence. In short, the 1958 constitution emerged from a consensus of constituents broadly representative of the mainstream of the French parliamentary tradition and was designed to serve as the basis for a parliamentary regime.

Three approaches are used to present this argument. The first describes the drafting process. This includes, for each step, the occasion, the participants, the activity, and the outcome. The next examines the expressed intentions of the principal framers, especially as they bear on the choice between parliamentarism and presidentialism. The third will consider the compatibility of the text of the constitution with those two basic forms of the executive–legislative relationship.

Thus, the framers' design and the general character of the Fifth Republic were squarely parliamentary. However, a number of specific provisions in the constitution had implications for that character that could be assessed only in the light of their practical application. Some of them will be examined in the next five chapters.

THE DRAFTING PROCESS

The drafting of the 1958 French constitution began with consultations in May that led to de Gaulle's investiture as prime minister. It ended with his public presentation of the final text on September 4. Between those dates more than a thousand persons representing all shades of French political opinion were involved. They included virtually all the top political party leaders of the Fourth Republic, its only two living presidents of the Republic, the leading officials of French Africa, interest association officials, both parliamentary chambers and their presidents, two parliamentary committees, a task force of experts, an *ad hoc* constitutional commission, the Council of State, the Cabinet Council, and the Council of Ministers. In addition, the general public debated the initial draft for more than a month between its publication on July 29 and the government's approval of the final text on September 3. Every step in that process had some effect on the content of the constitution.[6]

The Pre-Parliamentary Phase

De Gaulle's return to power after the May 13 crisis was not automatic. A series of consultations and negotiations between de Gaulle and his supporters, on one hand, and leaders of the Fourth Republic, on the other, paved the way. De Gaulle's plans for constitutional reform, including those affecting the executive-legislative relationship, were among the matters discussed.

The first step in that process seems to have been initiated by the president of the Republic, René Coty. On May 4, Gilbert Grandval, a "leftwing" Gaullist and former resident general in Morocco, called on Olivier Guichard, de Gaulle's *chef de cabinet*. He told Guichard that Coty had sent him to ask what de Gaulle thought "of all that," referring to the current Cabinet crisis and the Algerian situation. De Gaulle told Guichard to have Coty "write him a letter." Later, Simon Nora, an *inspecteur des finances* and collaborator of former premier Pierre Mendès-France, came to see de Gaulle on the same matter and received "an evasive answer." [7]

Four direct consultations with de Gaulle by top Fourth Republic leaders followed. They were a two-and-a-half-hour visit to Colombey-les-Deux-Eglises by former conservative premier Antoine Pinay on May 22, a two-hour conference in St. Cloud with incumbent MRP (*Mouvement républicain populaire*)* premier Pierre Pflimlin on May 26, and two meetings in St. Cloud with Socialist André Le Troquer, president of the National Assembly, on May 28. Le Troquer was accompanied by Diomède Catroux, Gaullist former deputy and minister, on the first visit and by Radical Gaston de Monnerville, president of the Council of the Republic, on the second. Socialist ministers Guy Mollet and Jules Moch would have joined Pflimlin if de Gaulle had disavowed in writing the insurrectionary landing in Corsica.

* For key to abbreviations used in this book, see p. ix.

The influence of those consultations was parliamentarist, at least implicitly. Published reports reveal little about any discussion of constitutional questions at those meetings, except that de Gaulle told Le Troquer and Monnerville that he wanted "a government which governs, which is strong and which lasts, a solid Executive." Also, he reassured Pflimlin that he would seek office only in accord with the existing constitution, which was, of course, parliamentary. In any case, all his interlocutors were committed parliamentarists. The 1952 Pinay government had been the principal bar to overthrow of the Fourth Republic by de Gaulle's presidentialist RPF political movement. The Mollet and Pflimlin governments had been just as staunch on the same stand. Le Troquer and Monnerville headed parliamentary chambers. Despite Catroux's RPF (*Rassemblement du peuple français*) background, he had served in the solidly parliamentarist Mendès-France government. Surely, de Gaulle knew of their commitment and of its bearing on his prospects and plans. If not, Le Troquer and Monnerville made it clear by insisting that any new constitution would have to be "made by Parliament or, if not, by an organism in which would sit members of Parliament delegated by the Assemblies." [8]

On the basis of those consultations, Coty initiated the constitutional process for de Gaulle's investiture as premier in the conventional parliamentarist manner. He called de Gaulle to the Elysée Palace on May 29 to invite him to form a government. De Gaulle assured him that he would adhere to the provisions of the 1946 constitution in soliciting investiture and the authority to introduce constitutional reforms. Also, he agreed to associate Parliament in the constituent process through a Consultative Constitutional Commission (CCC). Coty "did not dare to make him specify" the details of the constitutional reforms he contemplated and de Gaulle's public statement after the meeting said only that he intended to make changes "especially concerning the separation and balance of powers." He did not say that the constitutional reforms would require that the government be responsible to Parliament.[9] That implied a departure from parliamentary government, but the CCC would ensure substantial parliamentary influence in the drafting process.

Next, de Gaulle undertook to obtain the support needed for investiture, without engaging in the customary round of political party consultations. However, he wanted a substantial parliamentary majority, which was impossible without the outspokenly parliamentarist Socialists. Therefore, he made an exceptional effort to win their votes.

That elicited his first clearcut commitment to establish a parliamentary regime. On May 30, he met with three leading Socialists, first with former president of the Republic Vincent Auriol and then jointly with Mollet, general secretary of the party, and Maurice Deixonne, chairman of its National Assembly caucus. He responded affirmatively to Auriol's question: "In the future constitution, will the government be responsible to the National Assembly?" [10] He assured Mollet that his constitution would require the prime minister to go "before the Assembly to obtain its confidence" immediately after appointment by the president of the Republic. Also, he told Mollet that the president "must not be elected by universal suffrage; I have learned that unhappy experiments have been made with that form. Let's not repeat them." Instead, the president should be elected by "an Assembly larger than Parliament," including the General Councils, mayors, and representatives of overseas France. Finally, he said that ministers might be selected from among MPs, but would have to resign their seats.[11]

De Gaulle refused to consult separately with leaders of the other political parties, but held a joint meeting for them at the Lapérouse Hotel in Paris on May 31. Twenty-six representatives of twelve parties attended the seventy-minute session. Only the Communists stayed away.[12] De Gaulle provided information about his plans and responded to questions. He "presented . . . the points that he deemed essential to introduce in the future constitution." He affirmed that he "did not intend to install a presidential system" and that his constitutional reform "would respect and reinforce the two fundamental principles of democracy, namely that the executive branch as well as the deliberative branch issue from the national sovereignty and that the government must be responsible to the Assembly elected by universal suffrage." Also, he intended to create an "incompatibility between the function of minister and the parliamentary mandate," his only remark that evoked *mouvements divers* at that meeting. De Gaulle asked the parties to let him know by 5 P.M. whether they would support his investiture. By 6:30 P.M., he informed Coty that he had the requisite backing.[13]

De Gaulle's next step was to form a government. He consulted at least twenty-three persons for that purpose. Any of them could have refused to join his government unless he furnished assurances on constitutional issues. Most of them were MPs, among them well-known advocates of parliamentarism. In addition to Auriol, Mollet, Pinay, and Pflimlin, they included former premiers Paul Ramadier and Georges Bidault.

None of them have reported posing such conditions, but the composition of the cabinet had a strong parliamentary cast. For instance, it included a minister of state from each of the principal parties in the parliamentary coalition. Major party factions were recognized by offers of portfolios to both Mollet and Auriol in the SFIO and Pflimlin and Bidault in the MRP. The Radical-Socialists and Independents were mollified in the traditional way of French parliamentary government by giving Education to a Radical and Finance to a Conservative. On the other hand, de Gaulle broke with that tradition by naming five non-MPs to his fifteen-member initial cabinet.[14]

The participants in the pre-parliamentary phase of de Gaulle's return to office were preoccupied with the incipient insurrectionary situation. De Gaulle's constitutional intentions did not loom large in their considerations. However, most of them were convinced parliamentarists and, so far as the issue arose, their influence flowed in that direction.

The Parliamentary Phase

The parliamentarist current entered the constituent process in force when de Gaulle appeared in the National Assembly. MPs pressed for a parliamentary system and de Gaulle responded sympathetically. This occured in the investiture debate, but especially in the National Assembly's consideration of his request for exceptional constitutional reform authority.

Investiture

De Gaulle's investiture address included this statement on executive–legislative relations in the constitution to be drafted:[15]

> Executive power and legislative power must be separated effectively in such a way that the government and the Parliament assume, each for itself and on its own responsibility, its functions fully. The government must be responsible to Parliament.

Scorning Fourth Republic custom, de Gaulle left the chamber immediately after his speech. However, a debate that lasted for six and a half hours took place in his absence. Eighteen deputies representing nine parliamentary groups participated.

The speakers gave remarkably little attention to constitutional reform. Only five debaters referred to it. Their comments were brief and parliamentarist.[16] Pierre-Henri Teitgen (MRP) was the most explicit. He said that de Gaulle's Lapérouse statement on "the two fundamental principles of democracy" was one reason that the MRP had decided to support his investiture. Pierre Mendès-France (Rad.) and Jean Masson (Rad.) advocated "separation of powers," but also endorsed parliamentarism.[17] Jacques Duclos (PCF) warned against concentrating "the legislative power as well as the executive power and the constituent power" in the hands of one man. Pierre Courant (Indep.) said that the Executive should govern and the legislature should legislate, "but only on important matters and no longer on everything."

The Assembly had ample opportunity to impose conditions respecting constitutional reform and had a large parliamentarist majority. However, it seems to have been overwhelmed by the crisis situation. It produced no qualifying resolutions, exacted no governmental statements, and voted investiture, 329 to 224, with 39 deputies not voting for various reasons.[18]

The Universal Suffrage Committee of the National Assembly

The Assembly's Committee on Universal Suffrage gave the government's constitutional projects more substantial and critical attention. It reviewed the government's bill for urgent revision of Article 90 (amendment) of the 1946 constitution. After rapid but thorough deliberation, it recommended significant changes of parliamentarist import.

The government project had three main parts: [19]

> a. The bill itself proposed to replace Article 90 by a provision authorizing the Council of Ministers to submit a "draft constitutional law" to popular referendum after obtaining the advice of the Council of State.

b. An accompanying *exposé des motifs* included a promise to consult "qualified personalities" during the drafting process.

c. A separate statement affirmed that the constitution would be inspired by these principles:

1) Universal suffrage is the only source of power.

2) The executive branch and the legislative branch must be separated effectively in such a way that the government and the Parliament each assumes on its part and responsibility the fullness of its attributions.

3) The government must be responsible to Parliament.

4) The judicial branch must remain independent.

5) The constitution must permit the organization of the relations of the Republic with the peoples who are associated with it.

The committee's deliberations were serious and intensive. It met continuously from the Assembly's recess at 11:30 P.M., June 1, until 6:00 A.M., June 2, and again on the afternoon of June 3. Its concerns were both substantive and procedural. The ministers of state in the new government (Mollet, Pflimlin, Jacquinot, Félix Houphouët-Boigny) met with the committee at 2:30 A.M. for nearly two hours. About 42 of the 48 committee members took part in the proceedings.

The committee majority (PCF, SFIO, Rad.) opposed the bill, mainly because it omitted Parliament from the process of drafting and approving the new constitution. The government responded by revising its bill to provide that the draft constitution be reviewed by a consultative commission of MPs designated by the appropriate parliamentary committees. That was not enough for the committee majority. It adopted a counterproposal, 21 to 11 with 9 abstentions, to eliminate the consultative commission and require that the draft constitution be submitted to Parliament for review and adoption by an absolute majority in each chamber within three months. If it failed to pass Parliament, the government might submit it to popular referendum, with or without amendments adopted by Parliament. Also, the committee added these points to the government's statement of principles:

a. At least one house of Parliament shall be elected by direct universal suffrage and the government shall be responsible to it.

b. "The functions of president of the Republic and of president of the council shall be distinct."

c. Constitutional laws to amend the new constitution shall be submitted to popular referenda if they do not receive qualified majorities in each house of Parliament.

Finally, the committee proposal required that the government submit to popular referendum a bill enacting an electoral system for the National Assembly, choosing between a majority system and proportional representation.[20]

The committee disdained the reticence exhibited by the Assembly in the investiture debate. It addressed the constitutional issues squarely and forcefully and recommended heavier involvement of Parliament in the drafting process and a more parliamentary flavor for the final product. The government responded with some small steps toward accommodation. However, it stood firm on the major points.

The National Assembly Debate on Constitutional Revision

The Assembly debate was substantive and pertinent, but the government prevailed with little difficulty. Thirteen deputies joined the two-and-a-half-hour deliberation. It began with a speech by Albert de Bailliencourt (Rad.), *rapporteur* of the committee, opposing the government bill, and a response by de Gaulle.[21]

De Gaulle intervened four times later in the discussion. He insisted that the Assembly reject all of the committee's proposed changes. He furnished no explicit information about his intentions for the contents of the new constitution, but implied that it would include at least one popularly elected chamber and distinct functions for president and prime minister. Also, he called his stipulation that the government be responsible to Parliament "incompatible with a presidential regime." [22] However, he rejected the Communist proposal to write those specifications into the bill.

The debate avoided discussing substantive constitutional issues. Only Duclos broached the matter. He conjectured that de Gaulle would adhere to the "presidentialist" principles of his 1946 Bayeux speech. The bill passed in form satisfactory to the government, 350 to 163, 41 votes more than the three-fifths majority required for enactment of a constitutional amendment by Parliament alone.

Assembly action had several parliamentarist effects. It wrote the CCC into the bill and obtained oral assurances from de Gaulle on other parliamentarist features. Finally, it ensured that the bill incorporated the parliamentarist statement of principles and that the preamble included the two parliamentarist sentences from de Gaulle's investiture speech.[23]

The Council of the Republic

The role of the Council of the Republic in the parliamentary phase of the drafting process was much less substantial than that of the Assembly. The Council was not, of course, involved in the de Gaulle investiture and its action on the constitutional amendment bill was formal and perfunctory. What muffled noise it made was distinctly parliamentarist.

The Council's action in plenary session on June 3 took barely half an hour. Its Universal Suffrage Committee reported favorably on the bill. The *rapporteur*, Jean Gilbert-Jules (GD), provided no information on the committee's deliberations. He interpreted the government's intentions to be "to settle the question of the relations between the executive branch and the legislative branch and not to harm the legislature itself, to permit the parliamentary regime to renovate itself by according to the executive branch the indispensable authority that it needs." De Gaulle confirmed that interpretation from the podium, using the term "balanced powers" for the branches of government. The only speaker in the general discussion was the Communist spokesman, who merely parroted Duclos' remarks to the Assembly. Two other deputies made brief suggestions to the government. One asked that the presidents of the general councils be consulted during the drafting process, the other that a majority electoral system be adopted for the National Assembly. De Gaulle accepted the former and ignored the latter. The bill passed, 256 to 30.[24] Thus, the parliamentary phase of the constituent process ended less than 44 hours after it had begun.

The juggernaut's only significant sputter had been caused by the Assembly's Universal Suffrage Committee. The only substantive change effected by Parliament was inclusion of the CCC in the drafting process. However, the two Chambers made enough other parliamentarist noises that their position was clear. They let de Gaulle know that he could avoid important, perhaps fatal, opposition from France's political elite in the Autumn referendum only by presenting a constitution for a parliamentary regime.

Governmental Phase

The process of forming the new regime moved now into its governmental phase. The chambers adjourned, confident that they would not meet again in the Fourth Republic. They had empowered their committees to meet and transact business with the government, but that was expected to mean only that the Universal Suffrage Committees would select the parliamentary representatives for the CCC. Otherwise, the government could prepare its constitutional project without reference to or control by Parliament.

In fact, governmental work on the draft constitution had begun during the pre-parliamentary phase. About May 26, Michel Debré, who had been the leading Gaullist constitutional theoretician for some fifteen years, had begun to confer privately and informally with Raymond Janot, general secretary of the Council of State, and Jean Mamert, an *auditeur* there, on the possible content of a new, Gaullist constitution.[25] However, apparently, he was not yet in touch with de Gaulle on the matter.

Debré's role as constitution-maker had become official on May 31 when de Gaulle had invited him to join his government for the express purpose of supervising the drafting of the new constitution.[26] In that capacity, he and Janot had drafted the constitutional revision bill and had negotiated its modification and adoption.[27] However, serious work on the project did not begin until Parliament had adjourned.

Then, constitutional reform became a major preoccupation of the government. A task force of experts gave it full time. An interministerial committee (IMC) spent thirteen long meetings working over the task force's recommendations. De Gaulle, Debré, and Janot conferred as necessary. It consumed the attention of six Cabinet Council and two Council of Ministers sessions. Each group helped significantly to mold its final form.

Task Force of Experts

The first step in the governmental phase was the organization of a task force of experts to assist the government in preparing a draft text. It began "several moments after" the final Assembly vote in the investiture process when de Gaulle, in his first official act, met with Debré and Janot to assign them responsibility for directing that project.[28] Janot became *chargé de mission* on de Gaulle's staff and Debré recruited Mamert for the same position on his staff.

The task force was assembled quickly. Janot became vice chairman, chairing meetings in Debré's absence and ensuring liaison with de Gaulle. Mamert and Jérôme Solal-Celigny, another Council of State *auditeur*, served as secretaries. Each of the four ministers of state plus Berthoin, the only Radical-Socialist in the government, nominated an associate to the task force.[29] A member of the legal section of the Foreign Ministry and one from the political services section of the Interior Ministry joined the task force as observers.[30] Twelve other members were appointed.[31] The twenty-one experts on Debré's list included three law professors (Foyer, Luchaire, Portemer), one prefect (Gerbod), and seventeen members of the Council of State. None held national elective office. Only Luchaire had a reputation as a constitutional law specialist. Five were active in Catholic political and social organizations.[32]

The task force worked on the draft constitution full-time for about a month and intermittently for another seven weeks. Debré began to organize it on June 5 by picking Mamert as his assistant. On June 7, he met with Janot and Mamert and on June 12 the task force held its first plenary session. It divided at once into groups of two or three members, each working on a different title of the constitution, but continued to hold plenary meetings several times a week until about July 11. Then, over the long July 14 weekend, Debré, Janot, Mamert, one other task force member, and a stenographer retreated to the Château de la Celle–St. Cloud and wrote a complete working draft. After that, the task force met at the call of the government to work out the details of revisions until the final draft was approved by the Council of Ministers on September 3.[33]

In some respects, the task force had greater influence over the contents of the constitution than any other group. It spent more time on the project and was more fully immersed in its details. For instance, it invented the Constitutional Council, contrary to de Gaulle's longstanding aversion to anything that smacked of a supreme court. Also, working with Gilbert Devaux, Director of the Budget, at the instigation of Pinay, it devised the special provisions for dealing with the budget.[34]

Of all groups in the drafting process, the task force was the least parliamentarist. Among its members, only Debré had a solid parliamentary background and orientation. Luchaire has written that "many minds–notably in the group of experts which assisted the government in its work ... preferred a presidential regime." Janot has been identified explicitly by Mollet and inferentially by Pflimlin as the only "presidentialist" who attended Interministerial Committee meetings.[35]

However, the task force was clearly subordinated to the government, in close liaison with it, and loyal to it. At the outset, Debré held a series of meetings with de Gaulle "in order to become well acquainted with the details of his ideas, and in order that I might give him my suggestions on a certain number of provisions on which his reflections had not yet borne in a profound way." In one of those meetings, de Gaulle told him and Janot, "The regime will be parliamentary or will not be." Given French traditions and the existing situation, he believed that a presidential system "would turn quickly into a dictatorship." During the drafting process, the representatives of the ministers of state and of the premier met individually with their sponsors, Debré conferred "three or four times" with de Gaulle, and Debré and Janot attended Interministerial Committee meetings.[36] Possible presidentialist influence by members of the task force was attenuated further by their realization of the gauntlet their product had yet to run: Interministerial Committee, government, public discussion, CCC, Council of State, popular referendum.

The Interministerial Committee

The Interministerial Committee (IMC) was formed at the same time as the task force and supervised its work. De Gaulle chaired all or most of its meetings.[37] The other principal members were Mollet, Pflimlin, Jacquinot, Houphouët-Boigny, Pinay, and Debré. Bernard Cornut-Gentille, minister of Overseas France, joined the committee when his concerns were under discussion. Attending *ex officio* at least some of the time were Janot; Belin, general secretary of the government; Georges Pompidou, de Gaulle's chief of staff; and René Cassin, head of the Council of State.[38] Debré was *rapporteur* and Janot took and distributed notes of the first two meetings.[39]

The IMC pursued its task diligently. It first met on June 13 for two hours and decided "to meet periodically, probably every ten to twelve days." [40] However, it soon found that a much more intensive schedule was required. Two-hour meetings were held on June 23, 26, 30; and 90-minute sessions were held on July 7, 8, 9, and 10. A similar meeting on July 11 was postponed pending the results of the Celle–St. Cloud weekend. More meetings were held July 16, 17 (3 1/2 hours), 18 (1 1/2 hours), 19, and 19–20 (into the wee hours).[41] The aggregate time of those meetings was 25 to 30 hours. After the IMC reported back to the Cabinet Council on July 20, it met at the call of the premier to consider changes proposed by the Cabinet Council, the CCC, and the Council of State.[42]

De Gaulle began the first meeting by reviewing "the broad principles that must inspire the reform and that are consecrated by the constitutional law of June 3, 1958." The government should emanate from the president rather than Parliament and ministers should not hold seats in Parliament. Governmental instability should be prevented by "organizing" the mechanisms of ministerial responsibility to Parliament. The president should have "an essential role," but that of an "arbiter . . . not involved in the details of policy." He would be "elected by a very broad college," not by Parliament or universal suffrage and would be responsible for ensuring "the regular functioning of the political branches of government," especially by using the power of dissolution and the referrendum. Then, de Gaulle invited each minister to present his views and questions, to which he responded.[43]

At the second meeting Debré presented a draft of a portion of the constitution and de Gaulle elaborated somewhat on his views. In "exceptional" circumstances, the president should be able to dismiss the government. Normally, he would be "an arbiter," but "in case of national peril, he must be able to take the measures necessary for the continuity of national life" in his capacity as "guarantor of national independence, of the integrity of the territory and of respect for treaties." Two articles on the presidency and the presidential electoral system were discussed at length.

Mollet claims that "by the second meeting of the IMC, the essential choice had been made" to establish "a parliamentary regime." [44] The minutes of those two meetings do not disclose any remarks by the ministers that bore directly on the executive–legislative relationship. However, a number of comments by de Gaulle, Debré, Mollet, Pflimlin, and Cassin concerned it indirectly. In particular, the relationship between the president and the prime minister was discussed at length. All present seemed to agree that the president "must be truly an arbiter and not the chief executive," not intervening in political life except in extraordinary circumstances. The prime minister would be the chief executive. Because he would be responsible to Parliament constitutionally and the president would not be, that status would give the regime a parliamentary character.

The next six meetings examined partial drafts prepared by the task force, article by article and title by title. That procedure proved inefficient, because questions settled at one meeting tended to be reopened at another. Nevertheless, the task force had assembled piecemeal a nearly complete draft by the end of June.[45] On July 16, Debré presented the Celle–St. Cloud draft to the IMC.[46] The IMC meetings of July 16–20 discussed and revised that draft extensively.

IMC members have reported that the deliberations were serious and influential. Newspapers at the time mentioned "animated" meetings with "controversy" among "several members of the committee." [47] Debré called them "the center of reflection and of orientation, even of the drafting of different articles" and said that "undoubtedly" they "counted the most" of any of the meetings in determining the content of the constitution. "It was really there that the doctrine was elaborated, that the essential mechanisms were worked out." He called the meetings "long, serious, and well-prepared. General de Gaulle allowed discussion without watching the time." [48] Mollet and Pflimlin agreed, the former calling the IMC decisions "determining." [49]

The issue of executive–legislative relations consumed more IMC meeting time than any other matter. Until July 7, it discussed hardly anything else and it returned to the issue frequently thereafter.[50] The "provisions concerning the relationship between the government and the Parliament were born" in the IMC.[51]

Those deliberations proceeded through three distinct steps. First, the IMC members agreed on the basic principles of those relations. Then they defined "the competence of each" branch, distinguishing "the domain of law from that which belongs normally in regulations." Next, they worked out the legislative process, including the government's involvement, by following its steps hypothetically. This included a "grammar lesson" by de Gaulle on verb usage in French legal terminology. Another part of that deliberation was a "tense" discussion on the use of ordinances, which led to agreement on three limitations on which Mollet and Pflimlim insisted.[52]

The features introduced into the constitution by the IMC resulted from a variety of influences and reflect the importance of the parliamentarists. De Gaulle provided the conception of the Chief of State as arbiter above politics, but empowered to ensure that the machinery of government work properly; the emergency powers clause; the ban on MPs holding ministerial office; and the referendum. Debré proposed the provisions on questions of confidence, control of parliamentary rules by the Constitutional Council, the presidential electoral system, and the procedures to protect governments from excessively predatory parliaments. Mollet contributed the distinction between the "domain of law" and "the domain of regulation" and the principle of unicameral ministerial responsibility. Pflimlin suggested the devices of "passive enactment" of legislation and an absolute majority for censure.[53] Pinay was the main source for the provisions concerning the budget, as was Houphouët-Boigny for those on the relations of France with her overseas possessions.[54]

The IMC members have stressed the compromise and consensual character of the process. Debré has described in detail the concessions that he and de Gaulle made.[55] Pflimlin told the MRP that the text incorporated "all the principles that we proclaimed." [56] Mollet assured the SFIO at the time that no decision on the content of the constitution "was taken without my agreement" [57] and the National Assembly two years later that the text had resulted from a process of accommodation.[58]

The impact of parliamentarist influences in the IMC seems clear. Mollet, Pflimlin, Jacquinot, and Pinay had impeccable parliamentarist credentials. Debré was an articulate advocate of "reformed parliamentarism." De Gaulle was the only member of the government on the IMC who had presidentialist leanings. Of course, the constitution had to be acceptable to him, but, as he said later, he was inhibited by political considerations. He feared that if the parties represented by Mollet, Pinay, and Pflimlin did not support the constitution in the referendum, it would be defeated and, at age 68, he would lose his last chance to lead France. Therefore, he gave his collaborators what they considered essential, a parliamentary regime.[59]

The Cabinet Council

When the IMC completed its draft text on July 20, it reported back to the full Cabinet Council, which was heavily parliamentarist in composition.[60] It now consisted of twenty-three ministers plus de Gaulle. Only two were Gaullist politicians. Thirteen were politicians of other orientations (three SFIO, two Radicals, four MRP, three Independents, and one African). Seven were high civil servants (including an active Socialist) and one was a man of letters. This added the Radical political family to those on the IMC. Also, Soustelle had become so closely identified with the extreme Right that he and Debré represented quite different Gaullist factions. Thus, of the six main French political currents, only the Communists lacked a voice in the government.

The Cabinet Council reviewed the text at four long meetings on July 23 and 25-26, totaling about twelve and a half hours.[61] De Gaulle read aloud each article of the text in turn and Debré commented on it. Then, the ministers could comment, propose revisions, and ask questions. The discussions were "very free and sometimes lively." [62] The meeting notes record remarks by every Cabinet member except Pelletier. The most frequent speakers were Mollet (17 times); Pflimlin, Berthoin, Michelet, and Couve de Murville (12 each); and Soustelle (11). The politicians of the parliamentary Fourth Republic were much the most outspoken members. Every one of them said something. Not including Debré, they intervened 102 times (a 7.3 average), compared to 37 (4.6 average) for the others. Without Couve, the latter averaged only 3.6. Forty-five of the seventy-seven articles were discussed and thirty-nine were changed as a result.

Executive-legislative relations occupied the lion's share of the cabinet's attention. Thirty-five (81.4 percent) of the articles discussed pertained to that matter. So did twenty-seven (71.1 percent) of those changed. However, many were amendments of form rather than substance and others were not consistent in effect. Some strengthened parliamentarist features; others weakened them.

The emergency powers article was an especial bone of contention, consuming more than an hour of discussion time. Pinay, Lejeune, Malraux, Soustelle, Couve de Murville, Michelet, Buron, Mollet, and Pflimlin intervened. De Gaulle held "more firmly to this article than to any other." He said it had capital importance for the future and referred to the crises of 1940 and May 1958. Two modest changes were made. One broadened its scope; the other added the Constitutional Council to the list of institutions to be consulted by the president of the Republic before invoking its powers. [63]

The Cabinet deliberations were consequential. Many disagreements were expressed and many changes made in the text. All the members accepted the product. None resigned when the draft was published as approved by the Cabinet. This attests eloquently to the parliamentarist perception of the framers, given the fact that Soustelle and Janot were the only avowed presidentialists[64] among them and that others had insisted that parliamentarism was an essential condition for their support.[65]

External Consultations

The government produced the initial draft behind closed doors, but not in complete isolation. During the process, its members conferred with outsiders, especially other high officials, party activists, and interest-association representatives. Those consulted tended to be identified with parliamentarism.

They included such leading Fourth Republic politicians as President Coty and Monnerville, conservative leader Paul Reynaud, and Radical-Socialist Pierre Mendès-France. Coty expressed reservations about the provisions for the power of dissolution, the ban on ministerial office-holding by MPs, the *suppléant* system, and the presidential electoral system. However, he approved of the new constitution in general.[66] Monnerville met with de Gaulle and Debré, but has not disclosed the content of those meetings, except to say that "all the constituents, without exception," considered Article 89 to be the only amending provision of the constitution.[67] The content of the meetings with Reynaud and Mendès-France has not been divulged. Both of them were strongly parliamentarist in background and orientation.

Also, de Gaulle consulted on the new constitution with interest-association representatives. On June 12, he met with a large group, including officials of the Christian trade union federation (CFTC), most of the major farm organizations, the federation of "middle-class' associations, and independent trade unions. Later, the largest farm organization (FNSEA) and associations representing craftsmen, the middle classes, and small and medium-sized businesses (PME) sent him a letter on some aspects of the constitution. Finally, he discussed the provisions on the relationship between France and her overseas possessions with their leaders on an African tour in early July and during their visits to Paris for the Bastille Day festivities.[68]

The other members of the IMC seem to have consulted mainly with their fellow partisans. Houphouët-Boigny conferred with the leaders of the other two African political parties in Parliament. Pflimlin participated in an MRP study group on constitutional reform. Mollet joined an SFIO "study day" on the constitution on July 6.[69] Very likely, less formal consultations were not reported publicly.

Conclusions

The governmental phase was the longest, most decisive, and most secretive part of the drafting process. Yet it included much interplay among diverse political forces. All major parliamentary political parties and interest associations, except the Communists, had substantial involvement and influence.

That phase ended with the publication of the draft text on July 29. Of course, the government's work was not completed. It continued to be engaged heavily in its task by reviewing the text in light of the public discussion and the advice of the CCC and Council of State. However, after nearly two months of intensive effort, its main job was done.

Public Discussion

The French political public debated the draft text fully and freely for more than a month before the Council of Ministers approved the final text. Indeed, a certain amount of public discussion had preceded release of the initial draft. Some politicians outside the official process believed that they could have the greatest influence over the contents of the new constitution by speaking out publicly during the drafting process.[70]

However, the publication of the actual text unleashed a flood of comment. The media were filled with analysis and opinion. Ministers made statements and met with individuals and groups to explain, defend, and discuss their project. Political parties took stands (Socialist and Radical-Socialist parliamentary caucuses, dissident Socialists, Mendèsist Radicals, Communists) or tried to (MRP), but others deferred action pending publication of the final text. A delegation of Socialist leaders explained their reservations to de Gaulle. Most interest associations preferred to await the final text, but the CFTC (favorable), a civil service association and a veterans' group (both hostile) were exceptions. *Ad hoc* citizens groups were formed during August to crystallize opinion on the draft and, perhaps, influence its final form.[71]

Five weeks were available for public discussion before the final text was approved. The August doldrums were used by those who wished to affect its character. That debate occurred during the time that the CCC, Council of State, and government were deliberating and making final recommendations and decisions on the text and, presumably, remained susceptible to such influence.

Consultative Constitutional Commission

The official political organ for review of the constitutional reform work of the government was the Consultative Constitutional Commission (CCC) that had been required by the June 3 law. A decree set forth the details of its organization and operation.[72] The CCC was responsible for reviewing the draft text and submitting a recommendation to the premier within twenty days.

The CCC had thirty-nine members. In a July 22 meeting, the Universal Suffrage Committee of the National Assembly selected sixteen of its members to represent it. Its Council of the Republic counterpart named ten of its members in a July 17 meeting. The government appointed thirteen persons, none of whom held ministerial portfolios. The parliamentary delegations included six Independents, five Radicals, four Socialists, four Africans, three MRPs, two Gaullists, one Poujadist, and one unaffiliated. Thus, all major parliamentary parties, except the Communists, were represented.[73]

The government's delegation was a varied lot. It included the original political sponsor of both de Gaulle and Debré (Third Republic premier and Fourth Republic minister Paul Reynaud), a Fourth Republic deputy (Léon Noël), a member of de Gaulle's wartime Consultative Assembly (Maxime

Blocq-Mascart), two members of the Assembly of the French Union (Alfred Bour, Roger Frey), a member (René Chazelle) and a former member (Bour) of the High Council of the Magistracy, an ambassador (Noël), two interest association officials (André Malterre, CGC; Fernand Van Graefschepe, FNSEA), three educators (Marc Lauriol, Algiers Graduate School of Commerce; Marcel Waline, Paris Faculty of Law; Hamza Boubakeur, Paris Moslem Institute), and two high civil servants (Blocq-Mascart and Roland Pré). Those with known partisan political affiliations were two Gaullists, an MRP, a Socialist, an Independent, and a rightwing activist.[74]

The government provided the CCC with ample resources. It assigned Janot for liaison between de Gaulle and the CCC, Mamert as general secretary, Solal-Celigny as staff expert, and Luchaire, Guldner, Chandernagor, Foyer, and Plantey as "government commissioners." It allocated space to the CCC in the quarters of the Economic Council, some of whose staff members were placed at its disposal. Also, it made available staff assistance from the National Assembly, the Council of the Republic, the Council of State, and the "central administrations." [75]

The government assured the CCC that it would consider its advice seriously. The scope of its deliberations was to have "no limits" and the government would examine "in depth" all its suggestions, "even those that emanate from only a few of its members." De Gaulle wanted the CCC to be "associated fully in the work of the government." He spoke of the "extreme importance of your work" and assured it that the government would "examine with the greatest care . . . all your . . . suggestions." [76] More concretely, Debré announced that "several provisions have been left 'open' in the draft constitution" pending CCC advice. They included the composition of the presidential electoral college, the boundary between the domains of law and regulation, and the institutions joining France with her overseas possessions.[77] Also, Debré spent eleven and a half hours with the CCC in four formal sessions plus innumerable corridor conferences, and de Gaulle met with it twice for about one and a half hours.[78]

The CCC rose to the challenge. At its first meeting, it elected Reynaud chairman and Dejean and Montalembert vice chairman. Two days later, it divided into two committees, one of nineteen members on the relationship between the Republic and overseas France and one of twenty members on the institutions of the Republic (*les pouvoirs publics*). The following day, it named an eight-member subcommittee on the constitutional status of political parties. The committees met from 10 A.M. until 5 P.M. the day following their appointment. The Overseas France committee met six more times and the Republic committee four more times, each time for about ninety minutes. In addition, both committees held meetings one weekend. The subcommittee seems to have met only once. The committees were organized with chairmen and *rapporteurs*. They formulated resolutions and alternative phrasing and, in a general way, played influential roles in the CCC's deliberations and decisions.[79]

The full CCC worked equally hard. It met eighteen times in seventeen days, recessing twice for three-day weekends. The total meeting time was fifty-two hours and twenty minutes, an average of about four hours and forty-five minutes per day. When the meeting time of its committees and informal conferences is added, the group spent two very full weeks on the project. More than half (52.3 percent) of the plenary meeting time was spent on the executive and legislative branches and their relationship.[80]

CCC discussion was full and animated. All but two members (Nayrou and Raybaud) took part in its debates. It addressed the presidentialism-parliamentarism issue directly and at length. Nineteen members spoke on that question.[81] None of them advocated a presidential regime or argued that provisions in the draft should be altered to make it more presidential. Some opposed presidential government explicitly. For instance, Coste-Floret criticized "the admirers of the so-called presidential regime." [82] Also, he called the first draft "a compromise between a presidential regime and a parliamentary regime" and implied that he preferred pure parliamentarism.[83] Barrachin shared those views and insisted that "presidential regimes" have "nothing to do with ours." [84] Reynaud reminded them that "General de Gaulle's declarations to the National Assembly gave the impression that he was for the parliamentary regime, not for the presidential regime." [85] Every member who spoke to the point referred to the proposed system as "parliamentary" and assumed that the prime minister would be the chief executive and would be responsible to Parliament. The only exception was when Coste-Floret criticized the draft for making "the president of the Republic the true chief of the Executive" and Janot replied at once: "No, if he were, the position of the prime minister would be untenable." [86]

To allay residual fears on that question, de Gaulle returned to the CCC and responded to a direct question by Reynaud on whether the prime minister could be dismissed by the president of the Republic. His reply deserves quotation *in extenso*: [87]

> No! For, it if were like that, he could not govern effectively. The prime minister is responsible to Parliament and not to the Chief of State in what concerns policy matters. The Chief of State has as his essential role to ensure the regular functioning of the branches of government. So, he names the prime minister, as under the constitution of 1875, which is what eliminates the investiture, without excluding the use of the question of confidence. The prime minister, then, forms his government and the president of the Republic signs the decree, but he does not take the initiative for the decision on his own. If it were not like this, the balance would be compromised. The president of Republic, I insist on this, is essentially an arbiter who has the mission of ensuring, no matter what happens, the functioning of the branches of government.

With de Gaulle still present and not dissenting, Reynaud said that his answer "will appease the fears of those who wondered whether the first draft was inspired by the spirit of the presidential regime." [88] Teitgen affirmed that conclusion by saying that de Gaulle has "declared very firmly" his preference for a parliamentary regime.[89]

In Debré's appearances before the CCC, he discussed executive–legislative relations only once. He called the attempt to maintain "the responsibility of the government to Parliament" while ensuring "absolute governmental stability" "the problem of squaring the circle." He contended that its solution lay in the "mechanisms by which ministerial responsibility is called into play: the question of confidence and the motion of censure." [90]

Janot bore the brunt of the government's defense before the CCC. His comments on executive–legislative relations are lengthy and to the point. His general exposition on the topic of the political branches of government called the proposed system "a purified parliamentary regime" because the government remained responsible to Parliament but was given the means to avoid instability and to govern. To support that generalization, he insisted that "the chief executive is the prime minister" who is responsible to Parliament and not to the president.[91]

The CCC recommended changes in fifty-four (68.4 percent) of the seventy-nine articles in the draft text. It reported on changes to three more articles proposed in the commission but not endorsed by it. Forty-six of the fifty-four (85.2 percent) articles concerned the political Executive, the Parliament, their powers, or their relationship. So did all of the unendorsed proposals.

Some CCC recommendations proposed major changes. They included:

1. The specification of details for the composition of the presidential electoral college (Art. 4). [Accepted by the government with additional representation provided for cities over 30,000]
2. That the prime minister be made "responsible for the national defense," instead of simply having "at his disposal the administration of the armed forces" (Art. 19). [Accepted]
3. That the president be able to invoke emergency powers only after the Constitutional Council has expressed the opinion that a crisis exists (Art. 14). [Rejected]
4. That the president not be able to dissolve the National Assembly during the exercise of emergency powers (Art. 14). [Accepted]
5. That MPs becoming ministers be required to take leave from their seats rather than be replaced (Art. 21). [Rejected]
6. That the list of matters in the "domain of law" be expanded by some twenty items (Art. 31 and 65). [Referred to the Council of State]
7. That if no presidential candidate receives a majority of the electoral college votes in the first two ballotings, the choice be made by the members of Parliament and the presidents of the general councils and of the Assemblies of the overseas territories meeting together (Art. 4). [Rejected]
8. That a provision be added requiring political parties and groups to "respect the democratic principles" of the constitution (Art. 2). [Accepted in principle]

9. That the steering committees of the chambers as well as the prime minister or a majority of MPs be able to call special sessions of Parliament (Art. 27). [Rejected]
10. That the government be able to make changes in provisions of law only after the Council of State has been consulted and the Constitutional Council has declared them to be regulatory (Art. 33). [Accepted in substance for Fifth Republic laws]
11. That ordinances be made subject to parliamentary ratification (Art. 34). [Accepted in substance]
12. That the Economic and Social Council "be composed of persons designated by reason of their competence, especially by the most representative trade union, professional, and social organizations of the Republic" and that the government be obliged to consult it on the periodic economic and social plans (Art. 36). [Rejected]
13. That those restrictions on parliamentary procedure be deleted that:
    a. limited the number of parliamentary committees to six in each Chamber (Art. 38). [Rejected]
    b. provided for "blocked votes" (Art. 39). [Rejected]
    c. reserved one sitting each week for question period and, instead, to permit each Chamber to decide how to use that time (Art. 44). [Rejected]
14. That all rules of order by Parliament be reviewed by the Constitutional Council, not just those referred to it by the president of a Chamber (Art. 57). [Accepted]
15. That the institutions of the Community be defined more specifically and flexibly (Arts. 66–73). [Accepted in principle]

Most of those changes would have had the effect of shifting the balance of power from the Executive toward Parliament, "of bringing the new system closer to a true parliamentary regime".[92]

The CCC adopted its final report with no dissenting votes. Thirty members voted in favor. Four of the five Socialists abstained, as did two Radicals and one African. Reynaud, as chairman, did not vote and one African was absent.[93]

The government kept its promise to consider carefully all the CCC recommendations. De Gaulle reviewed its report over the August 16–17 weekend. He had the task force study it on Monday. Then the IMC worked on the text in a marathon session from 3 P.M. Tuesday until after 2 A.M. Wednesday. De Gaulle chaired it and the other members were Debré, Mollet, Pflimlin, Soustelle, Malraux, and Janot. Their recommendations went to a Cabinet Council meeting Wednesday morning and a full Council of Ministers meeting that afternoon.[94]

The government accepted, at least in substance, about half of the significant CCC recommendations. Perhaps the most influential CCC proposal concerned the broadening of the domain of law. Although the government did not accept the CCC recommendations explicitly, it referred the matter to the

Council of State, with much the same result. Of similar importance were the various additional restrictions that the government accepted on the use of emergency and delegated powers. In sum, the CCC accepted the basic character of the new constitution, but wanted its parliamentary character to be more clearcut. The government moved about halfway in response.

At this step in the process, also, a key issue concerning the parliamentary character of the regime came to a head. Mollet believed that parliamentarism required that the prime minister be the chief executive and responsible only to Parliament. He recognized that de Gaulle as president was bound to be boss, but thought the constitution should ensure that his successors would be arbiters on the Coty model. On the other hand, de Gaulle wanted it clear that his prime minister would depend on him and Debré considered it imperative that the constitution be designed to survive de Gaulle.[95]

The issue focused on the provision for the appointment of the prime minister. As approved by the Cabinet Council on July 23, it read: "The president of the Republic shall appoint the prime minister."

The CCC did not propose any change in that wording, but the government's review of its report precipitated further consideration of it anyway. Dejean, leader of the Socialist CCC delegation, had suggested that a prime minister should "remain in office as long as he has the confidence of the National Assembly." [96] To ensure that prime ministers could be removed by Parliament but not by the president would, of course, guarantee the parliamentary character of the regime. The CCC rejected Dejean's view, but Mollet raised it again in the IMC on August 19. The Gaullists would not yield.

The impasse was referred to an *ad hoc* committee of the four ministers of state plus Debré, Cassin, Janot, and Pompidou. They began work at 10 P.M. About midnight, Pompidou produced the solution. The provision would read: [97]

> The president of the Republic shall appoint the prime minister, he can remove him from office only on presentation by the latter of his resignation.

Pompidou argued that its terms would "become clear in the hands of its users." In other words, de Gaulle could extract resignations from whomever were his prime ministers, but his successors would not be so intimidating and a normal, parliamentarist relationship would emerge.[98] Everyone seemed to agree that the regime would be presidential in practice while de Gaulle could not be prevented from making it so, and parliamentary in text and in practice thereafter.

The Council of State

The Council of State review came next. Of course, prominent Council members had been involved in the task from the outset. Debré was a *maître des réquêtes*, Janot was its general secretary, and Cassin its head. Eighteen of the twenty-two members of the task force (including Debré) were on the Council. Pompidou had been. So were two ministers (Chenot and Boulloche), a deputy on the Universal Suffrage Committee (Brocas), a speaker in the investiture debate (Bonnet), and a CCC member (Blocq-Mascart). However, the Council did not become involved officially and institutionally until de Gaulle referred the draft to it on August 21.

The review took about one week. An *ad hoc* committee of ten councilors appointed by Cassin did preparatory work on August 25 and 26. The General Assembly (six section presidents, fifty-two councilors in ordinary service, and eight councilors in extraordinary service) met for five hours on August 27 and 28. Its deliberations opened with speeches by the committee *rapporteur*, André Deschamps, and Debré. The Assembly discussed the articles in turn, considered proposed changes in them, and voted on them separately. Some votes were "close." [99]

Debré described the first purpose of the constitutional reform as being "to renovate the parliamentary regime," rather than to found an "assembly regime" like its predecessor or a "presidential regime." The new system would be characterized by "the collaboration of the branches of government—separate Chief of State and Parliament, framing a government that issues from the first and is responsible to the second." Certain constitutional provisions were intended to ensure that it not degenerate into another Assembly regime. On the other hand, because universal suffrage had been rejected as a basis for election of the Chief of State, it would not become a presidential system.

The Council was concerned especially with technical drafting matters, but considered substantive matters as well. It sought to ensure that the text would serve the government's intentions, checked it against the conditions set by Parliament, and reviewed it for conformity to French constitutional traditions and standards. Also, it responded to a specific request of the government to propose a synthesis of the wording of the initial draft and of the CCC recommendations in defining the domain of law.[100]

The Council recommended changes in sixty-one of the eight-nine (68.3 percent) articles of the draft. Many were formal, but quite a few were substantive. Among the more significant was the Council's delineation of the domain of law. It went well beyond its mandate to "propose a synthesis." For one thing, it grouped the policy areas into categories:

1. Those in which the law would make policy
2. Those in which it would determine the "general framework" of systems
3. Those in which it would lay down the rules

Second, it deleted three items that had been included by both the government and the CCC (the organization of the branches of government, rights of personal security, the ratification of treaties). Third, it added six items that had been omitted by both (rules concerning bequests, the system of issuing money, some aspects of the taxation system, "publication, effects, and application of laws," disciplinary guarantees for state functionaries, nationalization of enterprises). Fourth, the Council retained seven items that had been added by the CCC (electoral system, denationalizations, syndical rights, matrimonial system, legal capacity of persons, the property system, national defense) [101] and deleted nine others (civil responsibility, civil procedure, social security allowances, family subsidies, control of public finances, management of nationalized enterprises, the national economic plan, presentation of state accounts, the definition of the government's economic and financial powers). Fifth, it changed the scope of some items that had been included by both.[102] Finally, the Council added an "elastic clause," providing that the law might pertain to "all matters recognized as legislative in nature by an organic law." [103]

The effect of the Council's recommendations on the domain of law is difficult to assess. The concept of "general framework" narrowed its scope in some cases. On the other hand, it added more items to the government's list than it deleted. On balance, probably the Council's "domain" was broader than that of the government and maybe that of the CCC, even without considering the latitudinarian effect of the elastic clause it proposed.

Also, the Council proposed a revision of the article that was numbered 49 in the final text to provide that the prime minister might pose votes of confidence to the Senate as well as the National Assembly. In the process, it changed "shall pose" (*engage*) to "may pose" (*peut engager*). It reasoned that a new government might be required to present itself to the Assembly but its presentation to the Senate should be optional.

The only other Council recommendation of substantial importance was its deletion of the clause on political parties that the CCC had proposed. Otherwise, its recommendations were matters of detail and form. Thus, the least parliamentary organ in the constituent process exerted parliamentarist influence, at least on the highly important "domain of law."

The government received the Council of State report on Friday, August 29, becoming the center of action again. De Gaulle forewent his usual weekend at Colombey to remain in Paris and confer individually with his "closest collaborators." Debré presented a "proposed solution" to the IMC when it met at 3 P.M., September 1, for six hours.[104] In the light of that deliberation, he revised the draft for a Cabinet Council Wednesday morning, September 3, and a Council of Ministers that afternoon. Together, they consumed about four and a half hours, "the longest deliberation at the Elysée since the formation of the de Gaulle government." However, even that effort did not end the government's task. Assisted by experts, Debré continued to work on the text, polishing it, especially eliminating redundancies. He had not finished by the morning of September 4, although de Gaulle was scheduled to make the text public that afternoon. During the final governmental review, de Gaulle conferred on the constitution with Monnerville and received comments from Coty. Also, apparently the *Cour de cassation* was consulted for its interpretation of the "public liberties" clause. Thus, the last week of the drafting process was exceptionally busy.[105]

The final flurry of activity produced several substantive and many formal changes. Debré recommended acceptance of the Council of State version in almost every particular. Aside from matters of form and detail, he disagreed on only two points. He wanted to retain the provision concerning political parties, using phrasing proposed by the Council of State's committee, and insisted that questions of confidence be posed only before the National Assembly.

The government accepted all of Debré's final recommendations, except that, on Mollet's initiative, it added a clause giving the prime minister the option of asking the Senate for a vote of confidence on a declaration of general policy.[106] Also, it made several other changes, mainly formal, transitional, or dealing with the Community. The only change of significance for executive–legislative relations added a list of offices to which the president might make appointments only in the Council of Ministers.

De Gaulle presented the proposed constitution with a speech in the Place de la République on the afternoon of September 4, the place and date of the proclamation of the long-lived Third Republic, 88 years earlier. He summarized his perceptions of the character of the executive–legislative relations as defined in the document as follows:[107]

> So the country may be led effectively by those whom it mandates and may accord them the confidence that animates legitimacy. So there may exist, above the political struggle, a national arbiter, elected by the citizens who hold public office, responsible for ensuring the regular functioning of the institutions, having the right to appeal to the judgment of the sovereign people, in case of extreme peril answering for the independence, the honor, the integrity of France and the welfare of the Republic. So there may exist a government which is made for governing, which is given the time and the possibility to do so, which is not distracted from its task by anything and which, therefore, merits the support of the country. So there may be a Parliament destined to represent the political will of the nation, to vote the laws, to control the Executive, without presuming to exceed its role. So government and Parliament may collaborate but remain separate in their responsibilities and so no member of one may be a member of the other at the same time. That is the balanced structure in which power must be vested.

All evidence indicates that all the other participants in the constituent process agreed in that description of the new system. Although he did not use the term nor spell out its traditional principles, de Gaulle was describing a parliamentary regime.

The drafting process was complex and difficult. It departed from the French tradition of constitution making in omitting Parliament as the principal constituent organ. Nevertheless, Parliament and its representatives in the government and the CCC were involved deeply and influentially. At every step, important changes were made in the proposed text, generally tending to render its basic parliamentary character more pronounced and explicit. That commitment to parliamentarism was evident, not only in the activities and outcome of the drafting process but also in the intentions of the framers expressed then and later, as shall be shown in the following pages.

THE FRAMERS' INTENTIONS

Review of the drafting process for the 1958 constitution has disclosed the pervasiveness of parliamentarist influences and assumptions. Examination of the intentions of the framers as expressed outside that process leads to the same conclusion. The remarks they made at the time and retrospectively confirm overwhelmingly the view that they regarded the new regime as parliamentary.

Charles de Gaulle

De Gaulle's later recollections show that he had agreed to a parliamentary constitution in 1958 from political necessity. He seems to have intended to make the regime more presidential as soon as possible. He claimed to have accomplished that latter objective through his manner of exercising the office of president and through the 1962 constitutional amendment that introduced the system of direct popular election of the president.

De Gaulle did not disclose those latter intentions in his early public statements. In January 1959, he called the president only "an arbiter . . . to set things right" if the government were to stray from its constitutional assignment "to accomplish its arduous mission" or the Parliament from "devoting itself to its legislative task." He made similar comments in November 1960.[108] However, in April 1961, he complained about the "exegetes who do not adjust to being unable to make the constitution fit one of . . . two rigid molds," either "assembly regime" or "the system of the United States." Instead, the constitution, in its text, "is both parliamentary and presidential" and "is being applied in its spirit and in its letter." [109]

His long-term intentions began to emerge in his descriptions of the regime during the 1962 referendum campaign. On September 13, he told the Cabinet, "We have remained in a parliamentary regime, since Parliament has kept the right to overthrow the government," but the "president is the essential cornerstone of the constitution of 1958, the keystone . . . , the head of the State, and not the arbiter." [110] A week later, he called himself publicly "the head of the State and the guide of France . . . who . . . takes all the important decisions of the State." However, the regime retained its "parliamentary character," because "Parliament deliberates and passes the laws, controls the government, and has the right to overthrow it." [111]

During that same campaign, he explained why he had concealed his more presidentialist sentiments in 1958. He had believed that "the events of history" had given him personally sufficient authority to carry out the responsibilities of the presidency. Therefore, he had not attached "particular importance to the mechanism accompanying his designation." On the other hand, "taking into account political sensitivities, . . . I preferred, at that time, that there not be a sort of formal plebiscite on me." Nevertheless, "from the beginning, I knew that I would have to propose" direct election of the president "to the country, before the end of my term," in order to ensure that his successors have authority comparable to his.[112]

Later, he explained his maneuver more fully. His memoirs report that he had intended that the president's role be "all-powerful," contrary to the wishes "of the adherents of the outgoing regime." He alleged that they had allowed him to implement his interpretation at first because they had wanted him "to relieve them of the millstone of Algeria" and that they had intended to drive him from office when he had accomplished that task and to make the president "an arbiter ... who may not choose." [113] Instead, he said, he had been able to make his interpretation prevail permanently by use of the 1962 referendum.

He expressed similar views in a 1966 interview that was published post-humously. He said that he had thought since his Bayeux speech of 1946, "that the president of the Republic must govern, but no one had wanted that!" in 1958. Therefore, "I could not say so. Then, gradually, we got there, with precautions, with detours, but, in the end, without much difficulty." [114]

The importance that de Gaulle attached to the effect of the 1962 referendum in legitimating his interpretation is evident in remarks he made fifteen months later. He contended that "the indivisible authority of the State is conferred in its entirety on the president by the people who elected him," implying that the authority of that office had been less complete in the original constitution. Nevertheless, even the amended constitution did not establish a "presidential regime." [115]

Thus, de Gaulle implied clearly that the original regime had been parliamentary. He had agreed to that in order to avoid endangering his retention of office, but changed it to something more presidentialist as soon as possible. His initial acceptance, rather than his concealed intentions, must, it would seem, be used to measure the character of the 1958 constitution. That leaves the parliamentarist perception intact.

Michel Debré

Debré's public reflections on the character of the 1958 constitution began to appear during its drafting and have continued to be expressed over the years since then. In the early years, his perceptions almost always were emphatically parliamentarist. Recently, he has been more equivocal.

During the drafting period of 1958, Debré made somewhat inconsistent statements in two published interviews. In one, he said that "the ministry collectively as well as each minister individually is responsible to the Chief of State," but that they "can be called to account before Parliament only in exceptional conditions and according to exceptional procedures." This seemed to imply that the regime was presidential routinely and parliamentary exceptionally.[116] In the other interview, he called the new system "a parliamentary regime with a pre-eminent dual Executive," rather than presidential, because "a constitutional regime is presidential when the Chief of State, who is also the head of the Executive, is elected directly by universal suffrage." [117]

During the same period, he was more firmly parliamentarist in two speeches in his senatorial constituency. He argued that "we must not depart too far from the parliamentary regime" by adopting "a presidential democracy in the American style," but also, "we must not fall into the excess of a false parliamentarism." [118] The new regime would be "parliamentary" [119] because the government would be "named by the Chief of State [and] responsible to Parliament." [120]

In the 1958 referendum campaign, his public pronouncements made similar points.[121] The new constitution was "a faithful attempt at a parliamentary regime" and rejected presidentialism.[122] The president of the Republic will be no more than "the arbiter of the republican institutions." [123]

As prime minister, Debré hewed consistently to that parliamentarist position. In his investiture debate, he said that the 1958 constitution "establishes a governmental regime of parliamentary type ... perhaps, even, for the first time in several generations." [124] He made the same point repeatedly and emphatically in an official commentary on the constitution that was published soon after he took office, calling the regime parliamentary and not presidential and its chief executive the prime minister and not the president of the republic.[125] At about the same time, he explained what he meant by "parliamentary regime." He enunciated to the Senate these principles of an "authentic parliamentary regime": [126]

1. "The division of responsibilities [between executive and legislature] is clearly established."
2. "Parliamentary control operates ... by voting laws, ... voting the budget ..., by ... automatic and regular questions."
3. The government is responsible to one or the other of the parliamentary chambers "in clearly determined conditions."

And he defined "the parliamentary regime" for the National Assembly: [127]

1. "The free character of the elections to the National Assembly."
2. "The precise and detailed division of powers between government and Parliament."
3. "The powers of the national arbiter who is the president of the Republic."

He elaborated on the second point in the latter definition by listing these elements in that division:

1. The government must receive the approval of Parliament for its program; it must have the confidence of Parliament.
2. The government may be censured by Parliament.
3. Laws must be enacted by Parliament.
4. The State budget must be passed by Parliament.
5. The government is subject to control by Parliament through question period.

And he summarized: "That is the balance between government and Parliament, a precise balance that is the law of the parliamentary regime." In a similar summary statement later in 1959, he said that the framers had "wanted, in accordance with . . . the laws . . . of the parlimentary regime, to remedy . . . the insufficiency and the instability of the executive branch." [128]

Since then, his recollections of those intentions seem to have evolved somewhat. As late as 1965, he continued to call the regime "parliamentary" and denounced proposals to make it more presidential.[129] However, in 1973, he rejected the parliamentary label for "the constitution that we drafted beginning with the text of 1958, even before the fundamental reform of 1962." [130] His description of the 1958 constitution requires quotation at length.

> Certainly, there exist in the constitution mechanisms that are found in a great many parliamentary regimes; for example, those which concern the passage of laws as well as a certain number of provisions concerning the relations between the government and the National Assembly. But the elements of a parliamentary regime come in second place and within the framework of a whole structure which is above all a system—that I would not label presidential, because the law professors have a habit of giving to this word a certain content which is not at all ours—but a system founded on the eminent responsibility of the Chief of State. In short, it is a question of a mixed regime which does not fall into any of the juridical categories presented by the law professors. It is an original construction. . . .

Five years later, he included a "parliamentary system" among the "three truly basic attributes" that he had believed had been required to reform the French governmental regime, but "an Executive with its own authority" was another.[131] At one point in that statement, he said emphatically that, *"The parliamentary system was instituted"* in 1958 and defined that regime as

> meaning on one hand a cabinet backed by a majority within an assembly and thus able to guide this majority as well as head the administration, but also, on the other hand, a Parliament that could carry out its legislative duties and act as a control without infringing on the executive and . . . , above all, that the Cabinet is based on a majority in Parliament and is responsible to that majority.

However, later in the same statement, he argued that "there are two possible readings of the constitution," one presidential and the other prime ministerial, that both are "completely correct," that both had been put into practice at different times, and that he favored "the more parliamentary application." [132]

Debré's perceptions of the intentions of the framers are not easily summarized. His early recollections seem to be the most reliable and the most parliamentarist. Later, he equivocated and tended to disdain labels, but his parliamentarist inclinations remained prominent. Perhaps "reformed parliamentarism" is the term that reflects his perceptions most accurately. The reforms faced in a presidentialist direction, but the basic character of the regime, as Debré saw it, was parliamentary.

Other Members of the Government

The non-Gaullist constituents were more steadfast in their recollections of the parliamentarist character of the 1958 constitution. Chief among them was

Mollet, who was especially insistent on that reading of his collaborators' intentions. During the 1958 referendum campaign, he said that the new constitution "establishes unequivocally the regime of a parliamentary Republic." [133] During the 1962 referendum campaign, he reaffirmed that view by noting that the constitution "assumed a real responsibility of the government to Parliament." [134] Speaking only for himself, in 1968, he affirmed that he was "not a partisan of a presidential regime" and had never been.[135]

In Mollet's main effort to explain retrospectively the intentions of the framers, he identified the constitutional views of the principal constituents: [136]

> M. Debré defended the traditional thesis of the RPF, that of Bayeux. President Cassin, M. Pflimlin, and I showed a greater inclination for the parliamentary regime. If, among those present, there were partisans of the regime called "presidential," they kept quiet; never did anyone speak up to advocate the institution of such a regime and the most severe condemnations were those pronounced by General de Gaulle and Debré.

The product of those intentions, Mollet believed, was unequivocally parliamentary. It had the essential parliamentarist quality, in that "the responsibility of the government before Parliament is ensured," [137] and that neither the prime minister nor the government can be dismissed by the president "as long as the government retains the confidence of the National Assembly." [138] Mollet had discussed that interpretation with de Gaulle "several times" and had expressed it to his party and publicly without hearing from de Gaulle or any member of the IMC "the least objection." [139] Mollet distinguished between "the 'parliamentary' regime in which the separation of powers is corrected by the responsibility of the government to Parliament and the 'presidential' regime in which the separation of powers is complete." [140]

Pflimlin agreed with Mollet on the intentions of the framers. In the months following the completion of their work, he called the new system "a parliamentary regime" with a strengthened executive branch.[141] Later, he expressed some misgivings over the amount of strengthening.[142] In any case, he refused to advocate "the presidential regime *à l'américaine*" because he feared that, in French political conditions, it would become paralyzed.[143]

Georges Pompidou was the only other member of the IMC to discuss his intentions publicly later. He avoided categorizing it as parliamentary or presidential, but did describe the character of its executive–legislative relations. For instance, soon after he became prime minister, he told the National Assembly: [144]

> The constitution has defined . . . the obligations of the government in its relations with the Assemblies. Named by the Chief of State, therefore finding in him its source, the government is and remains responsible to the National Assembly. It must, consequently, enable the Assembly to exercise its control fully—that is to say, keep Parliament up to date regularly on its policies and actions.

While he was president, he told a press conference that "our constitution is halfway between a regime squarely presidential and a regime squarely parliamentary." None of his other comments are any more helpful in placing him in the parliamentarism–presidentialism debate.

Other members of the de Gaulle government have been even less articulate on this point. Soustelle has said that the "constitution . . . established a parliamentary regime." Though he had preferred a presidential system, he "was almost alone in my opinion." [145] Also, Sudreau and Buron have both described the 1958 constitution as parliamentary.[146]

Other Members of the Task Force

Three staff members of the task force have expressed publicly their perceptions of the intentions of the framers, in addition to those who contributed anonymously to the official commentary mentioned in Footnote 125. Luchaire wrote an official commentary on the responsibility of the government to Parliament under the 1958 constitution. Foyer made remarks in a Cabinet meeting that have been reported publicly and Chandernagor discussed the topic in parliamentary debates, a book, and a journal article.

Luchaire is unequivocal in the opening statement to his commentary:[147] "The Constitution of 4 October 1958 establishes a parliamentary regime and not a presidential regime, for it makes the government responsible to Parliament." Furthermore, he asserts that the provisions concerning "the responsibility of the government"—that is, those that gave the regime its parliamentary character—"received the broadest agreement and underwent no modification of substance throughout the drafting process." [148]

Foyer agreed on that interpretation in a Cabinet discussion on the draft bill for the October 1962 referendum. He argued that the "balance of powers in the 1958 constitution was not that of a presidential regime." Therefore, he warned, unless preventive measures were taken, Parliament would recover its former strength with the eventual departure of de Gaulle.[149]

Chandernagor was more outspoken and persistent than either Luchaire or Foyer. He has spoken on this question several times in National Assembly debates.[150] For instance, in June 1959, he said that "the constitution . . . was . . . parliamentary . . . in its initial conception and its inspiration. . . . A presidential regime . . . was not foreseen by the constitution." More specifically, the constitution required "the responsibility of the government to Parliament and . . . a balance of powers," which are among the "essential" characteristics of a parliamentary regime. Elsewhere, he wrote that the 1958 constitution had been designed to produce a system "founded essentially on the maintenance of a balance of power between the government and the Parliament" without "renouncing the parliamentary regime" [151] and that it was "a purified parliamentary regime." [152] Later, he referred to "the hybrid character of the constitution of 1958" and alleged that "although they pretended to install a parliamentary regime, they have, in practice, oriented it toward a principality." [153]

Members of the CCC

At least eleven members of the CCC have discussed retrospectively their understanding of the intended character of the original constitution. They are unanimous in recalling its parliamentary design. However, they vary somewhat in emphasis and consistency.

Remarks by five of them were reported publicly during the 1958 referendum campaign. Frey labeled the new regime a system of "parliamentary democracy."[154] Marcilhacy denied that the constitution would establish "one of those presidential regimes," but rather "it strives boldly to be parliamentary."[155] Mignot made the same point with special emphasis in a campaign pamphlet: "THE PARLIAMENTARY REGIME REMAINS, for the government remains responsible to the Assembly, which is the essential characteristic of the parliamentary regime." Thus, he rejected the reproach that the constitution "provides for the installation of a presidential regime."[156] Alduy and Teitgen made similar points less directly.[157]

Among CCC members who commented later, Marcilhacy was the most active, though not entirely consistent. In a 1959 article reprinted in 1963, he alleged that "the constitution of the Fifth Republic has affirmed the predominance of the Executive over the control of the legislature."[158] On the other hand, he has said that the framers "wanted a parliamentary regime"[159] and that "the constitution of 1958 is profoundly . . . parliamentary."[160]

Others agreed with that latter view. Coste-Floret argued that de Gaulle and Debré had "declared that the new constitution was a parliamentary constitution" and expressed his concurrence.[161] Valentin's reflections on the CCC discussions were consonant with Coste-Floret's: "The most official voices, when they sought to define the role of Parliament as conceived in the 1958 constitution, all proclaimed that" it had the parliamentarist mission "of controlling the executive."[162] Reynaud asserted that "it is indisputable that the regime of the Fifth Republic is a parliamentary regime" in its original design.[163] Barrachin recalled that "the constitution that was established [in 1958] . . . constituted . . . a parliamentary regime in which the strengthened executive was charged no longer with following an ill-defined majority, but of directing it."[164] David suggested the same by complaining in September 1959 that the system had changed since its installation and that "we have now entered a presidential regime because it is not the government which is responsible to us [deputies] anymore."[165] Triboulet,[166] Bruyneel,[167] Noël,[168] and Dejean[169] expressed similar conclusions about the parliamentary character of the original regime, although less squarely and usually by making direct popular election of the chief executive the defining characteristic of a presidential system.

Other Participants in Preliminary Phases of the Drafting Process

The men discussed in the sections above (plus the councilors of state) were among the framers of the 1958 constitution. Thus, their perceptions of their intentions are the most relevant to this inquiry. However, they worked within guidelines that had been negotiated and adopted earlier. One of the guidelines stipulated that the new regime be parliamentary. The opinions of participants in those negotiations may help to clarify the extent to which the framers adhered to those guidelines. Most of the forty-some persons whom de Gaulle consulted before confronting Parliament were involved in the drafting process or have not commented publicly on this point. Seven others have published remarks that bear on the question.

Most of them have agreed that the constitution conformed to the parliamentarist guideline. Coty expressed general satisfaction with the new constitution for "strengthening the Executive without damaging the essential prerogatives of Parliament." [170] Deixonne told his fellow Socialists that the new constitution's proclamation "that the government is responsible to the Assembly elected by universal suffrage is the essence of the parliamentary regime." [171] Ramadier was equally emphatic: "The regime that is proposed to us is incontestably a parliamentary regime. The chief of government is responsible only to the National Assembly." [172] Also, he called the constitution "parliamentary and . . . democratic." [173] Another Socialist, Courriére, told the National Assembly in 1962 that "the constitution of 1958 had indeed instituted a democracy of parliamentary type." [174] Even Mitterrand, who was the leader of the opposition throughout the Gaullist period, has said that on "the 28th of September 1958, the French people voted for the constitution of a parliamentary regime . . . in its essence and its principal characteristics." [175] On the other hand, a Gaullist, Michelet, responded to those who complained that the constitution was "neither presidential nor parliamentary" by calling it "both parliamentary and presidential." [176] Monnerville implied that he considered the original system parliamentary by alleging in 1962 that de Gaulle was moving "by steps toward a presidential regime." [177]

Only two speakers in the parliamentary debates of 1958 (not counting those discussed already in other categories) have expressed publicly their views on the character of the 1958 regime. Tremolet de Villers, a militant rightwing deputy, called the original system "parliamentary . . . in letter and spirit" and alleged in 1959 that de Gaulle's domination of the executive branch "has made the parliamentary regime into a presidential regime." [178] Brocas described the constitution during the 1958 referendum campaign and again during its first year of operation as "parliamentary" [179] and the following year said that the framers had "wanted to remain in a parliamentary regime" [180] and "we are still in a parliamentary regime, at least in law." [181]

Conclusion

The overwhelming weight of evidence drawn from the recollections of participants in the drafting process shows that the framers of the 1958 constitution, perhaps unanimously, intended that it have parliamentary form. In fact, de Gaulle seems to have been the only one of significant influence who did not intend that it retain that character. This confirms the view of the drafting process that was presented above. Now, the actual text of the constitution shall be examined briefly to see how accurately it reflected those intentions. This should lead to a clear conclusion on whether the regime was, in fact and intent, parliamentary at the outset.

THE CONSTITUTIONAL TEXT

Introduction

An understanding of the character of the 1958 constitution requires consideration of more than the drafting process and the expressed intentions of the framers. The text itself must be examined also. As many observers noted at the time, the original 1958 constitution was ambiguous with respect to the legislative–executive power relationship and, consequently, the basic character of the regime.[182] It combined essential elements of both parliamentarism and presidentialism. However, taken on its face and in the context of democratic legitimacy, its parliamentarist elements seemed predominant, at least in normal situations.

The legislative–executive relationship was the most prominent topic of the 1958 constitution. The longest of its titles dealt exclusively and directly with that matter. Four titles in all, filling more than half the text, were concerned with those institutions and their interrelationships and references to them abound in all of the other titles.

However, not all aspects of the topic require attention here. Those that are relevant include the provisions on the exercise of executive power in exceptional circumstances. Also, they include, with respect to normal situations, the sections that define the electoral bases of the presidency and prime ministership, the distribution of authority between those offices, and the prime minister's responsibility.

Exceptional Situations

The 1958 constitution differentiates rather clearly between exceptional and normal situations in the exercise of executive power. It seems to give the president the initiative and the greater authority in the former case. It recognizes two types of exceptional situations: emergencies and those requiring constitutional arbitration.

The emergency powers provisions are found in Article 16. Its terms have received so much attention that they need no detailed review here. Suffice it to say that they authorize the president to take "the measures" he deems necessary to deal with "grave and immediate" dangers to the nation's institutions, independence, territory, or international commitments when "the regular functioning of the constitutional organs of government is interrupted." He need do no more than consult the prime minister, the speakers of the two parliamentary chambers, and the Constitutional Council and inform the nation. However, Parliament meets by right and the National Assembly may not be dissolved while Article 16 is in effect.

Although Article 16 seems unequivocal in conferring all emergency powers on the presidency, it does not leave the prime minister completely helpless. If, while exercising the powers of Article 16, the president were to be challenged by a prime minister who enjoyed the confidence of the National Assembly, he could not prevail constitutionally. He could not dismiss the prime minister unless the latter presented the resignation of the government (Art. 8), dissolve the National Assembly to try to obtain a more congenial Parliament and government, nor rule without a government (Art. 20). In short, even Article 16 is not unequivocally presidentialist.

The president's arbitral powers are found in Articles 5, 11, 12 and 64. Article 5 makes him the guardian of the constitution, of national independence, of the territory, and of international commitments. Also, it requires that he "assure, by his arbitration, the regular functioning of the political organs of government (*les pouvoirs publics*) as well as the continuity of the State." Article 11 authorizes him to call referenda at the request of the government or Parliament on constitutional bills and treaties. Article 12 gives him the power of dissolution, requiring only that he *consult* with the prime minister and the speakers of the chambers. Article 64 makes him the guarantor for the independence of the judicial authority. In all of these cases, the constitution seemed to assume that conflicts would arise between the branches of government and that the president would be a disinterested and neutral observer, standing above political strife as the guardian of the higher interests of the State and intervening to ensure that the protagonists resolve their disputes for the greater good of France. It treated the prime minister as one of the disputants and, therefore, gave him roles only as petitioner, respondent, or consultant in the arbitrations.

Normal Situations

The presidential role in exceptional situations, no matter how pre-eminent, should not affect the identification of the character of the regime. Although the president was supposed to be the predominant executive in emergencies and arbitrations, he was expected to ensure return to normalcy as quickly as possible. Therefore, the character of the regime can be discovered only by examining the constitutional provisions that pertain to normal situations, in particular those that apply to the presidential–prime ministerial relationship. They fall mainly into three categories: those that concern the electoral bases of the two executive institutions, those that distribute authority and responsibility between them, and those that define the prime minister's dependency on the president.

Electoral Bases

Perhaps the most important single constitutional element in defining the character of a democratic regime is the electoral base of the chief executive. If the political chief executive is elective separately from Parliament, the regime is presidential. If that officer is elective by the legislature, the regime is parliamentary.

The 1958 constitution did not permit easy identification of the political chief executive. It could have been either the president or the prime minister. To resolve that ambiguity, the implications of concepts of democratic legitimacy need to be considered.

In a democratic context, such as France at mid-century, the institution with the most viable popular connection tends to wield the greater power. This was true, for instance, in the Third and Fourth Republics. The lower chamber of Parliament was popular elective and predominated over president, government, and Upper Chamber, none of which had that kind of popular base. The 1958 constitution provided the prime minister with the more viable popular connection because the National Assembly, to which he was made responsible, was elected more democratically than was the president under the original electoral system.[183]

The National Assembly was made elective by direct (Art. 24), universal, equal, and secret (Art. 3) suffrage. The president was made elective by a complex electoral college composed of the members of Parliament, of the departmental councils, and of the Assemblies of the overseas territories, as well as representatives of the municipal councils in varying proportions (Art. 6). For instance, the presidential electoral college for the December 1958 elections—the only ones held under that system—looked like this: [184]

—465 deputies, who had been elected by popular vote in November 1958
—115 senators, who had been elected in 1955, mainly by municipal councilors who had been elected by popular vote in 1953
—115 senators, who had been elected in June 1958, mainly by municipal councilors who had been elected by popular vote in 1953
—1,575 departmental councilors, who had been elected by popular vote in 1955
—1,574 departmental councilors, who had been elected by popular vote in April 1958
—63,925 municipal councilors, who had been elected by popular vote in 1953
—8,541 supplementary delegates, who had been elected in December 1958 by municipal councilors who had been elected by popular vote in 1953

Thus, the popular connection for 94.9 percent of the metropolitan electors dated to 1953, the tail end of the RPF period, when Guallism was in deep eclipse. Only 0.6 percent had issued from popular vote since the new constitution had been adopted. By contrast, all the deputies (implicitly, the electors for the prime ministership) had been placed in office by popular suffrage less than two months before they gave Prime Minister Debré a vote of confidence, 452 to 56.[185] This made the popular connection for the prime ministership more direct, closer in time, and, consequently, stronger and more viable than that of the presidency.

The constitution gave the prime ministership two other advantages in terms of popular connection. First, it provided that the National Assembly remain in existence throughout the tenure of the prime minister and not survive more than five years between elections, whereas the presidential electoral college would disappear as soon as it had cast its ballots and might not reconvene for seven years. This ensured greater continuity of popular connection for the prime minister than for the president. Second, the weighting of the electoral base of the National Assembly was more representative of French society than was that of the presidency. In particular, the overrepresentation of rural France was significantly greater in the latter body. For instance, in 1958, the most rural communes had 33.1 percent of the population and 34.4 percent of the seats in the National Assembly, but 39.1 percent of the votes in the presidential electoral college.[186] Thus, in terms of continuity and representativeness, as well as directness, of popular connection, the electoral base of the prime minister provided greater democratic legitimacy than did that of the presidency.[187]

Distribution of Policy-Making Authority

The 1958 constitution seemed to assign predominance over policy making in normal situations to the prime minister and government. It gave the presidency a much more limited role. It did that both explicitly and implicitly.

Explicitly, Article 21 declared that the "prime minister shall direct the action of the government," while Article 20 conferred on the government the authority to "determine and direct national policy" and placed "at its disposal the administration and the armed forces." Also, Article 21 gave the prime minister the responsibility and, presumably, commensurate authority to "ensure that the laws are executed."

Those explicit and general pronouncements were confirmed and given substance by many other provisions of the constitution. For instance, the entire title (V) that defined executive–legislative relations (Arts. 34-51) mentions the president only once (as recipient of the resignation of the government), but it mentions the government twenty-three times, the Council of Ministers five times, and the prime minister three times. In effect, that title made the government, under the direction of the prime minister, the manager of the legislative program of the French State and, hence, the principal formulator of policy. Furthermore, because the constitution distinguished between "the government" and "the Council of Ministers," it seemed to permit the prime minister or the ministers collectively, meeting in the absence of the president, to perform all the normal executive functions, except those that are conferred expressly on the president in the Council of Ministers (decree of states of siege, enactment of ordinances, consideration of government bills, discussion of motions of confidence). Even in the Council of Ministers under the chairmanship of the president, the prime minister could have dominated, as in the Third and Fourth Republics.

The president's policy-making powers in normal situations were quite limited in the 1958 constitution. Beyond those performed in the Council of Ministers, most of them concerned external affairs. He had various functions as president of the Community (Arts. 80, 82, 83) and was given the authority to "negotiate and ratify treaties" (Art. 52). Also, he "shall have the right of pardon" (Art. 17) and to send and receive ambassadors and envoys extraordinary (Art. 14). With respect to Parliament, his only discretionary powers in normal situtations were to send messages to it (Art. 18), to summon it, if necessary, to hear those messages (Art. 18), and to require it to hold a new deliberation on a bill or parts of one (Art. 10).

Finally, president and prime minister shared certain powers. The president was to sign all ordinances and decrees taken in the Council of Ministers, but the prime minister's countersignature was required on all texts, except those terminating his own appointment, submitting a bill or treaty to referendum, dissolving the National Assembly, invoking emergency powers, sending messages to Parliament or summoning it to hear them, referring bills or international commitments to the Constitutional Council for review, and appointing members of the Constitutional Council. Decrees not taken in the Council of Ministers could be signed by the prime minister with countersignatures only by the ministers responsible for implementing them. President and prime minister were to share the appointment power (Arts. 13 and 21), the very highest to be made by the president (with prime-ministerial countersignature) and the others by the prime minister. Besides heading the government, at whose disposal the armed forces were placed, the prime minister was "responsible for national defense" (Art. 21), but the president was "commander-in-chief of the armed forces" (Art. 15), authorized to "preside over the higher councils and committees of the defense establishment" (Art. 15), and designated "protector of the independence of the nation, of its territorial integrity, of respect for treaties" (Art. 5). Even when the president's portions of these shared powers are added to the normal powers conferred on his office alone, they are not as great as the normal executive powers bestowed on the prime minister and his government.

Prime-Ministerial Responsibility

Conceivably, the formal distribution of authority in a constitution could be nullified by other constitutional provisions making the executive with the greater authority dependent for his office on the other. In the case of the 1958 constitution, the formal distribution of greater policy-making authority to the prime minister and government could have been nullified by making the prime minister responsible to the president for his office. In fact, that did not happen.

The constitution (Art. 8) specified that the president "shall appoint the prime minister," but gave him no authority to dismiss him, except "on presentation by the latter of the resignation of the government." It provided him no means to compel such a presentation. On the other hand, it did not require parliamentary involvement in the appointment in any way, but gave it the means to force the government to resign by passing a motion of censure or rejecting a motion of confidence by an absolute majority in certain conditions (Arts. 49 and 50). Of course, the newly appointed prime minister could choose voluntarily to solicit a vote of confidence from the National Assembly.

Thus, the prime minister required only the confidence of the president at the moment of his appointment and only the confidence of the National Assembly thereafter. So far as the text of the constitution was concerned, the prime minister was dependent solely on the National Assembly much more of the time than he was dependent solely on the president. The constitutional provisions concerning prime-ministerial responsibility did not override the parliamentarist distribution of authority or electoral base.

The original 1958 constitution established a parliamentary regime. This was the result of the drafting process, the intent of the framers, and the clear meaning of key provisions in its text. The next six chapters will examine how some of those provisions worked out in practice.

2

Executive Councils and Committees

One cause of the initial confusion over the character of the 1958 constitution lay in the provisions that defined the political Executive and that gave it a bicephalic quality, as described in the preceding chapter. The prime minister was dependent on the National Assembly in the classic parliamentarist sense. The president had a separate constituent base in the traditional manner of presidential systems. Both offices seemed to have the constitutional means to prevail over the other. Commentators speculated on the likelihood that one of them would come to dominate, thereby determining the constitutional destiny of the Republic.

The constitution provided, explicitly or implicitly, for the existence of a variety of collective organs within the political executive. They included a Council of Ministers chaired by the president and a Government or Cabinet Council chaired by the prime minister. Also, the text assumed that other councils and committees would function at the policy-making level of the executive branch. In fact, as this chapter shall show, the presidentialist elements of the collective executive organs became dominant very quickly. As a result, those organs operated during the Gaullist period in a thoroughly presidentialist manner.

BACKGROUND

The Council of Ministers and Cabinet Council had long and varied histories in Republican France before 1958. The 1795 constitution forbade them both with a provision (Art. 151) that "the ministers shall not form a council." The 1848 constitution implied the rehabilitation of the Council of Ministers (Art. 64), but left the Cabinet Council in limbo. The 1875 Constitution reinforced the former[1] but continued to ignore the latter. However, the 1877 rupture between the president of the Republic and the government and the resultant political eclipse of the presidency left the Council of Ministers a formal, ratifying body for decisions hammered out in the Cabinet Council.[2]

The 1946 constitution institutionalized both councils more fully. It recognized the Cabinet Council constitutionally for the first time by mentioning the "Cabinet" in five articles (12, 45, 48, 49, 52). Also, it gave more elaborate attention to the Council of Ministers (Arts. 45–55). It gave prime ministers constitutional ascendancy over the presidents of the Republic, in addition to the political ascendancy they had held since 1877. This ensured the continued practical dominance of the Cabinet Council, although the Council of Ministers still functioned regularly and even enjoyed some modest efflorescence when the political orientations of president and government were similar and rapport between them was good.[3] Thus, the significance of the councils shifted with changes in the political importance of their chairmen and in the characters of the regimes. When the presidency of the Republic was powerful (the Second Republic and early Third Republic), so was the Council of Ministers. Otherwise, the Cabinet Council dominated. The more presidential the regime, the stronger the Council of Ministers; the more parliamentary, the stronger the Cabinet Council.

THE CABINET COUNCIL

Constitutional Status

The pattern of that historical background and the Gaullists' distrust of "assembly government" suggested strongly that the balance would swing away from the Cabinet Council when de Gaulle returned to power in 1958. However, the new constitution did not make that altogether clear. It did not mention the Cabinet Council by name, though it referred to "the government" thirty-seven times and many of them were the functional equivalent of "Cabinet Council." For instance, Art. 7 provided that "the government" may petition the Constitutional Council to certify "the incapacity of the president," hardly business to be transacted in the Council of Ministers with the president in the chair. In any case, the "government" was a collective entity and it functioned collectively only as Cabinet Council and Council of Ministers. When the constitution referred to it in that latter form, it used the label "Council of Ministers." Its other references to the government as a collective entity seem to mean the Cabinet Council.

Meeting Schedule

However the text may be read, Michel Debré, the principal author of the 1958 constitution and its first prime minister, seems to have intended that the Cabinet Council continue to function as a viable institution. He has said that he scheduled meetings for it about once a month.[4] Such an intention would seem to be consistent with his "reformed parliamentarism" concept of the Fifth Republic.[5]

The public record suggests that his intention survived for about two years of his three-year term. An inaugural meeting of his Cabinet Council held a long, serious discussion of substantive matters two days before the first session of the Council of Ministers.[6] It met, thereafter, about once a month for about one year.[7] After the fourth meeting (March 18), the government spokesman announced that "henceforth the members of the government will meet at least twice a month in Cabinet Council. ... These deliberations will permit the government to take the pulse of public opinion." [8] Apparently, the government took that pulse by other means, for it never kept its noble resolution.[9]

Its failure to keep a biweekly schedule did not deter it from announcing a weekly schedule. After a meeting on February 22, 1960, Debré said that the Cabinet Council would meet weekly "to provide for better coordination of governmental activities." [10] A week later, after another Cabinet Council, the announcement was repeated.[11]

Those intentions faded fast again. The Cabinet Council met once in March, three times in April, and eight times in the last eight months of 1960. Moreover, it met only four times in 1961 and the only meeting called by Debré in 1962 was a formal farewell session after he had submitted his resignation.

Debré's successors abandoned the Cabinet Council almost completely. Pompidou's only meeting was a formality for the inauguration of his first government.[12] Couve de Murville, Chaban-Delmas, and Messmer held no meetings at all except during the interim presidencies of Alain Poher. In 1969, when Poher and the government were barely on speaking terms, Couve called three Cabinet Council meetings. In 1974, relations were less hostile and only two such meetings convened. The first met on April 3 instead of the Council of Ministers for which Pompidou had signed a delegation as his last official act. The second was a half-hour session the next day. Friday morning, a special Council of Ministers met and the following Wednesday morning, at the usual time, a regular Council of Ministers was held, after which Poher announced that all governmental measures during the interim presidency would be decided, in the normal way, in the Council of Ministers. No Cabinet Council meetings were held during the remaining five weeks of the interim, but Councils of Ministers were held every Wednesday morning (except May Day) in accordance with the established schedule. Also, after Debré, "Plenary Interministerial Committees" that were, in effect, Cabinet Councils continued to be called occasionally to prepare the annual State budget.[13]

Meeting Contents

The Cabinet Council dealt mainly with parliamentary, political, and fiscal matters, although Couve de Murville gave a foreign affairs report at least once. The imminent opening of the parliamentary session was an especially favored occasion for the Cabinet Council to review extensively the status of the government's legislative program. Major parliamentary bills of high political sensitivity provided the grist for two noteworthy meetings in December 1959: an attempt to work out a compromise on the school-aid bill, and a discussion of a bill to reform the electoral system for municipal councils.[14] Taxation and budget matters were standard agenda items. Other topics that received extensive attention were administrative reform, farm prices, social security, Overseas France, judicial reform, Algeria, foreign policy, and some of the 1959 ordinances. The first session after Pompidou's death dealt mainly with his funeral. The topics tended to be broad, to have political sensitivity, and to involve the relations of the government with Parliament.

Meeting Style and Form

The style and form of the meetings varied considerably. The session on school aid, for instance, included serious deliberation and negotiation. Other meetings were entirely one-man shows. This was especially true of the pre-parliamentary meetings. One such session was "long and important," yet consisted of a lengthy speech by Debré and written notes by ministers on their legislative plans, but no discussion.[15] Debré told another meeting: "Each of you may make your views known. I will gather up your reflections in order to be able to take them into account when appropriate."[16] Two others were "show and tell." Eight ministers one week and nine the next reported on their current activities, plans to use special powers, and proposed bills for the forthcoming parliamentary session.[17]

Conclusions

The brief continuance of the Cabinet Council reflected the parliamentarist side of the ambivalence of the early Fifth Republic. Its survival could have provided the prime minister with the organizational means to challenge or erode the political powers of the Chief of State as had happened after 1877 and in nineteenth-century Britain. The 1958 constitution implied that the Cabinet Council would function. Debré wanted it to be viable and tried repeatedly to pump life into it. He announced active meeting schedules and avoided the appearance of conflict with de Gaulle by ensuring that its agenda skirted the "presidential reserve." He experimented with various meeting formats in search of one that would suit any natural function it might develop.

Nothing worked. The Cabinet Council never really functioned. Its demise may be seen as both cause and symptom of the development of a more presidential system. The concomitant emergence of the Council of Ministers as a viable collective organ of executive leadership tended in the same constitutional direction.

COUNCIL OF MINISTERS

Constitutional Status

The 1958 constitution referred to the Council of Ministers in eight articles (9, 13, 21, 36, 38, 39, 49, 92). They provided that the president of the Republic would chair its meetings, specified the conditions in which the prime minister might serve in his stead, and required that certain executive decisions be taken in the Council. Their main import was to make the Council a consultative body in which key decisions of the president and government would be made officially in a formal setting with the principal officers of the Executive present. However, they did not require that it function as a *collective* deliberative and decision-making body.

Membership

Decisions on categories of members for Gaullist Councils of Ministers seem to have been made with a view to strengthening it as an executive instrument of the presidency. De Gaulle departed from the practice of the Third and Fourth Republics, which had included only the president of the Republic, the prime minister, and all full ministers in its membership. Secretaries of state (junior ministers) had attended only when responsible for agenda items.[18] De Gaulle included the secretaries of state on a regular basis to reinforce governmental solidarity.[19]

Practice varied during the Pompidou presidency. The Chaban-Delmas government reverted to the practice of the preceding republics, except that the secretaries of state for the budget and as government spokesman attended regularly. The change was not explained officially, but may have resulted partly from the size of the government. Its eighteen ministers and twenty secretaries of state totaled eight more than any previous Fifth Republic government. Also, Chaban-Delmas experimented with "apprentice-ministers," secretaries of state assigned to senior members to be trained as ministers. Their solidarity with the government may have been viewed as derivative and, therefore, not requiring their presence in the Council.[20] To compensate for their absence from the Council, Chaban-Delmas announced at the inception of his government that he would meet with them fortnightly to review the business transacted in the

Council and to give them an institutionalized opportunity to air grievances and aspirations.[21] However, only about two such meetings were held per year and the experiment was not repeated by his successor.[22]

The first two Messmer Governments restored de Gaulle's practice, but the third excluded all secretaries of state.[23] The former change was not explained officially, but Messmer gave size as the reason for the subsequent exclusions, claiming that government by sixteen rather than thirty-eight "will certainly be more rapid and consequently more effective." [24] Undoubtedly, the deterioration of Pompidou's health was another factor in that change.

Also, the Council of Ministers varied in size as a result of changes in the number of full ministers. Their number ranged from 15 (Messmer III) to 23 (Pompidou V) and the total size of the Council from 17 (Messmer III) to 32 (Pompidou V and Couve de Murville). (See Table 2.1.) The average total was 27.6 and the median was 29.

Probably, the Council was too large (except Messmer III) to deliberate and make decisions collectively with optimal efficiency. The frequent changes suggest a search for that optimum. Whether the Council was being enlarged for wider "solidarity" or reduced for greater efficiency, the changes were justified as increasing its effectiveness and, therefore, of strengthening the presidential leg of the regime.

Another change in attendance at Council meetings served the same purpose. For the first time, a presidential staff member was present. During the Third Republic, no staff member attended. In the Fourth Republic, the general secretary of the government took minutes under the prime minister's direction, as the constitution required.[25] Under the Gaullists, he was joined by the general secretary of the presidency.

The two secretaries sat with the government spokesman at "a very small table" in a corner of the room and kept notes of the proceedings but, of course, never spoke. The general secretary of the government submitted draft notes of each meeting to the general secretary of the presidency for review and approval by the president. The minutes were confidential, the only copy being placed in the presidential archives.[26] These staff arrangements helped make the Council a more effective instrument of presidential governance.

Members rarely missed Council meetings. Official travel abroad and genuine serious illness seem to have been the only acceptable excuses for most members. Antoine Pinay was the only apparent exception. Occassionally, he simply preferred to stay home in Saint-Chamond. Presidents missed only four meetings,[27] but prime minister Pompidou and Chaban-Delmas were absent fairly often. Donnedieu les Varbres, the general secretary of the government, 1964–74, missed only one meeting, an emergency session called suddenly while he was traveling abroad.[28]

Table 2.1. Size of Councils of Ministers and of Governments, 1959-74

	Debré	Pompidou					Couve	Chaban		Messmer		
		I	II	III	IV	V		a.	b.	I	II	III
President of the Republic	1	1	1	1	1	1	1	1	1	1	1	1
Prime Minister	1	1	1	1	1	1	1	1	1	1	1	1
Ministers	20	21	21	17	21	23	18	18	20	19	21	15
Secretaries of State attending	6	7	4	10	7	7	12	2	2	10	16	-
Size of Council of Ministers	28	30	27	29	30	32	32	22	24	31	29	17
Secretaries of State not attending	-	-	-	-	-	-	-	18	19	-	-	13
Size of the government[c]	27	29	26	28	29	31	31	39	42	30	28	29

[a.] As of June 23, 1969
[b.] As of January 7, 1971
[c.] Not counting the president
All figures refer to size at the time the governments were formed.

Meetings

Schedule

In keeping with the significance the Gaullists sought to give them, Council of Ministers meetings were scheduled to be frequent and regular. They met frequently and with increasing regularity. Through 1963, the schedule called for meetings at 3 P.M. every Wednesday. In practice, the Council met almost weekly, except for vacation periods, but less than two-fifths of the time (38.3 percent) on Wednesday afternoons. It missed eighteen non-vacation weeks, usually because de Gaulle was traveling. Nine times, it met twice in a single week. (See Table 2.2).

In January 1964, de Gaulle changed the scheduled meeting time to Wednesdays at 10 A.M.[29] Thereafter, the Council met more regularly. Nearly four-fifths of the meetings were held Wednesday mornings, more than ten times as many as any other half-day. Meetings were canceled or held twice in a week about as often as before. The regularity was broken only during May/June 1968.

Pompidou adhered to the same schedule even more closely, 85.3 percent of the meetings being held Wednesday mornings. He canceled fewer meetings and scheduled two meetings in only one week. In all three periods, two or three meetings were skipped in August and early September and one at Christmas.

The frequency and regularity of Council of Ministers meetings suggest the extent to which they were an important, institutionalized part of the Gaullist Executive. The rising regularity shows how that institutionalization increased with the passage of time. That, in turn, helped solidify the presidentialist element of the Executive.

Length

The Gaullist Council of Ministers consumed substantial and increasing amounts of time. About half of de Gaulle's meetings lasted two to three hours. The remainder were divided equally between longer and shorter sessions. About three-fourths of Pompidou's meetings were two and a half to three and a half hours long. Two-thirds of the remainder were longer and one-third shorter. Most of the latter occurred as he faded into his final illness.

The longest Gaullist meeting lasted six hours on February 4, 1959. It reviewed the last and largest batch of ordinances.[30] Two others lasted five hours. One concerned the 1969 referendum; the other the 1969 devaluation.[31] The shortest took thirty minutes to approve Couve de Murville's inaugural declaration to the National Assembly.[32]

The substantial length suggests substantial business. Substantial business suggests a substantial institution. That the length increased over time suggests that the Council (and presidentialism) became stronger.

Table 2.2. Frequency and Regularity of Council of Ministers Meetings

	Mon. AM PM	Tues. AM PM	Weds. AM PM	Thurs. AM PM	Fri. AM PM	Sat. AM PM	Total	Weeks Vacations	Skipped Other	Weeks With Two Meetings	Average Interval	Adjusted Average Interval[+]	% of Weeks With 1 Meeting	Percent. Weeks with Meetings Held On Schedule
De Gaulle until 1/22/64	2 5	9 12	85 95	16 10	4 9	0 1	248	18	9	9	7.4 days	7.7 days	89.8	35.7
after 1/21/64	2 1	9 3	197 10	18 1	4 0	4 2	251	23	13	5	7.7 days	7.8 days	87.2	69.9
Pompidou	0 0	3 0	186 7	13 2	6 1	0 0	218	21	4	1	8.0 days	8.0 days	89.7	75.7

[+]Omitting the second meetings in the weeks when they were held.
SOURCES: Newspaper clipping file at the *Fondation nationale des sciences politiques* and *Le Monde*.

Location

The Council always met in the president's Elyseé Palace, except that it met in the Hotel Matignon the four times the prime minister presided. Until October 7, 1959, it met in the ground-floor Salon des Ambassadeurs, one of the three rooms it used in the Fourth Republic. Then, de Gaulle moved it to the second-floor Salon des Fêtes, much nearer his office.[33] Pompidou wanted that room for Pierre Juillet's office. So, he moved the Council to the Salon Murat, another ground-floor room it used during the Fourth Republic. Its frequent moves at the president's behest suggest the extent of its dependence on him.[34]

Business

Its Constitutional Basis.   Much of the Council's business was required by explicit provisions of the constitution. It had to discuss all government bills and all decisions to pose votes of confidence (Art. 39, 48). All ordinances and states of siege had to be decreed there (Arts. 38, 92, 36). So did all appointments to the highest civil and military service (Art. 13). The Council was not required to decide these matters collectively. It simply had to discuss or be present. The president decided.

Also, the constitution conferred on "the government" certain functions that, to the extent they were performed collectively, fell to the Council of Ministers in practice. Among them were to "determine and conduct the policies of the nation," to ask Parliament for authority to issue ordinances, to propose referenda, to expedite reviews by the Constitutional Council, and to refer certain kinds of matters to the Economic and Social Council (Arts. 20, 38, 11, 61, 70). If a parliamentarist system had developed, the Cabinet Council would have been the natural locus for such deliberations. As things turned out, they were consigned necessarily to the Council of Ministers.

Other constitutional functions of "the government," however, could not conveniently be performed collectively on a routine basis. These included declaring proposed amendments to bills nonreceivable; sending bills to special committees; proposing, opposing, or accepting amendments and requiring "blocked votes"; declaring bills urgent and controlling their consideration thereafter; transferring stalled budget bills to the Senate; and setting parliamentary agendas (Arts. 41, 43, 44, 45, 47, 48). They all involved parliamentary procedural questions, often requiring spot judgments. The general situation might be discussed in the Council of Ministers, but usually only the prime minister or the minister responsible for the bill could make the necessary decisions in catch-as-catch-can consultation with his colleagues and MPs.

Its Extraconstitutional Basis.   The Council of Ministers transacted substantial amounts of business not required by the constitution. The most common type was the presentation of reports and policy statements by ministers. A second type, especially under de Gaulle, was the delivery of instructions by the president of the Republic to the Council. Finally, informal discussions of politics were held occasionally, especially under Pompidou.

The most frequent reports were those given weekly by the minister of foreign affairs on the international situation and the minister for the economy and finance on the economy. Also, Council members usually gave accounts of their official trips abroad and of visits by foreign dignitaries to France. The minister of the interior reported on each French election and the secretary of state for parliamentary affairs did so on each parliamentary session. Appropriate ministers reported on most other major political and governmental events.

Instruction-giving was less frequent. One example was de Gaulle's issuance of homework assignments on Algeria in 1959. Another was his order to the inaugural meeting of Pompidou III that the new ministers submit to him within two months "general reports outlining the activities of their departments and the reform projects and achievements they intend to carry out." [35]

Usually, the discussion of politics was unofficial and unreported. Only twice were such discussions mentioned in "the communiqué." The first occurred during the disorders of 1968 and the second during preparations for the 1973 elections.[36] Unofficial reports suggest that the Pompidou Council turned to politics fairly often in its more relaxed moments.[37]

The Types Of Business. Four basic types of business were transacted in the Council of Ministers:

1. Ceremonial. The first meeting of each government was devoted to taking the official group photograph, "pep talks" by president and prime minister, and basking in the glory of being among the annointed few.

2. Routine. The bulk of most meetings was taken up by the official tasks of the Council as they matured in the normal rhythm of governmental operations. Usually, they had been well prepared in advance, controversies had been resolved, and the deliberations were smooth and dull.

3. Emergency. On rare occaions, that rhythm was disrupted in a way that required Council action too urgently to await the next scheduled meeting. One example was Prime Minister Pompidou's amnesty proposal during the student disorders of 1968.[38] However, most emergencies concerned international monetary matters.[39]

4. Historic. When Gaullist presidents wished to consecrate an especially important policy departure, they used a special Council ritual that became part of the magic and drama of Gaullism. The ritual followed these steps: (a) the Council members were informed of the terms of the issue in advance and instructed to prepare recommendations; (b) during the meeting, the president polled all members individually, giving them full opportunity to present their recommendations, listening attentively, and asking probing questions; (c) after all members had spoken, concluding with the prime minister, the president announced his decision and instructed the members to support that policy actively or resign immediately.[40] At least twice, two successive lengthy meetings were required to complete the ritual.

Notable examples of "historic" business are: *1959*, self-determination for Algeria, church-school subsidies, tax reform; *1962*, the Evians Accords, presidential electoral reform,[41] *1968*, the May/June disorders, education reform; *1969*, regionalization and Senate reform, and economic recovery; *1972*, expansion of the European Community.

Conclusions.   The Council agenda tended to be dominated by business requiring formal, official action. The meetings afforded scant opportunity for the working deliberations that resolve disagreements and settle problems. Those were the tasks of other organs. The purpose of the Council was to satisfy the president that those organs had done their job and to provide him an official forum in which to announce his approval. Because the president emerged as the *de facto* chief executive, his approval was substantive, rather than merely *pro forma*, and the role of the Council was enhanced.

The Conduct of the Meetings

Preparing Them.   Council meetings were prepared elaborately. As business items percolated toward the top, the presidential and governmental secretaries called staff and ministerial meetings to ensure their readiness. When those meetings and appropriate telephone consultations seemed conclusive, the general secretary of the government placed the items on a draft agenda that he distributed the Friday evening preceding a Wednesday meeting to all members of the Council and to the general secretary of the presidency. The prime minister was master of the draft until it went to the president.[42]

The prime minister and president discussed the draft agendas at their regular Monday-morning meetings and the two general secretaries presented a second draft to the president that afternoon. At that time, the president gave the agenda its final form, often making revisions. The draft was distributed to all members, with special reminders to those responsible for its items. Finally, the prime minister consulted the president briefly in his office immediately before each Council meeting. Thus, the process gave the prime minister the initiative and the president the final say, unlike its parliamentarist predecessors, which gave the prime minister both.

Chairing Them.   The 1958 constitution provides that "the president of the Republic shall preside over the Council of Ministers" (Art. 9). However, it permits the prime minister, "exceptionally, to replace him as chairman of a Council of Ministers by virtue of an express delegation and for a fixed agenda" (Art. 21). In fact, the presidents almost always presided. Prime ministers chaired only four meetings. Before de Gaulle underwent prostate surgery in 1964, he prepared the agenda for the April 22 meeting and gave Pompidou the required delegation. Pompidou chaired the meeting and the two general secretaries reported to de Gaulle in the hospital, where he signed the decrees it had reviewed.[43] Similar arrangements were made for the meetings of September 30, 1964, and May 17, 1968, while de Gaulle was traveling in Latin America and Rumania, respectively.[44] Finally, Prime Minister Messmer presided on February 14, 1973, when President Pompidou was ill.[45]

At least five other delegations were made or planned for meetings that were cancelled. Two were second meetings during de Gaulle's trips to the Soviet Union and Somalia in 1966. Finally, on the evening of April 2, 1974, Pompidou signed a delegation for the April 3 meeting, three hours before he died.

The handling of the chairmanship underlies the rising dominance of the presidency. Presidents authorized meetings in their absence only when no alternative seemed feasible. Such occasions arose rarely.

Preliminaries. Most members arrived fifteen or twenty minutes before each meeting. They prepared their papers and water glasses and chatted until the arrival of the president and the prime minister was signalled by the entry of a *huissier* in formal attire. Chattering stopped and all members stood at their assigned places. The president and prime minister circled the table slowly, greeting and shaking hands with each member.[46]

Seating was formal and hierarchical by rank of office. The president and prime minister sat directly opposite at the center of each side, occupying the only two armchairs, the president's being the only one with a gold braid.[47] Ministers of state and other super-ministers sat to the right and then left of the president and, then, of the prime minister. The other full ministers were arranged similarly in descending order of the traditional status of their Ministries: Justice, Foreign Affairs, Interior, Defense, Economy and Finance, etc. The secretaries of state sat at the ends of the table.[48]

Format. The meetings were structured in accordance with the format set in 1947. *Part A* reviewed bills and decrees that had been approved by the ministers concerned. If other ministers objected, the texts were deferred pending resolution of the disagreements. *Part B* consisted of communications by the president, the prime minister, and other ministers and of personnel appointments. *Part C* reviewed preliminary important or controversial proposed bills and decrees. Also, "historic" business and politics were discussed in Part C.[49]

Aftermath. Immediately after each meeting, the official government spokesman used the notes of the general secretaries to revise a draft communiqué that the general secretary for the government had prepared in advance. During de Gaulle's presidency, it reported the official actions of the meetings in straightforward, factual phrases. Pompidou added editorial comment on occasion. The president reviewed, revised, and approved the communiqué and instructed the spokesman on oral comments to give the press. Information beyond the official communiqué and commentary was privileged. Finally, the general secretariat of the government prepared for the president's signature and distributed to the Council members a summary of the decisions taken.[50]

Style. The style of discourse in Gaullist Council of Ministers meetings was stiff and formal, especially under de Gaulle. He permitted no smoking or side conversations, although notes were passed and doodling took place. Late arrivals, lengthy presentations, technical arguments or explanations, and interruptions were bad form. Each member reported on his own affairs and avoided his neighbor's. Nothing was debated; little was deliberated; few dissents were expressed; routine meetings were dull.[51] One minister, emerging from his first meeting, asked another with amazed disappointment: "So, that is how it goes?"[52] Another first-timer exclaimed, in astonishment: "No one said anything." Still another minister called the meetings "funeral wakes with a difference: the corpse speaks."[53] Nevertheless, de Gaulle did try to encourage discussion. He told new members: "You are not only minister of Posts (for example), but a member of the government. You have the right and duty to express your views on every problem."[54] When some bold soul followed this instruction, de Gaulle listened attentively and spoke politely, but rarely heeded the advice.[55] Moreover, his austere presence intimidated more than his words emboldened. Also, Prime Minister Pompidou discouraged maverick comments, for they tended to disrupt the orderly presentation of business that he had arranged, often with great difficulty.[56]

President Pompidou's Council meetings were somewhat more relaxed. He allowed smoking and set the example. Ministers could leave the table to refill their water glasses. Discussion was freer, though side conversations still brought black looks from the president. Reports were presented more casually. Ministers were more prone to poach on their colleagues' domains, moves well designed to enliven meetings with debate, even squabbles.[57] Pompidou's more casual and open style may have lengthened the meetings. However, his control was no less complete than de Gaulle's. The agenda, the flow of business, the decisions were his as thoroughly as they had been de Gaulle's.[58]

Monologue was the standard form of discourse in both administrations. The elaborate preparations for the meetings discouraged questions and dissent. Members spoke only to present their reports. However, the monologues varied greatly in quality. Couve de Murville's delivery was barely audible in an austere, soporific monotone, reporting only what the daily press had already published. Nevertheless, one of his colleagues—who sat next to him—said that Couve added, "one word, one fact, one opinion which held all of substance."[59] Giscard d'Estaing was famous for the brilliance of content and presentation of his economic reports. Even de Gaulle admired them. He was confident, competent, articulate, perfect master of his domain, displaying his genius with swift, precise, authoritative flourishes that sparkled with statistics, facts, and analytic sallies.[60] André Malraux's rare interventions, characterized by literary elegance, a sense of drama, and his resonant voice, held his colleagues spellbound.[61] Under Pompidou, Maurice Druon took Malraux's literary and stentorian place briefly.[62]

Members differed, also, in readiness to offer dissent. In the early years, Pinay, Soustelle, Sudreau, Cornut-Gentille, and Pisani were noted for brashness.[63] Under Pompidou, Debré, Giscard d'Estaing, and Duhamel had similar reputations.[64] On the other hand, Guichard never spoke and rarely moved.[65]

A Gaullist president was challenged directly and forcefully only once in a Council of Ministers meeting. In November 1959, Minister of Finance Antoine Pinay responded to de Gaulle's comment that "Europe must organize its defenses." The exchange requires reproduction in full to show why no one emulated Pinay. Two months later, he left the government:

> *Pinay*: M. *le Président* [not *Mon Général*, as de Gaulle preferred], how do you reconcile this necessity, for the Europeans to provide for their own defense, with the speech that you just delivered at the *Ecole militaire*: National defense must be French? If I understand, you have condemned the very principle of NATO.
>
> *De Gaulle*: M. *le ministre des Finances* is interested in problems of foreign policy?
>
> *Pinay*: Yes, I am interested in problems of foreign policy. And, as few of my colleagues are informed about your speech, I will read the most interesting passages on which I hope that we may receive, if you will be so good, some light. [Pinay then read several key paragraphs from the speech.] Our allies are in consternation over your speech. Do you believe that, financially, technically, and militarily, we have the means to defend ourselves? For my part, I answer *no* at once, as far as the economic and financial domain is concerned. No, we do not have the means to defend ourselves alone. In a period of intercontinental missiles, it is senseless to pretend to act in isolation. We do not have the real possibility to create a striking force and we must prevent the Americans from leaving at all costs.
>
> *De Gaulle*: Of course, our defense, the establishment of the means, our conception of the conduct of war, must be combined with those of other countries. Our strategy must be coordinated with the strategy of others. On the battlefields, it is infinitely probable that we will be side by side with our allies. But each should have his part to himself.

The discussion moved to other topics. Then, de Gaulle turned back. He reminded Pinay that when de Gaulle had removed part of the French Mediterranean fleet from NATO command and sent memoranda to Eisenhower and Macmillan proposing to reorganize NATO, "*Monsieur le ministre des Finances* did not raise objections."

> *Pinay*: I beg your pardon, *Monsieur le Président*, I learned by newspaper that you were withdrawing part of the French fleet. . . . As to the memorandum to President Eisenhower and Mr. Macmillan, it is correct that you mentioned in the Council of Ministers the sending of that text. Perhaps you even said a few words about it, but you did not disclose its contents and, in any case, your decision had been taken. *Monsieur le Président*, do not look for cover. You are the one who taught me the laws of ministerial solidarity.[66] All ministers are together. Ministers who are in the minority on a question yield or resign. I do not have the same conception of ministerial solidarity as you do. Decisions must be deliberated, discussed, taken in common. But we are confronted by decisions that have been taken already.
>
> I do not want to sound you out on your intentions. I am not the depository of your thoughts. I have only one question to ask you, simple, clear, and precise. You declared at the *Ecole militaire*: "The system of integration is over." What does that mean?
>
> *De Gaulle, rising*: Thank you, M. Pinay. Gentlemen, the meeting is adjourned.

Later de Gaulle told Pinay: "I do not reproach you for saying what you think. I reproach you for saying it in the Council of Ministers." [67]

Though Pinay's persistence was unique, more moderate dissent was not unusual. Shortly before he was dumped as premier, Pompidou astonished his colleagues by making clear to a Council of Ministers that he had broad disagreements with de Gaulle. Debate was more impassioned on Algeria under de Gaulle than it had been on Indochina or Tunisia under the Fourth Republic.[68] Also, serious dissent was expressed on such issues as the 1959 school-aid bill, various agricultural issues, the 1968 university reforms, the miners' strike, and the reorganization of the Paris region.

Understandably, such dissent was more forthcoming when the presidents solicited opinions directly from individual ministers. The consideration of "historic" matters, as mentioned above, provided the most noteworthy occasions for such opportunities. However, both presidents used the device less systematically at other meetings.

Genuine deliberation was rare, if not nonexistent. The three-and-a-half-hour emergency meeting in November 1968 may have been as close as a Gaullist Council came to working out a major decision collectively. The international financial community agreed that devaluation was inevitable that weekend and the French government had only its size to decide.[69]

Finance Minister Ortoli opened the discussion by reporting on his negotiations in the European Community and listing three possible decisions: a large devaluation of about 15 percent, a small one of about 10 percent, or no devaluation. He expressed no choice at that time, but later made clear his preference for no devaluation. Then, de Gaulle asked each minister to state his preference. He began with a minister whom he knew would oppose devaluation eloquently. As each minister spoke, de Gaulle, "serene and relaxed," asked questions and commented. If a minister was unclear or equivocal, he asked: "Then, are you for or against the devaluation?" Only Chirac, Chalandon, and Marcellin favored devaluation.

Immediately after the meeting, de Gaulle announced his decision not to devalue. Clearly, this had been his preference at the outset, but persuasive arguments to the contrary by most of the ministers might have changed his mind.

The presidents' polling of the Council should not be mistaken for voting. Though they might tally the results, they did not feel bound by them. For instance, only four of twenty-four members in the Chaban-Delmas government favored the posing of a vote of confidence. Yet, Pompidou approved the request.[70] Also, more than half of the Council opposed reorganization of the Paris region, but de Gaulle approved it without change.[71]

The manner of concluding an item of Council business was invariable. When the president believed that a discussion had proceeded far enough, he announced the Council's decision that was, in fact, *his* decision or said that he would announce the decision after the meeting. In Pompidou's words: *"C'est moi qui decide."* [72]

Conclusion

The Council of Ministers under the Gaullist presidents became the chief collective body in the political Executive, yet its real importance was difficult to assess. Most meetings were formal and routine, with very little serious deliberation. Yet its review was the culminating step in the process of governmental decision making for the most important policy matters in the Executive. It attracted substantial serious attention from the presidents and prime ministers, and was an essential part of each minister's week.

Furthermore, this key executive institution became a major tool of the presidents. In earlier republics, presidents had chaired the Council formally, but in fact, prime ministers had controlled its business. De Gaulle and Pompidou transformed formal leadership into effective and virtually complete control. To use Walter Bagehot's terminology, the Council was converted from a "dignified" to an "efficient" institution of government and became one means by which the Fifth Republic was moved toward presidentialism.

OTHER COUNCILS AND COMMITTEES

Introduction

Committees rule democracies. No modern legislature or political executive can operate expertly at its most general level. Presidents, prime ministers, Cabinets, Parliaments must rely on specialized committees to prepare their decisions.

The collective elements of the Gaullist political Executive, then, included a committee system—standing and *ad hoc* committees in both the presidential and prime-ministerial spheres. Elaborate and important committee systems developed in both areas. Changes were especially significant in the presidential sphere. The establishment and growth of that presidential committee system may have been one of the key managerial factors in the development of presidential government.

Background

Very few presidential committees existed in the Fourth Republic. The only ones of consequence were created by the 1946 constitution. It made the president of the Republic chairman of the High Council and Committee of National Defense (Art. 33), the High Council of the Judiciary (Art. 34), the High Council of the French Union (Art. 65), and the Constitutional Committee. However, the High Council of National Defense met only rarely; [73] the High Council of the French Union did not come into existence for five years and then met only twice; [74] and the Constitutional Committee met only once. [75]

The High Council of the Judiciary was the most important presidential committee of the Fourth Republic, being responsible for ensuring the discipline and independence of French judges. It consisted of twelve other members (two appointed by the president) plus the minister of justice as vice chairman. It decided by majority vote, with the president having a casting ballot (Art. 83) and a virtual veto on appointments and promotions. Also, he exercised the right of pardon in the Council, though he was not bound by its judgment.[76]

The only other presidential standing committee of significance was the Committee of National Defense, which was composed of appropriate ministers and high-ranking military officers. However, the president's chairmanship was quite formal. The prime minister controlled its composition and staff and directed it "under the high authority of the president of the Republic." [77] In fact, the president was expected to refrain from expressing opinions,[78] though on occasion, he did.[79] In any case, the Committee never functioned very smoothly or effectively.[80]

In addition to those councils, Auriol called some *ad hoc* committee meetings on a few serious foreign affairs problems. However, they had little consequence, and were not repeated by his successor.[81] Otherwise, no presidential committees existed in the Fourth Republic.

In contrast, prime-ministerial committees were quite common in the Fourth Republic. Coalition politics thwarted an early effort to establish a system of standing committees in the government. Therefore, most of them were *ad hoc*, although some did become permanent, especially those dealing with defense and economic affairs. Usually, prime ministers appointed them to prepare matters for the Council of Ministers, to try to resolve disagreements that had surfaced in the Council of Ministers or Cabinet Council or to coordinate the implementation of governmental decisions. Such committees were mentioned frequently in Council of Ministers meetings. However, the fragility of the governmental coalitions rendered their work quite tentative and in the later years of the Republic, an effort was made to give the committees broader bases by working through mixed governmental-parliamentary-partisan *ad hoc* committees called "round tables." [82]

In summary, then, presidential committees had very little importance in the Fourth Republic and prime-ministerial committees were used very much, but with mixed results. In contrast, parliamentary committees were notorious for their overwhelming strength. The reversal of that power equation contributed greatly to the development of a structural basis for presidential government in the Fifth Republic.

Presidential Committees

Amount of Activity

Although the amount of committee activity was greater during the Gaullist administrations, it cannot be measured precisely. Many of the meetings were so informal that no records were kept. Also, only fragmentary data on the meetings have been published and neither of the secretaries has released additional information.

Nevertheless, the available material seems to provide a sufficiently solid basis for a generally accurate description. With respect to the presidential committees, it suggests that de Gaulle presided over an average of about 5.25 of them per month and that Pompidou chaired only about one per month. Initially, they had no regular schedule, but Prime Minister Pompidou tried to confine them to Tuesdays and Thursdays.[83]

Standing Committees

All presidential standing committees were created formally by official texts: constitutional provision, laws, or decrees.

The High Council and Committee of Defense. The 1958 Constitution provided (Art. 15) that the president "shall preside over the higher councils and committees of defense." A 1959 ordinance and a decree later that year spelled out the details, creating a Higher Council of Defense, a Defense Committee, and an Inner Defense Committee (*comité de défense restreint*), all chaired by the president, though he might delegate that authority to the prime minister for the Inner Committee.[84] The Higher Council contained as many as fifty members, including the prime minister, appropriate ministers, high-ranking military officers, civil servants, and private persons. The Defense Committee members were the prime minister; the ministers of foreign affairs, armies, interior, and finance and economics affairs; and such other ministers as the president might invite. The chairman of the joint chiefs of staff, the chiefs of staff of the three services, the general secretary of national defense, and the president's personal military chief of staff also attended its meetings and a member of the Elysée military staff served as recording secretary. The composition of the Inner Committee was decided by the prime minister, who also called its meetings.[85] A "general secretariat of national defense" reported to the prime minister. In theory, the High Council undertook studies of defense problems for the government. The Defense Committee made "decisions on the general conduct of defense." The Inner Committee made "decisions on the military conduct of defense."

In practice, defense policy was made by the president in the Defense Committee and was reiterated by him in the Council of Ministers.[86] The High Council was too large and inappropriately constituted. The Inner Committee hardly functioned, having been designed as a war council for major international hostilities. The Defense Committee met about once a month during the Algerian War and four or five times a year thereafter.[87]

Initially, some doubt existed as to whether the president or prime minister was pre-eminent in defense policy. However, the committee structure favored the president. Decrees in 1960 and 1962 removed that ambiguity in favor of the president.[88] Of course, de Gaulle's personal qualities and background expedited the clarification, but the situation did not change appreciably under Pompidou.

Council of Algerian Affairs. This institutionalized presidential council was created officially by decree during the "Barricades Crisis" of 1960, but it had developed out of earlier *ad hoc* meetings of appropriate officials on the Algerian problem.[89] Its purpose was to give the president the means to have an official, direct role in resolving the Algerian problem without resort to Article 16 emergency powers.[90] Therefore, it played an important role in French governmental affairs.

The founding decree designated as members the president, the prime minister, and the ministers of the interior and of the armies. It authorized the general delegate of the government in Algeria, the general secretary of Algerian affairs, the chief of staff of national defense, and the commanding general in Algeria to attend its meetings and empowered the president to include other members of the government. De Gaulle's principal staff adviser on Algeria says that the ministers of finance and foreign affairs were members also.[91] The general secretariats of the president of the Republic and for Algerian affairs provided the staff and administrative support. De Gaulle gave the general delegate the very unusual permanent delegation of authority to convene the other members, except the prime minister.[92] After the 1962 Evians Accords were signed, the minister of state for Algerian affairs and the high commissioner of the French Republic in Algeria replaced the ministers of the interior and the armies and the high functionaries "authorized" to attend no longer did so.[93] However, the Council met very little thereafter.[94]

The Council's mandate was to "make the decisions concerning Algeria so far as they are not taken in the Council of Ministers." In practice,

> Without replacing the Council of Ministers, the Committee prepared its deliberations and carried them further. Within it or after having consulted its members, General de Gaulle took . . . most of his important decisions concerning Algeria.[95]

Among those decisions were those that concerned the transfer of certain senior officials, the dissolution of some dissident defense units in Algeria, the suppression of the Psychological Warfare Bureau, reforms in the Algerian system of justice, the principal economic and financial policies for Algeria, the transfer of the general delegation outside Algiers, the preparation of the Evians negotiations, the creation and oversight of the Algerian *commissions d'élus*, the preparation of the 1961 referendum, and the implementation of its provisions.[96]

Council for African and Madagascan Affairs. This committee was an attempt to salvage something from the collapse of the ill-fated Franco-African "Community" of the 1958 constitution (Title XII).[97] By an exchange of letters in 1961, Prime Minister Debré and the president of the Community Senate acknowledged officially the demise of the original Community institutions.[98] Then, de Gaulle issued executive orders converting the general secretariat of the Community into a general secretariat to the presidency of the Republic for the Community and African and Madagascan affairs,[99] and creating this Council.[100]

The members of the Council were the prime minister, the ministers of foreign affairs and of cooperation, the secretary of state for foreign affairs, the general secretaries of the presidency and to the presidency for the Community, and other members of the government and high civil and military functionaries invited by the president. The Council was charged with making "the decisions concerning the relations of the Republic with the African and Madagascan states that issued from the former French Union insofar as they are not taken in the Council of Ministers."

The Council fared no better than its predecessor institutions. Relations between France and her former colonies became bilateral very quickly. Also, the secretariat and the successive ministers that dealt with the "Community" states usually operated more efficiently than the Council. By 1964, the Council was virtually moribund. It met on March 23, 1965 for the last time.[101]

Council of Foreign Affairs. Still another presidential council, the Council of Foreign Affairs, was announced in March 1960.[102] De Gaulle chaired its first meeting and the foreign minister and general secretaries of the presidency and of the foreign ministry attended also. This Council completed a network of presidential committees for the policy areas in the "reserved sector" (defense, Algeria, Community, foreign affairs).

However, the Council seems to have died aborning. No founding decree was issued. No later meetings were announced. Rather, its business seems to have wound up in the Defense Committee.[103]

High Council of the Judiciary. The 1958 constitution followed its 1946 predecessor by placing the president of the Republic in the chair for the High Council of the Judiciary (Art. 65). However, the first president of the Court of Cassation was to take the chair when it acted as "disciplinary council for the judges." Also, the minister of justice, as vice president of the Council, "may preside in place of the president of the Republic".

Despite the president's elimination from the process of disciplining judges, his authority actually increased substantially over matters within the purview of the Council. He became "the protector of the independence of the judicial authority" to be "assisted by the Council". He acquired the right to appoint all nine members of the Council (with some restrictions), rather than two of twelve as in the Fourth Republic. Finally, his authority over judicial appointments and promotions was increased at the expense of the Council.[104] Also, he retained the powers of pardon and reprieve, the Council having a consultative voice only.[105]

Ad Hoc *Committees*

Except the institutionalized councils described above, all Gaullist presidential committees seem to have been *ad hoc*.[106] The presidents called meetings as occasion required and invited participants as they deemed appropriate. Their appearance and growth in the Fifth Republic helped the presidency develop a decision-making infrastructure to tilt the regime toward presidentialism.

The *ad hoc* committees always included the prime minister and, usually, the finance minister, because finance touched so many policy areas. The most frequent other participants were the ministers of foreign affairs and defense. High functionaries attended meetings on matters for which they were responsible. For instance, the planning commissioner attended most meetings on economic and social affairs. Ministerial staff members never attended, although presidential and, during Pompidou's presidency, prime-ministerial staff members did.[107]

Meetings were initiated by the presidents or prime ministers or by members of the Elysée staff who used them to influence the ministers. Each meeting was organized by a technical councilor on the presidential staff in consultation with the prime-ministerial staff. He prepared the agenda, collected necessary supporting materials, and distributed them in advance to all participants. He attended the meeting, took minutes, distributed them to the members, and was responsible for follow-up.[108]

The *ad hoc* committees met in the same room as the Council of Ministers with much the same formality, though their smaller size made them less austere. The prime minister directed the presentation of business and the president arbitrated. De Gaulle "listened much and well, asked for explanations, provoked confrontations by posing hypotheses that did not always represent his own views. He concealed neither his ignorance nor his uncertainty."[109]

Ad hoc committee meetings had four main purposes:

(1) *Informational.* The officials who were mainly responsible for a matter explained it to the president.

(2) *Decisional.* The president resolved disagreements among officials when the prime minister had failed. His decisions were submitted to the Council of Ministers for ratification later.

(3) *Directive.* The president impressed upon his aides his insistence that they ensure execution of his high-priority projects.

(4) *Coordinating.* The president tried to ensure that the principal agencies in an area were acting in concert and in accord with policy.

Ad hoc committees met only for Algeria, defense, and foreign affairs during the Debré premiership. Thereafter, they met in all areas of policy,[110] although they tended to concentrate on the "presidential sector" and the economy. The most frequent topics were foreign affairs, the Common Market, the state budget, the economy, international monetary matters, and education. Other examples from de Gaulle's administration were aeronautical and space questions, atomic energy, computers, agriculture, population, the Paris region, administrative reform, and the judicial system. During the Pompidou presidency, modernization of the economy was the most frequent topic. For instance, during one eighteen-month period, two-thirds of the presidential committee meetings concerned that topic.[111]

These committees rarely dealt with matters of capital importance, though their cumulative significance may have been crucial in the evolution of the regime. The decisions on self-determination for Algeria, the 1962 constitutional referendum, the withdrawal from NATO, and the aborted 1968 referendum were not taken in such meetings, though their implementation may have been discussed there. Their domain lay "at the junction of the political and the administrative." [112] In short, they gave the presidents an important instrument for ensuring that their decisions in the Council of Ministers were prepared properly and implemented loyally.

Prime-Ministerial Committees

Amount of Activity

Committees chaired by the prime ministers or members of their staffs were even more active than the presidential committees. Debré and Pompidou chaired 599 committee meetings during the first seven years of the regime, an average of 7.11 per month, and members of their staffs chaired another 1,742, or 16.8 per month. Chaban-Delmas and Messmer chaired 429 meetings during the Pompidou presidency, or 7.27 per month.[113] The prime-ministerial meetings showed no consistent trend in frequency, but the staff-chaired meetings became much more numerous with the passage of time. (See Table 2.3)

Standing Committees

As with the presidential standing committees, most prime-ministerial standing committees were established by official texts. Their institutionalized character was enhanced further by assigning some of them offices and substantial staffs. Ten such committees existed in 1974, including: [114]

Interministerial Economic Committee. This committee was created by de Gaulle while he headed the provisional government after World War II[115] and was active and important throughout the Fourth Republic, with meetings scheduled weekly.[116] During the Debré premiership, meetings on economic matters were scheduled every Tuesday, though not necessarily by the Interministerial Economic Committee.[117] After that, the official committee declined in importance, meeting only a few times per year and being replaced by *ad hoc* economic committees, except that the standing committee was revived briefly while Debré was minister of the economy and finance in 1966–67.[118]

While Debré was premier, the standing committee was the object of a tug of war between a prime minister who "strove to be the real minister of the national economy" [119] and ministers who insisted on continuing the tradition that the rue de Rivoli rule the economic domain with an iron hand. The traditional view prevailed while Pinay was minister of finance, but the control of Wilfrid Baumgartner, who replaced him, was limited, though still substantial. If the committee's agenda contained only technical matters, Baumgartner presided, but if its business had political implications, Debré took over. However, Debré had delegated to Baumgartner authority to "coordinate" the activities of the

Table 2.3. Number of Committee Meetings Chaired by Prime Ministers and Their Staffs

	1959	1960	1961	1962	1963	1964	1965	1966	1967	1968	1969	1970	1971	1972	1973	1974
PM	33	57	118	88	87	100	116	129	118	94	92	147	121	100	73	82
Staff	23	61	142	154	283	394	356	329	318	322	307	530	592	583	501	534

SOURCES: Claude Dulong, *A L'Eliseé au temps de Charles de Gaulle* (Paris: Hachette, 1974); Michel Debré and Jean-Louis Debré, *Le pouvoir politique* (Paris: Seghers, 1976).

"technical" Ministries of Labor, Industry, and Agriculture and to arbitrate economic and financial disagreements among the other ministries.[120] Also, at that time, the committee was responsible for wage questions in the public sector.

Interministerial Committees on the Plan. Pompidou put new curbs on the Finance Ministry very soon after he became prime minister. He transferred the General Planning Commission from it to his office[121] and used its authority over long-term policies to control the short-term policies of the ministry. Four years later, he went a step further by replacing the *Interministerial Committee on the Plan for Economic and Social Development*, which had supervised the Commission since 1953,[122] with three new committees.[123] He chaired all three, as he had their predecessor. The other members of the *Interministerial Committee charged with Problems of Administering the Plan* were the minister of state for the civil service, the minister of the economy and finance, the secretary of state for the budget, and the general commissioner of planning. The *Interministerial Committee charged with Public Enterprise* had the same membership, except that it omitted Civil Service and added the Ministers of the armies, of industry, of facilities (equipment), and of scientific research. *The Interministerial Committee charged with Private Enterprises* was composed of the ministers of the economy and finance, of scientific research, and of social affairs; the general delegate for territorial improvement; and the general commissioner of planning. All three committees had high civil servants as "*rapporteurs.*"

Standing Interministerial Committee for Territorial Improvement and Regional Action. The second of Pompidou's "parallel" committees began as two committees created by Debré in 1960: the *Interministerial Standing Committee for the Paris Region*[124] and the *Interministerial Standing Committee of Regional Action and Territorial Improvement*.[125] The latter committee absorbed the former in 1963.[126] The merged committee was composed of the ministers of interior, finance and economic affairs, public works and transportation, industry, agriculture, labor, and construction, and the secretaries of state for finance and for domestic commerce. The general commissioner of planning attended some meetings. The committee had a secretariat.[127]

Pompidou attached the committee to an administrative agency that he created at the same time, the *Delegation of Territorial Improvement and Regional Action*.[128] The Delegation, in turn, was attached to his office. The Delegate chaired the committee and had a staff of about twenty persons.

The mission of the committee was to advise the delegate, whose task was to coordinate the work of the various ministers and other governmental agencies insofar as they affected "territorial improvement" and regional planning. He had the authority to require ministers to clear their programs with him, to investigate the investment programs of their ministers, to arbitrate among them on certain budget disputes, and to monitor the elaboration of the Plan. Certain key services in some ministries were placed at his disposal, though not under his direction, and some interministerial services were assigned to his administration. The Delegation had a substantial budget to promote its objectives by subsidizing the budgets of various ministries.[129]

The delegate for most of the Gaullist period after 1963 was Olivier Guichard. He was perhaps Pompidou's closest personal and political associate. Thus, when Pompidou moved from Matignon to Elysée, effective control of the Delegation and its committee went with him, a further manifestation of presidentialization in the committee structure of the Executive.[130]

Interministerial Committee on Tourism. The General Commission on Tourism had existed since 1935.[131] Soon after Debré became prime minister, he reorganized it to make it an instrument of control.[132] He created and chaired the committee, whose other members were the minister of state for cultural affairs and the ministers of finance and economic affairs, public works and transportation, foreign affairs, and the interior, with the general commissioner of tourism as a nonvoting member. Other persons attended by invitation of the prime minister. When Pompidou became prime minister, he transferred the General Commission from the Ministry of Public Works and Transportation to his office. The overlap of tourism with the concerns of such ministries as Transportation, Public Health, Construction, Commerce, Foreign Affairs, Interior, and Cultural Affairs made the committee a useful prime-ministerial tool for control and coordination. When Pompidou became president, he distributed its functions among several agencies, thereby weakening the premiership in that respect.[133]

Interministerial Committee for Questions of European Economic Cooperation. This was another Fourth Republic committee.[134] Its members were the prime minister as chair; the ministers of foreign affairs, of finance and economic affairs, and planning, and of industry and commerce: "the member of the government charged with European affairs and all interested ministers." The committee had its own secretariat. Two "interministerial technical committees" were attached to it to deal with the implementation of the EEC, ECSC, and Euratom treaties. The finance minister chaired the EEC/ECSC committee and the prime minister or the minister charged with atomic questions chaired the other. In 1964, Pompidou brought all three committees more directly under his authority by transferring their secretariat to his office. The approval of the original committee is required for all action by French officials in the EEC. Because so many ministers were affected by European economic integration, this arrangement strengthened prime-ministerial control. However, beginning in 1966 and especially after Pompidou moved to the Elysée Palace, this committee came increasingly into the hands of the president, another indication of the presidentialization of the regime.[135]

Interministerial Committee on Scientific Research. This committee and a consultative committee on scientific research were created in November 1958.[136] They were provided administrative support through a general delegation for scientific and technical research and a budget for research development was allocated to the prime minister's office. Initially, the committees were attached to the prime minister, who delegated his authority to a minister of state. However, when Pompidou became president, he transferred the Delegation (but not the committee) to a minister for industrial and scientific development. Then, the prime minister delegated his authority over the committee to the minister. This tended to diminish the coordinating authority of the prime minister to the net benefit of the presidency—and of presidential government.

Interministerial Committee for the Protection of Nature and the Environment. This committee was created in July 1970 as the Higher Committee on the Environment in DATAR and was transferred to the newly appointed "minister-delegate to the prime minister charged with the protection of nature and the environment" in February 1971, together with bits and pieces of pre-existing ministries. However, the ministry and its committee were spun off to autonomous status in April 1973. Its attachment to the premiership ran contrary to the Pompidolian penchant for shifting coordinating institutions away from that office, which may account for its early departure therefrom.[137]

Other Standing Committees. Several other prime-ministerial standing committees existed during the Gaullist period. Their value for control and coordination is suggested by their titles: Vocational Training and Social Advancement, Industrial Policy, Employment, the Family and Population, Atomic Energy, Equitation, Air Space, Highway Safety, For Participation for Workers in the Growth in the Capital of Enterprises Due to Self-Financing, Foreign Investments, for Information.[138] Of course, not all were chaired by the prime minister, but all were responsible to his office and served his purposes of control and coordination.

Significance

Prime-ministerial standing committees were more numerous, active, and important in the Fifth Republic than in the Fourth Republic. They were developed by Debré and even more by Pompidou as devices for centralizing control of the government in the prime minister, but when Pompidou became president, he took a number of steps to reduce their importance or to relax their attachment to the premiership. Not only did the prime ministers use them to work with ministers on matters where their authority converged but also they attached to them administrative agencies with independent authority paralleling, supplementing, and rivaling that of the ministries. Furthermore, the committee frequently included high civil servants, as well as ministers. Debré preferred to have high civil servants present, because, then, he "was more confident that the decisions would be implemented." [139]

Ad Hoc Committees

The second basic type of prime-ministerial committee was the *ad hoc* committee, which usually seems to have performed quite a different kind of function than the standing committee. The latter were instruments for coordination and control. The former were means for the prime minister to consult collectively, to arbitrate disagreements among his colleagues in the government, and to reach policy decisions.

The composition of the *ad hoc* committees was highly flexible and tended to be broader than their presidential counterparts. They included anyone invited by the prime minister on the basis that his presence would contribute to the search for a solution. They included members of the government, high civil and military functionaries, including ministerial staff members, and persons from the private sector. A prime-ministerial staff member served as a scribe. A presidential staff member attended all prime-ministerial meetings for the purpose of keeping the Elysée informed. Debré resisted this intrusion, but Pompidou accepted it as an essential element of the character of the regime. Also, he had two very practical reasons for favoring that practice. First, it seemed to him important for the cohesion of the relationship between the presidency and the government. Secondly, it permitted him to assume that a decision reached in one of his committees had been accepted by the president if he did not hear to the contrary within two days.[140]

At least during the Pompidou prime ministership, most committee meetings lasted from one to two hours. Pompidou called on each member to express his views, then summarized them and stated his own conclusions. He spent four or five hours a day in such meetings.[141]

A list of topics covered by prime-ministerial committees is virtually as long as that of the areas of governmental policy. Thus, to present a sampling here would serve little purpose. Also, no attempt can be made to discuss the even more diffuse subject of the interministerial working groups or *ad hoc* meetings not chaired by the prime minister.

CONCLUSIONS

The collective leadership elements of the Gaullist political Executive evolved in ways that contribute importantly to an understanding of the character of the regime. The parliamentarist Cabinet Council withered away, despite the first prime minister's repeated efforts to keep it alive. The Council of Ministers became more significant as a deliberative body and more thoroughly dominated by the presidents. Presidents and prime ministers developed a complex and active system of standing and *ad hoc* committees and councils. That change was especially dramatic for the presidency, which had lacked entirely such instruments of power before 1958. Even on the prime-ministerial side, the new growth had a very substantial centralizing effect, particularly during the Debré and Pompidou premierships. During Pompidou's presidency, the importance of prime-ministerial committees diminished.

All of those changes worked to bring governmental activities more closely under the president's control. Of course, that necessarily reduced the effectiveness of parliamentary oversight of the executive. A constitutional consequence of those changes was the dissolution of much of the original ambiguity in the system. Those structural developments helped to give the political Executive the autonomy necessary for it to emerge as a strong, independent branch of government. Especially, they reinforced and reflected the presidential character of that Executive and of the regime. The characteristic types of persons who staffed that Executive, especially in its most formative years, reflected and fostered that emergence also—as shall be seem in the next chapter.

3

Executive Personnel

Because a political system is people as well as institutions, its character may, in part, be formed by and reflected in the personnel that manage it. Thus, a study of the political Executive in the Gaullist Fifth Republic requires scrutiny, not only of the constitution and of the institutions in practice but also of the men and women who held office in it. In particular, this chapter examines the composition of the governments and of the presidential and prime-ministerial staffs during the Gaullist administrations in terms of age, sex, family background, education, occupation, nationality, and political activity.

In keeping with the focus of this book, this chapter seeks clues to the manner in which the Fifth Republic evolved toward presidentialism during the Gaullist years. It does so with the materials of collective biography. It argues that the personal and professional characteristics of the personnel of the political Executive were the sort that might well be expected to reinforce the presidentialist aspects of the regime. However, that character became less pronounced as the crisis atmosphere of the early years of the systems abated. This may be seen by examining each of the three categories of elites chronologically and in turn, moving from the most presidential to the most parliamentary (presidential staffs, prime-ministerial staffs, members of governments).

PRESIDENTIAL STAFFS

The presidential staffs were, quite naturally, the most presidentialist of the elites. They were the least parliamentary and political by background and characteristics. They were the most homogeneous and closed. However,

Pompidou's staff differed notably from de Gaulle's in some significant respects that gave it a less purely presidentialist cast.

Legal Framework

The presidential staff members depend on the incumbent president exclusively. This is so constitutionally, legally, politically, and practically. He appoints them, promotes them, transfers them, and dismisses them at will. No constitutional provisions or laws restrict him. They are not responsible, directly or indirectly, to parliament or any political party. In this, they differ from the prime minister, his staff, and his government. Of course, in practical terms, the president relies heavily on the general secretary of the presidency to manage that staff.

Presidential prerogative is confirmed by the absence of any official text defining the structure of the presidential staff, except that the general secretariat for the Community was established by ordinance.[1] Neither do such texts lay down qualifications or procedures for appointment or emoluments in office. Usually, though not invariably, new appointments are announced by *arrêté* of the president of that Republic in the *Journal officiel*. Unlike those issued in the Fourth Republic and unlike most presidential decisions, these *arrêtés* bear no ministerial countersignatures. Moreover, usually, departures from office are not announced officially.

Structure

Both de Gaulle and Pompidou organized their staffs with well-defined hierarchies, though their shapes were somewhat different. Both had three principal levels: executive, technical counselor, and *chargé de mission* (special assistant). Pompidou added a position at the super-grade of *chargé de mission auprès du président de la république* (special assistant to the president of the Republic; Pierre Juillet) and three positions between the executive and technical counselor levels: a deputy general secretary, a chief of the personal secretariat, and a *chef de cabinet* (staff administrator).[2]

De Gaulle followed Fourth Republic practice by organizing his staff into four services of fairly equal size: the general secretariat, the *Cabinet*, the military staff (*état major particulier*), and the general secretariat for the Community. All four were headed by executive staff members who reported directly to him. The general secretariat was responsible for "relations with the State," while the *Cabinet* was responsible for "relations with the nation." This meant that the former dealt with the ministries, the Parliament, and the courts while the latter handled the press, the mail, presidential travels, protocol, and various housekeeping chores in the Elysée Palace.[3]

Pompidou merged the *Cabinet* and the military staff in the general secretariat. Thus, his staff administrator (downgraded from staff director) and chief of the military staff reported to the general secretary. In theory, the general secretary and the general secretary for the Community reported to the president of the Republic directly. In practice, Juillet seems to have been an intermediary on political matters. This gave the Pompidou staff a much slimmer, more elongated structure than de Gaulle's.[4]

Size

Given the great importance of the presidency in the constitutional structure of the Fifth Republic, its professional staff was very small. Under the Fourth Republic, when the presidency was largely ceremonial, the staff included eighteen professional persons (seven civilians, six military officers, and five members of the French Union secretariat). (See Table 3.1.) At the outset of the Fifth Republic, it numbered thirty-eight (nineteen, fourteen, and five) and peaked at fifty-nine in 1960. Thereafter, it declined substantially during the remaining years of de Gaulle's administration, mainly through a drop in the size of the Community secretariat. Pompidou began with a still smaller staff—forty in 1969 and 1970—mainly by cutting the military staff, but it crept up slowly in his later years. (Of course, this does not include unofficial staff on loan from other agencies.) Still, it never recovered to the level set by de Gaulle. The failure of Parkinson's Law to operate and, indeed, its reversal, suggests a reflection of the evolution of the regime. The staff hit its peak size in the years of most acute crisis which, also, may have been the years when the leading problems facing the government were the type that fell most squarely in the presidential sphere.

More specifically, shifts in the size of the three services (civil, military, and Community) also paralleled changes in the importance of those policy areas. As the Community collapsed, its secretariat withered. As the Algerian War ended, the military staff declined. Concurrently, the civilian staff increased under the more civilian-minded Pompidou.[5]

Composition and Professional Characteristics

In a general way, the character of the staff became less closed and monarchical in the later years. This was true with respect to their tightness of loyalties, their professional backgrounds, and their personal characteristics. The changes were not great but they were discernible and quite consistent.

In general, the professional backgrounds of the presidential staffs reflected the independence of the presidency from Parliament. They were technical experts more than politicians and such politics as they had tended to be non-parliamentary. Their selection reflected the inclinations by de Gaulle and Pompidou to give the regime a presidential bent.

One of the most striking characteristics of de Gaulle's initial staff was the pervasiveness of an almost liegelike personal loyalty to de Gaulle.[6] His first general secretary was *Geoffrey Chodron de Courcel*, who could claim title as the

Table 3.1. Number of Professional Members on the Staff of the Presidency of the Republic, 1958-1974

	Coty	de Gaulle										Pompidou					
	1958	1959	1960	1961	1962	1963	1964	1965	1966	1967	1968	1969	1970	1971	1972	1973	1974
Special assistant to the president	-	-	-	-	-	-	-	-	-	-	-	1	1	1	1	1	1
General secretary	1	1	1	1	1	1	1	1	1	1	1	1	1	1	1	1	1
Deputy general secretary	1	-	-	-	-	-	-	-	-	-	-	1	1	1	1	1	1
Technical counselors to the general secretariat	-	6	5	4	3	6	5	4	4	4	4	6	6	8	8	9	9
Special assistants in the general secretariat	4	4	7	9	10	10	9	10	10	10	10	11	12	12	12	11	12
Director (or Administrator) of the presidential staff	1	1	1	1	1	1	1	1	1	1	1	1	1	1	1	1	1
Special assistants on the office staff	-	7	9	8	7	7	5	5	5	5	5	-	-	-	-	-	-
Total, civil professional staff	7	19	23	23	22	25	21	21	21	21	21	21	22	24	24	24	25
Chief of the military staff	1	1	1	1	1	1	1	1	1	1	1	1	1	1	1	1	1
Members of the military staff	4	9	12	11	11	9	9	9	9	9	10	4	4	4	4	4	5
Aides-de-camp to the president	-	3	3	3	3	3	3	3	3	3	3	2	2	2	2	2	2
Military commander of the Elysée Palace	1	1	1	1	1	1	1	1	1	1	1	1	1	1	1	1	1
Total, military staff	6	14	17	16	16	14	14	14	14	14	15	8	8	8	8	8	9
General secretary for the Community	1	1	1	1	1	1	1	1	1	1	1	1	1	1	1	1	1
Technical counselors to the Community secretariat	-	-	1	1	1	1	1	1	1	1	1	1	1	1	1	1	1
Special assistants in the Community secretariat	4	4	17	17	18	16	14	12	9	11	10	8	7	8	8	8	8
Total, Community staff[1]	5	5	19	19	20	18	16	14	11	13	12	10	9	10	10	10	10
Grand Total	18	38	59	58	58	57	51	49	46	48	48	40	40	43	43	43	45

SOURCES: 1969—*JO.LD.*, June 21, 1969, p. 6268, and June 26, p. 6516; 1974—*Le Monde*, March 22, 1974; all others, *Bottin Administratif* for the respective years.

[1]. The titles for 1958 were somewhat different and the designation of the "Community" changed several times.

first Gaullist. He had been assigned to Colonel de Gaulle as his aide-de-camp in 1939 and had joined his office staff when he became Undersecretary of State for War in June 1940. He alone had been with de Gaulle when he saw Pétain for the last time. He alone had accompanied de Gaulle when he fled to England. He alone had been with de Gaulle in the BBC studios when he broadcast his June 18 appeal. In 1940-41, he was de Gaulle's first *"chef de cabinet*, aide-de-camp, interpreter, and often-wise adviser." [7] He left that post in September 1941 to serve with de Gaulle's armed forces until 1943. Then, he returned to his staff as deputy director of his office staff in 1943-44. After the war, he returned to diplomacy, but he remained a loyal Gaullist and was appointed to two key governmental posts by Gaullist ministers of the Fourth Republic.[8]

The second executive on de Gaulle's original civilian staff was *René Brouillet*, director of his office staff. Brouillet had been staff administrator for Jules Jeanneney, president of the Third Republic Senate, 1939-40, and had first entered the Gaullist orbit as director of Georges Bidault's office staff while Bidault was head of the National Resistance Council, 1943-44. Then, he served de Gaulle directly as the deputy director of his office staff, 1944-46. When de Gaulle resigned, Brouillet followed de Courcel into diplomacy, but, like him also, remained a faithful Gaullist. When de Gaulle returned to office in June 1958, he appointed Brouillet general secretary of Algerian affairs and moved him into the office staff post when his predecessor, Georges Pompidou, returned to private life in January 1959.[9]

The third of de Gaulle's original civilian staff executives was *Raymond Janot*, general secretary of the Community, who did not fit the pattern of having bonds of personal loyalty to de Gaulle. Instead, he had not worked with de Gaulle at all until May 1958. At that time, he became de Gaulle's special assistant in charge of liaison with the working party that drafted the 1958 constitution. That appointment was made on recommendation of Pompidou, then de Gaulle's staff director, who had known Janot in the Council of State.[10]

However, despite Janot's executive status, he seems to have been less influential over Community affairs than *Jacques Foccart*, who was *"le fidèle d'entre les fidèles."* [11] Foccart handled Community affairs as technical counselor on de Gaulle's staff while he was prime minister and then president, until he replaced Janot in March 1960. The staff position he had held was abolished when he left it. Foccart remained general secretary for the Community throughout the de Gaulle and Pompidou presidencies.[12]

Foccart entered military Gaullism in 1940 as a Resistant (becoming a regional chief), political Gaullism in 1945 as an unsuccessful parliamentary candidate, and partisan Gaullism in 1947 as one of the founders of the RPF. He was an RPF officer throughout its existence, specializing in colonial affairs and serving as a member of the Assembly of the French Union after 1952 and as RPF general secretary after 1954. Perhaps no one worked as closely with de Gaulle as long as did Foccart. When he spoke in a meeting, all present understood that he spoke for de Gaulle, although he never said so.[13]

This characteristic of personal loyalty was evident also in the initial nonexecutive staff appointments. Four of the seven original special assistants in the office staff had worked for de Gaulle before. The most striking example was *Count Xavier de Beaulaincourt-Marles*, who was responsible for handling de Gaulle's correspondence. He had served as de Gaulle's personal secretary continuously since 1945 and remained in that job until de Gaulle's death in November 1970. He has been described as knowing "the life of the General better than does the General himself." [14] Even more durable though not so constant in job description was *Pierre Lefranc*. He had been a Gaullist since 1940, first in the Resistance, then, after 1942, in London. After the war, he continued as a Gaullist militant, serving as National Secretary for Youth throughout the life of the RPF and as staff administrator of de Gaulle's prime-ministerial office in 1958–59. Until he left the staff in 1963 to become a prefect, he was responsible for questions of domestic politics and the media. [15] Two other RPF veterans were *Raymond Labelle-Rojoux* and *Xavier de Babin de Lignac*. The former had been a member of the secretariats of the RPF and, then, the Social Republicans, 1948–58, and of de Gaulle's prime-ministerial staff in 1958–59. The latter had been editor-in-chief of the RPF newspaper, 1948–53, had served on the staffs of Gaullist ministers, 1954–58, and was appointed chief of the political service and editor-in-chief of the RTF (the French radio system) by Prime Minister de Gaulle. [16] Another longtime member of the office staff was *Col. Gaston de Bonneval*. Although he was an aide-de-camp rather than a special assistant and this study does not include the military staff, his responsibilities seem to have been those of a general factotum, rather than primarily military. Bonneval served de Gaulle in that capacity continuously from 1945 until he retired in 1965.

The original staff of de Gaulle's general secretariat was marked much less clearly by the Cross of Lorraine. Only *Olivier Guichard* and *Jean-Marc Boegner*, both technical counselors, had strong credentials of fidelity. Guichard, called "the General's shadow," began his Gaullist career in the Resistance in 1943. In 1947, he participated in the founding of the RPF as a special assistant, regional delegate, and member of the national steering committee. From 1951 until 1958, he was de Gaulle's staff administrator. During much of that time, he, Beaulaincourt, and Foccart were virtually de Gaulle's only full-time professional civilian staff members. When de Gaulle returned to the prime ministership, Guichard became his deputy staff director. During those "years in the desert" Guichard was "faithful in the pure, native, naïve state." [17] Boegner had been a professional Gaullist as early as 1941 when he defected from the Vichy diplomatic mission to Washington and joined de Gaulle in London. He had served on de Gaulle's office staff in 1944–46 and again in 1958–59. In between, he had pursued a diplomatic career. [18] *Bernard Tricot*, another technical counselor in the original general secretariat, had served in the Resistance, but had no other service of fidelity. [19] Neither of the other two technical counselors in the original general secretariat nor any of the four special assistants [20] seems to have had any position of responsibility in the Gaullist movement before 1958.

As time passed, the level of "fidelity" declined. Foccart and Beaulaincourt remained on de Gaulle's staff until he resigned. De Courcel resigned as general secretary in 1962 and was replaced by *Etienne Burin des Roziers*. Burin had been a Gaullist since resigning from the Vichy diplomatic mission in Washington in 1942 and joining de Gaulle, but he had served on de Gaulle's staff (as a special assistant) only in 1945–46. When Burin resigned, in turn, in 1967, he was succeeded by Tricot, who had been unknown to de Gaulle before 1958.

The same evolution occurred in the directorship of de Gaulle's office. Neither *Georges Galichon*, 1961–67, nor *Xavier Daufresne de la Chevalérie*, 1967–69, had had Brouillet's experience of working for de Gaulle before 1958, although Daufresne had fought with the Free French. After Boegner left de Gaulle's office in November 1959 and Guichard and Foccart followed suit in Spring 1960, Lefranc (left in 1963) and Beaulaincourt were the only members of the pre-1958 court among the forty-seven men who served as technical counselors or special assistants at the Elysée under de Gaulle.[21]

Personal service to Pompidou before 1969 meant something very different from personal service to de Gaulle before 1958. Before 1958, de Gaulle had been in the wilderness in one sense or another almost continuously since 1940. For most veteran Gaullists, loyalty had meant sacrifice. Before 1969, Pompidou had been prime minister or parliamentary leader of the majority party for seven years and for the previous eight years (except June 1958 to January 1959) he had worked for the Rothschild Bank. Before that, he had been a staff member himself. Because he recruited no one from the bank, previous service for him meant, essentially, staff membership in the premiership. Loyalty to Pompidou had meant a share of the power that de Gaulle had conferred on him. It had a less noble gloss.

The most striking case of personal service as a background for Pompidou's original staff was that of his highest-ranking aide, *Pierre Juillet*, special assistant to the president of the Republic. Juillet had been Pompidou's close friend and collaborator in Gaullist activities since 1947 and had served him as a technical counselor on his staff throughout his prime ministership. Almost identical in length was Pompidou's association with *Mlle. Madeleine Négrel*, head of his personal secretariat, who had worked for him in similar capacities continuously since 1947.

Pompidou's other original civilian staff executives had all served on his prime-ministerial staff, 1963–68, except, of course, that Foccart remained at the same post.[22] Those executives all remained in the same jobs throughout the Pompidou presidency, except that when Jobert became foreign minister in 1973, *Edouard Balladur* replaced him and was replaced in turn by *Jean-René Bernard*, who had served on Pompidou's prime-ministerial staff, 1962–68.

Five of Pompidou's original six technical counselors,[23] but only five of the eleven original special assistants, had worked on his staff before 1969. Also, *Henri Domerg*, special assistant, was his brother-in-law. As he appointed additional staff members and replacements, the element of prior service was diluted. None of those twenty-seven appointments went to persons who had served previously on Pompidou's staff,[24] although one special assistant was his niece, *Mlle. Anne Castex.*

Perhaps because of the importance the presidents attached to the personal nature of the prior service of their staff members and, in de Gaulle's case, a desire to signal clearly the break with the previous regime, very few of their aides had served their predecessors. Janot was the only member of de Gaulle's staff who had held a staff appointment under a Fourth Republic president (as legal counsel to Auriol, 1947–51). Foccart and *Gilbert Carrére*, special assistant in de Gaulle's secretariat and special assistant, then technical counselor, under Pompidou, were the only Pompidou aides with prior presidential staff service.

However, many presidential staff members had served earlier on the staffs of ministers, prime ministers, or the presidents of parliamentary-type assemblies. (See Table 3.2.) This was true of thirty-one de Gaulle aides (48.4 percent) and thirty Pompidou aides (69.8 percent). Some of them had occupied more than one such post. In fact, de Gaulle's staff had held a total of fifty-nine staff appointments (1.9 per person) and Pompidou's had held sixty-one (2.0).

Even more pervasive than personal loyalty as a characteristic of Gaullist presidential staff members was professional civil service status, especially membership in one of the *grands corps* of the French State (the Council of State, the finance inspectorate, the prefectoral corps, and the Court of Accounts) or the diplomatic corps. (See Table 3.3.) Two of de Gaulle's original staff executives were professional diplomats (de Courcel, Brouillet) and the third was a councilor of state (Janot). Their successors under de Gaulle came from the same two corps, also, except that Foccart had never had any civil service status, having always been a businessman, a party bureaucrat, or both.

De Gaulle's first six technical counselors included two party bureaucrats (Foccart, Guichard) and one member each from the Council of State, finance inspectorate, diplomatic, and university teaching corps. Of his first eleven special assistants, seven had similar civil service status,[25] while the other four had been RPF functionaries (Beaulaincourt, Labelle-Rojoux, Lefranc, de Lignac). Later, de Gaulle appointed forty-one new persons to technical counselor and special assistant positions of his staff. All of them were civil servants of one sort or another. Thus, the representation of civil servants increased from 70.0 percent in February 1959 to 90.9 percent in April 1969.

Unlike de Gaulle, Pompidou had been in the civil service himself before going to the Rothschild Bank. Yet civil servants were less dominant on his staff. His closest adviser, Juillet, was a lawyer. So was *Mme. Anne-Marie Dupuy*, his office head until January 1974. The other executives of his original staff included Foccart, *Michel Jobert* (Court of Accounts), Balladur (Council of State), and Mme. Négrel (professional stenographer). Only one-third were civil servants. However, five of his six original technical counselors and all eleven special assistants were civil servants.

Pompidou added twenty staff members later in his term. Fifteen (75.0 percent) were civil servants. This was a slight decline from the 78.3 percent at the

Table 3.2. Prior Service on Executive Staffs by Members of Presidential Staffs, Prime Ministerial Staffs, and Governments (Number of Appointments)[1]

	Number of persons who held given numbers of appointments					Total no. of persons who held previous staff appointments	% of staff/ministers who held previous staff appointments[2]
	1	2	3	4	5+		
Presidential Staffs							
de Gaulle	15	9	4	2	1	31	48.4
Pompidou	11	14	3	1	2	30	69.8
Total	26	23	7	3	3	61	68.5
Prime-Ministerial Staffs							
Debré	13	-	1	1	-	15	51.7
Pompidou	4	4	3	-	2	13	31.0
Couve	7	5	2	2	2	18	78.5
Chaban	8	8	3	1	2	22	50.0
Messmer	6	8	3	3	2	22	73.3
Total	38	25	12	7	8	90	59.3
Governments							
Debré	10	4	1	2	2[3]	19	48.7
Pompidou	6	3	2	3	-	14	23.0
Couve	1	-	1	1	-	3	10.0
Chaban	6	-	-	-	1	7	28.0
Messmer	2	2	1	1	2	8	43.7
Total	29	9	5	7	4[4]	51	42.7
Grand Total	93	57	24	17	15	202	

[1]Previous appointments to the category of staff being analyzed were not included.
[2]Unknowns were included in the total number of persons on the staff/ministry.
[3]"Several" such appointments.
[4]Including two who held "several" such appointments.

Table 3.3. Principal Occupations of Ministers/Executive Staff Members

	Presidential Staff					Prime-Ministerial Staffs						Ministeries				Original* Occupation
	de G	P	Tot.	D	P	C	Ch	M	Tot.	D	P	C	Ch	M	Tot.	
Professional civil service	58	32	88	26	37	20	42	30	139	21	22	14	17	25	54	56
Council of State	6	2	8	5	5	1	2	2	15	3	3	2	3	5	8	
Court of Accounts	2	2	4	3	4	2	2	1	11	-	2	1	1	3	3	
Finance, economist	7	3	10	4	5	2	5	3	19	3	3	1	2	3	6	
Interior	7	5	10	3	9	3	8	5	25	4	2	1	1	2	7	
Education	4	3	7	1	4	1	1	-	6	6	6	4	2	2	13	
Foreign service	17	8	25	3	4	8	7	4	21	1	3	2	2	5	6	
Justice	2	1	3	3	2	1	2	1	7	-	-	-	1	1	2	
Science, Engineering	4	4	8	-	2	1	5	1	7	3	2	1	2	1	5	
Other	9	4	13	4	2	1	10	13	28	1	3	2	3	3	5	
Political administration	4	1	5	2	1	-	-	-	3	1	3	1	1	1	3	
Business, industry	1	2	2	-	2	1	1	-	3	7	20	7	15	10	35	31
Journalism, Writing	1	2	3	1	-	1	1	-	3	4	5	3	2	2	7	9[2]
Law	-	3	3	-	2	1	-	-	3	4	9	4	6	4	13	11
Medicine	-	-	-	-	-	-	-	-	-	1	-	1	3	3	5	2[3]
Farming	-	-	-	-	-	-	-	-	-	1	1	-	-	1	2	2
Professional mil. service	-	2[1]	2	-	-	-	-	-	-	-	1	-	-	-	1	3
Other, unavailable	-	-	-	-	-	-	-	2	2	-	-	-	-	-	-	4[4]
Total	64	42	103	29	42	23	44	32	151	39	61	30	44	47	120	118

[1]Including one in a nationalized industry and one with no previous occupation (Pompidou's niece).

[2]Including "publicist."

[3]Not including Comiti, "agrégé de Médicine," who is included with professional civil servants.

[4]Including Mme. Suzanne Ploux, "mére de famille nombreuse."

*Pascale Antoni and Jean-Dominique Pascale, *Les Ministres de la Vᵉ République* (Paris: PUF, 1976), p. 27.

outset of the de Gaulle presidency to the 71.4 percent at the end. Overall, 76.7 percent of Pompidou's staff were civil servants, compared to 90.6 percent for de Gaulle.

Educationally, the staffs of the two presidents were identical in that only Foccart had no degree beyond secondary school. (See Table 3.4.) Also, both staffs were dominated by graduates of three institutions: faculties of law, institutes of political studies (or their predecessors), and the National School of Administration. Fifty-five of de Gaulle's sixty-four (85.9 percent) staff members and thirty-three of Pompidou's forty-two (78.6 percent) had degrees from at least one of those schools. In breadth of education, de Gaulle's staff was slightly more open. On de Gaulle's staff, 57.8 percent had at least one degree from schools other than those three, compared to 54.8 percent for Pompidou's staff.

2. *Political Involvement.*

The technocratic character of the staffs was not diluted very much by electoral political activities. (See Table 3.5.) Among de Gaulle's aides, only Guichard had held elective office before 1958.[26] Also, Foccart had been an unsuccessful parliamentary candidate in 1945. Magniny, Guichard, and Bas were the only members of de Gaulle's staff to run for Parliament later, the latter two successfully; and Janot, Guichard, and Bas won local offices. Only Guichard became a minister.

Pompidou's staff was somewhat more political in terms of running for office. Three members had run for Parliament unsuccessfully before joining his staff, including two who held local elective offices. Two did so while serving on his staff. Another (Chasseguet) was elected to Parliament later (in 1973). Only Jobert became a minister.[27]

Personal Characteristics

In certain personal characteristics, the Pompidou staff seems to have been somewhat more open than de Gaulle's. In particular, its social-class origins in terms of wealth and ties to nobility were somewhat broader. Also, it was less completely male, somewhat more diverse in terms of age, and a bit less purely French ethnically.

The nobility particle and other nominal indications of aristocratic affiliation, real or pretended, were conspicuously present on de Gaulle's staff. The two senior members of his staff in terms of service were *Count Xavier de Beaulaincourt-Marles* and *Count Gaston de Bonneval*. *Geoffrey Chodron de Courcel* organized his original staff. The only person he reappointed as a special assistant was *Count Philippe François Xavier de Maistre*, descendant of Joseph de Maistre. His technical counselors included *Baron Olivier Marie Maurice Guichard, René Georges François Maurice the Marquis de Saint-Legier de la Saussaye*, and *Count Xavier du Cauzé de Nazelle*. Other names of similar resonance were *Xavier Marie Emile Daufresne de la Chevalérie, Etienne Burin des Roziers, Bernard Léon Henri Jean Bailly du Bois, Xavier de Babin de Lignac*, and

Table 3.4. Higher Education of Ministers and Executive Staff Members

	Presidential Staff			Prime-Ministerial Staffs						Ministers					
	de G	P	Tot.	D	P	C	Ch	M	Tot.	D	P	C	Ch	M	Tot.
One or more of the Big Three[1]	55	33	86	23	35	22	33	25	123	23	37	20	24	30	70
Overseas France	9	1	10	1	2	3	5	8	15	-	-	-	-	1	1
Ecole Normale	5	6	11	1	1	3	1	-	5	3	2	-	1	3	5
Letters/Literature	20	7	27	4	11	4	8	7	28	10	15	8	9	10	5
Ecole Polytechnique/ Mines	4	4	8	-	2	1	3	2	5	3	1	-	1	1	3
Business, Economics	3	4	7	-	3	2	3	2	10	3	3	1	2	3	7
Other French schools	5	5	9	2	8	3	12	1	28	5	8	6	9	9	23
Foreign schools	1	-	1	1	2	1	1	1	5	-	3	-	1	1	5
No higher education, unknown	1	-	-	2	-	1	3	3	-	8	10	3	7	6	19
Total	64	42	103	29	42	23	44	32	151	39	61	30	44	47	120

[1]Faculties of Law, Institutes of Political Studies, and the National School of Administration.

Table 3.5. Number of Ministers and Executive Staff Members Who Were Candidates in Political Elections

	Presidential Staff			Prime-Ministerial Staffs						Members of Governments					
	deG	P	Tot.	D	P	C	Ch	M	Tot.	D	P	C	Ch	M	Tot.
Parliament, successful															
Before service	-	-	-	-	1[3]	1	-	-	2	26	27	3	18	20	94
During service	-	-	-	-	-	-	-	-	-	-	6	3	-	6	15
After service	2	1	3	2	7[3]	1	-	-	8[2]	26	34	-	14	4	78
Total[1]	2	1	3	2	7	2	-	-	10[2]	33	36	5	18	16	108
Parliament, unsuccessful															
Before service	1	3	4	-	2[3]	-	-	-	2	1	8	1	2	-	12
During service	-	2	2	-	-	-	-	-	-	-	1	-	-	-	1
After Service	1	-	1	-	1	-	-	1	2	4	4	-	-	-	8
Total[1]	2	5	7	-	3	-	-	1	4	4	10	1	2	-	17
Other															
Before service	1	-	1	-	-	-	-	2	2	10	21	4	20	20	75
During service	-	1	1	1	-	-	1	2	3[4]	2	5	-	1	-	8
After service	3	-	3	-	3	-	1	2	5	19	15	-	8	-	42
Total[1]	3	1	4	1	3	-	1	2	6[4]	19	25	4	17	13	78

[1]Totals do not include duplications.
[2]Chassequet served on both the Couve and the Chaban staffs.
[3]Roulland was unsuccessful in 1956 and 1962, successful in 1958 and 1967, on staff 1962-67.
[4]Martin de Beaucé served on both the Chaban and Messmer staffs.

Gérard Marie Le Saige de La Villésbrunne. Eighteen of de Gaulle's staff members bore such names and at least seven others had mothers or wives with nobiliary maiden names.[28] None of Pompidou's presidential staff members bore titles of nobility and only three had particles.

Such conclusions as can be drawn about the wealth of the presidential staffs must be inferred from the occupational status of their parents. (See Table 3.6.) None of them seems to have had parents who were manual laborers or peasants. The fathers of seven of them were farmers (*agriculteurs* or *exploitants agricoles*) or landowners. All the others were business executives or professional men, except for a watchmaker (*horloger*), two railroad agents, a bank employee, and a salesman. The two presidents had staffs of very similar family occupational backgrounds except that Pompidou drew slightly more from the professions. Information on parental occupations is not available for about one-fourth of the staff members.

De Gaulle never appointed a woman to his professional staff. Pompidou appointed four women (9.5 percent), three to his original staff and one (his niece) later. Furthermore, they filled important posts. One was the head of his office staff, and two were technical counselors. Only his niece was appointed at the lowest rank, special assistant. One of the technical counselors (Garaud) was regarded widely as the most influential member of his staff, excepting only Juillet.

Also, de Gaulle never appointed to his staff a man born elsewhere than in France or her possessions of Tunisia and Algeria or one who bore a non-French surname. Even during the early years of his administration, when he ordered his staff to exhort the ministries to hire more Algerian Moslems, he never employed one on his staff. Pompidou's staff was almost as simon-pure French, although Balladur had been born in Turkey and a spare sprinkling of Corsican (Marchetti and Saglio) and Basque (d'Iribarne) names appeared.

In terms of age, Pompidou's staff was distributed more evenly between 30 and 49 than was de Gaulle's, although the under-30s were represented somewhat more under de Gaulle's. (See Table 3.7.) Each president appointed only one person over 49.

PRIME-MINISTERIAL STAFFS

The staffs of the prime ministers were a bit more open and diverse than those of the presidents. They had a less purely executive air about them, they were less authoritarian and pretorian, more democratic and parliamentarist.

Structure

All the prime-ministerial staffs were organized on the same three-tier basis (executive, technical counselor, special assistant) as the presidential staffs.

Table 3.6. Principal Occupations of Parents of Ministers and Executive Staff members

	Presidential Staff			Prime-Ministerial Staffs						Ministers					
	de G	P	Tot.	D	P	C	Ch	M	Tot.	D	P	C	Ch	M	Tot.
Businessmen/industrialists	11	7	18	4	15	5	9	4	32	12	18	12	16	11	36
Professional civil servants	10	6	16	5	7	1	4	2	17	6	7	3	8	8	14
Engineers	7	4	11	2	3	1	2	1	8	1	2	1	1	4	7
Univ. or secondary teachers	5	1	5	3	2	-	3	1	9	2	3	1	4	1	7
Farmers, Landowners	6	3	7	3	2	1	-	2	8	-	-	-	2	1	3
Military or naval officers	4	3	7	1	1	1	1	3	6	3	6	2	3	5	10
Medical professions	3	1	4	4	4	2	3	2	11	-	2	2	3	3	5
Lawyers, judicial experts	2	1	3	-	1	-	-	1	2	3	6	4	3	6	10
Others	2[1]	1[2]	3	-	-	-	4[3]	1[4]	5	7	8	2	2	3	15
No occupation	1	1	2	1	-	2	1	1	5	1	1	-	-	1	2
Total	51	28	76	23	36	13	27	18	105	35	53	27	42	43	109
Not available	13	14	27	6	6	10	17	14	48	4	8	3	2	5	11

[1]Clergyman, watchmaker
[2]Salesman
[3]Man of letters, bank employee, two railroad agents
[4]Journalist

Table 3.7. Age of Ministers and Presidential and Prime-Ministerial Staff Members upon Initial Appointment to the Group Being Analyzed

	Presidential Staffs			Prime-Ministerial Staffs						Ministers					
	de G	P	Tot.	D	P	C	Ch	M	Tot.	D	P	C	Ch	M	Tot.
over 49	1	1	2	3	-	1	6	6	16	17	24	13	21	26	103
45–49	11	10	21	4	4	2	5	3	18	11	13	11	13	12	60
40–44	15	10	25	2	16	7	8	5	38	8	15	4	8	6	41
35–39	20	11	31	8	12	7	4	6	37	2	8	2	2	4	18
30–34	10	7	17	8	7	4	17	8	44	1	1	-	-	-	2
under 30	7	3	10	2	3	2	3	1	11	-	-	-	-	-	-
Total	64	42	106	27	42	23	43	29	164	39	61	30	44	48	224
Median	39	39/40	39	36	39	38	38	38	38	48	47	48/49	49	50	49
Unavailable	-	-	-	2	-	-	1	3	6	-	-	-	-	-	-

However, the details of their organization varied somewhat more among administrations and the executive tier was somewhat more differentiated.[29] On the Pompidou (until February 1967), Chaban-Delmas, and Messmer (until July 1973) staffs, the highest rank was *chargé de mission* (or *conseiller*) *auprès du premier ministre*, a position analogous to the one held by Juillet on Pompidou's presidential staff. Also, Chaban-Delmas and Messmer used special kinds of "counselors" as another super rank. Chaban had two "counselors to the prime minister," one for public relations (Roger Vaurs) and another for social and cultural affairs (Jacques Delors, then André Chadeau). Messmer had a "counselor for economic and financial affairs" (Jacques Friedmann, then Yves Sabouret) and a "counselor for social affairs" until March 15, 1974 (Sabouret). The other executive positions were staff director, deputy staff director (except July–October 1959 and January 1966–August 1968), one or two staff administrators (*chefs*), and (under Debré) a deputy staff administrator. Usually, the *directeur* was responsible for substantive matters, the *chef* for procedures.

Size

The prime-ministerial staffs varied considerably in size and were afflicted somewhat by Parkinson's Law. (See Table 3.8.) Félix Gaillard, last "normal" prime minister of the Fourth Republic, had had eleven members on his civilian professional staff. Debré started out with eighteen and finished with twenty-three, Pompidou began with twelve and ended with twenty-three. Couve de Murville cut back to eighteen. Perhaps manifesting presidential ambitions, Chaban-Delmas climbed from twenty-eight to thirty-three, the largest of any executive staff. Messmer drifted back down, from twenty-five to twenty-three. The median size through Couve was eighteen, but under Chaban and Messmer it rose to twenty-eight. This inflation may well have reflected the shift of public policy focus toward matters that lay primarily in the prime-ministerial domain.

Composition and Professional Characteristics

The importance of personal loyalty in appointments to prime-ministerial staffs varied considerably according to the prime minister's previous office-holding experience. Debré came from the opposition benches of the Senate (with a seven-month detour through the Ministry of Justice). Pompidou came from the Rothschild Bank. Neither had long-time official collaborators who fit the standard expectations for prime-ministerial staff members. Debré brought five staff members from the Ministry of Justice who had not worked with him, at least officially, before June 1958. They included *Yves Guéna*, his first deputy staff administrator, who was a cousin by marriage.[30] Also, *Constantin Melnik*, one of his technical counselors, had been secretary of the Gaullist group in the Council of the Republic in the Fourth Republic from February 1950 to August 1951, while Debré was vice president of that group, and they remained close political

Table 3.8. Number of Professional Members on the Staff of the Prime Minister, 1958-1974

	1958	De	1959	1960	1961	Po	1962	1963	1964	1965	1966	1967	1968	Co	1969	Ch	1970	1971	1972	Me	1973	1974
Special counselors	–	1	1	–	1	1	–	1	1	1	1	1	–	1	3	3	3	2	3	1	1	1
Staff directors	1	1	1	1	1	1	1	1	1	1	1	1	1	1	1	1	1	1	1	1	1	1
Dep. staff directors	–	1	1	1	1	–	–	1	1	1	1	–	1	2	1	1	1	1	1	1	1	1
Staff administrators	2	2	2	2	1	1	–	1	–	1	1	1	1	1	2	2	1	–	–	1	1	1
Dep. staff administrators	2	1	1	1	1	–	–	1	1	1	–	1	–	–	1	2	1	1	–	1	1	1
Technical counselors	3	4	2	2	4	6	6	6	5	6	6	6	6	7	7	8	10	12	9	9	9	9
Special assistants	3	9	9	11	15	3	3	10	9	11	11	13	15	9	10	14	16	17	15	10	11	10
Total	11	18	15	17	23	12	11	20	18	20	20	21	23	18	21	28	30	33	32	25	24	23

SOURCES: For columns by year, 1958 through 1973, *Bottin Administratif*; 1974, *Société générale de presse*. For columns by prime minister, *JO. LD.* for the first month of the new premiership. *Bottin Administratif* seems to lock up in March or April each year.

associates thereafter.[31] Then, too, the five aides Debré recruited from the Council of State had, of course, been his colleagues there. The only member of Pompidou's prime-ministerial staff who had actually worked *for* him previously was Mme. Négrel, head of his personal secretariat. However, Juillet (a technical counselor) and Guichard (special assistant to the prime minister) had worked *with* him closely in Gaullist affairs.

In contrast, the other three prime ministers had held high public office for long periods immediately prior to forming their Matignon staffs and had suitable aides to bring along. Couve de Murville had been foreign minister the ten previous years, Chaban-Delmas had presided over the National Assembly for more than ten years, and Messmer had held two major ministerial portfolios for a total of nearly eleven years. As a result, six of Couve's eighteen original staff members had served him before. So had six Chaban staffers, including one for twenty-five years. Messmer's original staff included nine with previous service for him, including one with twelve years' service.

Unlike the presidents, some prime ministers used their predecessors' staffs as a second important recruitment ground. This was not true of Debré or Pompidou. However, the seventeen members of Couve's staff who did not come from his own earlier staffs included eight who had served on Pompidou's prime-ministerial staff. Chaban-Delmas kept three from the Couve staff and Messmer appointed five of Chaban's and one of Pompidou's. Six other prime-ministerial staff members had served Fourth Republic prime ministers, including two who had worked for Prime Minister de Gaulle. In all, 22 of the 151 persons had served previous prime ministers.[32]

Prime ministers did share with presidents the predilection for recruiting former members of ministerial staffs. (See Table 3.2.) Of the 153 appointments made to persons who had not served previous prime ministers, 64 went to persons who had been on ministers' staffs.[33] Indeed, for some of them service on executive staffs seems to have been a kind of subcareer. The 90 persons with previous executive staff service had held 199 different appointments on the staffs of presidents of the republic, prime ministers, ministers, and presidents of parliamentary-type chambers—an average of 2.21 each. Two each had held six and seven such positions and five persons had held five each. Seventeen of the most striking career cases had served on such staffs during at least 80 percent of at least ten years immediately preceding the end of their appointments to a prime-ministerial staff.

Prime-ministerial staffs shared with presidential staffs the further characteristic of being overwhelmingly of civil service origin. (See Table 3.3.) Of the 151 persons who received such appointments and whose career backgrounds are known, 139 (92.1 percent) were professional civil servants. This percentage is even higher than for presidential staffs—85.4 percent.

However, those civil servants were distributed among the *corps* rather differently than on the presidential staffs, in a way that seems to reflect the different policy emphases of the two executives and the closer relationship of the prime ministership to the main concerns of everyday life. The greater presidential concern with the international affairs is indicated by the fact that the diplomatic service was its largest staff recruiting area, providing two-and-a-half times as many members as the prefectoral corps. In contrast, the prime-ministerial focus on domestic concerns appears in the fact that the prefectoral *corps* was its leading source of staff. The other domestic *corps*—Council of State, Court of Accounts, finance services, justice, but not education—were more important on the prime-ministerial than the presidential staffs. The composition of "other civil service" reflects the same difference. The most numerous element in that group was colonial administration for the presidential, but "civil administration" for the prime-ministerial staffs.

Educationally, the prime-ministerial staffs resembled those of the presidency closely. (See Table 3.4.) The Big Three (law faculties, institutes of political studies, ENA) dominated again. The distribution among other schools was similar, also, though the prime-ministerial staff ranged somewhat more into the unconventional institutions. All but one of the Couve staff were graduates of the Big Three and the other staffs all were at least 75 percent pure.

Political Involvement

Prime-ministerial staffs were notably more political than presidential staffs, as measured by electoral activities and ministerial appointments. (See Table 3.5.) By the end of the Gaullist period, ten of their members[34] had become deputies, seven [35] had become members of governments, and Chirac had become prime minister. In addition, four staff members[36] had run for Parliament unsuccessfully and six other persons[37] had held local office. Also, *Michel Jobert* plunged into partisan activities after Pompidou's death by launching a new political movement, and *Jacques Delors* had long been active in various political movements of the Catholic left and, after leaving Chaban's staff, in the Socialist party. These eighteen persons were, still, a relatively small part of the staffs, although they far outnumbered the "politicians" on the presidential staffs. "Politicization" varied considerably among administrations, Pompidou's staff being most political and Chaban's the least.

Personal Characteristics

In personal characteristics, the prime-ministerial staffs manifested much the same "closed" character as their presidential counterparts. Aristocratic names were slightly less common than on de Gaulle's staff but more so than on President Pompidou's. Twenty-six persons (17.6 percent) had that distinction. They included *Hélie de Noailles, Duc d'Ayen*, and *Prince Gabriel Marie Joseph Anselme de Broglie*, both of whom outranked any of the presidential nobility. Guichard and *Bruno de Leusse de Syon* were barons and *Ernest-Antoine Seillière de Laborde* was the son of a baron. No other titles appear on the list, but *Xavier Marie Norbet de Christen* and *Antoine Louis Guy de Clermont-Tonnerre* were sons of counts.

Several other members had distinctive family connections. *Nivet-Doumer* was a great-grandson of Third Republic President Paul Doumer. *Jacques Giscard d'Estaing* was a grandson of Third Republic President Sidi Carnot. *Mlle, Pucheu* was the daughter of Pierre Pucheu, who had been shot on de Gaulle's orders for serving as Marshal Pétain's Minister of the Interior. *Domerg* was married to Pompidou's sister. *Wiltzer* was the son of a prefect who had served on Edgar Faure's staff six times and *Philip* was the son of André Philip, Socialist minister in de Gaulle's wartime government and during the Fourth Republic.

Parental occupational data provide other evidence that prime-ministerial staffs were as closely upper-class in character as their presidential counterparts. (See Table 3.6.) The most common occupation of their fathers was corporation executive or industrialist (30.5 percent)—even more frequent than for the presidential staff. As with the presidential staff, the next most common parental occupation was administrative civil servant, slightly less common than in the Elyseé (by 15.2 percent to 21.1 percent).[38] Other state employees accounted for another 21.9 percent, the medical and legal professions for 12.4 percent, farmers and landowners (not peasants!) for 7.6 percent, and "no occupation" (not "unemployed") for 4.8 percent. This left only four "working-type" fathers—all white-collar—two railroad agents, a bank employee, and a journalist.

Unlike de Gaulle, prime ministers appointed female staff members, though at a lower rate than President Pompidou (6.5 percent to 9.5 percent). Also, prime-ministerial staffs were slightly less purely French. Three were born in foreign countries (Switzerland, Egypt, Turkey) and eight were born in French North Africa. *Melnik* was a first-generation Frenchman whose grandather had been assassinated as the Czar's physician. One Moslem name (*Benzaïd*) appears, but both his mother and wife were French. Non-French (Epifanoff, Ramoff, Melnik, Grollemund) and ethnic minority (Sicurani, Wiltzer, Worms, Friedmann) names are somewhat more common. Still, the distinct aura of French closeness hangs over the prime-ministerial, as over the presidential, staffs.

The age pyramids of the two sets of staffs were closely parallel. (See Table 3.7.) The only notable difference was a greater willingness by prime ministers to appoint persons over 49 (9.8 percent compared to 1.9 percent). Still, the median age was one year older for presidential aides.

MEMBERS OF GOVERNMENTS

From the beginning, ministers were much more political and parliamentary than were presidential or prime-ministerial staffs, and they became notably more so as time passed. The "technocratic" characterization applied to Gaullist governments was accurate by comparison with Fourth Republic governments. However, the sharp contrast at the outset may have created an impression that became progressively less accurate.

Structure

Members of the government in the Gaullist presidencies bore four different types of titles. Full members, usually responsible for major departments, were designated "minister." Junior members, usually responsible for minor departments or for assisting in the administration of major departments, were called "secretaries of state." Super-ministers, usually appointed in acknowledgement of their personal standing or the importance of the political forces they represented, were "ministers of state," usually without portfolio. Finally, some members were given assignments in which the prime minister had a direct, special interest and were called "minister delegated to the prime minister" or "secretary of state to the prime minister."

A traditional hierarchy existed among the departments. This was reflected in the order of listing in the decrees announcing appointments. Justice was the top-ranking portfolio, followed by Foreign Affairs, Interior, Armies, and Finance, as the classic Big Five. Although some changes occurred in the designation and order of other ministries, usually they ran something like this: Education, Public Works and Transportation, Industry, Agriculture, Facilities, Labor, Public Health, Veterans' Affairs, and Information.

Composition and Professional Characteristics

The matter of previous personal service as a basis for recruitment was complicated in the case of ministers, because, in effect, they served two masters—the president and the premier. Each government contained a few members who were there because of their personal association with either the president or the prime minister. This was true, for instance, of *Malraux* under President de Gaulle, *Jeanneney* under Premier Debré, *Guichard* under Premier and then President Pompidou. However, because of the greater importance of political and parliamentary considerations in the appointment of ministers, personal loyalty was not as important as in the appointment of staff members.

Probably for the same reasons, ministers came from more diverse occupational backgrounds. (See Table 3.3.) Professional civil servants remained the largest category, but were only half as numerous as on the staffs. Fewer than half of the ministers were civil servants, compared to nine-tenths of the staffs. The overwhelming dominance of civil servants prevented significant representation of other occupational categories on the staffs. In contrast, business and industry provided substantial numbers of ministers.

Even those civil servants who did become ministers may have had different qualifications and motives than most of those who became staff members. Usually, the latter were selected because of the technical expertise they had acquired through their civil service careers. While such expertise was useful to ministers, political and parliamentary talents were even more valuable. The minister who lacked the former was less handicapped than if he lacked the latter. Furthermore, usually staff members looked on that service as a step on the route through an administrative career. Ministers tended to see the civil service as an entrance to politics, especially after the Debré government.

The greater diversity among ministers shows up also in their education profiles (See Table 3.4.) Nineteen of the 120 ministers (15.8 percent) had not received higher education. In contrast, only Foccart among the 235 staff members (0.4 percent) had no higher education. Also, ministers were somewhat more diverse in their selection of schools. Fewer of them received their education only in the Big Three schools and more of them attended a school in the miscellaneous category—mostly trade schools.

Fairly significant differences in the occupational background of ministers appear among the governments. In the Pompidou and Chaban-Delmas governments, fewer than 40 percent of the ministers were civil servants. Under Debré and Messmer, they topped 50 percent and, under Couve de Murville, they were about midway between the others. Thus, the two "most political" premiers—manifested by their presidential candidacies—had the fewest civil servants and the largest number of "politician" ministers.

Even within the civil service category, staffs and ministries differed significantly. Teachers were four times as frequent among the latter as among the former, while diplomats were half as frequent and finance was represented less well, also. In fact, teachers formed the largest civil service category among ministers. The nonadministrative quality of teaching diluted still further the technocratic element in the governments. Comparisions among governments disclose no significant difference in the distribution among civil service categories.

The most striking and revealing difference between the staffs and the ministries in terms of the careers of their members lies in the much more political character of the latter. (See Table 3.5.) Despite initial impressions, nearly all of them were involved in parliamentary electoral politics. This contrasted sharply with the staffs, in which such activities were exceptional, even when they were at their most political.

That initial impression was created by the Debré government. At the time of its appointment, one-third of its members (13 of 39) had never run for elective public office. This was noted widely at the time as contrasting with the Fourth Republic[39] and being a sign of the anti-parliamentary character of the regime. However, the expected trend never developed. In fact, the tide ran decisively back toward a parliamentary character for the ministers. For one thing, seven of the thirteen original "technocrats" were elected to Parliament later. Secondly, only one of the remaining six (Malraux) survived the Debré government and all their successors engaged in parliamentary electoral politics.

The parliamentary careers of most members of even the Debré government were substantial. *Jacquinot* had served in the Chamber of Deputies in the Third Republic (1932–40), the Reynaud government, both Constituent Assemblies of (1945–46), the National Assembly of the Fourth Republic (1946–58), and had been elected to the first Parliament of the Fifth Republic. *Pinay* had served in both the Chamber of Deputies and the Senate in the Third Republic, the second

Constituent Assembly, the National Assembly of the Fourth and Fifth Republics, several Fourth Republic governments, and had been one of its most respected and popular premiers. Five of Debré's ministers had been members of de Gaulle's Consultative Assembly of 1943-44 and ten had been elected to one or both of the Constituent Assemblies. Fifteen had been deputies, six had been senators, and twelve had been members of governments in the Fourth Republic. Eighteen had been elected to the new National Assembly and two to the Senate. Thus, a close look at even the most technocratic of the Fifth Republic governments shows it to have been dominated by members with parliamentary orientations (including the premier, who had been a senator throughout the Fourth Republic).

After the Debré government, the parliamentary–political element in the governments became even more dominant. In the Pompidou governments, ministers without previous experience as parliamentary candidates were only half as frequent as under Debré. Ten such ministers (16.4 percent) were appointed, of whom all but one ran for National Assembly seats later. In most cases, "later" meant by 1967, so the Pompidou government had only four such "technocrats" at the end. On the other hand, experienced MPs in the Pompidou governments included one survivor from the Third Republic Chamber of Deputies, eleven from the Constituent Assemblies, twenty-two from Fourth Republic Parliaments, and fifteen from Fourth Republic governments, including two premiers (*Pflimlin* and *Faure*).

Malraux was the only member of the Couve government who had not been elected to Parliament, and all members of the Chaban-Delmas government had been so elected. Two members of the Messmer governments were not elective politicians, but the circumstances of their appointment are suggestive. *Maurice Druon*, a popular writer, was appointed minister of cultural affairs, the job that Malraux had filled for ten years, suggesting a nonpolitical tradition for the position.[40] The other nonpolitician was *Michel Jobert*, foreign minister. Jobert was promoted from President Pompidou's staff to replace *Maurice Schumann*. Schumann and *René Pleven*, minister of justice, had felt obliged to resign because they had been defeated in the March 1973 parliamentary elections. The significance of Jobert's appointment was largely offset by that of Schumann's resignation, especially in light of the fact that Couve de Murville had remained in the same office after having been defeated in the 1967 elections. Also, Jobert showed his colors as a politician later when he formed his own political party after Pompidou's death and served as a minister in the Mauroy governments of 1981.

Not only were nonpolitician ministers very scarce after the Debré government, but they survived in only one ministry. Only cultural affairs was held by ministers who had neither pasts nor futures in parliamentary electoral politics (Malraux and Druon). Thus, during the last twelve of the fifteen Gaullist years, two portfolios were held by nonpoliticians for only eleven months, one was held for seven years, and the rest of the time all ministers were politicians.

On the other hand, the parliamentary character of Fifth Republic governments was evident, not only in the pervasiveness of MPs but also in their parliamentary longevity. More than one-third (38.6 percent) of Chaban's ministers had served in Parliament during the Fourth Republic, which had held its last election thirteen and a half years earlier. The same was true of 36.7 percent of Couve de Murville's ministers and 27.1 percent of Messmer's, including two Fourth Republic premiers (Pleven and Faure).

The parliamentarist character of the members of the government was enhanced further by practices they developed to bypass the "separation of powers" provisions of the 1958 constitution. Article 23 had declared that "membership in the government shall be incompatible with the exercise of any parliamentary mandate." In accordance with that prohibition, MPs appointed to the government ceded their seats (under Article 25) to the *suppléants* who had been elected as their running mates. However, most ministers continued to engage in many MP-type activities. They performed constituent errands for the districts that had elected them, retained the local offices (mayor, general councilor, etc.) that they had accumulated, held office hours in their districts, maintained their district electoral organizations, provided office space at their ministries for their *suppléants*, and so forth. Everyone assumed that they would contest their seats again and, if re-elected and returned to ministerial office, continue in that dual role.

If a minister left office between elections, his *suppléant* was expected to resign from Parliament to precipitate a by-election in which the ex-minister would be the candidate. In 1969, for instance, six ministers lost their portfolios. The *suppléants* of five of them resigned loyally from Parliament. All five of those seats were recovered by the ex-ministers in the by-elections. The ungrateful sixth *suppléant* (Couve de Murville's) refused to relinquish his seat.

Couve's reaction is suggestive of the growth of parliamentarism. He had had a long, distinguished career as a civil servant when he left the ambassadorship in Bonn to become de Gaulle's foreign minister in 1958. By 1970, he was one of eighteen *inspecteur générals de finance*, the highest civil service rank in the finance ministry, and one of eleven *ambassadeurs de France*, the highest civil service rank in the foreign ministry. Before 1967, he had never run for office, had never played a public role in a political party, and had no apparent interest in or inclination toward parliamentary politics.

Yet, once Pompidou and de Gaulle had dragged him, kicking and screaming, into the parliamentary arena, he fought desperately to stay there. He was defeated in 1967, losing the district in which the foreign ministry was located that had been won by a Gaullist in 1962. Then he won a neighboring seat in the Gaullist landslide of 1968. When his *suppléant* (another ambassador) refused to resign in 1969, Couve refused to return to his profession. Instead, another deputy was persuaded to resign from a "safe" Gaullist seat and Couve entered the by-election. He was defeated, 15,200 to 13,063 in the second round, by a leftist who had run third in 1968 and who lost to another Gaullist in

1973—26,275 to 22,531 on the second ballot. Undaunted, Couve returned to his old seat with an 11,448 to 10,473 second-round win in 1973. However, in five years, his first-round percentage had fallen from 53.1 to 33.2. After so much early reluctance, so much persistence in the face of such adversity with so little incentive suggests that parliamentarism was soaking deep into Gaullist flesh. Other examples, of reluctant parliamentry candidacy, such as Louis Joxe and Jean-Marcel Jeanneney, support that conclusion.

The process of socialization in parliamentarism was precipitated by de Gaulle's decision to require all ministers to become candidates for Parliament in the 1967 elections. Only Malraux and Jeanneney were excused. In 1968, only Malraux was excused. In 1973, in the Pompidou presidency, all ministers were candidates.

A corollary to the developing concept that all ministers must face the voters was the principle that those who are defeated lose their portfolios. In 1967, four ministers were defeated. Charbonnel and Sanguinetti were omitted from the next government. Messmer and Couve de Murville retained their posts. However, if Couve had won he might well have become prime minister a year sooner than he did.[41] If Couve had lost and Messmer had won in 1967, the latter might have become prime minister then rather than in 1972. In 1968, only Morandat was defeated and he disappeared from the government, even though he had held office only one month. In 1973, Schumann and Pleven were the only defeated ministers and both resigned from the government at once.

Personal Characteristics

Women were scarcely more numerous in the ministries than on the staffs. Only 3 of the 120 government members were women. Also, they served even more completely at subordinate rank, all of them being secretaries of state. The first was *Mlle. Nafissa Sid Cara*, daughter of a prominent Moslem Algerian official, whose appointment to the Debré government was a transparent ploy in the fight against Algerian nationalism. Next was *Mlle. Marie-Madeleine Dienesch*, veteran MRP deputy and specialist on social problems. She was the most influential of the women, perhaps the only one who had real political clout. The third was *Suzanne Ploux*, another specialist on social problems and a member of the steering committee of the UDR group in the National Assembly. Mlle. Dienesch had the longest ministerial career, serving from May 1968 until June 1974 under four prime ministers. Mlle. Sid Cara served through the Debré government and Mlle. Ploux was in office for one year.

On the other hand, the ministerial level was somewhat more cosmopolitan than the staff level. Ten (8.4 percent) had been born abroad. Moreover, four of the ten (Houphouët-Boigny, Sid Cara, Sanguinetti, and Pisani) had non-French parents. Names of Polish origin (Palewski, de Lipkowski, Poniatowski, Bokanowski) were fairly conspicuous and Alsatian (Messmer, Schumann, Nungesser, Bord, Pflimlin, Baumgartner) and Corsican (Comiti, Ortoli) names also figured prominently. Still, main-line ethnic French—born in France of French parents, reared and educated in France—dominated overwhelmingly in the ministries as in the staffs.

Aristocratic blood was less evident in the ministries than in the staffs, also—perhaps another manifestation of the effect of parliamentary politics at that level. Of course, *Baron Guichard* appears again. Other titles of nobility were sported by the *Princes de Broglie* and Poniatowski and the *Counts Pineton de Chambrun* and *de Lipkowski*. Six others had aristocratic names of more or less authenticity.[42] Another nine had married into such families.[43]

The ministries had other notable family connections. Both Giscard d'Estaing and his wife were descendants of Louis XV.[44] His great-great-grand-father had been a minister of public instruction in 1877–79 and his maternal grandfather had been a senator in the Third Republic, was appointed to Pétain's National Council,[45] and was a deputy from 1945 until he bestowed his seat on his grandson in 1955. The Poniatowski family had given a field marshal to Austria, a marshal to France, and a primate and a king to Poland. Guillaumat's father had been a minister of war in the Third Republic and minister of state in de Gaulle's first postwar government. Maurice-Bokanowski's father had been a Third Republic minister, Châtenet's father had been general secretary of the Finance Committee of the Chamber of Deputies. De Broglie numbered marshals, dukes, peers of the realm, Madame Staël, and the first premier of the Third Republic among his ancestors. Dumas' father had been a senator and de Chambrun's had been a deputy. Pisani's first wife was the daughter of André Le Troquer, Fourth Republic minister and president of the National Assembly, and his second was the daughter of Abel Ferry, Third Republic minister, and the grand-niece of Jules Ferry, Third Republic premier. Terrenoire's wife was the daughter of Francisque Gay, vice premier under de Gaulle, Gouin, and Bidault in 1945–46. Taittinger's father had been a deputy and chairman of the Paris Municipal Council. De Lipkowski's mother had been a Gaullist deputy from Paris, 1951–55, and a mayor, 1965–71. Nungesser was the nephew of the pioneer French aviator who was lost in the first attempt to fly the Atlantic. Achille-Fould's father was a deputy and minister in the Third Republic and his great-great-grandfather was Napoleon III's finance minister. Saintény married the niece of Albert Sarraut, deputy, Third Republic premier in 1933 and 1936, and president of the Assembly of the French Union under the Fourth Republic. Habib-Deloncle's great-uncle had been a senator.

Though the Gaullist ministers had important family connections to politics, their ties to wealth were even more impressive. (See Table 3.6.) Exactly one-third of them had fathers who were businessmen or industrialists, and more than half were from professional families (48.6 percent), were landowners (2.8 percent), or lived on independent means (1.8 percent). On the other hand, in contrast to the staff members, a substantial sprinkling came from modest circumstances. Six had craftsman fathers (Buron, printer; Bacon, saddlemaker/carriagemaker; Bord, lathe operator; Poncelet, mechanic; Dusseaulx, furrier artisan; Habib-Deloncle, jeweler) and one (Soustelle) was the only person among the 347

Gaullist ministers and staff members to list his father in a working-class occupation (*ouvrier*).[46]

Parental occupations are not the only evidence that Gaullist ministers tended to come from the French economic elite. Some thumbnail reviews of their family and professional ties should make that clear:

> *Jacquinot*, married Simon Lazard of the Lazard et Frères banking family.
>
> *Malraux*, son of banker.
>
> *Couve de Murville*, family of Protestant provincial gentry, Marseille bankers on one side, Bordeaux shippers and merchants on the other; married to the daughter of a banker; related to Baumgartner family (see below).
>
> *Pinay*, son and grandson of hat manufacturers with largest industry in locality.
>
> *Fontanet*, son of industrialist.
>
> *Giscard d'Estaing*, son of inspector of finance who was also president of International Chamber of Commerce and of a financial corporation and a director of several other corporations, including Thompson-Houston, which ranks in the top ten in France; grandson of a director of some twenty corporations.
>
> *Maurice-Bokanowski*, principal stockholder of several corporations, including Dralux-Boka and Grande Maison de Blanc.
>
> *Frey*, son of executive of Le Nickel, third largest French corporation in nonferrous metal mining, which dominates the economy of New Caledonia.
>
> *Flechet*, son of hat manufacturer and close friend of Pinay.
>
> *Sudreau*, son of industrialist.
>
> *de Broglie*, brother of the administrator of Crédit d'Escompte who was also a director of Campenon-Bernard (619-million franc business, 1968); married to a member of a wealthy industrialist family.
>
> *Marcellin*, son of banker.
>
> *Grandval*, father was industrialist; mother was member of publishing family.
>
> *Marette*, son of industrialist.
>
> *Dusseaulx*, associate of *Conseil national du patronat français*, the French "bosses" union.
>
> *Terrenoire*, son of glove manufacturer.
>
> *Messmer*, son of industrialist.
>
> *Chalandon*, son of industrialist; from an old bourgeois family in Lyons and Mâcon; son-in-law of administrator of Indochinese rubber corporation; general director of Banque commerciale de Paris, administrator of Bon Marché department store, Hauts Fourneaux (one of top ten steel producers), etc.; represents Dassault interests on various boards; wife related to Alain de Boissieu, son-in-law of de Gaulle and to Schneider steel trust family and a great-granddaughter of banker Stern.

Pleven, executive for multinational corporations before World War II.

Germain, corporation executive.

Bonnet, son of industrialist; corporation executive and trade association leader in canning industry.

Kaspéreit, corporation executive.

Vivien, son of industrialist; executive in family corporation.

Baumgartner, father from Alsatian Protestant *grande bourgeoisie*; mother from Bordeaux shipping and chemicals family; father-in-law represented Rothschilds and headed electricity trust before World War II. Bank and corporation executive.

Tinaud, son of landowner.

Taittinger, member of a leading champagne-producing family with interests in luxury hotels, foundries, and printeries.

Duhamel, son of general delegate of coal trust before World War II; son-in-law of president of Rousselot chemical corporation (350-million franc business).

Inchauspé, son of banker and industrialist in woolens; executive in family business and in trade association of woolens industry.

Duvillard, son of hotelman; director of public relations for Papéteries de France, second largest paper manufacturer in France.

Trorial, son of executive of Aciéries de Longwy steel plant.

Dechartre (pseudonym for Jean Duprat Géneau), business entrepreneur, forced to resign from the government because of his questionable involvement in a fraudulent housing enterprise.

Bord, married member of Monoprix chain-store family.

de Chambrun, corporation executive.

Bettencourt, corporation executive; married daughter of founder of Oréal chemical firm (1-billion franc business); stockholder in agricultural magazine.

Achille-Fould, corporation executive; from a leading French financial family.

Torre, corporation executive, especially in Moroccan sugar company.

Debré, stepmother related to de Wendel steel trust family; corporation executive; nephew of corporation executive.

Faure, lawyer for president of *Mines de Zellidja*.

Sanguinetti, corporation president.

Herzog, corporation executive, including Kléber-Colombes (second largest French rubber products manufacturer).

Billotte, married member of Shell oil family.

This list presents only the signs of wealth that are obvious from brief biographical notices. Undoubtedly, other members of Gaullist governments would appear on it if more complete information were available. Even so, it is impressive evidence of the importance of the French social and economic elite in those governments.

Ministers were significantly older than staff members. (See Table G.) Their median age was 49, ten years older than the median for the presidential staffs and eleven years older than the prime-ministerial staffs. Except for Giscard d'Estaing (at 32) and Chirac (at 34), both as secretaries of state, no one was appointed below age 35. Giscard d'Estaing was also the youngest full minister (at just short of 36). By contrast, more than one-fourth of the prime-ministerial staff appointments went to persons under 35. At the other end, only one person each of the presidential and prime-ministerial staffs was above age 55 at the time of appointment, but prime ministers appointed to their governments 58 (48.3 percent) persons who were 55 or over.

These differences are due largely, of course, to the hierarchical progression of the positions. However, they may also be explained partly by the more political character of the governments. The political position necessary to claim a place in the government takes longer to acquire than the technocratic competence needed for the staffs.

CONCLUSION

The Gaullist executive elite was narrowly drawn from a few easily identified backgrounds. Its members came disproportionately from aristocratic or bourgeois families of mainstream French origin. The staffs were composed overwhelmingly of civil servants issuing from three closely related types of institutions of higher education. Civil servants, businessmen, and lawyers predominated among the ministers. Almost all the elite were male.

The presidential and, to a lesser extent, the prime-ministerial staffs had little involvement in or inclination toward parliamentary politics. The opposite was true of the ministers. Although the technocratic element in the early Gaullist governments was substantial, especially in contrast to the Fourth Republic, parliamentary political leaders were always more numerous. With the passage of time, they took over completely. The initial reliance of technocrats may have been partly a response to the crisis situation which the president dominated so thoroughly and from which Parliament was largely excluded. As the crisis abated, parliamentary politics recovered and it became important to have persons of parliamentary background and inclination predominant in the part of the Executive that depended on the confidence of the National Assembly. However, the growth, power, and character of the presidential staff; the absence of parliamentary backgrounds in the prime-ministerial staffs; and the technocratic coloration of the early governments all contributed to reinforcing the presidentalist orientation of the regime during its early, most formative years.

II

LAW MAKING

4

Domain of Law

The preceding chapters have dealt with selected aspects of the institutional framework of the political Executive in the Gaullist Fifth Republic. They have reviewed the drafting of the 1958 constitution, the operation of the executive councils and committees, and the elite of the political Executive. They have shown that the constitution was parliamentary but that the regime was much more presidential in practice.

The following three chapters examine important facets of the executive–legislative relationship in law making. The first considers the constitutional definition of a "domain of law" and how it worked in practice. The second studies the exceptional legislative powers of the political Executive; and the third describes, analyzes, and assesses the constitutional authority of the Executive to intervene in the parliamentary legislative process. All three show that constitutional prescription did not determine the character of the system. In all three cases, constitutional provisions designed to transfer authority from the more parliamentary to the more presidential components of the system had relatively little effect.

The explicit constitutional delineation of "domain" of law and regulation was noted widely at the time as one of the most distinctive innovations of the 1958 constitution. Article 34 contains a long list of policy areas included in the legislative sphere of Parliament. Other articles identify certain other matters as legislative. Article 37 defines residual matters as regulatory. Article 37, 41, and 61 provide means by which the Executive can enforce the exclusion of parliament from the regulatory domain.

Those provisions were perceived in 1958 as likely to contribute significantly to strengthening the political Executive at the expense of Parliament in the crucial activity of making public policy. They were expected to restrict the scope of Parliament's authority and to transfer some parts of it to the Executive. Because of their restrictions on parliament, they seemed likely, also, to shift policy-making authority from that part of the Executive (the government) that was dependent on Parliament to the autonomous part (the president).

In fact, the definition of domains had very little effect on the law-making authority of the various branches of government. The following study will show that the constitutional design of the domain of law differed little from practice under the Fourth Republic. Where it did, government usually found it expedient to follow the parliamentary, rather than executive, route to law making. Thus, the constitutional text, in this respect, does not appear to have been the source of the emergence of the more presidential system of the Gaullist Fifth Republic.

This chapter will look, first, at the historical background of the "domains." Then, it will examine the drafting process that produced their definition in the 1958 constitution. Next, it will review actual practice with respect to the domains. Finally, it will summarize adjudicated interpretation of the domains by the Constitutional Council and the Council of State during the Gaullist period.

HISTORICAL BACKGROUND

Neither the constitutional laws of 1875 nor the constitution of 1946 distinguished explicitly between legislation and regulation. However, that distinction had become well established in French constitutional law and practice by 1958. As early as 1904, the Council of State had validated decrees on the grounds that they had been issued "within the limits of the regulatory power of the president of the Republic." [1] In 1906, it stated this general rule: [2]

> All questions relative, directly or indirectly, to the obligations to be imposed on citizens in an authoritative way without any contractual tie belong, by their nature, to the legislative power. . . . On the other hand, in principle, the executive power regulates the internal organization of the public services and the conditions of their functioning.

The decision gave as examples of legislation, "the right to command and to constrain, the organization of forces of order and judicial systems, the seizure of private property, the enactment of taxes and of public expenditures, etc." Its examples of regulation were "the rules for contracts between the Administration and its agents, their recruitment, promotion, discipline, dismissal, etc." Throughout the Third and Fourth Republics, the Council of State continued to refine its delineation of the domains.

During the Fourth Republic, Parliament joined the Council of State in defining the domains. It enacted several laws containing provisions to that effect.[3] The most notable was the law of August 17, 1948, which stipulated that in matters having by their nature a regulatory character, as determined in Article 7 below, decrees may be decided upon in the Council of Ministers after receiving the advice of the Council of State on the report of the Minister of Finance and Economic Affairs and the ministers concerned, to abrogate, modify, or replace provisions [of laws] in force.

Article 7 listed these matters of regulatory character:

1. The organization and operation of the administration of the State, of nationalized enterprises, and of certain enterprises receiving substantial state subsidies
2. The rules for operating and the means for financing the social security system
3. The conditions for issuing state loans and for managing the state financial portfolio
4. The regulation of the securities market
5. Price controls and the operation of economic controls
6. Energy utilization
7. Conditions for distributing raw materials and industrial products

Article 6 forbade the use of the regulatory power to create or alter criminal penalties. Article 8 contained a list of matters reserved explicitly for the domain of law. They all concerned the press and the broadcasting system.[4] These distinctions were made without time limit. Other Fourth Republic laws that made similar distinctions gave expiration deadlines. For instance, the regulatory area identified in the law of July 11, 1953 expired December 31, 1953.[5]

By 1958, the contents of the two domains were well articulated.[6] However, the regulatory list was permissive to the government, not restrictive to Parliament. Parliament could continue to legislate in a regulatory area. Also, it could remove a matter from the regulatory domain at any time by passing a law. The Fifth Republic constitutional concept was developed beyond that point.

DRAFTING PROCESS

The notion of an explicit constitutional distinction between legislation and regulation had deep roots in the thought of Michel Debré. He seems to have developed it first in articles he wrote for a World War II resistance journal and in a proposed constitution he drafted for the National Council of the Resistance.[7] In 1945, he expressed it in book form, arguing that a "domain reserved to Parliament" should be defined.[8] It should include "public liberties and the rules relative to the status of persons: freedom of conscience, individual liberties, freedom of the press, acquisition or loss of French nationality, amnesty, . . . the system of elections, functioning of Parliament, justice, administrative status of the territory, questions of economic and social structure, . . . [power] to declare war, to ratify peace treaties and international agreements." Outside that domain

Parliament could legislate, but "the decisions that it makes are not eternal; after a certain deadline the government would be free . . . to use its legitimate power to regulate."

It appeared, also, in a draft constitution that Debré prepared for General de Gaulle in January 1946. One of its articles conferred on Parliament "sole authority to enact measures concerning" certain individual liberties, internal parliamentary matters, the organization and functioning of the Council of State, the system of justice, and the local administrative system, while the "government shall exercise the regulatory power," which, however, was not defined or described.[9] Another constitutional proposal of his in 1948 omitted that distinction.[10]

The "domains" concept was in favor again in 1958 and was implied clearly in one of the first official steps in the preparation of the new constitution. The Constitutional Law of June 3, 1958 included as one of the principles on which the new constitution was to rest:

> The executive power and the legislative power must be separated effectively in a manner that the government and the Parliament each assumes for its part and on its responsibility the fullness of its attributions.[11]

That principle came up in the first meeting of the Interministerial Committee on the Constitution that included de Gaulle, Debré, Guy Mollet, Pierre Pflimlin, Félix Houphouët-Boigny, Antoine Pinay, and René Cassin. However, the discussion turned on a distinction of composition rather than activity or authority.[12] Later in the same discussion, this exchange occurred:[13]

> M. Guy Mollet believes that governmental stability is less important in the end than governmental authority and that it is of capital importance to settle the problem of the delineation of the domain of the regulatory power from the domain of the legislative power; to which M. Debré observed that it is less of matter of constitutional definition than a question of parliamentary discipline and of the organization of parliamentary work.

Mollet treated distinction between those domains as one application of the principle of separation of powers, others being the difference in modes of designation of Executive and Parliament and the system of incompatibilities in office holding.[14] Yet the first meeting of the team of experts that drafted the working text of the new constitution did not discuss it under that heading nor did the second meeting of the Interministerial Committee.[15]

The first draft of the 1958 constitution in early June incorporated the "domains" concept. One article listed as "reserved to the law questions relative" to the following matters:[16]

A1. The electorate
A2. The eligibility for membership in and the duration of the powers of the parliamentary assemblies and of the councils of the decentralized collectivities
A3. The boundaries of the administrative districts

A4. The rights of persons
A5. The definition of crimes, the penalties applicable to them, and criminal procedures
A6. The status of the magistracy
A7. Declarations of war
A8. Proclamations of states of siege
A9. Amnesty

Other articles in that draft added these matters to the domain of law:[17]

A10. The ratification of certain types of major international treaties
A11. The financial resources and obligations of the State.
A12. The organization of the High Court of Justice and its procedures

All other matters were declared to "present a regulatory character" and the "regulatory power" was conferred on the prime minister. Members of Parliament were forbidden to submit bills or amendments "bearing on regulatory matters." The government could enforce that ban by challenging any text in Parliament. Such a challenge halted consideration of the text automatically, permitting immediate appeal to a "Constitutional Commission." [18]

Those provisions included all basic elements of the final version. Nevertheless, a number of changes were made later in the drafting process. As Mollet said, those changes were "all in the same direction; to elaborate and render more precise the list of matters which are in the domain of law" and to expand that domain.[19] Some changes were made by the team of experts:[20]

B1. A1 and A2 were transferred from the "domain of law" article to other parts of the constitution and narrowed somewhat.
B2. A3 disappeared forever.
B3. "The organization of the branches of government [*pouvoirs publiques*]" was added to the domain of law.
B4. The definition of incompatibilities in office holding, the manner of replacing dual office-holders, and the setting of indemnities for MPs were added as matters of law outside the "domain of law" article.
B5. Additional categories of treaties were included as matters of law.

The Interministerial Committee had a substantial and expansive effect of the domain of law when it considered the draft:

C1. It broadened item A1.
C2. It lengthened the list of civil rights in item A4.

Also, it added the following items to the "domain of law" article:

C3. Fundamental guarantees accorded to citizens for the exercise of public liberties
C4. The distribution of authority between the State and the local collectivities

C5. The establishment of jurisdictions (new systems of courts or tribunals)
C6. Personal obligations imposed by national defense
C7. General principles of the organization of education
C8. Fundamental rules of social security and the principles of the right to work
C9. Parafiscal taxes

It identified as matters of law elsewhere in the constitution:

C10. The composition of the Economic and Social Council
C11. The list of civil and military offices subject to presidential appointment
C12. The manner of filling vacancies in Parliament
C13. Proxy voting in Parliament
C14. The creation of new territorial units of administration

Thus, it nearly doubled the size of the domain of law. It left the other parts of the system virtually the way Debré had conceived them originally. The Cabinet made very few changes with respect to the domain of law. It broadened the civil rights clause slightly and deleted "the organization of" from the education clause (C7).

The draft went next to the Consultative Constitutional Commission, (CCC).[21] An accompanying note, prepared mainly by Debré, explained the domain of law provisions:[22]

> In the contemporary political context, the governmental function necessarily includes the ability to issue general rules in a much broader domain than what is left to the regulatory power at present. Failing to have that possibility available normally, the governments of the past thirty years could try to escape from immobility only by constantly risking their existence to obtain from Parliament the enactment of laws indispensable for their action. The true mission of Parliament is to control governmental policy, to define the fundamental structures of the State and the society, and to ensure the protection of the fundamental rights of the citizens. That is the modern significance of the separation of powers, that is the [prerequisite] condition for governmental effectiveness and stability with respect for essential liberties.

Raymond Janot, the government's commissioner, explained it to the CCC:[23]

> Art. 31 does not tend to increase the powers of the bureaus immeasurably. It only tries to take into account the lessons of the past and to give the government the means to escape from immobility. It must be admitted: In recent years most of the important reforms have been made by decrees.

Also, he said that "the heart of the problem ... of the relations between Parliament and the government" was to ensure "the stability of the government and the continuity of governmental policy." One step toward that goal was to reform the process of holding governments responsible, but[24]

> it is still better to prevent that process from being set in motion uselessly at any moment. That is why we plan to replace the traditional distribution of authority, inherited from the nineteenth century, by another, better adapted to the role of the modern State, which must constantly issue texts of general effect for which parliamentary sanction must no longer be necessary; otherwise, the apparent respect for the separation of powers leads, in fact, to assembly government.
> That is so true that, despite being forbidden by the authors of the 1946 constitution, delegations of authority analogous to those used under the Third Republic between the wars had to be obtained several times. Facts triumphed over the written rule. Is it not time to learn the lesson and to recognize constitutionally a practice which, in fact, has become the common law of government? ...
> Thus, Article 31 enumerates the matters reserved to the competence of Parliament which are those that constant practice in recent years has reserved to it. All the other matters will have a regulatory character. About this enumeration, there may be some discussion. But the principle itself seems to me to be unassailable, since it is not, no matter what is said, a revolution—or at least it is one only on the level of juridical theory—for on the level of reality it is the consecration of a practice. (*Indications of disagreement.*)

The CCC discussed Article 31 (later 34) for more than two hours, more time than it spent on any other article in the draft constitution.[25] As Janot had urged, almost no one spoke against the principle of a constitutional distinction between law and regulation. In fact, the CCC explicitly accepted "a precise distribution of authority between the Parliament and the government" and "even agreed to the principle of a limiting enumeration of the matters falling in the legislator's domain." [26] However, the CCC found that enumeration to be "incomplete" and recommended twelve amendments to Article 31, mostly adding items to the domain of law. They were: [27]

D1. The electoral systems for Parliament, the Executive, and local councils
D2. The transfer of property between the public and private sectors
D3. Property, matrimonial, and civil responsibility legal systems
D4. The definition of public, civic, and trade union liberties
D5. Social security benefits and family subsidies
D6. The organization of the armed forces
D7. The control of public finance
D8. The management of nationalized enterprises and mixed corporations
D9. The rules of civil procedure
D10. The national economic plan
D11. The rules for presentation of the accounts of the State and of all public agencies
D12. The definition of the scope of and conditions for exercising the economic and financial powers of the State

Outside Article 31, the CCC recommended other additions to the domain of law: [28]

D13. Application of a requirement that political parties be democratic

D14. The consolidation and organization of local territorial units and the diminution of their "prerogatives"

D15. Ratification of commercial treaties

D16. Approval of decisions by Overseas Territories to change their status

Also, it recommended (D17) elimination of the replacement system for filling parliamentary vacancies and, thus, its deletion from the domain of law. It advocated (D18) incorporating into the constitution the definition of the presidential electoral college, except for Overseas France, thereby removing it from the domain of law. Finally, it recommended (D19) deleting the enumeration of offices under presidential appointment (C11) from the domain of law and replacing it by determination of the conditions in which he can delegate that right to the prime minister. [29]

In addition to those recommendations concerning the content of the domains, the CCC proposed that Article 33 (later 37) require that decrees modifying laws be reviewed by the Constitutional Council to determine that "they are not contrary to the provisions of Article 31." [30] Some members objected to the ban on parliamentary revision of decrees issued under Article 33, but they could not convince enough of their colleagues to make it a recommendation. [31] All those proposals amount to an addition to the domain of law as large as Debré's original proposal or as the additions made at the governmental level.

The government made no decision on the CCC recommendations concerning Article 31 pending review by the Council of State. It accepted the recommendation for Article 33, as well as D15, D18, and, with rewording, D16. With respect to D19, it retained the enumeration and added the conditions of delegation. It rejected D13, D14, and D17. Also, it added the conditions for filling vacancies in Parliament to the domain of law. [32]

The government's refusal to endorse any version of Article 31 (now become 33) to the Council of State departed from its practice with respect to every other article in the constitution. Rather, it made available all the versions prepared until that time. [33] Debré spoke to the General Assembly of the Council of State on August 27, after it had received a report on the draft from one of its committees. He gave considerable attention to "the article in which a definition of that domain of law is attempted" and expressed surprise that it was "among those that have provoked the greatest astonishment": [34]

From the viewpoint of principles, the definition is normal and it is the confusion of law, regulation, even of measures for individuals which is the absurdity. From the viewpoint of facts, our juridical system has reached such a state of confusion and congestion that one of the most constant, but vain, efforts in recent years has been the attempt to "disencumber" a parliamentary agenda crushed by the excess of laws passed for so many years in domains where Parliament has no legislative competence normally. An observer of our parliamentary life would have been able to notice between the wars, but especially since the Liberation, this double deviation by our political organization: a Parliament crushed by bills and racing in disorder to multiply its interference in details, but a government dealing without parliamentary intervention in the gravest national problems. The result of those two observations led to a double crisis: the impotence of the State because the administration was strangled by inadmissible laws, the anger of the nation because a partisan coalition in the government took grave measures that were decided without previously having undergone serious examination. To define the domain of law or, rather, of Parliament, is not to reduce parliamentary life, it is, also, by determining the responsibilities of the government, to ensure a necessary division of labor between the Ministry and the Assemblies.

The Council of State proposed a complete revamping of Article 33. Not a single line survived intact from the last previous governmental draft, though the basic concept and most of the content remained essentially the same. The Council of State recommended inclusion of a statement of general principle: "The law . . . lays down the principles and sets the general rules of which the government ensures the execution." Then it set up two categories of policy areas. In one, the law "determines the general framework of systems." In the other, it "sets the rules." The first category covered:[35]

E1. National defense and the obligations imposed by it on citizens in their persons and their goods
E2. The free administration of local collectivities and the determination of their authority and their resources
E3. Education
E4. Property, real estate rights, and civil and commercial obligations
E5. The right to work, trade union rights, and social security.

The second category listed:

E6. The publication, effects, and implementation of laws
E7. The electoral systems of parliamentary and local assemblies
E8. Civic rights and the fundamental guarantees accorded to citizens for the exercise of public liberties
E9. Nationality, personal status and capacity, the matrimonial, inheritance, and charity systems
E10. The creation of new categories of jurisdictions and the status of magistrates, the determination of crimes and offenses as well as the penalties which apply to them; penal procedure; amnesty
E11. The distribution, the rates, and means of collection as well as, when occasion requires, the assignment of all types of taxes imposed on the taxpayers; the system of issuing money
E12. The creation of categories of national public establishments
E13. The nationalization of enterprises and the transfer of the property of enterprises from the public sector to the private sector.

E14. The disciplinary guarantees of civil and military functionaries in the services of the State.

Also, the Council of State listed separately in Article 33:

E15. Determination of the resources and burdens of the State
E16. Prolongation of the state of siege beyond twelve days
E17. Declarations of war

In other parts of the draft, the Council proposed these changes that concern the domain of law:

E18. Addition of the conditions for the election of presidential electors from overseas territories
E19. Elimination of the listing of offices for presidential appointment
E20. Addition of the operating rules of the Economic and Social Council
E21. Addition of the rules of organization and operation of the Constitutional Council

The net effect of those proposals would have been a significant further expansion of the domain of law. Also, the Council of State recommended inclusion in the constitution of an "elastic clause" to permit later expansion of that domain through enactment of organic laws. This was a different and easier amending process than for any other part of the constitution.

Debré recommended to the Interministerial Committee that it accept most of the Council of State's work. He asked for elimination of the general statement of principles and broadening of the elastic clause: "The provisions of the present article can be made more precise and elaborated by an organic law." [36] He accepted the categorization, but wanted "general framework of the systems" changed to "fundamental principles." With respect to E1, he recommended removal of "national defense" and the transfer to the "rules" category of the rest of the clause. He proposed retaining the rest of the "fundamental principles" intact and, with some reordering, all the other items in the Council of State list, except E6, E14, and E19. Finally, he recommended that the spirit of the CCC's D10 (national economic plans) be incorporated as "Program laws shall determine the objectives of the economic and social action of the State."

The Interministerial Committee accepted Debré's recommendations intact, except that it added to the "rules" category in Article 33 (now become 34):[37]

F1. The fundamental guarantees accorded to the civil and military functionaries of the State
F2. The general organization of national defense

and elsewhere in the domain of law:

F3. The means of implementing the presidential electoral college.

The Council of Ministers reviewed and approved the final draft of the Interministerial Committee on September 3. It made only two minor changes in the delineation of the domains. It clarified the wording of the clause on presidential appointments (Art. 13) and added to the domain of law determination of the conditions in which the Superior Council of the Magistracy is consulted on pardons (Art. 65).

The constitution as approved by referendum on September 23 included twenty-one articles that identified matters in the domains of law or regulation. Those articles are set forth in Appendix A. Also, the Constitutional Council has included the Preamble, the Preamble of the 1946 Constitution, and the Declaration of the Rights of Man of 1789, and certain laws as defining "fundamental principles" that belong in the domain of the law.[38] They omitted the following items that had been proposed for inclusion at some point in the drafting process (the person or organism that first proposed each item is indicated in parenthesis):

G1. The boundaries of the administrative districts (Debré)

G2. The organization of the branches of government [*pouvoirs publiques*] (task force)

G3. The security of persons (task force)

G4. The organization of the family (Interministerial Committee)

G5. Social security benefits and family subsidies (CCC)

G6. The organization of the armed forces (CCC)

G7. The control of public finance (CCC)

G8. The management of nationalized enterprises and mixed corporations (CCC)

G9. The rules of civil procedure (CCC)

G10. The rules for the presentation of the accounts of the State and public agencies (CCC)

G11. The enforcement of a requirement that political parties be democratic (CCC)

G12. The consolidation and organization of local territorial units (CCC)

G13. The publication, effects, and implementation of laws (Council of State)

The definition of the domain of law was a profoundly serious deliberation that continued intensely over a three-month period and involved a substantial number of active participants. Probably, that task required as much effort and attention as any part of the drafting process. Debré, the task force, de Gaulle, the Interministerial Committee, the CCC, and the Council of State all had significant impact on the outcome. The Cabinet and the Council of Ministers produced minor changes. Even so, the final text did omit some rather substantial items that had been proposed for inclusion in the domain of law.[39] The effectiveness of those choices can be assessed on the basis of practical experience in their implementation during the Gaullist period.

THE "DOMAINS" IN PRACTICE

Statistical Indicators

Statistics provide a crude measure of the success of the effort to define the domain of law. The framers wanted to reduce the sweep of parliamentary law making. One indication of that sweep is the number of laws enacted by Parliament. By that test, they did well. In eleven and a half years, from November 28, 1946 until June 12, 1958, the Parliaments of the Fourth Republic enacted 2,668 laws, an average of 232 per year. In fourteen and two-thirds years, from April 28, 1959 until December 20, 1973, the Parliaments of the Fifth Republic enacted 1,376 laws, an average of 94 per year.[40] Moreover, although law making fell to 40 percent of its Fourth Republic pace, the number of executive measures did not increase correspondingly. In fact, the number of such measures[41] actually declined. The governments of the Fourth Republic, through the Pflimlin ministry, used 16,144 numbered decrees, 1,404 per year. The corresponding figures from the installation of the de Gaulle government until Pompidou's death were 20,221 and 1,277.[42]

The law-making rate of the Fifth Republic shows no significant trends. (See Table 4.1.) The rather wide differences among the years seem explicable by major

Table 4.1. Number of Public Measures Enacted in France, 1946-73 [a]

	FOURTH REPUBLIC					FIFTH REPUBLIC			
Year	*By Parliament*	*By the Executive*[b]	*Total*	*Laws as % of Total*	*Year*	*By Parliament*	*By the Executive*[b]	*Total*	*Laws as % of Total*
1946	11	132	143	8.3	1958	0	963	963	---
1947	246	2,205	2,451	10.0	1959	51	1,543	1,594	3.2
1948	331	1,723	2,054	16.1	1960	89	1,440	1,529	5.8
1949	276	1,401	1,677	16.5	1961	102	1,550	1,652	6.2
1950	257	1,378	1,635	15.7	1962	49	1,570	1,619	3.0
1951	272	1,256	1,528	17.8	1963	99	1,384	1,483	7.2
1952	184	1,247	1,431	12.9	1964	117	1,263	1,380	8.5
1953	239	1,137	1,376	17.4	1965	74	1,115	1,189	6.2
1954	237	1,115	1,352	17.5	1966	133	948	1,081	12.3
1955	197	1,531	1,728	11.4	1967	85	1,186	1,271	6.7
1956	140	1,340	1,480	9.7	1968	75	1,196	1,271	5.9
1957	198[c]	1,236	1,434	13.8	1969	78	1,198	1,276	6.1
1958	80	443	523	18.1	1970	97	1,251	1,348	7.2
Total	2,668	16,144	18,812	14.2	1971	115	1,038	1,153	10.0
					1972	130	1,148	1,278	10.2
					1973	82	1,150	1,232	6.7
					1974	0	278	278	---
					Total	1,376	20,221	21,597	6.4

[a.]Compiled from *JO. LD. Tables. Chronologique.*
[b.]Referendal laws, numbered decrees, DRAP, and ordinances.
[c.]Not including 45 "decisions" ratifying decrees.

political events. The low years (fewer than 80 laws) were years in which parliamentary sessions were interrupted: 1962 and 1968, dissolutions; 1965 and 1969, presidential elections. The only exception was 1959, de Gaulle's first year as president.

On the other hand, a significant correlation existed between the law-making rate and the size of the parliamentary majority. The rate was almost 50 percent higher for Assemblies with solid Gaullist majorities (II, 1962–67, and IV, 1968–73) than for those with marginal Gaullist majorities (I, 1958–62 and III, 1967–68). (See Table 4.2.) This suggests that the decline in law making was only partly a function of the constitutional change and depended partly on the size of the Gaullist majority. In effect, political factors bore importantly on the force of the constitutional change.

Table 4.2. Number of Laws Enacted by Legislature, 1959–73

Legislature	Number of Laws	Average Number per month
I	288	6.13
II	437	8.57
III	87	5.80
IV	492	8.36

The 1958 constitution reduced the scope and, thus, the rate of law making. Within that reduced scope, the rate has varied according to the strength of the Gaullist majority. Beyond mere rate, however, the framers wanted to affect the character of the laws. To evaluate their success in that respect, the content of the legislation must be examined.

Content of Legislation

The configuration of the "domains" worked out unevenly in practice. Every clause in Article 34 served as the basis for some legislation. No serious consideration seems to have been given to using the "elastic clause" to change its boundaries. However, few other law-making articles produced much legislation. Also, much material of clearly regulatory character appeared in laws. Thus, the stated purpose for Article 34 was not well served.

Much the most important basis for legislation was Article 34. Table 4.3 shows this clearly. It gives the number of laws enacted each year according to their constitutional basis. Because some laws appeared to have more than one constitutional basis, the total indicated by the table is greater than the total number of bills enacted during those years. Article 34 provided 1,099 of the 1,487 "constitutional bases," 73.9 percent. Nineteen other articles authorized laws. Only three of them served as the basis for a significant number of laws. Most of the others authorized organic laws that were, in effect, transitional measures and were enacted as ordinances during de Gaulle's personal dictatorship of 1958–59.[43]

Table 4.3. The Constitutional Bases of Law Enacted in France, 1959-73

	1959	1960	1961	1962	1963	1964	1965	1966	1967	1968	1969	1970	1971	1972	1973	Total
Art. 25. Legislatures length; status of MPs	0	0	2	1	0	0	0	1	0	0	0	0	0	0	0	4
Art. 34. Rules concerning:																
Civic rights, liberties; nat'l. def. duties	2	1	0	1	2	0	1	3	1	3	0	3	2	2	0	21
Personal status, matrimony, inheritance	0	2	3	0	5	1	4	5	3	4	3	6	3	4	1	44
Crimes, procedures, amnesty, judiciary	6	5	6	5	16	13	14	18	14	12	1	11	15	25	1	162
Taxes; system for issuing money	11	11	28	3	11	33	3	7	2	8	6	4	5	4	1	137
Local, parliamentary electoral systems	0	0	0	0	2	1	1	5	0	0	1	0	2	5	2	17
Creating categories of public authorities	1	2	1	0	2	3	1	2	2	1	0	0	1	1	1	19
Fundamental guarantees of functionaries	5	12	6	1	5	14	7	6	3	4	5	13	3	9	1	94
Nationalizations and denationalizations	0	1	0	0	0	0	1	0	0	0	0	1	0	1	0	4
Art. 34. Fundamental principles of:																
General organization of national defense	7	5	3	2	6	4	5	6	1	2	0	4	2	4	0	51
Local collectivities: admin., resources	1	1	3	0	3	9	1	5	3	3	5	6	5	5	0	48
Education	3	2	0	1	1	1	0	1	0	2	0	1	7	2	0	21
Property; civil, commercial obligations	5	13	4	11	14	14	16	30	18	12	17	37	26	33	4	254
Labor law; social security	4	5	8	3	7	6	6	14	6	5	4	9	16	28	3	124
Art. 34. State resources, expenditures	10	9	4	7	7	2	2	3	7	6	6	5	5	4	0	77
Art. 34. State social, economic action	3	3	5	4	0	2	2	1	2	0	0	2	2	0	0	26
Art. 38. Authorizations for ordinances	0	2	1	1	0	1	0	2	1	0	1	0	0	0	0	9
Art. 38. Ratification of ordinances	0	0	0	0	0	0	0	0	0	1	1	0	0	0	0	2
Art. 53. Ratification of int'l. agreements	2	18	18	10	21	24	15	28	19	10	26	25	23	30	0	269
Art. 72. Territorial collectives	0	0	1	0	0	0	0	0	2	0	1	2	1	2	0	9
Art. 73. O/S depts.: legis., admin. systems	1	5	3	3	3	0	4	4	1	5	3	2	1	1	2	38
Art. 74. Organization of O/S territories	5	1	5	2	6	3	0	7	7	3	6	2	1	7	0	55
Art. 85. Revision of Community (Title XII)	0	1	0	0	0	0	0	0	0	0	0	0	0	0	0	1
Art. 89. Revision of constitution	0	0	0	0	1	0	0	0	0	0	0	0	0	0	0	1
Totals	66	99	101	55	112	131	83	147	90	81	86	135	118	167	16	1,487

The other three major law-producing articles were 53 (ratification of international agreements), 73 (overseas departments), and 74 (overseas territories). They were the basis for 269, 38, and 55 laws, respectively. Five other articles served as the basis of laws. They were Articles 25 (duration of legislatures; MPs) with four laws, 38 (ordinance authority) eleven, 72 (territorial collectivities) nine, 85 (the Community) and 89 (constitutional amendment), one each.

No laws enacted during the period in question dealt with objects not included in the constitutional domain of law. However, many laws dipped to a level of detail that does not seem to have been intended by the framers. For instance, many of the 477 laws deriving from the "fundamental principles" category of Article 34 included matters too minor to merit that label. Laws on the "fundamental principles" of the "general organization of national defense" illustrate this. One of them did no more than authorize the government to give early release to conscripts in their last four months of service, rather than only in the last month.[44] Even the laws that have "fundamental" objects often seemed to defeat the purpose of Article 34 by including much minor detail. Note, again, defense legislation. More than fifty laws in that area were enacted during the Gaullist years. Some of them contained scores of articles and tens of thousands of words.

In other areas, too, the objects of some laws seem clearly regulatory. For instance, is control of the profession of dance instructor a "fundamental principle" of education? [45] Similar questions are raised by laws concerning audioprosthesists,[46] opticians,[47] physical education instructors,[48] orthophonists and orthophonist aides,[49] accounting experts,[50] judicial experts,[51] and wine labeling.[52] Also, were laws required to transfer General Catroux,[53] raise Paris bus and subway fares,[54] amend a 1681 ordinance on flags of convenience,[55] rescind special fishing privileges granted to the village of Fort-Mardych in 1773,[56] suppress the rights of "certain persons" in the Hautes-Alpes department to graze their livestock on the land of others,[57] define the status of *"chefs et sous chefs de musique"* in the military services,[58] and to modernize the "wolf-warden" corps? [59] If all matters of comparable consequence were encompassed in the domain of law, little would be left to regulation. Rather, it appears that the government chose to give a very generous interpretation to Article 34 when it approved of the policy proposed and preferred, for one reason or another, that the parliamentary route be pursued.

Another anomaly in implementing Article 34 arose from the clause that "program laws shall determine the objectives of the economic and social action of the State." This clause seems to have been the government's response to the CCC suggestion that the domain of law include national economic plans, even though they had always been promulgated as decrees in the Fourth Republic. Nevertheless, both the government's preliminary "reports on options" and the Fifth and Sixth Plans themselves were enacted as ordinary laws, rather than program laws.[60] On the other hand, program laws have dealt with such varied matters as atomic energy experimentation, the overseas departments, military facilities, electrical facilities, scientific and technical research, and historical monuments,[61] none of which seems to be described most accurately as "determining" the objectives of the economic and social action of the State.

Not only did laws intrude into the territory of regulations on one side and program laws on the other, but they seem to have held their own in the domain of law. Virtually all major domestic policy measures were enacted through laws. The only important exceptions were the economic and social ordinances of 1967 (which were authorized and ratified by laws) and some Algerian crisis measures. Early fears to the contrary notwithstanding, the domain of law remained intact in the Gaullist Fifth Republic.

ADJUDICATED INTERPRETATION

The Constitutional Council

The 1958 constitution differs from its predecessors in providing explicitly for third-party interpretation of the delineation of the domains of law and regulation. Three provisions authorize Constitutional Council rulings on that question. Under *Article 37*, laws and ordinances affecting regulatory matters "which have been promulgated since the present constitution went into effect can be modified by decree only if the Constitutional Council has declared that they have a regulatory character" upon petition of the prime minister. Under *Article 41*, if the prime minister declares a bill or amendment in Parliament to be regulatory in character and, hence, out of order, and the president of the chamber disagrees, either of them may ask the Constitutional Council for a ruling. Under *Article 61*, the Constitutional Council reviews for constitutionality all organic laws automatically and any other laws referred to it by the president of the Republic, the prime minister, or the president of either parliamentary chamber.[62]

Article 37 produced most of the cases. It served as the basis for seventy-seven (87.5 percent) of the eighty-eight such cases decided by the time of Pompidou's death.[63] In forty-nine (63.6 percent) of the Article 37 cases, the Constitutional Council ruled that the provisions in question were entirely regulatory in character. In twenty-two cases (28.8 percent), it ruled that they were partly regulatory and partly legislative. In only six cases (7.8 percent), did it rule against the government completely.

Article 41 produced eight cases. Senate President Gaston de Monnerville brought five of them. Prime Minister Debré brought one and Assembly President Chaban-Delmas brought two. The Constitutional Council ruled in favor of the government in six cases.[64] It ruled in favor of Monnerville in one case[65] and, in another of his cases,[66] ruled that the bills in question were partly legislative and partly regulatory. However, neither of the bills that the Constitutional Council saved ever became law.

Article 61 produced only three cases concerning the domains of law and rule. All three were brought by prime ministers. The government won two cases[67] and lost one.[68] The latter decision upheld a provision of a law that prohibited the reduction of the fiscal resources of local administration. That was the only instance of a law or part of a law that took effect despite the government's contention that it trespassed in the domain of regulation.[69]

In general, the Constitutional Council rulings supported the government's interpretation of the domain of law and, therefore, tended to be restrictive. Also, in one pair of decisions,[70] it held that governmental permissiveness in the parliamentary process did not, thereby, enlarge the domain of law. The government had included regulatory matter in a parliamentary bill deliberately and announced that on the floor of the Assembly.[71] The Constitutional Council held that it could, nevertheless, alter those matters later by decree.

Most of the Constitutional Council's jurisprudence in this area was interpretation of the substantive clauses of Article 34. An especially fertile ground for interpretation was the meaning of "fundamental" with respect to "guarantees" and "principles." The "fundamental" lay in the domain of law; the rest was regulatory. Some examples may clarify the manner in which the Constitutional Council worked in this area and the kind of effect its rulings had:

1. Only *laws* can change or create obligations imposed by the State, but *rules* may change the "precise object" or amount of an obligation.[72]
2. Only *laws* can grant authority to act in the name of the State, but *rules* may determine the procedures, means, and officials through which that authority shall be exercised, so long as they do not "denature" legislative intent.[73]
3. Only *laws* can create, change, or abolish types of rights or State benefits, such as social security and civil and military employment, and identify categories of beneficiaries; but *rules* may set conditions of eligibility, deadlines, procedures for qualifying, methods of calculation and accounting, rates of compensation, types of exceptions, etc., so long as they do not deny persons their basic rights. For instance, a rule could deny social security maternity benefits to mothers under a certain age with offspring conceived out of wedlock.[74]

The Constitutional Council delineated "fundamental" in other ways, too. It held that certain "fundamental principles" of property rights might be impaired by rules "to permit certain interventions deemed necessary by the public authorities"—in other words, for general policy considerations.[75] Also, rules may override "fundamental guarantees of public liberties" if promulgated to implement legislative decisions.[76] In other restrictive interpretations, the Constitutional Council held that military reserve officers not on extended active duty are not "functionaries of the State" in the meaning of Article 34[77] and that rules may establish penalties of imprisonment for *contraventions*, despite a traditional principle of French jurisprudence that a person can be deprived of liberty only under the authority of law.[78] Also, the Constitutional Council ruled that the boundaries of the domains of law and rule are the same for overseas territories as for France, except that matters delegated by Parliament to territorial assemblies necessarily fall in the domain of rules in the Republic's dealings with the overseas territories.[79]

Finally, two Constitutional Council decisions seemed to interpret parts of Article 34 broadly. One held that "new orders of jurisdiction" include new jurisdictions and tribunals incorporated in existing hierarchies and that "creation" means substantive as well as formal changes, both interpretations contrary to traditional French jurisprudence.[80] The other construed the "rules concerning . . . the nationalization of enterprises and the transfer of property of enterprises from the public sector to the private sector" to include the setting of deadlines for the liquidation of public enterprises.[81]

In summary, the Constitutional Council established itself as an active and viable interpreter of the constitutional meaning of the domains of law and regulation. Generally, it favored the government and, thus, helped to hold the line against parliamentary imperialism. However, the exceptions were frequent enough to protect the credibility of the Council. Also, its decisions helped to fill in detail and to clarify the substance of Article 34. Yet it did very little to change the meaning or the boundaries of the domains.

The Council of State

Council of State rulings also affected the law versus rule issue. Usually, they resulted from complaints filed by individuals or organizations alleging that governmental decrees had exceeded their constitutional authority by trespassing in the domain of law. In theory, the Council of State had no authority to review parliamentary acts, but occasionally its decisions had that effect if it believed that a decree was based on an unconstitutional parliamentary act. For instance, in 1961 it annulled a decree on the grounds that its authority derived from an ordinance that violated Article 34 by purporting to transfer to the government permanently the power to define the "fundamental guarantees" accorded to certain functionaries, and, thus, removing "certain administrative acts from any juridical control." [82]

Under that authority, the Council of State developed a substantial body of jurisprudence on the "domains" question during the Gaullist administrations. Indeed, its administrative sections spent about one-third of their time on that matter.[83] By the time Pompidou died, it had issued 102 decisions concerned with defining the "domains." [84] In sixty-five cases (63.7 percent), it upheld the questioned decree entirely. It annulled decrees twenty-four times and upheld some provisions and annulled others twelve times. Once it declared itself incompetent to judge.[85]

In amount of Council of State activity, the period falls neatly into two nearly equal parts. From 1958 through the presidential elections of 1965, the Council of State averaged 4.4 decisions a year, of which 48.4 percent upheld the government entirely. From then through Pompidou's death, it averaged nearly twice as many decisions per year, 8.6, and was nearly half again as favorable to the government, 70.4 percent. It seems almost as though the Council of State followed the 1965 election returns and decided that the Fifth Republic had come to stay. Indeed, in 1966, it made eleven decisions, all entirely upholding the government.

As with the Constitutional Council, most Council of State decisions on this matter wrestled with the definition of "fundamental," especially "fundamental guarantees." In that effort, the Council of State relied heavily on the traditional distinctions of French jurisprudence. That is, it tended to see as "fundamental" matters that had required legislation under earlier Republics and to view matters treated by decrees in earlier republics as not being "fundamental." This produced much greater similarity and continuity with the jurisprudence of the Third and Fourth Republics than the constitutional texts suggest.[86] Some examples of Council of State rulings in that area may clarify the character of its jurisprudence:

1. Only *laws* can decide that the funds of different social security systems be administered by boards elected separately by distinct constituencies, but *rules* can provide that they be placed administratively in the same ministry and subjected to the same inspection system.[87]
2. Only *laws* can impose restrictions on general categories of property, but *rules* can define those categories precisely.[88]
3. Only *laws* can prescribe the "nature of the conditions required for the attribution of benefits," but *rules* can define "their elements and means," so long as they do not "denature" those conditions.[89]
4. Only *laws* can define the rights of members of social security systems to choose among hospitals, but *rules* can prescribe the bases on which such choices may be made. Therefore, a decree might exclude the convenience of a member as a valid basis.[90]
5. Only *laws* can make age a condition of eligibility under labor law, but *rules* can specify what shall be the age.[91]

Many similar examples could be provided. In general, perhaps uniformly, they seem consistent with the principles derived from Constitutional Council decisions in the same area.

Decisions resting on other bases than the meaning of "fundamental" were less numerous and tended more to create new jurisprudence. Thus, the Council of State ruled that Articles 34 and 37 broadened the traditional domain of regulation with respect to control of markets,[92] *contraventions,*[93] parafiscal fees,[94] and nonpenal judicial procedures.[95] Also, its inclusion of economic "solidarity" with war victims among the "obligations imposed by national defense" was not required by previous tradition.[96]

Still other Council of State decisions seemed to prefer traditional definitions over the literal meaning of the constitutional text. For instance, it construed "magistrates" to mean "professional magistrates," [97] "new orders of jurisprudence" to include single courts or tribunals,[98] and "functionaries of the

State" to exclude mayors[99] and industrial workers in nationalized enterprises.[100] On balance, then, both the Constitutional Council and Council of State decisions tended to reduce the significance of Article 34 in changing the boundaries between the domains of law and regulation.

CONCLUSIONS

Despite widely expressed expectations at the time, the domain of law remained substantial in the Gaullist Fifth Republic, apparently adequate in the eyes of most people concerned. Little was said or done about revising the constitution in this respect, or even of using the "elastic clause" to change the boundaries of the domains. Indeed, those boundaries were very close to practice in the Fourth Republic.

The reasons for this are various. Political and administrative inertia may be one. The natural conservatism of the adjudicating organs may be another. Also, the government had important reasons for wanting to keep the domain of law intact and broad. Often, policy making through laws and Parliament was safer and easier than through decrees and the Council of State. Parliament was more reliably Gaullist than was the Council and laws were less vulnerable to Council depredations than decrees.

Thus, the domain of law was defined more by practical political realities than by constitutional provisions. It survived intact because the Executive trusted the Parliament. It found Parliament trustworthy because of its dependable Gaullist majority. That majority was dependable because of its cohesion and the cohesion reflected the greater cohesion of French society, as shall be shown in Chapter 7. The same relationships of constitution, society, and governmental practice may be seen in the other aspects of law making discussed in Chapters 5 and 6.

5

Executive Law Making

INTRODUCTION

One of the most striking and controversial features of the 1958 constitution was the inclusion of sweeping emergency powers for the political Executive. In effect, they empowered the Executive to enact laws without parliamentary consideration in certain, specified circumstances. They were widely perceived as strengthening the political Executive and creating dangerous possibilities for the abuse of power. In fact, this chapter will show that they had very little effect on the power equation of the two political branches of government. Such changes as occurred resulted more from political than constitutional factors. This will become apparent through review of the historical background of exceptional powers; examination of their use by de Gaulle as premier, 1958–59; and study of the basis, use, and parliamentary control of executive law making under Articles 16, 38, and 11 of the 1958 constitution. Throughout this chapter, ideology (as expressed principally through constitutional texts) and circumstances (mainly political) will be compared in their relative effect on governmental practices.

HISTORICAL BACKGROUND

The Third Republic

Ideology

The several texts that formed the constitution of the Third Republic did not deal explicitly with the matter of delegated legislation. However, parliamentary legislative exclusivity was implied by the provision that "the legislative power is exercised by the two assemblies: the Chamber of Deputies and the Senate." [1] Moreover, the constituent assembly had established the principle that its constituent powers were sovereign, unlimited, and exclusive. By analogy, the legislative assemblies had legislative powers of similar sweep.[2] Most constitutional law commentators supported that doctrine throughout the Third Republic.[3]

Practice

Despite that ideology, circumstance soon reared its insistent head. As early as April 3, 1878, Parliament passed an enabling act. It authorized the president of the Republic, on advice of the Council of Ministers, to declare a state of siege during the adjournment. However, Parliament had to convene "by right" within two days and either Chamber could invalidate the declaration.[4] Again, in December 1879, Parliament authorized the president of the Republic in the Council of State and with the approval of the Council of Ministers to issue decrees during its recesses to "appropriate funds provisionally," provided that the decrees indicated the sources of funds and were submitted to Parliament during the first fortnight of its next session. Until 1914, such enabling acts were used sparingly. One authority lists only three others before then.[5] Certainly, they were fewer, less important, and less sweeping than in later years.

That restraint evaporated in World War I. Expediency became addictive in crisis. Executive legislation became an almost normal part of governmental life. On August 2, 1914, the president of the Republic, invoking the 1878 law, proclaimed a state of siege throughout the French territory.[6] The Chamber of Deputies met for about 85 minutes on August 4; heard war messages from its president, the president of the Republic, and the prime minister; received the Budget Committee's unanimous recommendation for the passage of five government bills; considered thirteen others without reference to committee; and adopted all eighteen unanimously and without debate, including ratification of the state of siege.[7]

Parliament met next in special session December 22, sat for less than three hours, heard drum-beating speeches by its president and the premier, and adopted ten government bills—including one that ratified 34 decree laws—unanimously and without debate.[8] the regular session of 1915 was equally submissive. It passed a veritable cascade of bills, ratifying at least 133 decrees. All but one bill breezed through with no debate and no recorded opposition.[9] Parliament passed two more enabling acts on April 20 and 22, 1916.[10] The constitution to the contrary notwithstanding, the most important laws of those years were made by the Executive, subject to review by Parliament in only the most perfunctory way.

Emboldened by those successes and by British and Italian examples, the government attempted a long step forward. It submitted a bill authorizing it "until the end of hostilities, ... to take, by decrees rendered in the Council of Ministers, all measures which, by addition to or deletion from laws in force, are required by the needs of national defense with respect to agricultural and industrial production; port equipment; transportation; provisioning; public health and hygiene; recruitment of manpower; the sale, distribution, and consumption of provisions and produce." Any required funds were to be requested of Parliament within a week. The government could fix penalties for violation of the decrees up to six months in prison and 10,000 francs in fines.[11]

However, the government overplayed its hand. It told the Chamber that the decree powers would be used to solve "all the questions concerning national defense that laws are too slow to solve . . . in particular a grave question which can be settled only in wartime and the solution of which is important to the life of our country, to its welfare, the complete suppression of the consumption of alcohol." [12]

That was too much. The government threatened a Frenchman's most sacred right. The Chamber rebelled. Seven interpellation motions were submitted.[13] The government lost on a procedural vote,[14] and the bill was killed in committee, 23 to 2.[15] At least three more enabling acts were passed in connection with World War I, though prohibition was not mentioned again.[16]

As the wartime crisis passed, resort to decree laws was discarded, but the financial and economic crisis of the mid-1920s aroused yearnings for the easy leadership of the heady days of 1914. Governments requested decree powers fourteen times between 1924 and 1937. Parliament acquiesced ten times. The frequency increased with the passage of time. Eleven requests and eight grants came between October 1933 and May 1937. Between March 1, 1934 and July 1, 1940, France was ruled by decree laws for 31.5 of the 76 months.[17]

As another war approached, the pressure for delegated legislation increased still further. Enabling acts were passed for financial, economic, and defense affairs, four times between March 1938 and March 1939.[18] Then, in December 1939, Parliament went further than it had refused to travel in 1916—although prohibition was not mentioned. In one breath, it mouthed the established ideology: "For the duration of hostilities, the Chambers shall exercise their powers in legislative and budgetary matters as in peacetime." In the next, it yielded to circumstance: "However, in case of immediate necessity, the government is authorized to take, by decrees considered in the Council of Ministers, the measures imposed by the exigencies of national defense." The decrees were to be submitted to Parliament within a month or immediately after its reconvening.[19] The bill passed the Chamber, 318 to 175, after a key hostile amendment was defeated, 189 to 309, and breezed through the Senate, 259 to 23.[20]

The result of the December 10 enabling act was "the complete substitution of Cabinet for Parliament as the legislative organ of the French government." [21] Hundreds of decree laws poured forth. Virtually all cited the December 8 law. None were submitted for ratification, except that Marshal Pétain ratified eighteen by another decree under his dictatorial powers.[22]

Those powers had been granted by a joint meeting of the two chambers, which voted, 569 to 80, "all powers to the government of the Republic, under the authority and the signature of Marshal Pétain, for the purpose of promulgating by one or more acts a new constitution of the French State." That constitution was to be "ratified by the nation." [23] No Parliament ever met under Pétain and he never submitted any of his "constitutional acts" for ratification by anyone.

The Fourth Republic

Ideology

At the birth of the Fourth Republic, delegated legislation lay in deep disrepute because of its association with economic distress and foreign military occupation. Reacting appropriately, the framers of the 1946 constitution made explicit what had been implied by its departed predecessor. Article 13 read: "The National Assembly alone enacts laws. It cannot delegate this right." So pervasive was acceptance of that principle that discussion of Article 13 centered on whether the Council of the Republic should be included as a legislative chamber. The possibility of delegating legislative authority to the Executive was hardly mentioned.[24]

Constitutional law specialists at the time interpreted Article 13 as being intended to forbid decree laws, at least the Third Republic version.[25] One leading scholar wrote that the "Framers certainly intended . . . to proscribe any enabling act, delegation, injunction which would have restored the practice of decree laws directly or indirectly." [26] Most of the orators in a 1948 Assembly debate on the matter agreed that Article 13 banned decree laws.[27] Twenty years later an official parliamentary report asserted the same view.[28]

The Practice

Despite the explicit constitutional ban and a more fully articulated doctrinal commitment to parliamentary legislative exclusivity, the Fourth Republic founders were even more precipitous than their predecessors in skipping down the primrose path. Even before the 1946 constitution had been promulgated, Parliament was delegating legislative authority to the executive freely. During the thirteen-month-long Constituent Assemblies in 1945–46, at least eight laws granted the Executive the power to legislate by decree.[29] As in the Third Republic, the government invoked the necessity of circumstances, this time the economic and financial travail of postwar recovery.

As the immediate postwar crisis eased, so did reliance on enabling acts, although they were used more frequently than in the Third Republic. One or two were adopted in most years and the total for the eleven and a half years of the Fourth Republic was twenty-five.[30] The Fourth Republic Parliament was much more permissive toward enabling acts than had been its predecessor. Except for four successive rejections for four successive premiers or premiers-designate between May 12 and June 10, 1953, it honored all requests.[31] All groups in Parliament accepted their necessity. All of the last nine governments of the Fourth Republic were their beneficiaries. Usually, they were enacted when a new government was invested or very soon thereafter, so that France was under decree rule almost continuously in the last few years before de Gaulle returned to power.[32]

Also, the Fourth Republic outdid its predecessor at ingenuity in inventing new devices for delegating legislative authority. It produced at least four new devices. The first was the "domain of regulation" discovered legislatively by the Reynaud law of August 17, 1948. According to it, certain policy matters were "by their nature" subject to definition by decree rather than by law and required no parliamentary action.[33] Such matters included the organization of the nationalized enterprises and of the social security system; management of the State's borrowing power; control of the real estate market, the foreign exchange market, prices, energy use, and the distribution of raw materials and industrial products; and the mechanisms of economic control. Through 1954, about 350 decrees had been issued under authority of that law[34] and others appeared until the end of the Fourth Republic.

Laws in 1953, 1954, and 1955 broadened the scope of the "domain of regulation." This escalated the volume of decrees enormously. The average number of such decrees submitted to the Council of State each year rose from 59 in 1948–53 to 241 in 1953–58.[35]

A second Fourth Republic innovation was the framework law (*loi-cadre*). This was a major piece of parliamentary legislation that laid down the principles of long-term policy in a broad area and authorized the government to fill in the details in conformity with them during a stipulated period of time. Some decrees had to be submitted to Parliament for review. Others took effect without such submission. The framework laws differed from the Third Republic "laws of principles" of Doumergue and Blum in permitting decrees to abrogate or repeal laws.[36] They differed from the traditional enabling act in granting less general authorization to the government. In a framework law, the government specified "the objectives and the means of its action," whereas the traditional enabling act simply identified the policy area.[37]

The first framework law was the 1956 Defferre law that reformed the governmental system of French Africa.[38] Forty-five decrees were issued under its authority and submitted for parliamentary review by the deadline it set. All were reviewed in lengthy parliamentary deliberation. None were abrogated, but forty were modified.[39] Thus, the main effect of the framework law was to expedite decisions, not to escape parliamentary consideration of the policies.

The second framework law—the 1957 law for housing and public facilities construction—was less successful.[40] The law was very long (62 articles), poorly drafted, and susceptible to administrative sabotage. No decrees were issued under its authority before the Fourth Republic fell.[41] After de Gaulle returned to power, the framework law was absorbed by his "full powers" law and decrees finally began to appear.[42]

The third and final use of a framework law was hardly more successful. The Bourgès-Maunoury government fell on defeat of a bill for a framework law to reform the Algerian governmental structure. The succeeding Gaillard government obtained passage of an emasculated version of that bill.[43] At least twelve decrees were issued under the law and submitted for parliamentary review.[44] Three were discussed at some length in Parliament, but all twelve were passed without change.[45] Several other bills for framework laws were in process at that time, but died with the regime.[46]

A third invention of the Fourth Republic was the "state of emergency," a device designed to provide the government with somewhat the same authority in an insurrection that it would have in wartime under "state of siege." An April 1955 law created the device and declared it to be in force for Algeria for six months.[47] Decrees implemented it for part of Algeria immediately and the entire country a year later.[48] The declaration was renewed for another six months and the law strengthened in August.[49] Five decrees imposing martial law in Algeria were issued under the "state of emergency" between April 23 and November 14, 1955.[50] The state of emergency was extended to mainland France for a three-month period by a law of May 17, 1958.[51] The collapsing Pflimlin government issued three decrees to implement that law, but never managed to use them.[52]

While the regime was in those death throes, it attempted a fourth innovation by amending Article 13 of the constitution to remove the ban on delegated powers, thereby permitting government and Parliament to make a "majority contract" or even a "contract for the legislature" through the grant to the government of "extensive powers for a long period to execute a specified program," including the power "to issue decrees under the control of Parliament to take measures . . . required for the welfare of the country." [53] The amending resolution had passed the Assembly by voice vote after a key motion carried, 408 to 165. It lay in committee at the Council of the Republic when the regime collapsed.[54] The reform was an obvious and rather frantic effort to fend off de Gaulle. Two months earlier when his breath was not so hot on the necks of the MPs, they had approved a series of constitutional amendments that had left Article 13 intact, despite seven private members' resolutions for its amendment.[55]

Conclusions

The parliamentary legislative exclusivity that had been preached by the ideologies of both the Third and Fourth Republics was undermined and destroyed by the recurrent crises that afflicted both those regimes. World War I had undermined and the financial, economic, and military crises of the 1930s had destroyed Parliament's legislative dominance in practice. By 1937, all major French political parties had approved delegations of legislative authority in practice, and France was ruled by decree powers for 22-1/2 of the last 36 months of the Republic. In 1940, the Popular Front Parliament scrapped the ideology, too, by conferring all legislative and constituent power on the Executive.

The wheel turned full circle again under the Fourth Republic. At the outset, it borrowed the ideology of its predecessor and expressed it more articulately. It followed its predecessor, also, in failing to obey its own doctrines. Finally, it renounced its ideology *in extremis* as had happened in 1940. The overlapping crises of postwar recovery, financial insolvency, and colonial disengagement underlaid that evolution.

By 1958, then, the habits of delegated legislative powers were at least 44 years old and had been indulged almost continuously for some 25 years. The contrary ideology was virtually abandoned. That development was well suited to de Gaulle's views on governmental leadership. Thus, the ground was well prepared for new constitutional arrangements in which practice would conform with ideology. Transition from Fourth Republic required, on this point, a minimum of change.

THE DE GAULLE DICTATORSHIP

In birth, the Fourth Republic scorned the Third; its death copied it. Both committed suicide by overwhelming parliamentary vote, conferring dictatorial powers on the great French hero of the preceding war to escape an imminent military threat. In 1940, Charles de Gaulle had been enraged by Parliament's delegation of legislative and constituent powers to Marshal Pétain. In 1958, he insisted that it do the same for him. Parliament's previous moves in that direction, de Gaulle's personality and constitutional concepts, and the crisis situation all facilitated its acquiescence. Ideology and circumstance combined to produce de Gaulle's dictatorship of 1958–59, an interim regime that concentrated legislative authority in executive hands to a degree rarely exceeded in a major democratic State.

The Bases of De Gaulle's Dictatorship

The Law of December 13, 1957

Some provisions of a 1957 law granting limited decree powers to the government remained in effect through June 1958.[56] They authorized the government to legislate on certain economic and fiscal matters by decrees taken in the Council of Ministers after consulting the Council of State. No parliamentary ratification was required.

The Investiture Vote

De Gaulle was not satisfied with that limited legislative authority, however. In his investiture address to the National Assembly, he insisted that his government was undertaking an onerous task and needed "the means" to accomplish it. Those means were (1) "full powers . . . for a period of six months" and (2) "a mandate to draft, then to propose to the country through referendum, indispensable (constitutional) changes," based on the fundamental principles of "universal suffrage, separation of powers, the responsibility of the government to Parliament, and a new organizaiton of the relationship between France and her overseas territories." By voting to install de Gaulle as premier, 329 to 224 with 39 deputies not voting, the Assembly accepted his conditions.[57]

Algerian Special Powers

Parliament fulfilled those conditions quickly. The next day, it renewed the Algerian enabling act that had been passed for the Mollet government in 1956 and renewed for the three succeeding governments. The Assembly vote was 337 to 199 with 56 not voting. The Council of the Republic voted 267 to 24 with 25 not voting. Debate was perfunctory in both chambers.[58] In the circumstances, Parliament would have done the same for any government it installed.

The June law provided that the decree power expire with the de Gaulle government.[59] That provision was abrogated by an ordinance in October 1958, leaving the law with no termination date.[60] In fact, it expired with Algerian independence in July 1962.

Full Powers

The same day, Parliament passed a new enabling act, broader than any previous Fourth Republic law. Earlier enabling acts had granted "special powers"; this one bestowed "full powers." For six months, the government could issue decrees called ordinances to take "the legislative measures necessary for the recovery of the nation." Substantively, the ordinances had to "respect the fundamental public liberties." Procedurally, they had to be taken "in the Council of Ministers after advice from the Council of State" (except in emergencies) and had to be submitted for parliamentary ratification at the end of the six-month period.

In response to criticism from the Assembly committee, the government revised the bill to make explicit its authority to "abrogate, modify, or replace" existing legislation, to specify more fully the public liberties that were protected, and to require that, in emergencies, the ordinances would have to be submitted to the Council of Ministers at its next meeting.[61] The Assembly debated it for about 80 minutes, easily defeated amendment attempts by the Communists and the Extreme Right, and passed it without change, 319 to 231 with 42 deputies not voting.[62] The Council of the Republic discussed it about an hour but considered no amendments and voted adoption, 247 to 47 with 22 senators not voting.[63]

Constituent Powers

A third bill to meet de Gaulle's investiture conditions proposed to revise Article 90 of the 1946 constitution to provide the following amendment procedure:

The government of the Republic shall prepare in the Council of Ministers, after consulting the Council of State, a draft constitution which shall be submitted to referendum.[64]

Parliament passed the bill quickly with changes of form only.

For four months, those three laws were, in effect, the French constitution. The Fourth Republic was dead. The Fifth Republic was gestating. Parliament was in limbo. The executive branch held virtually unlimited legislative authority.[65]

Articles 90 and 92

Before the authority of those laws expired, the 1958 constitution was drafted, approved by popular referendum, and promulgated. Its Article 90 provided that Parliament could meet only at the call of the government until the National Assembly to be elected under the new constitution had convened. Article 92 conferred on the government the authority (1) to set up the new constitutional institutions, (2) to enact legislative measures to ensure the functioning of the existing governmental institutions until the new ones would begin to operate, (3) to establish the parliamentary electoral system, (4) "to take in all matters the measures that it deems necessary for the life of the nation, the protection of citizens, or the safeguard of freedom" until February 4, 1959.

That sweeping legislative authority imposed no substantive limitation. Its only procedural restriction was requirement that its ordinances be "taken in the Council of Ministers after consultation with the Council of State." As long as those meager formalities were observed, de Gaulle had the authority to do virtually anything legislative without responsibility to anyone. Even after the new Parliament convened, the ordinances were not subject to its review or ratification.

Legislation During De Gaulle's Dictatorship

The Legislation

Under Authority of Law. The de Gaulle dictatorship began its legislative career under the cover of an enabling act passed for the Gaillard government, one of the weakest of the Fourth Republic. It issued seven decrees of rather minor importance under that authority between June 24 and 28, 1958.[66] They all concerned commercial activities having developmental and foreign exchange implications and clearly fell within the frame of reference of the enabling act.

De Gaulle used the renewed Algerian enabling act more extensively. He issued nineteen decrees under that authority between June 28, 1958 and January 30, 1959.[67] All dealt with Algeria. Some had considerable importance. For instance, one promulgated the Constantine Plan for the social and economic development of Algeria. Others reformed the Algerian land tenure, electoral, and governmental systems.

However, the "full powers" enabling act was much the most important Fourth Republic basis for legislation during the dictatorship period. Each ministry had a "working group" of civil servants to pump out ordinances for issuance under that authority. By the time it expired on December 2, 1958, 75 ordinances had been issued under it.[68] They ranged across a wide variety of policy matters. Some were very important. None were challenged seriously as violating the public liberties protections or other limitations that the enabling act contained.

Under Authority of Article 92.   After the new constitution was adopted, de Gaulle no longer had to rely on Fourth Republic bases. Its Article 92 was ready-made to authorize the executive authority de Gaulle desired. He made much use of it. Two days after the constitutinal referendum, de Gaulle appointed a committee of nine experts headed by Jacques Rueff to initiate, expedite, and coordinate an economic and financial program to be implemented by Article 92 ordinances.[69] By the time Article 92 authority expired on February 4, 1959, it had served as the basis for 303 ordinances.[70]

The two sets of 378 ordinances touched virtually every area of public policy. "In several days, every single industrialist, businessman, wage-earner, farmer, family head, taxpayer, patient, educator, student, mere pupil, landlord, tenant—in short, everyone, absolutely everyone, saw the daily rhythm of his life changed" by the Article 92 ordinances alone.[71] Perhaps no legislative program has ever transformed French life so much so fast.

Many measures had been on hand in the ministries when de Gaulle returned to office, but had not gone to Parliament because of overloaded agendas or political hostility. Others, such as Debré's reform of the judiciary, were initiated by de Gaulle's government. A mere listing of the more important measures suggests the size and scope of the operation:[72]

1. Thirty-five international agreements were ratified.
2. The books were closed on the 1951 through 1956 state budgets.
3. The national defense system was reorganized.
4. The judicial system was reorganized.
5. A new general civil service statute was issued.
6. The compulsory schooling age was raised from 14 to 16 years.
7. The secondary education curriculum was revised.
8. The transfer of the Halles (Paris central) and Paris wine markets was begun.
9. The urban planning system was reformed.
10. The Cameroon and Togo governmental systems were reorganized.
11. The "Third Plan" for the national economy was approved.
12. Sweeping changes were made in the taxation system.
13. Establishment of the Paris District and of a plan for Greater Paris was begun.
14. The mammoth *Défense* urban development project was started.
15. Rent controls were relaxed.

16. Social security contributions were increased.
17. The unemployment insurance system was overhauled.
18. Some 600,000 war veterans were removed from the pension rolls.
19. Central control of local government was loosened a bit.
20. The 1957 framework law for housing was implemented.
21. Many State subsidies were reduced or eliminated.
22. The State radio-television system was reorganized.
23. The regulatory system for the pharmaceutical industry was reformed.
24. The Algerian marriage and real estate codes, educational system, and civil service were reformed.
25. The National School for Administration was reorganized.
26. State operational expenditures were trimmed and investments increased.
27. Price controls were stiffened.
28. The penal code was revised.
29. Obsolescent criminal code provisions were repealed.
30. Child adoption rules and procedures were streamlined.
31. The bankruptcy system was reformed.
32. State controls over public morality were tightened.
33. The 1959 State budget was enacted.
34. The Greater Paris public transportation system was reorganized.
35. The enabling act of March 16, 1956, was extended indefinitely.
36. The franc was devalued and made convertible.
37. A statute for the exploitation of Saharan oil was promulgated.
38. The hospital and public health systems were reorganized.
39. A system to encourage small businesses to consolidate was established.
40. The municipal council electoral system was reformed.
41. The parliamentary electoral system was reformed.
42. The constitutional system of the Fifth Republic was elaborated and put into place.
43. The establishment of worker–management committees in industry was encouraged.
44. The financial markets were reformed.
45. A State loan was floated.
46. Public housing administration was reorganized.
47. Regionalization institutions were reformed.

Those measures and other ordinances of lesser importance virtually revolutionized French life. Of course, not all became effective. Already at President de Gaulle's first Council of Ministers meeting, some measures required revision.[73] The measures to encourge worker–management committees and small-business consolidations had little effect. Construction of the *Défense* project was very slow. The original plan for the transfer of the Halles meat market was a $125-million disaster that had to be abandoned. The Paris District was stymied until the government backtracked and took it through Parliament.[74] On balance, however, the executive legislation of the de Gaulle dictatorship accomplished a tremendous amount.

Ratification of the 1958–59 Legislation

Most of the legislation of the de Gaulle dictatorship was never reviewed or ratified by Parliament. In the absence of ratification requirements in the enabling act of December 13, 1957, and Article 92, none of their measures ever came before Parliament. The Algerian enabling act required that decrees issued under its authority be submitted to Parliament within one year. In fact, only the last of its decrees that were issued during the dictatorship period was ever submitted to Parliament and the ratification bill that included it was never discussed or voted by Parliament.[75] The other eighteen were ratified by an Article 92 ordinance that never came before Parliament either.[76] The "full powers" law required that its ordinances be "submitted to the *bureau* of the National Assembly for the purpose of ratification" upon its expiration December 3, 1958. On that date, the National Assembly of the Fourth Republic had ceased to exist and its Fifth Republic successor had been elected but had not yet convened and, hence, had no *bureau*. Therefore, the government ratified them with an Article 92 ordinance and they never went before any Parliament.[77]

Parliamentary delegation of legislative authority to the de Gaulle dictatorship was a logical, though extreme, extension of the trend of the last few years of the Fourth Republic and a close replication of 1940. Although the enabling acts contained certain limitations, Parliament ceased to exist immediately after passing them and could not possibly have enforced them. Yet the dictatorship never breached constitutionality. It observed all the substantive and procedural limitations of its various grants of authority. Furthermore, the Parliament elected in November 1958 could have disavowed de Gaulle's measures by withholding its confidence from the Debré government. Nothing prevented that except de Gaulle's popularity, parliamentary acceptance of his measures, and the atmosphere of crisis that continued to hang over the land. Given the fractious character of French parliamentary life in the preceding years, the circumstances of crisis as pressure on the MPs may well have been the decisive factor.

THE FIFTH REPUBLIC

Executive legislation in the Third and Fourth Republics had been generated by circumstances, despite the ideologies and constitutions of the regimes. Executive legislation during the de Gaulle dictatorship rested on circumstance, ideology, and a constitution formed of a shifting patchwork of texts. As the dictatorship gave way to the Fifth Republic, circumstance and ideology changed little, but the constitutional basis became a single, cohesive, and reasonably coherent document. As the regime continued, ideology and constitution were stable, but the circumstances changed very appreciably with the end of the Algerian War and financial and economic recovery. This suggests that detailed examination of executive legislation and its parliamentary control during the Fifth Republic by comparison with its predecessors can help toward understanding the interplay of those factors.

Bases of Executive Authority to Legislate

The 1958 Constitution

Article 16. One provision of the 1958 constitution that loomed very large in early discussions of its character was Article 16,[78] which gave the president of the Republic very broad emergency powers, including legislative, in emergency circumstances without express delegation by Parliament—or even necessarily its consent. The notion that the president of the Republic might play constitutionally the role of national savior that de Gaulle had played *de facto* in 1940 was dear to his heart. He seems to have been more deeply involved in its drafting than he was for most other articles.[79]

De Gaulle seems to have intended Article 16 to be principally a protection against a recurrence of the debacle of 1940, believing that if President Lebrun had possessed similar powers, he could have carried French honor abroad with him instead of giving way to the ignominy of Vichy. In defending Article 16 to the Consultative Constitutional Committee (CCC), he stressed that event and stated his assumptions that, if Article 16 ever were used, (1) France would be confronted by such "tragic circumstances" as nuclear war, (2) crisis would prevent the government and parliament from functioning effectively to deal with it, and (3) the president would be able to act on his own.[80] The government's commissioner alluded only to 1940 in his presentation to the CCC.[81] However, de Gaulle also mentioned Clemenceau's appointment as premier in 1917 and the May 1958 crisis as historical occasions when Article 16 powers might have been used. Furthermore, he rejected Paul Reynaud's suggestion in the CCC to reserve that article explicitly for use in "foreign war or civil war." [82] Also, Debré told the Council of State that Article 16 might be used in "grave circumstances, interior or exterior" and in "other . . . cases" than those created by "modern forms of war."[83]

The constitution related Article 16 to Parliament in two ways. First, it required the president of the Republic to consult the presidents of the two chambers before invoking it. Second, it stipulated that Parliament meet by right and might not be dissolved during an Article 16 crisis.

The latter provision was paradoxical. Initially, de Gaulle had assumed that the president would require Article 16 powers because Parliament would be unable to meet. The first version of Article 16 had not required a meeting of

Parliament for three months after its invocation. The version submitted to the CCC provided that Parliament would "meet as soon as circumstances permit." [84] The CCC recommended that it meet at once "by right" unless prevented by "*force majeure*," apparently to exercise some control over the measures he would take.[85] The government accepted that recommendation. Then, it also accepted a recommendation by the Council of State to delete "except in case of *force majeure*." [86] Thus, what had been intended as means to be used because Parliament could not meet became means that could be used only while Parliament was meeting. Indirect parliamentary control over even the most sweeping powers of executive legislation became an official part of the constitution of the Fifth Republic.

Article 38. Article 38 was designed to deal more directly than Article 16 with the kind of problem that had given rise to so many delegations of legislative authority under the Third and Fourth Republics. In fact, the framers of the constitution seem to have assumed that such delegations would be routine.[87] Article 38 was a constitutional formulation of practice in the earlier Republics, permitting Parliament to delegate legislative authority by express decision for a specified period and requiring that measures taken under that authority be submitted to Parliament for ratification but not requiring that they actually be ratified in order to have legislative effect.[88] Article 69 authorizes but does not require submission of Article 38 ordinances to the Economic and Social Council for advice.

The implications of the ratification requirement are complex. The CCC expressly refused to recommend that ratification be required for validity "to spare the deputies difficult votes." [89] If the government fails to submit a ratification bill in time or Parliament rejects it, the ordinances become void. If the government submits a ratification bill in time and Parliament takes no action, the ordinances are valid and have the status of administrative acts rather than laws. This means that they are subject to review by the Council of State and may be modified or rescinded by decrees. If Parliament ratifies an ordinance, it acquires the status of a law and is not subject to review by the Council of State nor to revision or abrogation by decree. However, if the Constitutional Council, on petition of the prime minister, declares parts of an ordinance to be regulatory, they can be modified only by other administrative acts.[90] Ratification may be implicit through parliamentary action that, in effect, approves of the substance of an ordinance, even though it has not adopted the ratification bill. For instance, adoption of a budget appropriating funds to implement an ordinance is implicit ratification.[91]

Article 38 departed from previous practice in conferring on the government exclusive legislative authority in the area of delegation. In the Third and Fourth Republics, Parliament retained concurrent jurisdiction, but Article 41 of the 1958 constitution gives the government authority to declare "nonreceivable" any bill or amendment which it deems to be "contrary to a delegation accorded it by virtue of Article 38." Such a declaration may be appealed by the president of the chamber to the Constitutional Council.[92]

Article 11. The referendum provision of the constitution also contains a basis for the delegation of legislative authority to the Executive.[93] The text does not include such delegations explicitly as one of its purposes. Nor does it exclude them. Earlier versions of that article do not allude to delegations.[94] So far as has been disclosed they never were discussed by the framers.[95] However, they are certainly covered by the words "any bill" and an interpretation excluding them would seem very difficult to sustain persuasively.

Laws

Legacies. Some Fourth Republic enabling acts continued in effect during the Fifth Republic and provided its governments with law-making authority. One was the Algerian enabling act of March 16, 1956, that had been extended indefinitely by an October 1958 ordinance. Another was the "state of emergency" law of April 3, 1955. An April 1960 ordinance revised it to repeal the requirement that only a law might declare the existence of a state of emergency and to permit that to be done by decree for a twelve-day period. Beyond twelve days, a law was required.[96]

New Enactments. Articles 16 and 38 did not eliminate entirely the use of the earlier forms of enabling acts. Seven laws during the third and fourth legislatures granted legislative authority to the Executive without reference to Article 38. However, those delegations were much more limited that in the earlier republics.[97] One law (68–1248) authorized the expenditure of funds by decree for the free distribution of agricultural commodities. The others authorized reductions, suspensions, revisions, or refunds of specified taxes. Five had expiration dates at the end of the following year. The others had no expiration dates. None required that decrees be submitted to Parliament for ratification.

The Use of Executive Authority to Legislate

Under Article 16

The Circumstances. Article 16 was invoked only once during the administrations of presidents de Gaulle and Pompidou. The occasion was the abortive attempt by four retired French army generals to seize power in Algeria in April 1961. Some Foreign Legion troops under their command held control of parts of Algiers, Oran, and a few smaller towns temporarily, but no regular French units joined them and the *coup* fizzled quickly. Except that they occupied some government offices in Algiers for a few days and captured the commanding general of the French armed forces in Algeria, the top civilian official in Algeria, and the Minister of Public Works, who happened to be traveling in Algeria, their actions did nothing to fulfill the Article 16 crisis definition of interrupting the "regular functioning of the constitutional institutions of government." [98]

The government reacted swiftly. The *coup* began during the night of April 21/22. On the 22nd, de Gaulle declared a "state of emergency" throughout France, effective at midnight.[99] On the 23rd, he consulted the prime minister, the presidents of the chambers, and the Constitutional Council and had obtained from all of them agreement that the constitutional conditions existed for the use of Article 16.[100] That afternoon, he signed a "Decision" declaring Article 16 in effect and that evening he reported that act to the French people by radio-television broadcast.[101] Parliament was assembling to begin its regular spring session on April 25. De Gaulle reported his action to it by message, observing that Parliament was meeting both in regular session and "by right."[102] All the procedural steps required by the constitution had been accomplished. De Gaulle was free to "take the measures required by the circumstances."

Executive Legislation. De Gaulle had begun to issue "Decisions" under Article 16 already. Four were announced after the Council of Ministers meeting April 24. They (1) extended indefinitely the state of emergency that otherwise would have expired May 5, (2) authorized internment of subversives for fifteen days by prefects and indefinitely by the minister of the interior, (3) empowered the president to cashier or remove from office any rebellious member of the armed forces or civil servant, and (4) extended the limit for *garde à vue* from five to fifteen days. Six more decrees appeared in the next eleven days: (5) rebellious personnel lost their pension rights and other benefits, (6) irregular transfer of judges was authorized, (7), (8), and (9) two military courts were established to try Algerian insurrectionaries, and (10) subversive newsletters were outlawed. Four more Decisions appeared in June: (11), (12), and (13) provided for the irregular removal of civilian, military, and judicial functionaries from service or from Algeria, (14) permitted exceptional promotions for brigadier generals. Of the last three, issued in September, (15) extended the deadline of one of the June Decisions, (16) and (17) ended the exercise of Article 16 powers while extending the life of most Decisions until July 15, 1962, and made major changes in the composition of one of the military courts.[103]

The Decisions were used much. Ten military subversives were cashiered on April 24.[104] The military courts pronounced 938 sentences.[105] Transfers, suspensions, or removals were imposed on 1,108 military and 1,637 civil functionaries and 9 judges in Algeria. Twenty newsletters were banned.[106]

Whether the Decisions were appropriate to the circumstances that occasioned resort to Article 16 depends on the interpretation of those circumstances. If only the abortive *putsch* is considered, none of the Decisions issued after April 25 were necessary or, hence, appropriate. However, if the *putsch* is viewed as part of a web of conspiratorial resistance to governmental authority on Algerian policy, all the Decisions were appropriate.

Whether the use of Article 16 itself was appropriate depends on whether the letter of the constitution or the intentions of its framers is considered. The text is so broadly worded as to permit its use in almost any crisis situation and France in April 1961 was clearly in crisis. On the other hand, its drafters intended that it be used only when regular procedures, including Article 38, were not adequate. All evidence suggests that, in April 1961, Parliament would have responded with alacrity to governmental requests for any measures it deemed necessary and appropriate. Parliament's attitude makes that clear.

Parliamentary Control. The contradictions of Article 16 surfaced very soon. Despite de Gaulle's original expectation that he would use Article 16 only when Parliament was not present, it was doubly present in 1961, in regular session and in session "by right." De Gaulle sought to resolve that contradiction to his liking by informing Parliament that, "in the present circumstances, I believe that application of Article 16 will not alter the activities of Parliament: exercise of legislative power and control. Therefore, the relationship of the government and Parliament must function normally so long as the measures taken or to be taken under Article 16 are not concerned." Parliament was not to interfere in his use of Article 16.[107] Yet he and his government then explained and defended his Article 16 actions and asked for Parliament's help, implicitly acknowledging that those actions were at least partly and indirectly subject to its control.

No parliamentary vote or debate followed those statements, but public comments by parliamentary leaders left no doubt that de Gaulle had overwhelming support among the MPs.[108] Furthermore, for two months Parliament heeded his admonition against interference. A few ineffectual minority gestures were made. The Socialists and some Rightists raised points of order asking the government for a new declaration on Algeria, but they died aborning from lack of support.[109] Other MPs submitted questions asking when Article 16 powers would be relinquished, but each time the prime minister refused to answer on grounds that the question concerns "a power that the constitution confers on the president of the Republic" and the matter died.[110] A move by two senators to force the issue in the Senate Laws Committee produced no committee vote, no floor action, and a rebuke from the Senate president.[111] Appeals from the PCF, SFIO, and MRP national conventions in May were ignored in Parliament. Indeed, Parliament was so indifferent to its role as Article 16 watchdog that it recessed in mid-May for the cantonal election campaigns.[112]

In June, the Assembly's interest flickered briefly. The government requested suspension of the parliamentary immunity of a deputy on suspicion of complicity in the general's *putsch*. However, the government promised not to try him by an Article 16 tribunal and the Assembly acquiesced without attempting to broaden the issue.[113]

Parliament passed up another major opportunity to review the Article 16 decisions later in June. Both chambers debated a governmental declaration on Algeria. Thirty-seven deputies and twenty senators spoke for about fifteen hours. Most of their remarks concerned governmental policy on the future status of Algeria. No speaker gave his principal attention to review of Article 16 action. The occasional passing references to it were mainly criticism of the government for using it "to punish Frenchmen whose only offense was patriotism." No votes followed the debate.[114] The chambers recessed July 22 when the regular spring session ended, indifferent to their Article 16 right to remain in watchdog session.

That indifference was cast into sharp relief later that summer by intense concern of the MPs over a farm price crisis. Backbenchers and opposition forced a very reluctant parliamentary leadership to recall the chambers despite the government's objections. A storm of parliamentary protest greeted de Gaulle's announcement that, because Parliament would be meeting under Article 16, it would be "contrary to the constitution that the announced meeting of Parliament have a legislative outcome."[115] The danger of a successful censure motion loomed and the use of Article 16 would have deprived de Gaulle of the retaliatory power of dissolution. To recover that weapon and deter censure, de Gaulle renounced Article 16.

In the very act of renunciation, however, de Gaulle extended the life of some Article 16 measures and brought them more explicitly under parliamentary control. Four Decisions and a decree were extended until July 15, 1962, "except as may be decided by law." Additional suspects might be arraigned before Article 16 military courts "until such date as is set by law." [116] Only one attempt was made to use those opportunities for parliamentary control. On October 13, eight rightwing deputies introduced a bill to abrogate all Article 16 Decisions.[117] The bill died in committee.

Parliament never made a serious effort to control the use of Article 16 in 1961. The circumstance of an approaching solution to the Algerian war restrained any inclinations the parliamentary majority might have had in that direction. However, Article 38, offerred a more likely object of parliamentary control because of the more substantial constitutional involvement of Parliament in its application and because, usually, it was invoked in calmer circumstances.

Under Article 38

Article 38 was used more often than Article 16, although it did not become the "normal" part of French parliamentary life that its sponsors had expected. The de Gaulle administration used it eight times. Pompidou used it once, for a minor matter, in 1969.

The "Barricades Crisis."

(1) *The circumstances.* Article 38 was used first in connection with an armed insurrection of European settlers in Algeria that erupted on January 24, 1960. The government marked time for several days, apparently doubtful of the loyalty of the police and armed forces. Then, on January 29, de Gaulle asserted his authority dramatically in a radio-television address and the revolt collapsed within hours. Only then did the government decide, on the afternoon of February 1, to call Parliament into special session and request Article 38

authority. The immediate crisis had abated, even more than in 1961, but the underlying problem remained.[118]

(2) *The enabling act.* The bill was sweeping. For a year, the government was to be "authorized to take by ordinances in the conditions provided by Article 38 of the constitution, the measures necessary to ensure the maintenance of order, the security of the State, the pacification and the administration of Algeria." A ratification bill was due in Parliament by April 1, 1961.[119]

The Assembly committee recommended that the bill be amended to (1) limit the authority explicitly to the incumbent government acting on President de Gaulle's signature, (2) provide that its authority end upon dissolution of the Assembly, (3) insert "and of the constitution" after "the security of the State," (4) protect certain basic rights explicitly, (5) limit the duration to eight months with the ratification bill due one month later.[120] The Assembly debate lasted about five and a half hours. Premier Debré accepted the first three changes that the committee had recommended, but rejected the others. However, he assured the chamber that the authority would not be used to effect economic, social, or institutional reforms; establish special tribunals; promulgate retroactive penal laws; jeopardize essential liberties, or deprive the Assembly of its legislative and budgetary powers or its rights of control and censure. Then, he invoked the "blocked vote" procedure of Article 44 and the bill passed, 441 to 75 with 35 deputies not voting.[121] The Senate committee recommended a November 1, 1960, expiration date, to be extended to February 1, 1961, if Parliament did not vote to end the special powers before then. The government rejected the amendment, imposed another "blocked vote," and the bill passed, 225 to 39 with 43 senators not voting.[122] Although the votes had been lopsided, the debates had been acrimonious at times and de Gaulle had been so uneasy about the outcome as to receive "for the first time in the history of the Fifth Republic ... the chairmen of the parliamentary groups in order to ask Parliament to pass the bill." [123]

(3) *Executive legislation.* De Gaulle issued thirty ordinances under the February 4 law.[124] The first two did not appear until February 13, well after the immediate crisis had ended, and only one other was issued in February. The last twelve were published in the last three days before the authority expired February 2, 1961.

Most of the ordinances seemed to conform to the letter and spirit of the enabling act, but some were questionable. One overruled a Constitutional Council decision on the liquidation of the state newspaper printing enterprise.[125] Another that forbade the destruction of automobiles was not restricted to Algeria.[126] Still another permitted the forced transfer or dismissal of civil servants for disturbing the public peace in overseas departments, not including Algeria.[127]

(4) *Parliamentary control.* The government submitted the ratification bill April 25, 1961, nearly a month late.[128] Parliament never debated it or voted on it. However, one ordinance was debated in Parliament twice in other contexts.

That ordinance was 60-1101. Twenty-five civil servants were transferred under its authority in 1960–63 and one in 1968. Seven others were dismissed for refusing transfers.[129] In 1964, Parliament nearly abrogated it through an amendment to a government bill on the general status of functionaries. The Assembly vote was 268 to 187 with 26 not voting and the Senate vote was 115 to 65 with 94 not voting.[130] Then, in 1972, it passed a government bill abrogating the ordinance. A parliamentary move to restore rank and seniority to the disciplined functionaries was thwarted by the government invoking the Article 40 ban on private members' amendments that would increase expenditures. In both cases, the ordinance was the object of a full parliamentary debate and vote.[131]

"Social Scourges."

(1) *The circumstances.* The next use of Article 38 was directed against alcoholism and prostitution. A number of French governments under both the Third and Fourth Republic had tackled these problems and Premier Debré was especially committed to dealing with alcoholism, partly because of the influence of his father, a distinguished physician and medical scientist who had long been active in anti-alcohol campaigns. In 1959, Debré had introduced an anti-alcohol bill that had passed the Assembly but died in Senate committee. In 1960, he revived his project under cover of Article 38.[132]

(2) *The enabling act.* The bill authorized the government to issue Article 38 ordinances for four months to combat "cancer, heart disease, and tuberculosis, as well as alcoholism and prostitution." [133] A procedural move on the floor of the Assembly blocked a favorable committee report until Debré agreed to limit the bill to alcoholism and prostitution and described some of the measures he planned to take. Then, the Assembly agreed, 284 to 142 with 125 deputies not voting, to receive the report. The following debate lasted four and a half hours with fourteen deputies speaking.[134]

The responsible minister gave additional details on implementation plans and threatened to enforce a more rigorous 1954 decree if his bill were defeated. He accepted amendments, mainly writing some of those plans into the text, softening its provisions against home distillers slightly, and setting a December 15, rather than December 31, 1960, deadline for submission of a ratification bill. The revised bill passed, 290 to 163 with 98 deputies not voting.

The Senate committee took no position on the Assembly bill, a rare occurrence. The Senate debate lasted two and a half hours with five speakers taking part. The government accepted further amendments, preventing changes in existing wine industry legislation and authorizing bans on some alcohol advertising. The amended bill passed, 159 to 92 with 57 senators not voting.[135] The Senate bill passed second reading in the Assembly without debate or change, 323 to 131 with 96 deputies not voting.[136]

(3) *Executive legislation.* Seven ordinances were issued under the "social scourges" law. The most important placed restrictions on the home distillers and

introduced measures designed to reduce their number and the number of fruit trees used for producing alcohol. As a result, the number of home distillers fell from 1,912,171 in 1960 to 1,285,691 in 1972 and about 3 million fruit trees had been destroyed by 1973. Other ordinances banned labor contracts providing for payment in kind with alcoholic beverages, reduced the number of vendors of alcoholic beverages, and banned certain kinds of advertising of alcohol.[137] The other two ordinances revised French law in conformity with a 1949 international covenant on prostitution.[138] All the ordinances seem compatible with the terms of the enabling act.

(4) *Parliamentary control.* The government submitted its ratification bill the day before the deadline,[139] but refused to place it on the agenda. Louis Briot, the Assembly spokesman for the home distillers, moved the previous question.[140] To prevent adoption of that motion, which would have blocked consideration of the government's Paris Region bill, Debré agreed to defer application of the ordinances until April.[141] Parliament also showed its displeasure over the ordinances by deleting from the 1961 state budget funds to implement one of them.[142]

On July 18, 1961, the previous question was moved again to force out the ratification bill.[143] This time, the government had its agenda protected otherwise and, also, benefited from a favorable committee report on the ratification bill.[144] Nevertheless, the government made further concessions. It agreed to eliminate from the list of institutions to be protected by zones free of liquor outlets places of worship, cemeteries, most types of hospitals, dispensaries, schools, and youth centers, leaving only "sanitariums, convalescent homes, hospitals for the chronically ill, retirement homes, and psychiatric clinics." [145] Also, Debré promised to meet with parliamentary leaders at least twice in October on the matter. However, he refused to bring forth the ratification bill and lost on the previous question, 290 to 168 with 93 deputies not voting.[146]

The ratification bill remained off the agenda in the Fall 1961 session. The Assembly retaliated by deciding, 250 to 248 with 52 deputies not voting, to delete Article 38 authority from another government bill. The government stood firm and a week later parliament relented and restored Article 38 authority to the other bill.[147]

Occasional attempts were made to repeal or modify the ordinances later. They slackened after the government won a more reliable parliamentary majority in the 1962 elections. A final attempt was made in the Senate to bring them up through a clause in the 1965 budget. When that failed, the fight was abandoned. The ordinances remained on the books, unratified and unamended, although Parliament had exercised some control over them in other ways.[148]

Repatriation Aid.

(1) *The circumstances.* Article 38 was used next in a 1961 bill for aid to repatriate overseas Frenchmen. Ostensibly, the bill was aimed at Frenchmen returning to Morocco, Tunisia, and tropical Africa. Its real purpose was to

prepare for Algerian independence. A small government bureau had dispensed about $260 million in such aid already, but was expected to be inadequate for the forthcoming task. A secretariat of state for repatriates was established in August 1961[149] and brought forward a bill in September.

(2) *The enabling act*. The bill authorized the government to issue Article 38 ordinances for one year "to integrate repatriated Frenchmen [and certain foreigners] into the economic and social structures of the nation," especially through "loans, subventions, temporary or long-term aid" to resettle them and retrain them vocationally. The state budget was to provide funds and allocation procedures. A ratification bill was required within three months after the authority expired.[150]

The bill was introduced in the Senate. The principal committee and three advisory committees recommended significant limitations on its Article 38 authority.[151] Robert Boulin, the responsible minister, gave oral assurances to the committees to meet their objections, but the Socialist, Democratic Left, Independent Republican, and Communist groups opposed the bill. They numbered 203 of the 305 senators and, undoubtedly, individual UNR senators were opposed also. In the face of that opposition, Boulin withdrew the bill.[152]

Boulin met with the principal committee again and Debré held a "long meeting" with it and with the chairmen, *rapporteurs*, and amendment authors of the other committees at which he answered "many questions." In the words of the principal *rapporteur*,

> These working sessions permitted a dialogue to develop between the government and the representative of our assembly thanks to which it has been possible to identify more precisely the objectives to assign to the governmental action and to envisage more concretely the means to be put to work to attain them.
>
> These results have been translated into new amendments . . . which constitute a sort of synthesis of the modifications, presented by our colleagues, which have seemed likely to improve the content of the bill without altering its meaning. . . .
>
> The secretary of state and his collaborators have given an especially receptive welcome to the concerns expressed by many senators.[153]

His committee withdrew its objections, but asked the government to make "a public declaration . . . promising . . . to use its right of priority if necessary . . . to ensure that a discussion will be held next session" on the ordinance. Also, it asked "the real collaboration . . . by the government . . . with our assembly on . . . this bill . . . continue beyond its adoption and, especially, that the advice of its representatives will be requested during the elaboration of the implementing measures." The other *rapporteurs* expressed similar views, one of them adding that, although "as parliamentarians we are shocked *à priori* by delegations of power . . . , we wonder if, in a pre-electoral period, it is not better not to ask Parliament to take certain courageous measures, but . . . , in return, the government must have the courage to take them." [154]

Boulin agreed "to take a certain number of measures, even if they may appear unpopular" and accepted "the limits on the delegation of powers proposed by your committee." Also, he reminded Parliament that it could control the government's use of Article 38 authority through review of the State budget and promised to place a ratification bill on the agenda. Finally, he described in some detail the measures he planned to take under Article 38 and under the government's regulatory authority.[155]

Senators proposed twenty-six amendments. The government's final position prevailed on twenty-three, although it had made earlier concessions on some of those. In particular, it accepted restrictions on its Article 38 authority with respect to the indemnification of repatriates. Boulin closed the debate by acknowledging that Senate consideration "has led to an obvious result: considerable improvement of the original bill." [156] The amended bill passed by voice vote.

Boulin repeated to the Assembly committees his pledge to have the ratification bill "effectively placed on the agenda" of parliament and supplied more details on his plan for ordinances and decrees.[157] After long discussion, the principal committee recommended approval because of the limited character of the delegation, the urgency of the problem, and the promise of a ratification debate.[158] Another *rapporteur*, a Gaullist, commented that the Senate deliberation "attests to the benefits that can and must be gained from constant dialogue between the Executive and the legislature which, in a republican regime, must be the rule" and to the fact that "the government's doctrine" on the repatriation problem "was not totally established." He recommended that specific obligations be added to the bill, including that any government committments not executed by ordinances must be covered by parliamentary bills submitted in the following six months.[159]

In floor debate, Boulin, reiterated his pledge of a ratification debate and described in detail the "regulations we intend to issue in order to set up the practical mechanisms for serving the repatriates," the steps taken already, and examples of ordinances to be issued. He concluded by expressing a "desire to collaborate with your Assembly and . . . to examine in the most liberal way the amendments that you wish to propose." Only the Socialists criticized the use of Article 38, although others regretted the vagueness of some government committments for its use, especially on indemnification for the repatriates.[160]

Thirty-four amendments were proposed. Fifteen were adopted, two over the opposition of the government. One amendment, produced by dissatisfaction over the anti-alcohol ordinances, deleted the Article 38 clause, 250 to 248 with 52 deputies not voting. That killed the bill, but President de Gaulle used his Article 10 powers to require reconsideration.[161]

Upon reconsideration, the principal Assembly committee recommended against restoring the Article 38 clause. To save it, Boulin accepted three amendments curbing the Article 38 authority. Also, he promised to schedule the ratification debate for July 1962. Thus amended, the Article 38 clause was restored by voice vote and the bill passed. 365 to 168 with 47 deputies not voting.[162] A further reading in each chamber, joint conference committee action, and final passage in both houses were required to iron out some details of the bill, but the Article 38 clause was not changed.

In final discussions, both the Assembly *rapporteur* and Boulin commented on the "fruitful dialogue of Parliament and government" and Boulin admitted that it had improved his bill.[163] In fact, besides the oral commitments Boulin had made, the duration of the Article 38 clause had been reduced from twelve to five months, the ratification bill deadline had been shortened from three months to two, and its scope had been limited to "the fundamental guarantees accorded the civil and military services of the State as well as the fundamental principles of the right to work and of social security," instead of all matters covered by the bill, as originally.[164] Parliament had shown clearly its ability to exercise prior control over the use of Article 38 powers.

(3) *Executive legislation.* Six ordinances were issued under the repatriates law.[165] One ordinance established more flexible arrangements for early retirement from the civil service, apparently to open more places for repatriates. Two others gave repatriates exceptional eligibility for health insurance, maternity benefits, unemployment benefits, and family allocations. Another guaranteed them priority consideration for jobs in firms regularly employing fifty or more workers. The last two facilitated the integration of Algerian civil servants into the French civil service and repatriates from Morocco and Tunisia into public and private employment in France. All fell well within the terms of the enabling act and were compatible with the intentions expressed by Parliament.

(4) *Parliamentary control.* The government submitted the ratification bill on June 6, 1962, well within the deadline.[166] Boulin did not keep his promise. The bill never appeared on the agenda. However, no MPs ever made any serious effort to place it there, either.

In any case, Parliament had adequate other recourse if it had wanted to attack the ordinances. The repatriation program was very expensive. By 1965, nearly $2 billion was spent assisting about 720,000 persons.[167] A serious parliamentary threat to that budget could have forced the government to bring the ratification bill forward. None ever came.

EEC Harmonization.

(1) *The circumstances.* Four Article 38 enabling acts have concerned the implementation of European Economic Community agreements. They gave the government the authority to make by ordinance changes in French law that were expected to be required by EEC decisions then under discussion. In fact, these enabling acts had little policy significance. France was bound by valid international agreements to effect the changes, but they did simplify the government's task.

(2) *The enabling act.* The first of the EEC acts was a clause in the 1962 agricultural orientation law.[168] The original government bill authorized the use of Article 38 powers "to ensure the implementation of the common agricultural policy" by imposing taxes on agricultural products and by revising the laws regulating agricultural and food markets except for the determination of offense

and penalties. The authorization was to expire December 31, 1963, and a ratification bill was due by March 31, 1964.[169]

A special Assembly committee recommended deletion of Article 24 by "virtually unanimous" vote. It feared that "so general a delegation" would permit imposition of a production tax, toward which "Parliament has expressed its hostility many times already." Also, the "principle of the superiority of international law already gives to the government the necessary powers" to implement the treaty. Any further legislative measures required should "be submitted to Parliament in the normal way." [170]

The government sought accommodation with the committee. "A certain number of confrontations . . . during the afternoon, in the evening, and in the night between the government and the committee" led to "an agreement . . . between the majority—if not the virtual unanimity—of the committee and the government" on the clause. The government agreed that (1) its taxation authority be limited to taxes which were "the direct consequence of the decisions of the" EEC, (2) its authority be broadened to include measures to assist agriculture to conform to the terms of the treaty, (3) it be required to consult with the appropriate parliamentary committees before issuing ordinances, (4) the termination date be June 30, 1963, and (5) the deadline for the ratification bills be three months after each ordinance. The revised clause was adopted by the Assembly by voice vote.[171]

The Senate committee expressed reservations over the scope of the delegation in the Assembly bill, but recommended only one change, that the expiration date be set at October 31, 1962. Also, it asked that the agricultural minister reiterate to the Senate his promise to the Assembly not to use ordinances "to call into question existing legislation but to stay in a straight line with the modifications that are the consequences of the Brussels decisions." [172] He did. Also, he persuaded the Senate to accept the June 30 deadline and the clause passed by voice vote.[173].

The second EEC enabling act came in 1964. A government bill authorized the use of ordinances to bring French legislation into line with EEC decisions requiring that the nationals of all EEC countries have equal right to pursue occupations in all EEC countries. It set a January 1, 1966, expiration date and a ratification bill deadline of April 1, 1966.[174]

The Assembly committee recommended adoption of the bill without change.[175] Assembly debate on the bill was remarkable only for a dialogue between the Socialist and government spokesmen over the handling of ratification bills.[176] Chandernagor complained that the government refused to put them on the agenda and prevented its majority from doing so. Foyer responded that "the government has never opposed the ratification of the ordinances by the Assembly" and that "no democratic country" gives "the minority mastery over the agenda of Parliament." The bill passed on voice vote without amendment.[177]

The Senate committee *rapporteur* used the occasion for a long juridical discourse on the theory and practice of delegated legislation and concluded with a recommendation for adoption without change.[178] The short floor discussion followed virtually the same script as in the Assembly and the bill passed without change by voice vote.[179]

In May 1966, the government filed a bill to extend the deadlines of the 1964 law to 1970.[180] The Assembly committee approved of this in substance, but recommended a new law, rather than an extension of the old.[181] The government agreed and its bill passed by voice vote without change.[182] The Senate committee recommended passage of the Assembly bill and the Senate concurred by voice vote.[183]

In December 1969, the government submitted a bill to renew the enabling act until 1974.[184] The Assembly committee recommended that the expiration date be set at December 31, 1972, and that ratification bills be required by March 31 of the year following publication of an ordinance.[185] The government agreed and the revised bill passed by voice vote without discussion.[186]

The Senate committee first proposed to revive the requirement in the 1962 agriculture law that the government consult with parliamentary committees in drafting ordinances, but was persuaded that that arrangement might "be contrary to the spirit of Article 38." It did obtain from the minister an assurance that he would "keep us informed on the drafting of the measures to be taken" and the Assembly bill passed by voice vote.[187]

(3) *Executive legislation.*   Neither the 1962 or 1964 EEC enabling acts produced ordinances, apparently because EEC decisions were tardy.[188] The 1966 law produced five ordinances, all of which conformed to the terms of the law.[189] The 1969 law produced two ordinances.[190] They concerned persons eligible to operate liquor outlets in France and identity cards for foreign merchants. Both fit the law.

(4) *Parliamentary control.*   The ratification bill for the 1968–69 ordinances was submitted March 20, 1970. It never appeared on the parliamentary agenda.[191] The ratification bill for the 1972 ordinances was submitted March 28, 1973.[192] It was reported favorably by the Senate committee and adopted by voice vote without discussion or change.[193] The same scenario was played out in the Assembly.[194] No one said whether the government had kept its commitment to inform parliamentary committees on the drafting of ordinances. Thus was affected in the most tranquil circumstances the only parliamentary adoption of a ratification bill during the Gaullist period, except for the 1967 social security measures.[195]

The Somalia Referendum.

(1) *The circumstances.*   When President de Gaulle visited French Somalia in 1966, he was greeted by nationalist demonstrations. This offended him so that he announced then and there that Somalia could choose independence if it wished. After his return to Paris, the government decided that its choice would be made by referendum. This gave rise to another resort to Article 38.[196]

(2) *The enabling act.*   The government bill authorizing the referendum provided for Article 38 powers to take such measures "as are justified by the

situation" following it until such time as "parliament will have spoken" in response to the referendum. The ratification bill deadline was December 31, 1967.[197] The Assembly committee—with Gaullist constitutional law expert René Capitant as *rapporteur*—recommended unanimously that Article 38 be used only if Somalia chose independence and that the expiration date be April 2, 1967, rather than July 1, 1967.[198]

The government got very huffy. It invoked emergency procedures on the floor, refused to accept any amendments, and required a blocked vote. Neither the responsible minister nor Prime Minister Pompidou would explain why special powers might be needed if Somalia rejected independence but neither would they renounce their availability. Nevertheless, the bill passed without amendment after a six-hour debate, 283 to 0 with 196 not voting.[199]

Another Gaullist constitutional law expert, Marcel Prélot, was the Senate *rapporteur*. His committee agree with the Assembly committee, except that it preferred an October 2, 1967, expiration date.[200] The government still refused an explanation and invoked the same emergency procedures. The bill passed after a three-hour debate, 64 to 0 with 213 not voting, including Prélot.[201] Somalia voted against independence and no ordinances were issued.

Economic and Social Reforms.

(1) *The circumstances.* The opportunities for parliamentary control of Article 38 authority were most apparent in the 1967 economic and social reforms. The EEC was due to eliminate internal tariffs on July 1, 1968, requiring changes in French law and practice. Prime Minister Pompidou was determined to legislate France into a modern industrial State. The social security system was nearly bankrupt. Yet the government had only a paper-thin parliamentary majority after the March 1967 elections.

That Fourth Republic situation produced a Fourth Republic solution: an enabling act. "Social security reform cannot be a popular operation," Pompidou explained: "it requires that one cut across various electoral interests whose strength is known to everyone." In the absence of "a solid majority," the "classical parliamentary method" had to be abandoned.[202] President de Gaulle agreed.[203]

(2) *The enabling act.* The government bill authorized Article 38 ordinances until October 31, 1967, to (1) reform the unemployment insurance system and improve the system for retraining workers, (2) "ensure the participation of workers in the fruits of the expansion of businesses," (3) reform the social security system and ensure its financial equilibrium, (4) promote the adaptation of businesses in preparation for the EEC change, and facilitate the modernization or reconversion of outmoded economic sectors or regions. The ratification bill deadline was December 31, 1967.[204]

Publication of the bill precipitated intense and extensive opposition. The major labor unions called a one-day general protest strike. The opposition political parties agreed to submit a joint motion of censure. Valéry Giscard d'Estaing, whose forty-four member parliamentary group was essential to the governments' majority, criticized the government sharply, especially for failing to consult the Liaison Committee of the Majority. Edgard Pisani, Minister of Facilities, resigned in protest. Pro-Gaullist Centrists such as René Pleven and Jacques Duhamel objected strenuously. Pompidou responded by meeting with the Giscardians twice, once for "several hours" and with the UDR for "more than two hours." He made no concessions of substance, but offered to consult with them on the drafting of the ordinances and agreed that recourse to Article 38 "should not be considered an habitual method of government." [205]

In the Assembly, Pompidou invoked emergency procedures and sent the bill to special committee. He and two ministers met with the committee. He explained that he needed Article 38 powers to act rapidly, but above all, "because of the difficulty of carrying out coherent overall action on matters where the regulatory and legal domains are so thoroughly intermingled." He promised not to oppose discussion of the ratification bill and pointed out that Parliament would be able to control much of the program through the budget. The committee split, 15 to 15, and was unable to elect officers or agree on recommendations.[206]

On the floor, Pompidou added details on his plans for ordinances and promised to "initiate a general debate on . . . economic and financial policies . . . before the end of the present parliamentary session." Also, he accepted an Independent Republican amendment setting the expiration date as "the opening of the discussion of the 1968 budget." Finally, he declared the bill urgent under Article 49 on the grounds that a previous question motion had been posed. This meant that the bill would pass automatically unless a motion of censure were submitted within 24 hours and adopted and that the debate was adjourned for 24 hours.[207]

Five minutes after adjournment, the opposition submitted a motion of censure.[208] Thirty-six speakers joined the fifteen-hour censure debate. Most asked for information and commitments on the government's intentions, especially about the social security reforms. The government gave a few more details on its social security plans and promised not to use ordinances to "modify the fundamental conditions for the exercise of the medical profession," to ratify treaties, to deal with agricultural or housing policy, or to "go beyond the very precise and very limited domain for which we ask special powers." Pompidou evaded a question on whether he would place the ratification bill on the agenda. The censure motion required 244 votes to pass. It received 236, so the bill was adopted passively.[209]

Only the two ministers met with the special Senate committee, Pompidou turning down three insistent invitations. They told it that parliamentary ratification would be solicited for all the ordinances in order to give them full legislative character and promised that ordinances would not impose the participation of workers in the management of firms, change the general or local taxation systems, alter the grain market organization, or touch the "rights of war veterans or victims."[210] Nevertheless, the committee recommended, 19 to 2 with 3 abstentions, that the government bill be rejected outright.[211] Twenty-three senators—only three of whom voted for the bill—and only one junior minister spoke in the ten-hour Senate debate. The minister added a few assurances. He said that the government contemplated no fiscal measures, except to increase incentive payments to firms with worker participation, and would not tamper with the Alsatian social security system. The Senate defeated Article 1, 30 to 215 with 24 not voting, and the bill as a whole by voice vote.[212]

The government sent the bill to joint conference committee under Article 45, which rejected it, 9 to 5.[213] Pompidou posed a question of confidence under Article 49.[214] Half an hour later, the opposition submitted another motion of censure.[215] Four opposition deputies and Pompidou spoke in the two-hour debate. Pompidou added nothing substantive, except that the general debate on economic and financial policy would be held "five days from now." The second censure motion received the same number of votes as the first.[216] The Senate discussed the bill for ten minutes, rejected Article 1, 33 to 223, and Article 2 by voice vote.[217] The Assembly repeated its second-reading performance, the third censure motion receiving one more vote than the first two, after a 45-minute debate.[218] Thus, the bill became law by passive enactment, no changes having been made.[219]

(3) *Related parliamentary action.* Parallel to the parliamentary deliberation on the enabling act and closely related to it was an oral question with debate on unemployment and the use of ordinance powers in dealing with it. Eighteen deputies and a junior minister spoke in the four and a half hour debate. The minister gave no real information or commitments on the ordinances beyond promising that they would be designed to provide the workers with "the means to adjust to an industrial society in rapid change." [220]

Also, the economic and financial debate was held as promised, before any ordinances were issued. Forty-six speakers, mostly opposition, debated twelve and a half hours. Yet, none addressed the enabling act directly and specifically.[221]

(4) *Executive legislation.* The 1967 law produced thirty-five ordinances.[222] Four dealt with unemployment and working conditions. Three promoted workers participation. Four reformed the social security system. The other twenty-one concerned various economic matters, including agriculture.[223]

The 1967 ordinances introduced major changes into some aspects of French economic and social life. All seem to have fit the framework of the enabling act and the promises made to Parliament, with two possible exceptions. One reformed the system licensing grain brokers[224] and another allegedly increased the levies on cooperatives,[225] both in apparent conflict with governmental promises. Also, the agricultural reforms conflicted with an early pledge that was withdrawn before the act was passed.

(5) *Parliamentary control.* The ordinances came before Parliament the first time only four days after the last one was issued and eight days before the expiration date through a motion of censure posed by the Communists and the Federation of the Left.[226] Eighteen orators debated for eight and a quarter hours. The Centrists and the Independent Republicans urged revision of the

ordinances, but did not vote censure. Pompidou admitted that they might require revision: "The government will, no doubt, be led to propose some itself. And if constructive private members' bills that are financially sound and economically and socially useful, are submitted we will be quite ready to agree to discuss them." Censure drew 207 votes, 37 short of adoption.[227]

Parliament voted on the ordinances again the very next day. A Communist motion to recommit the State budget to permit prior deliberation on a ratification bill was defeated, 199 to 246 with 42 not voting.[228] Also, at least fifteen speakers in the budget debate in the Assembly and eight in the Senate referred to the ordinances, especially those on social security, employment, and agricultural cooperatives. They helped defeat some sections of the budget in preliminary consideration.[229]

Parliamentary questions also dealt with the 1967 ordinances. Eight deputies and a minister discussed an oral question with debate on the social security ordinances for about one and three-quarter hours and two ministers responded to seven oral questions without debate on the unemployment ordinances in a two and a half-hour session.[230] In the Senate, two oral questions with debate on the social security ordinances occupied a two-hour session and oral questions without debate came up on the "participation," social security, and employment ordinances.[231] Finally, at least thirty-four written questions by deputies and one by a senator were submitted on the ordinances.[232]

A ratification bill for all the 1967 ordinances was submitted on December 28, 1967. Despite the demands of some MPs, however, it did not appear on the agenda.[233] Then, the Grenelle Accords that Pompidou signed with the labor unions and employers associations to end the disorders of May 1968 contained a government commitment to schedule a parliamentary debate on ratification of the social security ordinances during the session then meeting. The dissolution prevented fulfillment of that pledge but the government submitted another ratification bill, this time on the social security ordinances only, on the second day of the session following the elections and scheduled it for debate ten days later.[234]

Gaullists had by far the largest parliamentary majority in the history of republican France. Yet the government obtained ratification only at the cost of substantial concessions. In a series of meetings at the outset, it told leaders of the major labor unions and professional associations and the Assembly committee that it would revise the ordinances, provided the administrative efficiency and financial solvency of the system were not jeopardized.[235] The committee responded by recommending 37 amendments, some of great importance.[236] A total of 116 amendments were submitted. Owing to withdrawals and combinations, only 35 committee amendments, 32 private members amendments, and 15 government amendments actually came before the Assembly.

The Assembly debated the bill for about fifteen hours, including four on the amendments. It adopted thirty-two amendments and eight others were withdrawn in return for government promises. The amended bill passed, 312 to 102 with 73 deputies not voting.[237]

The Senate committee voted 11 to 0 with 7 abstentions to recommend abrogation of the original ordinances and 19 to 1 with 1 abstention against the Assembly bill. That report was rejected by the Senate 95 to 164 with 12 not voting. Twenty-two amendments to the Assembly bill had been submitted by the time the Senate debate began and others were put down later. Eighteen came up for floor consideration. Three amendments unacceptable to the government passed, leading it to invoke cloture and require a blocked vote on the Assembly bill with three additional amendments that it accepted. It was defeated, 46 to 169 with 56 senators not voting.[238]

The government then sent the bill to joint conference committee.[239] The committee recommended the Assembly bill with minor changes accepted by the government. The government presented eleven additional amendments in the Assembly. Four passed, 355 to 4 with 128 not voting, and the others were approved by voice vote.[240] The Senate accepted five of the government amendments, but balked on the sixth, 39 to 153 with 78 not voting. The government again invoked a blocked vote on the unamended Assembly bill and again lost, 47 to 159 with 65 not voting.[241] The Assembly passed its bill on third reading by voice vote and the Senate rejected it again on blocked vote, 46 to 162 with 63 not voting.[242] Because the Assembly vote was decisive, the bill became law after about seventeen hours of debate in the Assembly and eight and a half in the Senate.[243]

The ratification law made thirty-seven changes in the ordinances, all but two or three substantive. It required additional administrative consultations with representatives of interested groups, increased the agency's autonomy from the government, changed the composition of administrative councils, restored some insurance benefits, revised the financial and administrative systems, and introduced a means test for the amounts of family allocations. Also, it required that the Sixth Plan program social security planning and that the government report to Parliament on the financial status of the social security system. The reforms that the government had called essential remained intact, the system's beneficiaries lost their majorities on the administrative councils, and its solvency was ensured.

One of the social security ordinances (67–828) came before Parliament again. Three articles were added by law. However, no effort was made to repeal it or revise its existing provisions.[244]

Under Article 11.

(1) *The circumstances.* The Evians Accords ending the Algerian war provided for a referendum in Algeria on independence and assumed that the outcome would be favorable.[245] Organization of the referendum and implementation of transitional arrangements required French legislation. President de Gaulle, on recommendation of the government, called a referendum under Article 11 of the constitution to obtain the necessary authority to legislate by ordinance.

(2) *The enabling act.*   Article 2 of the referendum bill authorized the president of the Republic to "take by ordinance or ... decrees taken in the Council of Ministers all legislative or regulatory measures relative to the implementation" of the Evians Accords "until the new political organization ... has been put in place.[246] Neither the Evians Accords nor the referendum bill required formal parliamentary action. However, de Gaulle convened Parliament in special session to receive a message from him on the matter. The Assembly debated his message for about ten hours and the Senate did so for about eight. Neither debate concluded with a vote. Most of the discussion concerned the Evians Accords and the government's past Algerian performance, but the proposed delegation of legislative authority by referendum was mentioned also by several speakers.[247]

Parliament then adjourned. It did not meet until after the referendum. The voters approved the government's referendum bill, 17.5 million votes to 1.8 million.

(3) *Executive legislation.*   Fifty-two ordinances were issued under the April 13 law.[248] All seem to have had the purpose of working out the problems of the transition to Algerian independence. Therefore, they all conformed to the terms of the enabling act.

(4) *Parliamentary control.*   The referendal law did not require that the ordinances be submitted for ratification. However, they came under parliamentary scrutiny in other ways. For one thing, they figured prominently in three debates on other matters that were held in the three months following the referendum. First, they were much discussed by the thirty-seven participants in the thirteen-hour debate on Pompidou's investiture as premier.[249] It concluded with a vote of confidence, 259 to 128 with 164 not voting. Second, the Assembly held a general debate on Algerian policy that lasted thirteen and a half hours, heard fifty-four speakers, and ended with a censure motion vote that drew only 113 ballots, 163 short of passage.[250] Third, several speakers in the debate on the supplemental State budget for 1962 criticized the provision of funds to implement some of the ordinances. Yet, when the government invoked Article 49, no motion of censure was submitted and the budget was adopted passively, ordinance funds and all.[251] All three results were implicit acceptances of the ordinances.

Moreover, the ordinances also received explicit approval by Parliament. One ordinance had established a Court of Military Justice to replace the High Military Tribunal which had been set up under the February 4, 1960, enabling act.[252] In October 1962, a decision of that court was struck down by the Council of State and, on appeal by the Court of Cassation.[253] The government submitted two bills replacing the Court of Military Justice by a Court of State Security, meeting the principal objections of the Council of State, and making very significant changes in the ordinance.[254] Also, one bill contained a provision ratifying the ordinance to give it the full force of law and remove it from Council of State purview.

After long debate, the Assembly committee recommended, by 18 to 8 and 11 to 1, approval of the bills with extensive revisions.[255] It proposed fifty-one amendments of which fifteen were purely formal, but another proposed ratification of all the ordinances. Also, fifty-nine private members' amendments were submitted. Forty-eight committee and eleven private members' amendments were adopted, including the one on ratifications. Twenty-seven orators, including the leading jurists of the Assembly, debated the bills for nearly fourteen hours. They passed, 240 to 188 with 53 not voting and 233 to 190 with 58 not voting.[256] Even more drastic revision had been staved off only by long meetings of the minister with the committee and many corridor meetings between him and individual deputies.[257]

The Senate committee recommended twenty-two amendments, eleven purely formal.[258] Also, eight private members' amendments were proposed. Nine of the committee's substantive amendments and five private members' amendments were adopted and the revised texts were adopted, 128 to 109 with 34 not voting and 126 to 109 with 36 not voting, after a seven-hour debate with thirty speakers participating.[259] The Senate bills were "entirely different on all the essential points from those adopted by the deputies," moving still further from government's wishes.[260]

After two difficult meetings, the joint conference committee reported back bills closer to the Senate than the Assembly version, 9 to 3 with 2 abstentions.[261] Both chambers adopted the conference report, the Assembly after an 85-minute debate with seven speakers by 263 to 186 with 33 not voting and the Senate after 50 minutes and five speakers by 115 to 108 with 48 not voting.[262] The differences between the original ordinance and the bill passed by Parliament were considerable.

Only one speaker in any debate commented on any other ordinance than 62-618. He raised a question about an ordinance on early retirement of judges, received a courteous answer, and that was that. No one in Parliament mentioned any other ordinances.[263] One of them, however, was repealed by Parliament at the request of the government as being needed no longer. In neither chamber was there either discussion or opposition.[264]

Under Ordinary Parliamentary Laws. The 1956 Algerian special powers law that had been renewed in June 1958 was used fairly extensively under the Fifth Republic. More than fifty decrees were issued under it between February 1959 and May 1962. All dealt with the Algerian troubles and, consequently, fell within the scope of the enabling act. All were included in ratification bills submitted to Parliament as required.[265] No ratification bill ever came up for parliamentary action. The government never put any on the agenda and no MP ever made a public effort to force it to do so.

The enabling acts passed by Fifth Republic Parliaments have had little significance. The Assembly has no record of any decrees being issued under any of them prior to 1973. However, the 1972 law was used as the authority for a decree suspending the value added tax on beef for 1973. No ratification was required and it never came under parliamentary review.

CONCLUSIONS

The problem of exceptional powers lies at the heart of executive–legislative relations in France. Constitutional dictatorship exists to the extent that the legislature invites or at least permits the Executive to perform functions that normally are parliamentary. Thus, in a sense, it marks the boundary between the spheres of authority of those two branches of government. This makes it a good indicator of their relative power and authority. It tells some interesting tales about the Fifth Republic.

First, it says that the Executive of the Gaullist Fifth Republic was not so much more authoritarian than its predecessors as its reputation suggests. Indeed, its resort to legislative powers was less frequent and less extensive than that of any previous regime since 1933. Articles 11, 16, 38 were invoked an average of once every 16.3 months in 1959–74, compared to an enabling act passed on an average of once every 5.9 months in 1933–40 and every 5.5 months in 1946–58. The frequency was, of course, even greater in 1940–46 and 1958–59. Nor was the extent of its use any greater under de Gaulle and Pompidou than under their predecessors. Four of the six important enabling acts concerned Algeria, and the others dealt with "social scourges" and economic and social matters. The Third Republic enabling acts covered broader areas of economic and financial matters as well as defense affairs. The Fourth Republic enabling acts concerned major economic and financial matters and, also, Algeria. Not in number, frequency, importance, nor range did the enabling acts of the Gaullists exceed those of the earlier regimes.

Second, it says that Parliament was not the passive and impotent victim of executive legislation that it has been called sometimes. Every significant Gaullist use of an enabling act was influenced by Parliament in important ways. After months of tacit acceptance of de Gaulle's use of Article 16 in 1961, Parliament forced its termination. The Assembly obtained significant amendments to the "Barricades Crisis," "Social Scourges," and the EEC harmonization bills. It debated and voted on one of the "Barricades" ordinances and the "Social Scourges" ordinances. It ratified two of the seven EEC ordinances. It considered four censure motions on the economic and social problems bill and its ordinances and, after making substantial amendments, ratified four of its ordinances. It debated, amended extensively, and ratified the Evians ordinances. No evidence exists to indicate that so much as a sizable minority of the deputies wanted even to debate other ratification bills. When deputies were interested in the ordinances, they found other ways—especially parliamentary questions, budget debates, and previous question motions—to worry the government. In all these ways, Parliament imposed controls on executive legislation, despite the existence of a Gaullist majority in the Assembly throughout the period. Clearly, if Parliament had been less Gaullist it would have been more inclined to give greater effect to the control mechanisms available to it. Parliament was relatively restrained, not by necessity but by choice, not by oppression but by common interest and general accord with the Executive.

The experience of constitutional dictatorship in France tells us, also, some interesting tales about the interplay of ideology and circumstance in executive–legislative relations. It shows that usage of executive legislation correlates more closely with circumstance than ideology. The Third and Fourth Republics preached against it, but the circumstances of crisis forced them to practice it. The Gaullists preached it, but—as crisis abated—practiced it less and then not at all. During the de Gaulle dictatorship, ideology, crisis, and heavy usage coincided. In the face of crisis—especially external threats such as the two world wars and Algeria—political opinion drew together toward greater unity of interest and the strength of the Executive grew. As crisis abated and less consensual issues dominated the political stage, the executive–legislative power boundary drifted back toward Parliament.[266] Power flowed toward the institution best suited to the circumstances of the moment, regardless of the assumptions and constraints of constitutional text or ideology. That phenomenon may be observed, also, with respect to executive involvement in parliamentary law making, as the next chapter will show.

6

Parliamentary Law Making

INTRODUCTION

When Michel Debré presented the draft of the 1958 constitution to the Council of State, he told it:[1]

> Ah! if we had the possibility to make a clear and constant majority spring up tomorrow, . . . it would not be necessary to impose order and stability by cutting the ties between the parties and the government. . . . But . . . no one has the right in France, at the present time, to issue a check against a future that we know too well will be marked for a long time yet by political divisions—that is, by majorities menaced too readily by collapse and which must be forced to be wise. *Because, in France, governmental stability cannot result initially from the electoral law, it must result, at least in part, from constitutional regulation.*

Acting on that assumption, the framers included in the constitution provisions designed to give the government greater control over parliamentary law making. Some were designed to give governments the means to control the course of the legislative process in Parliament. This chapter studies the extent to which those innovations were successful. It argues that few of the devices were genuinely new and that they had less effect than did the social changes that underlaid the "clear and constant majority" that emerged in the new regime. Also, it shows how collegial was the process. This aspect of the 1958 constitution was neither the pure and unadulterated manifestation of Debré's "reformed parliamentarism" nor the 1958 Fourth Republic constitutional reform proposals warmed over. Each constitutional device is examined in turn, its historical background, its drafting, and its use in actual practice being considered. Especially, experience in legislatures with marginal Gaullist majorities is compared with that of legislatures with decisive majorities for indications of the impact of social and political circumstance.

HISTORICAL BACKGROUND

The constitution of the Third Republic had provided for very little executive involvement in the parliamentary process. What there was emphasized the president rather than the prime minister or government. In practice, parliamentary rules and custom permitted much more such involvement. Also, in practice the prime minister and government were responsible for the relationship of the Executive with Parliament, while the presidency became an almost purely ceremonial office.

The ability of the Executive to provide leadership in the legislative process was limited less by the constitution and rules, however, than by the political reality of a heterogeneous, undisciplined, and shifting parliamentary majority. That reality made executive involvement in the parliamentary process difficult and uncertain. Indeed, those difficulties partly inspired the development, even in the Third Republic, of some of the devices that were incorporated in the 1958 constitution.

The Fourth Republic constitution was designed, in part, to provide the government with greater means to lead Parliament in its law making. It recognized the shift in real authority by transferring procedural means of control from the president to the premier or the government. Also, it introduced devices to neutralize the effects of unreliable majorities, to stabilize governments, and to permit greater leadership by them. Nevertheless, contrary to expectations, Fourth Republic presidents played more active roles in parliamentary law making than had their predecessors, although the government remained the focal point of executive leadership. Also, the governments continued to be plagued by uncertain majorities, because the constitutional devices had little practical effect. Nevertheless, some progress was made. Governments did have somewhat more control of the legislative process and, in 1954 and 1958, Parliament accepted constitutional changes intended to increase that control.

General de Gaulle and his followers were constant critics of the weakness of Fourth Republic Executives in their parliamentary relations. Naturally, then, their constitution making of 1958 reflected that concern. However, nothing in the text or debates on de Gaulle's constitutional reform bill of June 1958 indicated that the new system would give the government greater means to participate in parliamentary law making.[2] Nevertheless, the matter came up at the very beginning of the drafting process, both in Michel Debré's first meeting with the team of experts assigned to assist him in preparing the draft[3] and in de Gaulle's first meeting with the Interministerial Cabinet Committee on the

Constitution (IMC).[4] In the latter meeting, Debré stressed the importance of "parliamentary discipline and the organization of legislative work." [5]

The published records of the drafting process shed little light on the reasoning that inspired such provisions in the constitution. However, Debré did tell the Council of State: [6]

> Our legislative and budgetary-procedure was one of the clearest marks of the assembly character of our democratic system. The draft submitted to your deliberations proposed modifications which may appear secondary to some; in law and in fact, they are fundamental.

More eloquent than such general statements are the amount and detail of the "modifications" to which he referred.

PROCEDURAL DEVICES

Organizing Parliament's Business

The Convocation of Parliamentary Sessions

Article 29 of the 1958 constitution authorized the prime minister to summon Parliament into special session. This is a traditional executive power in France. The 1875 constitution gave it to the president of the republic upon countersignature by a minister, as well as to a majority of the MPs.[7] It was used frequently, always on the initiative of the government. By 1913, special sessions had "become as common . . . as the ordinary sessions," being held every year, mainly to debate the State budget.[8]

The 1946 constitution (Art. 12) transferred that authority to the steering committee of the Assembly, though one-third of the deputies or the premier could require that it be exercised. Usually, it did so on the initiative of the government for brief sessions in January, mainly for budgetary purposes.[9]

Despite that tradition, the constitutional drafts that Debré submitted to Premier de Gaulle and the Interministerial Committee in early June 1958 contained no reference to this matter. It appeared first in a draft that Debré submitted to the Interministerial Committee in late June:[10]

> Parliament shall meet in special session for a designated purpose at the call of the prime minister or of the majority of the members composing the two Assemblies. The special sessions shall be opened and closed by decree of the president of the Republic.
>
> When the special session takes place at the call of the members of Parliament, the cloture decree cannot be issued before Parliament has exhausted the limited agenda for which it was called.

That wording remained intact until the Cabinet reviewed a draft for the first time on July 25. Then it became the object of one of the few real Cabinet debates on constitutional provisions. After a discussion involving Jacques

Soustelle, Jean-Marie Berthoin, Maurice Couve de Murville, and Guy Mollet, the third paragraph was revised:[11]

> When the special session takes place at the call of the members of the *National Assembly, a new session cannot be called before the expiration of an interval of one month after the cloture decree.* The cloture decree *shall take effect as soon as* the agenda for which it was convened has been exhausted *and no later than one week from the date of the first meeting.*

Only a minor stylistic change was made before the draft article went to the CCC on August 14. However, its provisions attracted an unusual amount of attention from the CCC, which proposed several substantive changes: (1) It asked that the steering committee of the Assembly also be able to call special sessions; it suggested (2) that the "one-week" maximum length be extended to "twelve days"; and (3) that it be extended still further if a motion of censure was being processed; finally, (4) it wanted the prime minister to be able to call a new special session within one month after the cloture of the previous one.[12] The Interministerial Committee accepted the second, third, and fourth proposed changes and transformed the second paragraph into a separate article before the draft went to the Council of State.[13]

The Council of State proposed rejection of the third CCC recommendation and the addition of this phrase at the beginning of the former paragraph 2: "*Except for cases when Parliament meets by right*, the sessions. . . ." Debré recommended the Council of State version to the Interministerial Committee. The Interministerial Committee and the Council of Ministers agreed, with two minor changes in style.[14]

Special sessions of Parliament may convene automatically as a result of executive action under a provision of the emergency powers article of the constitution (Art. 16). That provision appeared first in a draft of articles dealing with the presidency of the Republic that Debré presented to de Gaulle in early June. It stipulated that when the president invoked emergency powers, "Parliament shall meet as soon as circumstances permit."[15] The clause remained the same in the draft that went to the CCC.[16]

The CCC recommended rewording that clause: "Parliament shall meet except in case of *force majeure*." Also, it asked for the addition: "During the exercise of the exceptional powers provided by the present article, the National Assembly cannot be dissolved."[17] The Interministerial Committee accepted the CCC changes with some words reordered. So did the Council of State, except that it recommended deletion of "except in case of *force majeure*." Debré recommended acceptance of the Council of State version. The Interministerial Committee and the Council of Ministers agreed.[18]

Automatic convocation of Parliament may result, also, from exercise of the presidential power of dissolution. That provision appeared first in the draft that Debré submitted to de Gaulle in late June: "The Assembly shall meet by right the third Thursday following its election after a presidential dissolution." It disappeared completely from the next draft, but reappeared in the draft he submitted to the Interministerial Committee about June 30 and remained in identical terms until the Interministerial Committee accepted the CCC recommendation that "third Thursday" be changed to "second Thursday." Also, the Interministerial Committee added this sentence: "If that meeting takes place outside the periods set aside for regular sessions, a special session shall open by right for a duration of fifteen days." [19] The Council of State and the Council of Ministers accepted that draft as revised.[20]

Thus, the constitutional provisions involving the Executive in the convocation of special sessions of Parliament were seriously debated throughout the drafting process. They underwent m.., changes. The final product was a joint effort of many hands.

In practice, fewer special sessions were called in the Gaullist period than earlier. Parliament had held ten special sessions under Art. 29 by the time of Pompidou's death.[21] All were called by the president of the Republic on recommendation of the prime minister. A majority of the deputies called for a special session under Art. 29 once, in March 1960, but de Gaulle refused to issue the opening decree and it did not meet.

Two distinct periods may be identified with respect to the frequency of Art. 29 special sessions. Between January 1959 and December 1962, six such sessions met, an average of one every 8 months. From January 1963 through March 1974, only four sessions met, one every 33.8 months. In fact, 52 months elapsed between the ninth and tenth sessions and the tenth seemed to be more the product of Pompidou's deteriorating condition than of any political or governmental needs. All of this suggests that the special session was an important constitutional device only during the early period of the Fifth Republic when a crisis situation was combined with a marginal majority in Parliament.[22]

Measured by the amount of meeting time, the special sessions were not very important either. More than half the total amount of time (185 hours) spent in special sessions came in the December 1962 session, which was really makeup time for the Fall session that had been interrupted for two months by dissolution. Otherwise, the longest special session (December 1959) was 42 hours, less than one-third the length of the shortest regular session that went full term (Spring 1959, 145 hours).[23] The aggregate total amount of time devoted to special sessions was only 367 hours, 4.6 percent of the total sitting time of the National Assembly. The percentages were 15.6 in the first four years and 1.1 thereafter.

When examined for the character of the business they transacted, the special sessions seem scarcely more important and the impression of decline after 1962 is reinforced:

January 1959. To permit newly appointed Prime Minister Debré to present his Cabinet and program and to obtain a vote of confidence. Because no doubt existed that the Assembly would accept any premier that de Gaulle appointed, this purpose was unnecessary. Also, Debré may have wished to set a precedent with respect to the procedure to be followed when a new prime minister takes office. If so, he was unsuccessful, since his example was followed only by Chaban-Delmas in 1969.

December 1959. To permit Parliament its constitutionally allotted time to consider the 1960 budget, which Debré had submitted late. The same session enacted the *loi Debré* providing state aid to church schools, one of the most important pieces of legislation in postwar France.[24]

February 1960. To enable Parliament to delegate law-making powers to the government under Article 38 in order to deal with the "Barricades Crisis." In fact, the crisis ended before the powers were granted. Also, Article 16 could have been invoked for that purpose, as in a similar situation a year later.

March 1962. To meet the constitutional requirement that Parliament be in session at the time de Gaulle called the referendum for approval of the Evians Accords granting independence to Algeria. In fact, the session played no significant part in that decision. The regular Spring session was scheduled to begin thirty-five days later.

July 1962. To enact agricultural legislation that could have been submitted in time for deliberation during the regular session that had ended the previous day. It amounted to a two-day extension of the regular Spring session.[25]

December 1962. To obtain enactment of the 1963 budget and seven other bills that had been squeezed out of the regular Fall session by the two-month interruption occasioned by dissolution and to elect judges to the High Court of Justice. It enacted all eight bills[26] plus two other[27] and elected the judges.[28]

December 1965. To obtain enactment of a tax reform bill[29] that had been omitted from the regular Fall session by the abbreviation occasioned by the presidential elections.[30]

September 1968. To obtain enactment of the orientation law for higher education and of laws on investment aid and corporation tax relief[31] that were legislative responses to the disorders of the preceding summer. In fact, the session met for two days (9 hours) immediately before the regular Fall session, which met for 356 hours—substantially less than some other Fall sessions.[32] It seems likely that those 9 hours could have been fitted into the regular session. The investment and tax laws were enacted in the special session and the education law in the regular session.

September 1969. To permit recently appointed Prime Minister Chaban-Delmas to present his Cabinet and program. As in 1959, no one doubted that he had the support of a majority of the National Assembly.

January 1974. To permit the government to make a declaration to Parliament on monetary policy following the recent devaluation of the franc.

Executive action precipitated two other special sessions, also. One resulted from de Gaulle's use of Article 16 emergency powers in April 1961. The other was required by Article 12 after the 1968 election had been produced by de Gaulle's dissolution of the Assembly. The other presidential dissolution (1962) was timed so that the new Parliament simply "resumed" the regular Fall session with no reference to Article 12.

The Article 16 session happened to coincide with the regular Spring session until its scheduled end on July 22, but de Gaulle continued Article 16 in force thereafter. As a result, he was obliged constitutionally to permit Parliament to meet again for a two-day session (seven hours) in September to discuss a farm-price crisis. However, he prevented the MPs from either giving their views legislative form or considering a motion of censure against the Debré government.

The Article 12 session met for sixty-two hours. It permitted the chambers to organize; to receive a declaration of general policy from the new prime minister, Couve de Murville, and one on education policy from the minister of national education, Edgar Faure; and to enact eleven laws.[33] Some of the laws were first-rate in importance, including some that fulfilled governmental promises that had enabled it to negotiate an end to the May/June disorders. Another granted amnesty for offenses committed during the Algerian War.

The balance sheet for the special sessions is not rich. The only sessions of consequence under Article 29 were December 1959 (Debré law, budget) and December 1962 (budget, ten laws). The only really important special session was July 1968. If it had not been required by Article 12, it probably would have been called under Article 29. Probably the others were unnecessary. Furthermore, special sessions called by the Executive certainly had played a bigger role in the parliamentary lives of the Third and Fourth Republics, despite the weaker position of the Executive. Therefore, this device was neither very original nor very important in changing the operations of French executive–legislative relations.

Executive Sessions of Parliament

The next point of executive involvement in parliamentary affairs concerns executive sessions. Article 33 provided that "each Assembly may sit in closed session at the request of the prime minister or of one-tenth of its members." This was an innovation in constitutional phrasing, although it reflected previous parliamentary rules.[34]

The 1875 constitution had provided that "each Chamber may sit in closed session, at the request of a certain number of its members, set by the rules. It shall decide later, by absolute majority, if the sitting must be held again in public on the same subject." [35] The 1946 constitution said simply that "each of the two Chambers may sit in closed session" (Art. 10). The Third Republic rules specified five senators or twenty deputies. The Assembly rules in the Fourth Republic specified twenty-five members, the government, or the Conference of Presidents. In all cases, the request had to be approved by vote of the Chamber.[36]

The Third Republic Parliament held closed sessions only on rare occasions during the two world wars.[37] The Chamber of Deputies met in closed session eight times between June 16, 1916, and October 10, 1917, and once each on

February 9 and March 19, 1940. The Senate held four such sessions between July 9, 1916, and July 21, 1917, and another on March 14–15, 1940. All of them seem to have been initiated by MPs for the purpose of questioning the government on the conduct of the wars.[38] The Fourth Republic Parliament never met in closed session. Thus, the Executive never called Parliament into closed session in either earlier republic.

Nevertheless, very early in the drafting of the 1958 constitution, the Executive was included in that action explicitly in the wording given above. That provision remained intact from the late June draft until final approval. Neither the CCC nor the Council of State commented on it.[39] The device was never used in the Gaullist period. No prime minister or group of MPs ever called for a closed session and none was held.

Control of the Parliamentary Agenda. Article 48 of the 1958 constitution provides that "the agendas of the Assemblies shall include, by priority and in the order that the government has set, discussion of the government's bills and of the private members' bills accepted by it." That clause stands in logical progression from the situations in the Third and Fourth Republics. It represents an evolution of tradition, rather than a departure from it.

The 1875 constitution did not mention parliamentary agendas.[40] However, the parliamentary rules gave government bills an assumption of priority. Before standing committees were established, government bills went directly to the Chamber, while private members' bills went to special committees. Also, defeated government bills could be reintroduced at once, but a private member's bill had to wait at least three months.[41] In 1911, proposal of the agenda was transferred from the Chamber president to a Conference of Presidents and the government was represented on the Conference.[42]

Proposed agendas required approval by the Chamber. Often, this became the occasion for a vote of confidence through a device called "interpellation." In effect, an interpellation motion, debate, and vote passed judgment on the government before proceeding to the agenda by deciding whether to approve an agenda acceptable to the government. More governments fell on interpellations than on votes on legislative and financial measures. Even so, most agendas were adopted without interpellations, sometimes against the government's wishes.[43] However, if a government felt strongly about an agenda and was challenged, it became a matter of interpellation. Interpellation, then, gave the government control of the agenda as long as it retained the confidence of the Chamber.

The government's hold on the agenda was strengthened somewhat during the Fourth Republic. The 1946 constitution was silent on this matter and the parliamentary rules were basically the same as in the Third Republic, although the government benefited from a 1955 rules revision that weighted voting in the Conference of Presidents proportionate to the number of MPs represented. Interpellations continued to be important, although they were permitted less freely and were less deadly.[44]

The value of the government's priority on the agenda was diminished somewhat by the role of the committees. A bill could not come before the House until the appropriate committee was ready to report on it. A committee had a limited time in which to report (three months in the Fourth Republic). Thereafter, the government could force it to report. Use of that power, however, might antagonize the committee and precipitate the report of an unsatisfactory bill.[45]

The 1958 constitution transformed the government's practical priority into constitutional right. That change reflected a longstanding Gaullist idea. As early as his 1946 draft, Debré had proposed a provision that "the government shall hold a right of priority for the discussion of the bills that it submits to the deliberations of Parliament." [46] Apparently, however, he did not discuss that device at the first meeting of the team of experts.[47]

A reference to agenda control appeared first in the late June draft: "The agendas of the Assemblies shall include, by priority, discussion of government bills. However, one sitting each week shall be reserved for questions by members of Parliament and responses by the government." [48] The June 30 version added "in the order set by it" at the end of the first sentence.[49] The Interministerial Committee inserted "and private members' bills formally accepted by it" immediately before that phrase.[50] The Cabinet dropped "formally." [51] The CCC asked that the second sentence be revised to read: "However, the agenda for one sitting per week shall be left to the discretion of each Assembly, especially for the responses of the government to the questions of the members of Parliament."[52] The Interministerial Committee rejected that suggestion, but accepted a Council of State recommendation that "by priority" be inserted after "reserved" in the second sentence. So did the Council of Ministers.[53]

While establishing the principle of government control of the agenda, however, the framers also adopted provisions that conflicted with it, notably in Articles 26, 44, 47, and 49. Those provisions authorize or require access to the agenda for specified purposes, apparently whether or not the government approves. In practice, they are exceptions to the government's control and override it.[54]

Article 26 provides that "detention or prosecution of a member of Parliament shall be suspended if the Assembly to which he belongs requires it." Unless it were to override Article 48, the government could make a dead letter. This provision was invoked twice. In 1960, the government gave a high agenda priority to a resolution requiring it to suspend the detention of a deputy who had been involved in the "Barricades Crisis." However, the Assembly noted the irony of the situation and revised its rules to require that such motions be scheduled, by priority, on the Friday agenda.[55] In 1963, in an apparent courtesy gesture, the Assembly voted to require suspension of prosecution of a deputy who was being sued for libel by a political rival. However, the suspension was to end with the cloture of the session, only twenty-four hours later.[56] Those cases intruded very little on the government's control of the agenda, for they consumed a total of only about four hours of floor time.

Article 44 provided "the members of Parliament" with "the right of amendment." [57] That right, too, would be nugatory if overridden by Article 48.

On the other hand, some amendments might be the functional equivalent of bills. If they were permitted freely, the government's general control of the agenda could be vitiated.[58] The government had some protection through parliamentary rules requiring "germaneness," etc., and from the Constitutional Council with respect to some objects of amendments. However, the principal protection was political, a reliable parliamentary majority that prevented the amendment power from being abused in that way.

Article 47 accords the Assembly forty days and the Senate fifteen days to act on the State budget. In theory, this restricts the government's agenda control substantially. In practice, of course, the government wants its budget to be considered.

Budget debates consume substantial portions of the agenda. Through the last session before Pompidou's death they required about 31.2 percent of all parliamentary time and 35.0 percent if question time is deducted. Indeed, the burden of budgetary deliberations increased. The percentages rose from 29.0 (all) and 32.9 in the first two legislatures to 33.5 and 37.5 in the next two and reached 34.2 and 37.7 in the first year of the fifth legislature.

Furthermore, significant differences existed between the legislatures with marginal majorities and those with decisive Gaullist majorities. Legislatures I and III had marginal majorities and devoted less time to budgets (24.0 percent and 27.5 percent) than did II and IV (32.6 percent and 35.0 percent). However, the marginal fifth legislature was an exception during its first twelve months, with a 34.2 percentage.

The government is limited further by the practical requirement that budgetary deliberations always occur in the Fall session. As a result, during the Fall terms (including the special December sessions of 1959 and 1962), only about 45.5 percent of the total time (39.1 percent, with question period excluded) was available for nonbudgetary business.

Article 49 gives a majority of deputies the right to overturn a government by passing a motion of censure; this right would evaporate if the government's control of the agenda could exclude such motions. However, the Assembly rules[59] require that motions of censure be brought up for discussion by the third parliamentary day following the forty-eight-hour reflection period that Article 49 requires between the submission of the motion and its debate. The priority status of censure motions is implied also by Article 51, which requires that cloture of sessions be delayed, if necessary, to allow enough time to complete a censure process that has begun. That provision operated twice under the Gaullists, for the Spring 1962 regular session and the January 1974 special session.

This exception has been a minor intrusion on the government's agenda control. Through March 1974, twenty-one motions of censure had been submitted and discussed. They consumed about 1.9 percent of the total floor time. On the average, one was submitted every 8.7 months, but that average concealed significant variations among the legislatures. The legislatures with marginal majorities (I, III, and V) averaged one censure motion every 5.0, 2.5, and 6.5 months. The others averaged one censure motion every 25.5 and 28.0 months. The only successful censure motion (October 1962) was passed by a legislature with a marginal majority—that disappeared thereby. Clearly, the political character of the Chamber affected critically the operation of censure and, therefore, its impact on the government's agenda control.

That control was eroded, also, by practical as well as constitutional conflicts. For one thing, the Assembly must transact a certain amount of "housekeeping" business. It must adopt rules; select officers, committees, and representatives; consider points of order; eulogize deceased members, and so forth. All those matters escape the government's agenda control.

None of that business required much time under the Gaullists. Assembly rules were debated in 1959 when the original rules were adopted, in 1969 when they were revised extensively, and in 1963. The debates required 31 hours 45 minutes in 1959, 6 hours 15 minutes in 1969, and 1 hour 30 minutes in 1963. Also, the Assembly used 11 hours 10 minutes to organize originally in 1958–59. All of that totaled only about 49 hours.

The selection of officers, committees, and representatives took even less time. From one to three hours were spent electing officers and committees at the beginning of each legislature and of each Spring session.[60] Also, from time to time, a few minutes were taken to choose representatives to such organizations as the Council of Europe and the European Parliament and members of the High Court of Justice. They totaled perhaps 31 hours.

Points of order were raised rather frequently, but required little time. The *Journal officiel* annual indices list 556 from January 1, 1962, through April 2, 1974.[61] However, 213 were submitted in 1973 alone. Leaving aside that bumper crop, they averaged 30.5 per year. The rules allow 5 minutes apiece for discussion of points of order, but the actual average time used seems to have been about 4 minutes. In the aggregate, then, they consumed about 37 hours of agenda time.

All other kinds of housekeeping business required perhaps another 55 hours. The aggregate total for housekeeping, then, amounted to about 172 hours. This was about 2.2 percent of the total floor time.

Governmental agenda control was modified, also, by the existence of a "complementary agenda." The Conference of Presidents prepared it, alongside the priority agenda. However, it existed only by grace of the government, which could snuff out its feeble life at any time by shoveling still more priority business into the Assembly's hopper. On the other hand, a resolute Assembly could have fought back by scheduling sittings for mornings, early afternoons, Mondays, and weekends—which were virtually unused. In fact, the Assembly showed little inclination to escape the government's control in that way.

Few complementary agendas were adopted and fewer were the basis for the transaction of business. Eighty-three were adopted in the period under review, an average of 5.4 per year. They led to discussions that occupied about 120 hours of agenda time. However, about 87 hours were used for nonlegislative purposes and only about 33 hours were spent discussing bills.

Twenty-eight bills actually came up for debate and another five appeared on the agenda but never reached the floor. Thirteen measures were adopted on the complementary agenda. Five others were adopted from priority agendas in later years. Also, one Senate bill was debated on a complementary agenda but not passed. Nine other bills were defeated definitively.

Some fitful signs indicate that the complementary agenda may have acquired slightly more substance late in the Gaullist period. Eleven of the thirteen successful bills were enacted in 1971–73. By contrast, between November 6, 1959, and December 10, 1969, not a single bill was enacted from the complementary agenda. The complementary agenda produced few headline-makers: [62]

1959.	Re-evaluation of life annuities among individuals
1969.	The declassification of the Place de Lille
1971.	The protection of young animals
	Modernization of the office of master of the wolf hunt
	Nationality of residents of Alsace-Lorraine born before 1918
	Regulation of the profession of expert-in-court
	Abolition of certain legal servitudes
	Revision of the commercial lease law
1972.	Control of election polling operations
	Unemployment insurance for airport personnel
1973.	Creation of a Superior Council of Sexual Information, Birth Control, and Family Education
	Early retirement for former prisoners of war
	Honorariat for mayors

Complementary agenda bills that passed later on the priority agenda were:

1959.	Revision of a child adoption statute (adopted 1960)
	Revision of commercial lease law (adopted 1960)
1962.	Regulation of the profession of optician (adopted 1963)
	Big-game-hunting development (adopted 1964)
1968.	Fourth week of paid vacation (adopted 1969)

The ten bills that were discussed and defeated were:

1959.	Gifts and bequests of farms
	Jointly owned intermediate property (*mitoyenneté*)
1962.	Crop damage caused by game animals
	Electoral law changes to prevent fraud
	Aid to the blind and very infirm
1972.	Creation of an office of family information and education
	The safeguard of business performance bonds
	Social security for young persons
	Regulation of work by adolescents
	Regulation of insurance subagents

In sum, despite some flickers of life in the last three years, the complementary agenda did not intrude appreciably on the government's control of the agenda. It used only about 1.5 percent of the floor time. Even that amount was available by grace of the government to discuss matters which it supported or toward which it was indifferent.

In addition to the implicit and practical exceptions to the government's control of the agenda, one exception is mentioned explicitly in the constitution. Article 48 reserves one sitting each week in each chamber "by priority for questions by members of Parliament and responses by members of the government." The framers saw that as a counterpart to the government's general control of the agenda.[63]

In practice, question period operated fairly well and became an important, well-established element in parliamentary life, but did not attract the amount of interest and attention that its framers had expected. The Assembly reserved Friday afternoon for question period. Friday afternoon proved to be a poor time to attract good attendance. Provincial MPs tended to leave Paris early for the weekend in their constituencies. In December 1963, the Assembly tried to remedy that by shifting to a mid-week morning with an hour added from the afternoon sitting to keep the same amount of time, but the Constitutional Council disallowed it on the grounds that it violated the constitutional provision that only "one sitting a week" shall be reserved for question period.[64]

The Conference of Presidents organized the question period. A representative of the government attended and was consulted, especially on the availability of ministers, but had no vote or official role in the deliberations or decisions. The basic organizing principle followed by the Conference was access to question time by the parties proportionate to their parliamentary size.[65]

Question period was a regular and moderately substantial part of parliamentary life. It continued at very much the same level throughout the period. An average of 18.3 sittings were devoted to questions each year. With two exceptions,[66] their number ranged between eighteen and twenty-three each year. About 11.2 percent of all floor time was devoted to question periods. Even so, only about one-fifth to one-half of the questions put down each year were answered and the fraction fell as low as one-tenth for oral questions with debate.

During the first three years, questions were answered individually.[67] Beginning in 1962, they were grouped by "themes." Over the next eight years, an average of 87 such questions were answered each year, distributed about equally between those followed by debate and those that were not. The average for those two categories rose to 99 per year for the following four years. A new category of "questions on current topics"[68] was introduced in April 1970 and averaged 134 questions per year thereafter.[69]

Question topics ranged widely. In concept, oral questions with debate dealt with the broadest topics, oral questions without debate were narrower, and questions on current topics were very precise and topical. Some typical questions are indicated by the following list:

Questions on Current Topics

Wine in the Common Market	French journalist jailed in Greece
The Nancy–Metz turnpike	Franco–Soviet cultural exchanges
China's admission to the UN	Strike by customs personnel
The stock market crisis	Extradition of Klaus Barbie
Indemnities for repatriates	Stevedores in Marseilles
Urban automobile traffic	Skyjacking
Credit restrictions	Family allocations
A cyclone in Reunion	Auxiliary teachers
	New towns

Oral questions Without Debate	*Oral Questions With Debate*
Pork	Employment problems
Loire Valley industrialization	Highway accidents
Responsibilities of local collectives	The state broadcasting system
The state telephone system	Forestry
Immigrant workers	War veterans
Indemnities for repatriates	Agricultural problems
Retirement pensions	Sports policy
The price of wine	Public health
Aid to Bengalis	Environmental policy
Amnesty for Algerian War offenders	Reform of the judiciary
Employment in the Douai region	
Drug abuse	
Housing policy	
The organization of the Paris region	

The dividing line among the categories was not at all distinct. Some topics appeared under all three headings. Some "current topics" were broader than the objects of oral questions. Some topics in all categories were perennials. Most questions seemed directed toward the special interests or views of a limited audience, but a few got general attention and had true importance. The April 1964 debate between Pompidou and Mitterrand on the powers of the premiership and the one on student unrest in May 1968 that helped fuel the disorders of that month were notable examples. Other major question-time debates dealt with foreign aid, education, social security, and the Ben Barka affair.[70]

If question period rarely throbbed with excitement, neither was it sterile and pointless. It provided a substantial shelter from which deputies from all parties, treated equally, could take potshots at the government beyond its control of the agenda. Only the will of Parliament prevented it being more.[71]

The government's control of the agenda was not so complete, then, as Article 48 suggests. The following percentages of the total sitting time of Parliament must be deducted to get a clear picture:

Annual budget	31.2
Censure debates	1.9
Assembly governance	1.7
Points of order	0.5
Complementary agenda	1.5
Oral questions	11.2
Total	48.0

Even within the remaining 52.0 percent of the agenda time, the government was limited by political and practical realities. It consulted closely with the Conference of Presidents, committee leaders, and the parliamentary groups of the majority as it worked out the agenda. Usually, they reached agreement. Sometimes, the government yielded to an adamant majority on the Conference. For instance, at the insistence of the Conference, it delayed consideration of the Fourth Plan for six months and it rescheduled a special session to enact the 1962 agricultural orientation law. Also, it "used fully its veto over the agenda only against a small number of important bills that—it believed—were of such a nature as to interfere seriously with the policy that it had the mission to determine and conduct." [72]

The government exercised that control enough that it moved its legislative program along the parliamentary tracks expeditiously. Its successful bills were enacted in less than a third of the time required for successful private members' bills.[73] That, of course, was the aim of the framers. Given the fact that Fourth Republic governments controlled the agenda as long as they retained a parliamentary majority and the fact that Fifth Republic governments lost their majority only once (October 1962), the effective difference resulting from the constitutional provisions is very difficult to identify and measure. At any rate, the fact of control is less important than the use made of it. Other constitutional provisions facilitated that use.

Executive Communications to Parliament

Four articles in the 1958 constitution mention communications by the Executive to Parliament explicitly and some others authorize or require that it take actions that imply such communications. Article 16 requires that the president of the Republic consult the presidents of the Assemblies before invoking emergency powers. Article 18 authorizes him to "communicate with the two Assemblies by messages that he has read for him." Article 31 provides that the members of the government "shall be heard [by the two Assemblies] when they ask to be." Article 49 authorizes the prime minister to present the program of the government to the National Assembly and a "declaration of general policy" to either Chamber.

Nothing comparable to Article 16 existed in the constitutions or practice of either of the two previous regimes. However, Article 18 had counterparts in both of those constitutions. The 1875 constitution authorized the president of the Republic to communicate with Parliament via messages countersigned and read for him by a minister.[74] MacMahon used that authority freely during his effort to wield real political power from the presidency. However, after his fall, it lapsed, except for the most routine and nonpolitical matters. When Millerand attempted to revive it in 1924, he was forced to resign within forty-eight hours.[75]

The 1946 constitution provided that the "president of the Republic communicates with Parliament by messages addressed to the National Assembly" (Art. 37) with the countersignature of the premier and a minister (Art. 38). President Vincent Auriol (1947–54) never sent such a message. Neither did René Coty (1954–58), except for his threat to resign if de Gaulle were not invested as premier, an important step in de Gaulle's return to office.[76]

Given the wishes of the framers of the 1958 constitution to enhance the authority of the president of the Republic, their retention of his message power is no surprise. It appeared in both of Debré's proposed constitutions of the early Fourth Republic[77] and at every step in the 1958 drafting process. However, the content did evolve somewhat. The first draft that Debré prepared in 1958 said: [78]

> The president of the Republic shall be able to have read before the two Chambers of Parliament communications which shall give rise to no discussion.

The principal issue discussed throughout the drafting process seems to have been whether he might read such messages in person. That possibility was written in four times and taken back out again each time. The CCC recommended its restoration. However, by that time the Cabinet was settled against it and the Council of State and Council of Ministers concurred. The final text differed in substance from the first draft only by the addition of a sentence: "If not in session, Parliament shall be convened especially for that purpose." [79]

The constitutional authorization for the members of the government to be heard by Parliament when they wished was traditional also. It appeared explicitly in both the 1875 and 1946 constitutions.[80] Neither constitution mentioned ministerial appearances before parliamentary committees.

In practice, ministers in both Republics exercised fully and freely their right to speak to Parliament and, upon invitation, to its committees.[81] Early in each session, the premier presented orally to Parliament a "ministerial declaration" outlining in a general and usually innocuous way the policies of the government.[82] Thereafter, the ministers played major roles in all important debates and appeared before committees on behalf of all government bills and concerning most private members' bills that were considered seriously. For instance, thirteen members of the government appeared a total of twenty times before nine committees of the Chamber of Deputies in 1932–33.[83] However, ministers were required to withdraw before the committees began to deliberate.[84]

The founders of the Fifth Republic had no apparent wish to change that situation. Debré did not mention it in his 1946 or 1948 drafts nor in his notes of the June 12 meeting of experts. Nor was it discussed in the June 13 or 23 meetings of the Interministerial Committee. However, it appeared in the first 1958 draft in these words: "The members of the government shall have access to the two Chambers and to the Committees. They must be heard when they ask to be." No such provision is in the second draft and the reference to committees was omitted in the third draft, "must" became "shall," and "Chambers" became "Assemblies." Thereafter, no changes were made, except that the Interministerial Committee added a sentence in late July: "They may be accompanied by government commissioners." The CCC did not discuss it. The Council of State recommended restoration of the reference to committees and Debré agreed, but the Interministerial Committee and the Council of Ministers did not.[85]

The "declaration of general policy" authorized by Article 49 was intended to serve as one of two possible bases for a vote of confidence in the government. That device had direct antecedents in the Third and Fourth Republic. The 1875 constitution was silent on that point, but, in practice, each new government made a declaration of general policy and that was followed by a vote of confidence. That practice was incorporated into the 1946 constitution (Art. 45). In both of those Republics, the procedure was invoked only at the time a government was being installed. Article 49 imposes no such limit.

That provision appeared first in Debré's second draft of 1958: "During the regular October session [of Parliament] the government shall make a declaration after which a debate may be held." In the June 30 draft that element was linked with the delegation of legislative authority: "Approval by the Assemblies of the general policy program presented to it by the prime minister shall include authorization for him to issue ordinances. . . . " When it reached the Cabinet, the link to ordinance making was broken and a connection was made to votes of confidence: "The prime minister shall be able to engage the responsibility of the government, after deliberation in the Council of Ministers, by asking for approval of its program or of a general policy declaration." The only substantive change made thereafter restricted that action to the National Assembly, rather than Parliament.[86]

The consultations required by Article 16 occurred only once. On April 23, 1961, President de Gaulle summoned Assembly President Jacques Chaban-Delmas and Senate President Gaston de Monnerville to the Elysée Palace separately and told them that he intended to invoke Article 16.[87] The consultations seem to have been mere formalities without political significance. Certainly, the conduct of neither the president nor of the Assemblies were influenced by them.

Article 18 was used more frequently. De Gaulle sent six messages to Parliament. Pompidou sent three. Four were formal greetings. De Gaulle sent greetings for the openings of the first and second legislatures. Pompidou did the same for the fifth. Also, Pompidou sent greetings to the Assemblies on the closing of the Spring 1969 session, the first after he was elected president.[88] Each presented and discussed the policies of the president in a very broad and general way. None had any specific legislative object.

The other five messages were specific. On April 25, 1961, de Gaulle informed the Assemblies that Article 16 of the constitution was in effect. The other four messages informed Parliament of the president's intention to hold referenda.[89] Three of them were simple formalities. The exception concerned the October 1962 referendum revising the presidential electoral system. That message precipitated the passage of the only successful motion of censure under a Gaullist president. Otherwise, the message power of the president had no real political significance.

The Article 31 requirement that members of the government be heard by the Assemblies when they ask was exercised in three principal ways. First, prime ministers made formal declarations of policy on behalf of their governments. Second, members of the government took part in Assembly debates. Third, members of the government met with Assembly committees.

The constitution required that formal declarations be discussed in the Council of Ministers before delivery. Usually, they dealt with major or general policies, especially at the beginning of a government's tenure. In those cases, sometimes they led to a sort of investiture debate and a motion of confidence or censure.

Formal declarations were made rather frequently—66 in fifteen years. The average of 4.4 per year concealed significant differences among the Legislatures. The marginals (I, III, V) averaged 5.9, 10.2, and 9.0 per year. The decisives averaged 1.9 and 3.4 per year. The governments seemed to use declarations like whips, cracking them more often for the skittish and cantankerous than for the congenial and obedient, another example of the effect of political factors on constitutional practice.

The declarations concerned a wide variety of matters, though a distinct pattern emerges. Comparison between them and the subjects of motions of censure is suggestive about the relative priorities and perceptions of strengths and weaknesses of government and opposition. Eleven declarations concerned general policy or the government's program. The others were concentrated heavily in three areas, as shown in Table 6.1. The government's declarations emphasized external affairs, while the opposition gave more attention to

Table 6.1. Subjects of Governmental Declarations and Motions of Censure, 1959-74

Subject	Governmental Declarations	Motions of Censure	Total
General policy or government program	11(16.7)	4(19.0)	15(17.2)
Foreign policy, Algeria, Community	23(34.8)	1(4.8)	24(27.6)
Economic and social matters	12(18.2)	8(38.1)	20(23.0)
Defense policy	1(1.5)	5(23.8)	6(6.9)
Education and youth	9(13.6)	1(4.8)	10(11.9)
Constitutional amendment	0(0.0)	1(4.8)	1(1.1)
Nationalized enterprises	1(1.5)	1(4.8)	2(2.3)
Others	9(13.6)	0(0.0)	9(10.3)
Total	66	21	87

economic and social matters and defense policy. Also, the government stressed education and youth more than did the opposition.

Governments issued declarations frequently during the Gaullist administrations. Yet, that device was not a Fifth Republic innovation. In fact, they were more numerous as the parliamentary majority was more similar to the Third and Fourth Republic situations. They do not seem to have had any significant impact on changing legislative–executive relations.

The Gaullists also used extensively the second mode of communication covered by Article 31, participation in Assembly debates. Most debates were led and managed by a member of the government. Under parliamentary rules, the sponsor of a bill—in the case of a government bill, a member of the government—began the general discussion immediately after the committee report or reports had opened the deliberation. Also, he closed the general debate. Then, he remained on the front bench during the discussion of amendments to present the government's position. He raised objections on the basis of the Assembly's rules or the constitution and called for votes as appropriate. Often, he negotiated with the committee *rapporteurs* and others to work out satisfactory compromises, especially on the details of bills.

Members of the government took part in an average of about 137 Assembly debates and other plenary-session transactions each year.[90] Annual averages did not vary significantly among legislatures.[91] Usually, a minister made at least two major statements and several minor interventions in a debate. Sometimes, the minor interventions numbered in the dozens over several sittings.[92]

Ministers addressed the Assembly about 80 to 90 hours per year. This consumed about one-fifth of the debate time of the chamber.[93] In addition, they spent several times as much time on the front bench.

Thus, despite the presidential aspects of the regime, the government behaved in a very parliamentarist manner on the floor of the Assembly. It was deeply involved in the minute-to-minute transactions of the legislative process. Its behavior resembled closely that of many Fourth Republic governments. Although it spoke with the assurance that it had more powerful constitutional support, its main advantage was its more reliable majority.

The third form of Article 31 communication flowed naturally from the floor role of the government. Members of the government appeared frequently before Assembly committees, mainly to support and defend bills that they would sponsor later in plenary debate. All such appearances resulted from invitations by the committees.

Ministers attended more than one-fourth of all committee meetings, 1,153 of the 4,205 meetings, 1958–74.[94] This was almost double the number of appearances by other outsiders (595). The amount of ministerial participation rose slightly late in the period. After holding steady in the first three legislatures with the number of appearances averaging 68.5, 64.9, and 69.6 annually, it rose to 91.6 in the fourth and 81.0 in the first year of the fifth. The percentage of meetings attended by ministers increased also. It had dropped from 29.5 to 25.2 to 23.1 then rose to 28.2 and 27.2.

Under established practice, a committee did not invite a minister to meet with it concerning a bill until it had held one or two preparatory meetings or, more frequently, a subcommittee-type "working group" of five or six members had done so. Usually, the working group was chaired by the prospective *rapporteur* for the bill. Often, the ministers met with working groups also, although they held no official status and made only oral reports to the committees.

The ministers' meetings with the committees and their subgroups were serious working sessions. Much of the legislative work of the regime was accomplished there. Out of the glare of publicity and before battle lines had hardened, constructive criticism, accommodation, and compromise were easier. Discussion focused on the bill—usually drafted or endorsed by the government—but most of the possible amendments were considered at that point, also, and the government indicated which ones it would accept. In the committees as on the floor, the relationship between the Executive and Parliament followed most of the forms and practices in effect before 1959. Again, the big change was in the character of the Assembly majority.

Governments made declarations of general policy under Article 49 six times: once each in 1959, 1962, 1969, 1970, 1972, and 1973. Each time, they "engaged" their "responsibility" and received decisive votes of confidence. The closest margin was 254 to 206 in 1973. The average margin was 249 votes. Thus, although that device was not used frequently, it manifested the government's strength on strategically chosen occasions. Without that reliable majority, however, it would have had little value.

Preliminary Steps in the Parliamentary Process

The Introduction of Bills

Article 39 of the 1958 constitution provides that "the right to initiate bills shall belong to the prime minister and to the members of Parliament concurrently." In the 1875 constitution it had belonged to the president of the Republic with the countersignature of a minister and two MPs.[95] In practice, the government was the sponsor of most legislation that had a reasonable prospect of enactment.[96]

The 1946 constitution transferred that right from the president to the prime minister (Art. 14). Prime ministers exercised it actively. In eleven years, 3,234 government bills were introduced, an average of 294 per year, compared to 11,037 private members' bills, 1,033 per year. Parliament enacted about 58.2 percent of the government bills and 7.1 percent of the private members' bills. Government bills constituted about 22.7 percent of all bills submitted and about 70.4 percent of the legislative output.[97]

The framers of the 1958 constitution decided very early to adhere to the Fourth Republic principle on this point. Debré's proposals of 1946 and 1948 stated or implied that the government and MPs would share the power of legislative initiative.[98] At the first meeting of his team of experts, he said, "It is the government which shall draft the bills," but it seems unlikely that he meant that private members' bills would not be permitted.[99] The first 1958 draft offered an option between having the president of the Republic or the prime minister share initiative with the MPs,[100] but the late June draft mentioned only the prime minister and MPs[101] and initiative was not included among the presidential powers in a draft of those articles prepared by Debré about the same time.[102] The next two drafts retained the wording of late June[103] and this was approved with only stylistic changes by the Cabinet on July 25.[104]

A CCC member proposed that the president of the Republic be given power of initiative, in view of the fact that "everything in the draft constitution makes the president of the Republic the true head of the Executive." However, the government's commissioner rejected that on the ground that "if he were that, the position of the prime minister would be untenable." Another CCC member asked if the government would accept a change from "prime minister" to "government." The commissioner responded that this would be weaker than the 1946 text and the CCC approved the provision as presented to it.[105] That wording was approved by the Cabinet, the Council of State, and the Council of Ministers, and appears in the final text.[106]

Gaullist governments availed themselves of that right freely. They introducd 1,391 bills, an average of 92.7 per year. They constituted about 29.0 percent of the total number of bills submitted.[107]

However, government bills weighed far heavier in the legislative scales than those figures suggest. First, they formed a larger proportion than that of new bills, because fewer government bills than private members' bills were reintroduced from the preceding legislature. For instance, 27 of the 74 (36.5 percent) private members' bills on agriculture submitted to the second and third legislatures were duplicates of bills submitted earlier.[108] Secondly, some private members' bills were duplicated by provisions of more general government bills that absorbed them. Third, government bills tended to be longer, more complex, and more important than private members' bills. The average government bill was about three times as long as its private counterpart.[109]

However, the dichotomy between government bills and private members' bills should be regarded cautiously. Some private members' bills were inspired or even drafted by the government, although that happened less often with bills than with amendments. On the other hand, some government bills were prompted by MPs, hoping thereby to improve the prospects of a pet measure. Others included provisions supplied by MPs who might have submitted them as separate bills otherwise.[110] Finally, some private members' amendments to government bills were really thinly disguised bills whose authors found more convenient or expedient to submit in that form.[111]

Of course, the most striking difference between the two categories of bills and the one that gave the government bills such importance was their greater success rate. About 84.8 percent of government bills became law under the

Gaullists, compared to 5.4 percent of the private members' bills. About 86.6 percent of the laws derived from government bills. Those rates differed significantly among legislatures. (See Table 6.2.)

Table 6.2. Success Rate of Bills, by Category and Legislature, 1959-73

| | Legislature | | | | | |
	I	*II*	*III*	*IV*	*1973*	*Total*
Number of government bills introduced	362	421	100	424	91	1,398
Number of government bills passed	271	382	69	406	57	1,185
Percentage of government bills passed	74.9	90.7	69.0	95.8	62.6	84.8
Number of private members' bills introduced	612	674	427	765	622	3,100
Number of private members' bills passed	20	55	18	79	14	186
Percentage of private members' bills passed	0.3	8.2	4.2	10.3	2.2	0.6
Total number of bills introduced	974	1,095	527	1,189	713	4,498
Total number of bills passed	291	437	87	485	71	1,371
Percentage of all bills passed	29.9	39.9	16.5	40.8	10.0	30.5
Percentage of government bills among bills introduced	37.2	38.4	19.0	35.7	12.8	31.1
Percentage of government bills among bills passed	93.1	87.4	79.3	83.7	80.2	86.4
Number of government bills passed per year	72.2	80.4	63.7	86.9	57.0	77.7
Number of private members' bills passed per year	5.3	11.6	16.7	16.9	14.0	12.2
Number of bills passed per year	77.5	92.0	80.4	103.8	71.0	89.9

As Table 6.2 shows, government bills fared better in legislatures with decisive majorities. So did private members' bills. The existence of a homogeneous parliamentary majority favored both the bills that the government sponsored and those that it tolerated. The effect of the political character of the majority on the constitutional authority was clearly discernible.

The Exclusion of Private Members' Bills

Under Articles 40 and 41 of the 1958 constitution, the government can prevent the receipt of private members' bills on the grounds that they would increase expenditures, reduce revenues, or trespass in the domain of regulation.

This was a constitutional innovation. Neither preceding constitution contained such a provision.

In the early Third Republic, neither parliamentary rules nor practice impinged seriously on the MPs' powers in that area and often the governments' financial projects were butchered in Parliament. However, in 1910 and again in 1920, the Chamber revised its rules to restrict the power of the deputies to amend the governments' budgets. In 1934, the restrictions were extended by law to bar private members' bills or amendments "susceptible of directly or indirectly increasing public expenditures or of diminishing treasury receipts" unless they also provided the means for closing the gap.[112] In practice, the governments increased their ability to prevent destructive parliamentary assaults on their budgets gradually during the Third Republic, but they remained highly vulnerable, especially if they lacked a solid majority or if an election were approaching.

The 1946 constitution expressly authorized deputies to propose expenditures, except "during the discussion of the budget, the estimates or supplementary budgets" (Art. 17). However, parliamentary rules and, after 1949, legislation weakened that authorization somewhat. The situation became similar to the Third Republic after 1934.[113] Still, effective application of the restrictions required a resolute government, a cooperative Finance Committee, and a reliable majority, conditions that were not always present.

Provisions to strengthen the government in that respect appeared in the drafts of the 1958 constitution from the outset. The first draft had these clauses:

> ... the members of Parliament shall not be able to submit any bill or present any amendment concerning: (1st variant) regulatory matters, (2nd variant) the matters having been the object of a transfer of competence to the government in the conditions provided for in Article D7 above.

> Bills and amendments formulated by members of Parliament shall not be receivable if their adoption would have the consequence of reducing revenues or increasing the expenditures of the State.

The second and third drafts retained the second of those clauses, but the first of them was omitted from the second draft and appeared in this form in the third draft:

> (1st variant): Bills presented by members of Parliament shall not be receivable if they concern matters within the competence of the government. ...
> (2nd variant): The matters covered by Article 2 shall remain within the competence of the regulatory power even if they have been the object of measures taken in legislative form.

They were combined in one article again in the drafts that were approved by the Interministerial Committee, the Cabinet, and the CCC. The Council of State separated them into two articles again and gave them their definitive phrasing. The desirability of these provisions seems to have been accepted throughout the drafting process, despite their constitutional novelty, though their form was a matter of some deliberation.[114]

The Gaullist governments used those provisions freely, though with declining frequency. Whether the decrease resulted from greater caution by the deputies or greater tolerance by the governments is not clear. In any case, the change was dramatic, as Table 6.3 shows. Indeed, the rate declined from 33.1 percent in 1959 to 2.2 percent in 1971–73.[115]

Table 6.3. Bills Declared Out of Order, 1959-73

	Legislature					
	I	*II*	*III*	*IV*	*1973*	*Total*
Number of private members' bills introduced	771	730	479	1,118	593	3,691
Number of private members' bills out of order	177	89	60	47	13	386
Percentage of private members' bills out of order	22.8	12.2	12.5	4.2	2.2	10.5
Annual average, number of bills out of order	47.2	20.9	55.4	11.1	13.0	25.3

The value of this constitutional device seems clear. The decline in the number of out-of-order bills suggests that it trained the MPs in the proper use of their right to introduce bills. The availability of the Constitutional Council to assist at enforcement meant that the government did not depend solely on the docility of its majority. Nevertheless, significant differences between marginal and decisive legislatures remained. Marginal legislatures I and III averaged 47.2 and 55.4 out-of-order bills per year. Decisive legislatures II and IV averaged 20.9 and 11.1. The first year of the marginal Vth was the only exception, with 13 out-of-order bills. Even here, with one of the most successful constitutional provisions, politics still counted heavily.

Referral to Special Committees

Under the 1958 constitution, the government shares with the Assembly the right to require that a bill be "sent for consideration to a committee especially appointed for that purpose" (Art. 43). Otherwise, it would go to one of the six subject-matter standing committees. This departs from constitutional precedent.

Neither the 1875 nor the 1946 constitution mentioned special committees. However, the parliamentary rules and customs of the early Third Republic provided that the only committees to review bills were special committees. Practice evolved gradually toward the use of standing committees and, in 1902, the Chamber established a standing committee system to consider bills and used special committees for unusually complex special assignments of oversight or inquiry.[116] The same general arrangements prevailed in the Fourth Republic.[117]

Despite the long eclipse of the special committee system, Debré's 1946 proposal provided that bills might be sent to "special and temporary committees" and by 1948 he was so disgusted with the powerful standing committees of the Fourth Republic that he wanted to eliminate all but one standing committee, for the budget. Various nonparliamentary or quasi-parliamentary "councils" would review various categories of bills and residual private members' bills would go to special committees. In 1958, he proposed to the first meeting of the team of experts that all but the major parliamentary committees be abolished, but he did not mention special committees. The late June draft contained a provision that "any bill may be sent to a specially constituted committee for a recommendation before discussion." Special committees were not mentioned in the next two drafts, but the one that was approved by the Cabinet on July 23–26 stipulated that

> bills shall be sent, at the request of the government or the Assembly, to be examined by committees especially designated for that purpose. Bills for which no such request has been made shall be sent to one of the standing committees of which the number shall be limited to six in each Assembly.

The CCC proposed, with the concurrence of the government's commissioner, that the number of standing committees be unlimited and that special committees be used only for bills that did not lie entirely within the competence of one of them. The Cabinet rejected the advice of the CCC and the Council of State concurred.[118]

Desipte that insistence, the Gaullists used few special committees. "All authors and politicians agree that the framers regarded the special committees as the rule and resort to standing committees as the exception." [119] Yet, Gaullist governments requested only ten such committees and the Assembly itself requested another twenty-nine. They fall into no pattern by legislatures. The government requested four in the first legislature, one in the second, none in the third, three in the fourth, and two in 1973.

Thirteen government bills were referred to them. Nine were enacted in the same session, three were enacted in later sessions, and one was never enacted. The casualty was a 1970 bill on establishing corporations to invest in agricultural land. Another bill, on farm tenancy, that went to the same committee was defeated also, but went to another special committee in 1973 and was enacted. Two other agricultural bills that went to that same 1970 committee were adopted without delay. Two "orientation" bills (for artisanry and for commerce) were submitted to separate special committees eleven days before session end in Fall 1972, died there, were exhumed in 1973, combined in a single bill, sent to another special committee, and enacted after a grueling battle.[120]

Perhaps the most important bill sent by the government to a special committee was the Complementary Law for Agricultural Orientation of 1962. This was an omnibus reform bill to complement the Agricultural Orientation Law of 1960. The sponsoring minister, Edgard Pisani, expected it to be controversial, so deliberately asked for more than he needed and made a show of intransigence. In the end, he accepted most of the committee's changes and the bill passed.[121]

The government sent six other bills to special committees. They were social welfare, 1959; three cooperation agreements with Mali and Madagascar, 1960; pre-emption authorization for urban zoning, 1961; and regulation of apartment construction enterprises after the Garantie foncière scandal, 1963. All were adopted within the session.

Several considerations explain the relatively slight use of special committees. For one thing, they had a comparatively low success rate, although this resulted in part from the controversial nature of the legislation referred to them. Also, special committees were cumbersome. Unlike standing committees, they had to be assembled from scratch and organized. Their members were unaccustomed to working together or with the minister and were unknown quantities to him. They were alien elements in a functioning system.

Chiefly, however, they were not used because they were not needed. They had been designed as alternatives to powerful and hostile standing committees. In fact, because of the emergence of a homogeneous majority in the Assembly, the governments and committees developed generally comfortable working relationships and still another constitutional innovation of the Fifth Republic proved to be unnecessary because of the political change.

The Use of the Government's Bill as the Basis of Deliberation

The 1958 constitution (Art. 42) requires that the Assembly use the government's version of any of its bills as the basis of floor consideration. Under the Third and Fourth Republics, the version of the principal parliamentary committee reporting on it had served that purpose. That requirement was not stated in either constitution but was included in the parliamentary rules. Invariably, practice conformed.

Reversal of that system seems to have been accepted throughout the drafting process in 1958, despite its long establishment and the absence of concern on that point in Debré's 1946 and 1948 proposals. Debré included in his initial presentation to the team of experts the statement that "Parliament must discuss the government bill." A provision to that effect appeared in the late June draft and remained essentially unchanged through the rest of the process.[122] Even the CCC raised no objection.[123]

That unanimity survived intact in practice. The records of the Assembly disclose no instance of the government waiving that right. Indeed, it does not appear to be constitutionally possible. However, probably most government bills that came up on the floor contained provisions that were dead but not buried. The government had agreed to changes, but could not give them effect until the bill was on the floor. Also, without a homogeneous majority, the government bill would melt quickly in the noonday sun of heated opposition and the initial advantage would amount to little.

Nevertheless, the constitutional requirement remained an asset to the government. To be able to lay the basis for discussion was to take a large step toward winning it. Also, the government was better assured of having a coherent document to work with. In both respects, this provision improved the position of the government compared to the previous Republics.

The Amending Process

The Right to Submit Amendments

Under Article 44 of the 1958 constitution, the government shares with the MPs the right to propose amendments to bills. This was not so in the Third and Fourth Republics. Although their constitutions were silent on that point, parliamentary rules and practice reserved to private members the right to propose amendments. Of course, governments could and did arrange for friendly members to do so on their behalf.[124]

The 1958 constitution brought that practice out of the closet. The first draft included the provision that "the members of Parliament and the government shall dispose of the right of amendment." It survived verbatim through all drafting stages and was not even mentioned by the CCC or the Council of State.[125]

Gaullist governments used that right freely. They submitted more than 3,000 amendments, about 200 per year.[126] The adoption rate for their amendments was high, about 84.2 percent.[127] Nevertheless, only about 22.2 percent of all amendments adopted were the governments'.[128] However, a substantial proportion of the committee amendments that were adopted (3,718 in 1967–73) had been worked out with the government and had its approval.[129] The same was true of a lesser share of the 1,138 succssful private members' amendments.[130] Conversely, no doubt, some government amendments had a parliamentary inspiration.

Comparisons among legislatures have limited value because of the unavailability of statistics for the first two legislatures. Nevertheless, differences among legislatures III and IV and the first year of V are suggestive. (See Table 6.4.)

Substantially more amendments of all origins were adopted per year in the decisive IVth legislature than in the marginal IIIrd or Vth. Also, the committee share of successful amendments was higher and the private members' lower in the IVth. This suggests that the government accepted amendments more freely and worked more fully and seriously with the committees when it was confident of its majority.

Differences of intent among the categories of amendments should be kept in mind. Invariably, government amendments were intended for adoption. So were most committee proposals, though some were propagandistic or bargaining tokens. However, a very large share of the private members' amendments were not intended for adoption. They were duplicates of other amendments and intended mainly to express the author's sentiments; or they were legislative blackmail designed to extract some sort of price from the government in return for a timely withdrawal;[131] or they provided vehicles for questioning ministers, calling attention publicly to a problem, complaint, criticism, or ambition. Finally, of course, some private members' amendments did have legislative intent.[132]

Table 6.4. Success Rate of Proposed Amendments by Category and Legislature, 1967-73

			Legislature		
		III		*IV*	*1973*
	Per yr.	*Tot.*	*Per yr.*	*Tot.*	*Tot.*
Government amendments submitted	149.6	162	279.8	1,329	143
Government amendments adopted	133.9	145	232.4	1,104	122
Percentage of government amendments adopted		89.5		83.1	85.3
Committee amendments submitted	449.7	487	929.3	4,414	589
Committee amendments adopted	333.3	361	640.2	3,041	316
Percentage of committee amendments adopted		74.1		68.9	53.7
Private members' amendments submitted	456.1	494	1,016.6	4,829	887
Private members' amendments adopted	105.3	114	171.4	814	155
Percentage of private members' amendments adopted		23.1		16.9	17.5
Total number of amendments adopted		620		4,959	593
Government amendments adopted as percentage of total		23.4		22.3	20.6
Committee amendments adopted as percentage of total		58.2		61.3	53.3
Private members' amendments as percentage of total		18.4		16.4	26.1

The government introduced amendments for three main purposes. First, it had decided to permit enactment of some private members' bills, provided they were revised in certain respects, and it submitted amendments to that effect. Second, it responded constructively to criticism of its own bills. Third, it implemented compromises or concessions to stave off defeat of its bills or corrosive confrontations.

The right of governments to introduce amendments, at least indirectly, was not new in 1959. Nor did it guarantee their adoption. This depended largely on the character of the parliamentary majority. Moreover, it was facilitated by another constitutional device, the "blocked vote."

The "Blocked Vote"

Under Article 44 of the 1958 constitution, the government can require that the Assembly "take a single vote on all or part of the bill under discussion, retaining only the amendments proposed or accepted by the government." This is commonly called the "blocked vote." It introduced a new concept into the French constitution.

The constitutions of neither preceding Republic included such a provision. However, practice developed a functional equivalent. Governments sometimes posed elaborate motions of confidence that had the same effect. They gathered up in one motion the various positions on amendments that they considered essential to the survival of the government's program and required that the Assembly make its commitment on that basis. For instance, in July 1957, Premier Maurice Bourgès-Maunoury posed and passed this motion of confidence:

> for the adoption . . . of Arts. 2, 3, 4, and 5 in the text of Report No. 5542 as modified with respect to Art. 2 by Amendment No. 22 of M. Mérigonde and against every other motion, every request for separation, and all other amendments and sub-amendments of a nature to modify the import of the date of implementation, and for the adoption of the bill as a whole.[133]

Premier Félix Gaillard provided a similar example five months later:[134]

> For adoption of Arts. 1 to 13 of the budget bill for 1958 as presented in the reports . . . of the Finance Committee, modified and completed: 1. By taking under consideration and adopting Arts. 2 and 6 of the government's bill . . .: 2. By Amendment No. 10 of M. Gaumont to Art. 7; 3. By Amendment No. 9 of M. Max Brusset to Art. 8; Against any other motion and all other amendments; And for adoption of the bill as a whole.

The blocked vote did not appear in Debré's 1946 or 1948 draft proposals, nor was it mentioned in the preliminary discussions of 1958. It appeared first in the June 30 draft: "The government may, at any moment, request a single balloting on all or part of the bill under discussion, retaining only the amendments that it proposes or accepts." That text, with no substantive changes, survived the early stages of drafting, but the CCC objected to it on the grounds that it "abolishes purely and simply the right of amendment." [135] The government and the Council of State rejected the CCC advice and the provision entered the final draft basically as it had first appeared.[136]

The blocked vote was one of the most frequently and effectively used constitutional devices to provide executive leadership of Parliament. The government invoked blocked voting 125 times through 1973.[137] Frequency varied considerably among legislatures, though not in the usual pattern. The annual averages for the legislatures were: I, 6.1; II, 16.0; III, 16.6; IV, 2.7; 1973, 3. De Gaulle's governments used them much more frequently than did Pompidou's—11.0 per year, compared to 2.2.

The government was defeated on blocked votes only six times. Five defeats were in marginal legislatures: one in I, three in III, and one in 1973. One was in the decisive IV legislature. The success percentages were 95.7, 100.0, 66.7, 92.3, and 66.7.[138]

The blocked vote was especially important in protecting the annual budget. Forty-five (36.0 percent) of all blocked votes came on annual budgets. Every Gaullist annual budget, except 1961, 1970, and 1971, benefited from at least one blocked vote. Another seven blocked votes came on supplemental budgets and at least twenty other blocked votes concerned other financial measures, so three-fifths (59.2 percent) of all blocked votes concerned state finance.

Blocked votes were used on other important bills, also. The agricultural reform legislation of the early 1960s was the object of ten blocked votes. Others assisted creation of special state security courts during the Algerian War, the 1964 ORTF statute, and the Debré law on aid to church schools.

The full force of the blocked vote was exerted rarely. It was used to exclude all amendments only twelve times and was used on private members' bills only four times. Even so, deputies complained frequently about its "abuse" and, on at least one occasion, rebelled against it by refusing to vote for a government bill they favored.[139]

The blocked vote was new as a constitutional device under the Gaullists, but was an innovation in practice only to the extent that it no longer required a vote of confidence. Of course, the constitutional sanction legitimized and strengthened it. An even greater strengthener, however, was the homogeneous majority. Without it, the blocked vote might well have been a dangerous and unreliable weapon.

Excluding Amendments

The 1958 constitution permits governments to exclude certain kinds of amendments from parliamentary consideration unless challenged successfully before the Constitutional Council. Article 40 forbids any amendment whose "adoption would have the consequence of reducing public revenues or creating or increasing public expenditures." Article 41 does the same for any amendment which "is not in the domain of law or is contrary to a delegation accorded by virtue of Article 38" and, under Article 44, the government can exclude any amendment "which was not submitted previously to the Committee."

The Article 40 provision is another example of a parliamentary rule developing into a constitutional provision. The Third Republic constitution gave the government no authority to exclude amendments. However, by 1900, the abuses in the financial area had become so troublesome that parliamentary rules were developed gradually to provide some protection against spendthrift MPs.[140] By the 1930s, the pertinent rule read: "Every amendment or additional article presented during the course of the discussion shall be referred without question to a committee for examination if such a request is made by a minister. . . ." [141] Also, the Finance Act of 1934 forbade amendments "susceptible of directly or indirectly increasing public expenditures or of reducing treasury receipts" except "within the context" of government finance bills.[142]

The Fourth Republic constitution included a provision (Art. 17) that could be invoked by a minister, forbidding deputies from submitting amendments "entailing an increase in the expenditure prescribed or creating new expenditure . . . during the discussion of financial bills." If the government objected on that basis, the amendment was made a separate bill and referred to committee. No such bill was ever reported out of committee.[143]

The Article 41 provision (concerning amendments in the domain of regulation) was entirely new. The Executive in both the Third and Fourth Republics had rule-making authority under laws, but could not exclude Parliament from enacting laws in the areas covered by that authority. Nor was Parliament prevented, legally or constitutionally, from recovering law-making authority that it had delegated. Therefore, it would have been quite inappropriate for the government to be able to exclude amendments of rule-making character or that would have trespassed on the territory of a previous delegation.

Article 44 has precedent. In the Third Republic, the government had authority under parliamentary rules to exclude from floor consideration any amendment not reviewed previously by the committee reporting on the bill.[144] That right was simply made constitutional in 1958.

Proposals to empower the government to exclude amendments appeared throughout the 1958 drafting process. Debré's 1948 proposal denied MPs "the initiative for expenditures." His first 1958 draft included a ban on amendments (1) increasing expenditures, (2) reducing revenues, (3) trespassing in the rule making or (4) delegated legislation areas. His second draft covered only (1) and (2), but all four appeared in the next three drafts. The right of the government to exclude amendments not reviewed by a committee did not appear until the July 25 draft.[145]

The CCC discussed all these provisions at length. It accepted the first two as, in the words of the government's commissioner, "being intended purely and simply to constitutionalize the *loi des maxima*" of the Fourth Republic. A proposed amendment to delete (3) was defeated in the CCC by voice vote. The Council of State approved of their substance also, but divided them into three articles and reworded portions. The Council of Ministers accepted the Council of State version.[146]

Gaullist governments freely used their power to exclude amendments. They declared 1,484 amendments out of order at the time they were submitted and 212 others later in the process, totaling 1,696 or 138.4 per year, about 6.6 percent of all amendments submitted. Such declarations occurred about 50 percent more often in marginal legislatures: I, 8.6 percent; II, 5.3 percent; III, 7.6 percent; IV, 5.3 percent; 1973, 11.1 percent. Private members' amendments were hit harder than committee amendments, 696 (11.2 percent) of the former and 111 (2.0 percent) of the latter having been excluded in the 1967–73 period.[147]

MPs from groups in the majority suffered the least from out-of-order declarations, although the differences were surprisingly small. The UDR and Independent Republicans lost 9.2 and 9.1 percent, respectively, compared to 14.6 and 11.9 for the Communists and Socialists. Centrists fared most poorly, with 15.6 percent. Majority deputies submitted substantially more amendments that the Left opposition, so the losses in absolute numbers were about the same—290 to 297.

By far the most frequent grounds for excluding amendments was that it violated Article 40 (revenues). That accounted for 1,662 of the 1,696 total (98.0 percent). Of the remainder, 25 were charged under Article 41 (regulatory) and 9 under Article 41 (bypassed committee).

Although declarations of nonreceivability were used often and with effect, that success depended on a tolerant majority and a chamber president disinclined to challenge the government in the Constitutional Council. The chamber could have defeated the government's bills when its amendments were excluded. The president could have tied up the government's legislative business by requiring Constitutional Council rulings. Also, in all likelihood, most government's declarations were well founded on constitutional grounds, which, in turn, were accepted as desirable by most deputies.[148]

Facilitating the Enactment of Bills

Declarations of Urgency

In case armament is not sufficient protection for government bills against parliamentary ambush, the constitution provides a high-speed forward gear, called a "declaration of urgency" (Art. 45). This procedure had existed in parliamentary rules since the early Third Republic and had been referred to (though not spelled out) in the 1946 constitution (Art. 20). Such declarations had been exceptional under the Third Republic, but, at times in the early years of the Fourth Republic, more urgent than ordianry bills were enacted. Overuse of that device led to restrictions and it became exceptional again, though still viable.[149]

Declarations of urgency in the 1958 constitution are part of the procedure through which the two Chambers and the government seek agreement on the text of a bill, especially by using a Joint Conference Committee (JCC). In particular, an "urgent" government bill may go to a JCC after only one reading in each chamber rather than two.

That provision appeared first in the late June draft, although a similar device had been mentioned in Debré's 1948 proposal. It survived with only stylistic changes through all phases of the drafting process. Although the CCC proposed changes in Art. 45, it accepted the reference to urgency. So did the Council of State and the Council of Ministers.[150]

Declarations were used rather frequently by Gaullist governments, the rate varying considerably among legislatures. They totaled 131, an average of 8.6 per year. Table 6.5 shows the distribution among legislatures.

Table 6.5. Declarations of Urgency, by Legislature, 1959-73

	Legislatures					
	I	*II*	*III*	*IV*	*1973*	*Tot.*
Number of declarations of urgency	5	39	5	74	8	131
Annual average number of declarations of urgency	1.33	9.18	4.62	15.85	8.00	8.59
Declarations of urgency as percentage of government bills adopted	1.8	10.2	7.7	15.5	13.8	11.1

Typically, I and III form one set, II and IV form another, and 1973 rides in between. Declarations of urgency were used more frequently with decisive than with marginal Gaullist majorities. In this case, however, there appeared a trend toward greater usage. Each valley was higher than the previous valley, each peak was higher than its predecessor.

Success may account for its popularity. No "urgent" bill failed of adoption in the same session. Nearly half (48.0 percent) were adopted in form acceptable to the government on the next reading.[151]

Declarations of urgency were used mainly for major, controversial legislation.[152] They were never used for bills ratifying international agreements. Article 47 of the constitution forbids their use for the annual budget, nor were they used for any supplemental or Algerian budget. Among typical objects of "urgent" bills were: complement to agricultural orientation law, the Court of State Security, public service strikes, ORTF statutes, military program law, reform of the added-value tax, amnesty, the 1967 special powers authorization, higher education orientation law, social security ordinance ratification, the new rural code, trade union rights, rent control, the authority of local government, military conscription, local tax reform, and improvement of working conditions.

By itself, a declaration of urgency did little more than announce the serious intentions of the government. An incohesive or hostile majority would not have been intimidated so easily. However, it also opened the way to the use of another procedural innovation of the Fifth Republic, the Joint Conference Committee (JCC).[153]

Joint Conference Committee

Article 45 of 1958 constitution established the JCC as a means to expedite or shorten the shuttle of a bill between the two chambers. The government can require referral to a JCC whether or not it has declared the bill urgent. The JCC is one of the clearest examples of a constitutional innovation in the legislative–executive relations of the Fifth Republic.

Neither the 1875 nor the 1946 constitution contained such a device. One had existed in the parliamentary rules of the Third Republic, but had been rarely used and did not survive into the Fourth Republic.[154] Instead, a bill "shuttled" back and forth between the chambers indefinitely until they agreed on a version. The shuttle was unlimited in the Third Republic, but changes were made to hasten its conclusion in the Fourth Republic

Already in 1948, Debré had proposed a "Joint Commitee" to conclude shuttles. Unlike the 1958 version, it did not represent the Chambers in parity. Rather, the Assembly had three-fifths and the Upper Chamber two-fifths of the membership. A similar committee appeared in the early 1958 drafts and the parity principle was introduced in the July 25 version.[155] When the CCC reviewed that article, Debré made one of his few direct interventions in its deliberations. He called the JCC "in its principle, a return to the system initially imagined in 1875" and compared it to similar devices in the United States and West Germany. He pointed out that, unlike the Third Republic version, it was at the disposal of the government rather than the chambers. Although the CCC proposed some changes of detail, it accepted the concept.[156] The government accepted some of those suggestions, but rejected others that would have required it to share the right of referral. The Council of State recommended only changes of style and the government retained the Council of State text.[157]

Article 45 provides the government with three routes to avoid a parliamentary impasse: (1) it can allow the shuttle to continue indefinitely, pending resolution of the differences; (2) if two readings in each Chamber (one reading each, if "urgent") fail to produce agreement on an acceptable text, it can refer it to the Chambers for approval; (3) if route 2 is followed unsuccessfully, it can ask for another reading by each Chamber and, if no acceptable text emerges yet, it can require the Assembly to decide, using the JCC version or the Assembly's last version with such Senate amendments as the government accepts.

Each Chamber appoints seven members to each JCC. In the first legislature, the Assembly sent delegations representing the parliamentary groups proportionately. Later, when the Gaullists acquired a homogeneous majority, it sent homogeneous delegations most of the time. Occasionally, it included an opposition member to bring pressure on the government. Such a move produced concessions on the 1964 added-value tax reform and the 1963 Court of State Security bill.

The government has no formal role in the JCC. Initially, it held aloof, its members attending meetings only as observers and counsel. Later, it became involved much more actively. Its members spoke officially to fourteen of the forty-nine JCCs in the second legislature and joined in drafting acceptable texts. For instance, the Court of State Security and medical insurance for farmers bills were drafted that way.[158]

In legislatures III and IV, formal appearances by the government decreased, but informal collaboration continued. Ministers spoke to none of the thirteen JCCs of legislature III and to eight of the seventy-five of legislature IV. On the other hand, informal preparatory meetings between the sponsoring minister and *rapporteurs* of the two chambers became standard procedure.[159]

Gaullist governments required 160 JCCs. They were little-used in the first legislature, 13 (3.5 per year). Thereafter, usage was fairly stable: II, 49 (11.5); III, 13 (12.0); IV, 75 (16.1); 1973, 10.

As time passed, JCCs tended to be combined with declarations of urgency. The percentages of such combinations rose, by legislature, from 15.4 to 36.7 to 38.5 to 46.6 to 50.0. A similar trend appeared in the weight of JCC bills in the total legislative output. The percentage rose from 4.4 to 11.2 to 13.8 to 15.5, but dropped to 13.9 in 1973.

Some of the most important measures of the Fifth Republic passed through JCCs. They included all annual budgets, the agricultural reforms of the early 1960s, two ORTF statutes, creation of the nuclear striking force, creation of the Paris Region, repatriation from Algeria, the Court of State Security, regulation of public service strikes, the Fifth Plan, added-value tax reform, the higher education orientation law, rural code reform, trade union rights, creation of the system of regions, the urban land-use orientation law, repatriates indemnification, and creation of the office of *médiateur*.[160]

The JCCs worked very well. They failed to produce a bill in only 24 of 160 cases (15.6 percent). In 23 of those failures, the government obtained final enactment of the Assembly's bill and in one case it used the Senate's version.

When the JCC agreed (136 times), both chambers usually accepted its text, either verbatim (72 times) or as amended by the Assembly (32) or by the Senate (1). Thirty times the Assembly adopted the JCC bill, either verbatim (11) or with its own amendments (19), but the Senate rejected it. The reverse was never true and only once did both chambers reject a bill (the conscientious objectors bill of 1963). When the Assembly accepted and the Senate did not, the government used its power to select the bill for final decision to obtain enactment of the Assembly version intact twenty-seven times and with Senate amendments three times. Also, it obtained enactment of the Assembly version of the conscientious objectors bill intact. In these 160 cases, then, the JCC version was adopted intact 45.0 percent of the time, the Assembly version was adopted intact 51.9 percent, and Senate amendments were accepted 3.1 percent.

The 1966 bill reforming corporation law is an extreme example of the JCC in operation, but is, nevertheless, suggestive of its character of accommodation. The Senate considered 533 amendments to the Assembly's bill, including 72 proposed by the government. It adopted 487, including 58 of the government's. The Assembly accepted 378 of those. The JCC considered 44 more, accepted 29, defeated 10, and incorporated five in compromises.

The JCC system carried further the reforms of the "shuttle" that had been made by the Fourth Republic. It worked well and was used successfully for many important bills. However, this resulted largely from a circumstance contrary to the expectations of its inventors, the presence of a cohesive parliamentary majority.

Passive Enactment

When parliamentary deliberation ends and voting begins, the government has other constitutional weapons at its disposal. Under Article 49, it can "engage its responsibility" on passage of a bill. If it does, the bill is adopted automatically and passively, without a vote, unless a motion of censure is submitted within twenty-four hours and adopted by an absolute majority of the deputies.

This was a clear innovation. No such device had existed in law or practice in either preceding Republic. However, occasionally in the Fourth Republic, Parliament had provided in laws that certain administrative texts issued in pursuance of them would have the effect of law if submitted to Parliament, unless Parliament renounced them explicitly before specified deadlines.[161]

Passive enactment was not a feature of Debré's proposals of 1946 and 1948 nor did it appear in the first six drafts of 1958. However, the draft reviewed by the Cabinet on July 25 contained this clause:

> When, after deliberation by the Council of Ministers, the prime minister engages its responsibility on the vote of a bill, it shall be considered to be adopted if, within three days, no motion of censure has been passed.

That version was reviewed, discussed at length, and approved by the CCC and, with two minor changes, by the Council of State. In the final review by the Cabinet, significant changes were made. The time period was reduced to twenty-four hours and a phrase was added to provide that only the votes favorable to a censure motion would be counted. This meant that negative votes and abstentions could not be distinguished from each other.[162]

The "responsibility" of Gaullist governments was "engaged" ten times on the adoption of a government bill (the 1960 budget; the military program law of 1960, three times; the supplemental budget for the nuclear striking force, three; special powers for economic and social legislation, three). Motions of censure were submitted eight times. The only omissions were two of the readings on the nuclear striking force. No motion of censure passed. Thus, four government bills were adopted passively.[163]

Passive enactment was not very useful. Its greatest accomplishment was to ensure the creation of the nuclear striking force. The 1960 budget did not need its help. The 1967 special powers were largely overridden later. By the time of Pompidou's death, it had not been invoked for seven years.

Enactment of the Annual Budget by Ordinance

If the National Assembly fails to act on the annual budget within forty days after receiving it, the government may refer it to the Senate, which must act within fifteen days. If Parliament fails to complete the action on it within seventy days, the government may enact it by ordinance (Art. 47).

The 1875 constitution contained no reference to the budget, nor did parliamentary rules or practice establish such a procedure. However, a constitutional revision proposal by the Doumergue government in 1934 would have authorized the government to enact the budget by decree if Parliament did not pass it by December 31.[164]

The Fourth Republic constitution did mention the budget explicitly, but not any sort of deadline or executive enactment. However, a 1956 decree, authorized by Parliament, estabished a procedure that moved in that direction. If the budget were submitted by November 1 but not enacted by January 1, the government could make certain kinds of appropriations by decree, subject to veto by the Assembly's Finance Committee.[165]

Executive enactment of the budget was not mentioned in Debré's proposals of 1946 and 1948, but appeared in his first version of 1958. It survived through all later drafts with only minor changes. The CCC approved the principle, even referring favorably to the 1956 decree, but proposed substantial editorial changes. So did the Council of State. The government accepted them and made a final change, revising deadlines slightly.[166]

This procedure was never used during the Gaullist period because Parliament always acted on the budget by the constitutional deadline.

Last Resorts

New Deliberations

Under Article 10 of the 1958 constitution, the president of the Republic can request "a new deliberation of a law or of any of its articles" within fifteen days after it has been transmitted to him upon "final adoption." The request cannot be refused. This provision is a sort of last resort by which a president can delay and possibly prevent a bill he opposes from taking effect.[167] The constitutions of the Third[168] and Fourth[169] Republics included similar provisions. No Third Republic president ever asked for a new deliberation.[170] Fourth Republic presidents did so twelve times, several times killing bills.[171]

Debré included "new deliberation" authority in the draft of articles on the presidency that he prepared for de Gaulle in early June 1958. It breezed through the drafting process without substantive change. The CCC did not even discuss it and the Council of State and Council of Ministers accepted it.[172]

Neither de Gaulle nor Pompidou ever used that authority, nor did they need it. The other defenses had held. No law was passed that they considered unacceptable.

Referrals to the Constitutional Council

Article 61 of the 1958 constitution authorized the president of the Republic, the prime minister, and the presidents of each Chamber to refer bills that had been passed by Parliament to the Constitutional Council to be reviewed for constitutionality before being promulgated.[173] Because as the Constitutional Council was a new institution, the previous Republic had not estabished comparable authority. However, a "Constitutional Committee" had been created by the 1946 constitution (Art. 91, 92, 93). It had been composed of the president of the Republic as chairman, the presidents of the Chambers, seven non-deputies elected by the National Assembly, and three non-senators elected by the Council of the Republic. It reviewed laws passed but not promulgated to ascertain if they required revision of the constitution. Laws could be referred to it only by joint decision of the president of the Republic and the Council of the Republic. Only one law was ever referred to it (in June 1948). On that occasion, it obtained reconsideration of the bill and revision of the parliamentary rules of both Chambers.[174]

Neither Debré's proposals of the 1940s nor the first deliberations of 1958 mentioned a similar institution. However, in the June 30 draft a "Constitutional Committee" could prevent the promulgation of a law it deemed unconstitutional. The president of the Republic and the president of each Chamber could refer laws to it for review. In a later draft, the institution's name became "Constitutional Council" and some of its characteristics were changed, but not those relevent here, except that the prime minister was added to the list of officials who could "seize" the Council.[175]

During the Gaullist years, four measures were referred to the Constitutional Council by prime ministers to be reviewed for constitutionality before promulgation.[176] They were: (1) an article in a 1960 law extending the social security medical insurance system to farmers, (2) a 1961 organic law on proxy voting in Parliament, (3) a 1963 law reforming the real estate stamp tax, (4) an article in the 1970 supplemental State budget that required the government to consult parliamentary committees on the preparation of decrees. The Constitutional Council invalidated the first and third measures on the grounds that they violated Article 40 of the constitution (reduced state revenues or increased expenditures). It struck down the fourth for violating "the principle ... of the separation of legislative and regulatory competencies and [being] thereby contrary to the constitution. It found the second measure to be partly valid and partly contrary to Article 27 of the constitution (voting in Parliament). Thus, in all four instances, this constitutional feature served to strengthen the Executive in ways not possible in earlier Republics.

Dissolution

The ultimate means of executive influence over the legislative process is, of course, dissolution. The 1958 constitution confers that power on the president of the Republic via Article 12. The only limitations are that he must consult the prime minister and the presidents of the Assemblies and that at least twelve months must have elapsed since the most recent previous dissolution.

Dissolution of the lower house of Parliament had been provided for in the 1875 and 1946 constitutions, but had been used only once in each regime. The 1875 document conferred that power on the president of the Republic with the concurrence of the Senate and the countersignature of a minister.[177] President MacMahon dissolved the Chamber in 1877. The pretext was legislative (disagreements between the prime minister and the Chamber over pending bills on local government and the press), but the real issues concerned the basic political orientation and structure of the regime.[178] Those circumstances tainted dissolution with the flavor of rightist coup and it was never invoked again.

The 1946 constitution transferred the dissolution power from the president of the Republic to the Council of Ministers, eliminated the Upper Chamber from the procedure, and imposed strict conditions on its use. It could be undertaken only after two governments had been overthrown by absolute majorities on formal votes of confidence within an eighteen-month period after the first eighteen months of a legislature and after the president of the Assembly had been consulted. In December 1955, that provision was used by the Edgar Faure government, which had been overturned by the Assembly on the legislative question of parliamentary electoral law reform.

The 1958 constitution returned the power of dissolution to the president and removed most of the limitations on its use. In his 1946 proposal, Debré had conferred it on "the government ... by decree taken in Council of Ministers," but his 1948 proposal returned it to the president with restrictions that tied it tightly to legislative disagreements. Dissolution was prominent in the minds of the framers from the outset of their 1958 deliberations, being mentioned both in Debré's first meeting with the team of experts and de Gaulle's first meeting with the Interministerial Committee. It appeared in the first draft in this bold phrasing:

> The president of the Republic ... at any moment, on proposal of the prime minister, shall be able to pronounce the dissolution of the National Assembly.

Later drafts added restrictions requiring consultation with the presidents of the assemblies and a year's interval between dissolutions. The CCC accepted this article after rejecting an amendment that would have required the concurrence of at least two of the three officials consulted. The Council of State and the Council of Ministers agreed.[179]

President de Gaulle dissolved the National Assembly twice, in October 1962 and May 1968. In neither case was a legislative question at issue.[180] Nevertheless, the existence of that powerful weapon may have kept the majority in line on some controversial legislative issues. However, the requirement of a one-year interval meant that if its first use had been unsuccessful in subduing a recalcitrant Assembly, it could not have been used again for so long a time that the Executive probably could not have survived without accepting Parliament's ascendancy. Thus, dissolution was used less as a legislative weapon under the Gaullists than in the earlier Republics and had very limited potential value as long as the majority remained basically cohesive and friendly.

ADJUDICATED INTERPRETATION

Two articles of the 1958 constitution provide authorizations for the Constitutional Council to protect the procedural devices described above. Article 41 authorizes the government or the president of either Assembly to appeal to the Constitutional Council if they disagree on whether a private member's bill, resolution, or amendment "is not within the domain of law or is contrary to a delegation of authority made in accordance with Article 38." Thus, the Constitutional Council is charged with protecting the government's power to exclude measures that violate those rules. Article 61 requires that "organic laws, before their promulgation, and the rules of procedure of the houses of Parliament before their implementation, must be submitted to the Constitutional Council which shall decide on their conformity with the Constitution."

The Constitutional Council used those authorizations on a number of occasions. It ruled on eight cases under Article 41. They are discussed at p. 116 above. Also, in five opinions pursuant to Article 61, it invalidated rules of the houses of Parliament on the grounds that they conflicted with constitutional provisions granting the executive controls over parliamentary procedures. Three concerned the National Assembly and two the Senate. Several of the decisions invalidated more than one provision of the rules.

The Constitutional Council found that one or more of the provisions in question infringed on eight of the procedural protections. According to its decisions, rules that imposed a five-minute time limit on orators in some circumstances,[181] limited participation in certain debates to specified categories of deputies,[182] or permitted each orator to speak only once[183] violated the constitutional guarantee to the members of the government to "be heard when they so request" (Art. 31). Rules that permitted the committee version of a bill to serve as the basis for discussion on second deliberation[184] were invalidated as violating the constitutional requirement that government bills serve as the basis of deliberation (Art. 42). Debates on the acceptance of the minutes cannot take priority over the government's control of the agenda[185] (Art. 48), nor can the Conference of Presidents override that control by altering the schedule of sittings.[186] The Constitutional Council interpreted assignment of a bill to a special committee as being exclusive, preventing its referral to standing committees, even for advisory opinions,[187] and it construed censure as the only means by which Parliament may "orient or control the action of the government." [188] Finally, with respect to the amending process, rules may not limit the applicability of the ban on private members' amendments that would increase expenditures or reduce revenues,[189] the flexibility of the blocked vote,[190] or the type of amendments that the government may introduce.[191] The direct impact of those rulings may not seem to have been substantial, but indirectly they made clear to the chambers that they could not use their rules to undermine the constitution.

CONCLUSIONS

The 1958 French constitution defined executive–parliamentary relations in law making more fully than had either of its predecessors. Especially, it contained more provisions that conferred legislative authority on the executive. However, many of its innovations were elevated from earlier practice or parliamentary rules.

The few clear exceptions were the use of the government's bills as the basis of floor consideration, the Joint Conference Committee, and the Constitutional Council. Other procedural devices were taken over virtually intact from one or both of the precedent constitutions. They included the powers to call special sessions, to request closed sittings, to introduce bills, to require review of proposed amendments by committee, to require a new deliberation on a bill, and to dissolve the Lower Chamber. The others were not found in those constitutions but had emerged earlier in parliamentary rules or practice, although some of them were developed further for the 1958 constitution.

The basic continuity may account for the ease with which most provisions sailed through the drafting process. Few substantive changes were made in the initial formulations. The CCC persuaded the government to ease its curbs on

Parliament somewhat and the Council of State tidied up the text quite a bit. Most of the substance, however, came from Debré, his team of experts, and de Gaulle's Interministerial Committee.

The controls of procedure varied greatly in effectiveness. Some devices were never used (executive sessions, the enactment of budgets by ordinance, new deliberations). Others were used so little that their importance was doubtful (Article 16 consultations, presidential messages, special committees, exclusion of certain kinds of amendments, passive enactment), they were not used for legislative purposes (dissolution), or they were used less than in earlier Republics (special sessions, declarations of urgency). Still others were much used, but had existed in some form in earlier Republics also (control of the agenda, executive access to committees and debates, introduction of bills by the Executive, exclusion of certain kinds of bills and amendments, submission of amendments, blocked vote). Finally, a few new devices had a significant effect (the use of government bills as the basis of deliberation, the Joint Conference Committee, referral to the Constitutional Council).

The importance and utility of many of those constitutional features were related closely to the character of the parliamentary majority. They tended to be used more frequently and to work better or, alternatively, to be less needed in the legislatures that had decisive Gaullist majorities than in those that had marginal majorities. Also, their effective functioning in many cases was obviously dependent on the absence of a hostile or neutral majority.

In sum, then, this description of the operation of the key means through which the Executive has been involved in parliamentary law making has shown that the political circumstances—especially the existence of a homogeneous majority—had more effect on those operations than had the designs of the framers of the constitution. Nevertheless, it seems true, also, that the constitution clarified, systematized, and legitimated those relations more than it changed them and perhaps that is a sounder and more viable purpose for a constitution anyway.

III

GOVERNMENT AND SOCIETY

7

The Transformation of French Society, 1944-1962

INTRODUCTION

The preceding chapters have examined various aspects of executive–legislative relations in Gaullist France with a view to discerning the extent to which they were determined by provisions in the 1958 constitution. They have shown that, in most respects, that text affected governmental practice relatively little. The text was squarely parliamentary, yet practice veered toward presidential government. The presidential components of the collective Executive became predominant very rapidly. Staffing at the policy-making levels reinforced that trend. In the distribution of policy areas between the domains of law and regulation, in the exercise of exceptional executive law-making powers, and in the use of devices for the intervention of the executive in the law-making process of Parliament, practice in Gaullist France seemed to be more responsive to political forces than to constitutional prescription.

In particular, governmental practice seems to have responded sensitively to the transformation of the parliamentary political party system. After 1958, the parliamentary parties underwent, a triple change. In the first place, they fell in number. During the Fourth Republic, six major political currents had substantial parliamentary representation. During most of the Gaullist period, only four did so. Second, those four coalesced rather quickly (by late 1962) into two broad, stable parliamentary alliances, unlike the shifting coalitions of the Fourth Republic. Third, the larger of those alliances held a majority throughout the remainder of the Gaullist period with the larger of the partners in it (the Gaullist party) holding a majority or near-majority. As was shown in the chapter on parliamentary law making, executive intervention tended to vary according to the strength of the majority alliance.

The party system in presidential electoral politics formed along a similar model. The necessity to contest a single, winner-take-all election conferred a very valuable premium on the formation of broad electoral alliances. However, because of the two-round balloting system, the alliances tended to act on the basis of anticipated first-round results and undergo hasty revisions between the rounds. In any case, presidential electoral politics tended to reinforce the dichotomous trend in parliamentary partisanship.

This chapter will examine the social basis of those changes in the structure of the political party system. It assumes that the party system was not auto-nomous, that it responded to the needs of the French people for effective political expression. Before 1962, the French tended to attach greater import-ance to their particular interests than to their general interest, to borrow Rousseau's terms. Thereafter, they tended to be more sensitive to the interests that their particular groups shared with other particular groups. Of course, this change did not occur instantaneously. It developed over a long period, but 1962 was the watershed year, for the presidential popular election system was adopted then and a homogeneous parliamentary majority emerged for the first time in French history. The following pages will show that the new partisan, political, and constitutional structures rested on and responded to a social foundation that was dramatically different from the character of French society when France emerged from World War II in 1944 or when the Fourth Republic was founded in 1946.

The general character of the changes that occurred in French society during that period is familiar to all students of contemporary French affairs. This short chapter does not purport to offer a significant new interpretation of that trans-formation. Rather, (1) it presents in concentrated form an array of information, especially statistics, to support that interpretation as tangibly and precisely as possible; and (2) it suggests a relationship between those changes and the character of the political and governmental system of the Fifth Republic. It attempts to explain the impact of France on the Fifth Republic—on its birth and on its ability to survive and to combine effective governance with valid representation of society.

THE TRANSFORMATION OF FRENCH SOCIETY, 1944-62

The long history of French social, economic, political, and constitutional conflict and instability after 1788 is well known. From the end of the *ancien régime* to the end of World War II, France was marked deeply by an almost continuous record of revolution, civil strife, war, and economic crisis that left society riven and politics and government weak and lacking in consensus. Furthermore, the latter part of that period produced little evidence to suggest that the situation was likely to improve. In fact, in many respects, the dozen years preceding the establishment of the Fourth Republic in 1946 had been the most divisive period in French history since the Terror. The riots of 1934, the Great Depression, the Popular Front governments, the defeat in 1940, Vichy, the Occupation, the squabbles in exile, the Resistance, the Liberation, the civil strife and purges, the surge of Communist strength, Stalinism and the Cold War, the human and material losses of World War II, the postwar inflation and economic recovery problems, the erosion of empire, the fall from Great Power status—all tore at the social and political fabric.[1]

The next dozen years reversed those effects dramatically. Behind the continuing colonial losses and Cold War, French society acquired a very different character. It became much more affluent, modern, and cohesive. By the time the 1962 referendum introduced direct election of the president of the Republic, it had become sufficiently cohesive to provide an adequate social base for an independent, coordinate political executive. Conversely, it needed a political institution, such as the presidency, that could express that greater unity. France had become much more tightly integrated socially through (1) the modernization and homogenization of the economy, (2) urbanization, (3) increased affluence, (4) a waning in the intensity of religious feeling, (5) depoliticization of the press, and (6) greatly improved social communication.

Economic Modernization

The 1944–62 changes were evident most strikingly in the economy. The least modern sectors of the economy shrank, while the most modern grew the fastest. The same kinds of change occurred within each sector as among them. In all areas, major technological innovations furthered the modernization process.

The primary sector, dominated by agriculture, was the largest and least modern in 1944. It employed 38.4 percent of the labor force, compared to 35.3 percent in manufacturing and transportation and 26.2 percent in the services.[2] Although agriculture's share was lower than when statistical data first became available, the decline had been slow and intermittent. From 1850 until 1901, it had fallen from 60.0 to 41.8 percent, an average drop of 0.38 percentage points a year. By 1946, it had fallen to 38.4 percent, a further average drop of only 0.08 percentage points a year. Nor was the post-1901 decline continuous. The percentage was higher in 1906 than in 1901, in 1921 than in 1911, in 1946 than in 1931 or 1936[3] Thus, the French in 1946 might conclude quite reasonably that agriculture not only was remaining the most important economic sector, but that its lead was increasing.

By 1962, the picture had changed spectacularly and with unequivocal finality. Agriculture had fallen from the top to the bottom of the sectorial heap, with 19.6 percent of the labor force, compared to 43.3 percent for the industrial sector and 37.1 percent for services.[4] It had declined at an annual rate of 1.18 percentage points, nearly 15 times as fast as during the preceding 45 years.

In general, the smaller farms were the least modern. Therefore, the modest but perceptible decline in the number of small farms during the early postwar period contributed further to the modernization of agriculture. In 1946, 55.8 percent of French farms had been smaller than 10 hectares (24.7 acres). By 1963, that percentage had fallen to 48.0.[5]

Also, modernization correlated highly with compactness. The extreme parcellization of farms, so prevalent in traditional French agriculture, impeded modernization. Governmental programs to consolidate such holdings had operated since 1919. During the first decade, they had involved an average of about 165,000 acres per year. From 1929 until 1945, that figure had dropped to about 60,000. However, in 1946–62 the rate jumped nearly ninefold, to about 518,000 acres per year, and operations involving another 4,577,000 acres were in progress.[6]

Technology reached deeply into the French countryside during the period in question. France had had 28,000 farm tractors in 1944 and 46,000 in 1946.[7] Thus, in the latter year, France had one tractor for every 160.2 persons employed in agriculture. By 1962, France had 900,000 tractors, one for every 4.3 persons in agriculture. The number of other farm machines increased similarly.[8] Finally, the agricultural use of chemical fertilizers grew about 3.5 times at about the same time.[9] As a result of this modernization, the efficiency of the average French farmer doubled. In 1946, he fed five persons. By 1962, he fed ten.[10]

Changes in the other two economic sectors had similar effects. Both increased in size. The more modern of them, services, grew the faster, by 11.9 percentage points compared to 8.0 for the industrial sector. Moreover, the most modern parts of each sector had the greatest growth. The older industries (mining, textiles, clothing, leather) fell from 34.3 percent of the labor force of that sector in 1936 to 18.9 percent in 1962. Also, domestic service dropped from 3.8 percent of the total labor force in 1936 to about 2.6 percent in 1964 and small shopkeepers declined from 90 percent of the distribution market in 1950 to 83.8 percent in 1962.[11]

This veritable revolution in the French economy in sixteen years reduced the pre-industrial sector from primary weight and importance. The farm vote had become much less significant in the electoral panorama. The interest community represented by the agricultural associations had become much smaller and, therefore, packed much less lobbying clout. The same was true of the extractive, forestry, and fishing industries and of the less modern parts of the manufacturing sector. Furthermore, the farms, mines, fishing vessels, factories, and the like, that remained in those industries were, in general, more modern than those that had disappeared from the economy. Consequently, the differences among the sectors in politically salient terms were greatly reduced. For instance, the surviving farms were able to compete more effectively on the international market and, thus, were not so likely to oppose the low-tariff policies of the most advanced manufacturing industries as had been the earlier agricultural industry. Of course, this had important implications for politics. It eliminated a major political division. Perhaps symbolically, the designation "peasant" disappeared from the National Assembly in 1962, after having loomed very large for some time.

Urbanization

A parallel process of modernizing homogenization transformed the urban–rural balance during the same period. In 1946, France was almost evenly split between urban (53.2 percent) and rural (46.8 percent) inhabitants. In 1962, the former had reached 63.5 percent and the latter had fallen to 36.5 percent. A gap of 6.4 percentage points had increased to 27.0. Furthermore, the cities had grown much more rapidly than the towns. Places of more than 50,000 inhabitants increased by 127.6 percent compared to 11.4 percent for France as a whole.[12] As a result, rural France in 1962 was much less of a drag on the more dynamic urban France than it had been in 1946 and another political division was reduced.

Affluence

A record period of economic prosperity in postwar France and the accompanying improvement in material comfort contributed further to the development of a viable foundation for presidential government. In currency of constant value, French per capita gross domestic product was $511 in 1946 and $1,358 in 1962.[13] The index for per capita national revenue rose from 78 to 167 (1938 = 100) with an uninterrupted trend of eighteen years by 1962. Only once before in the twentieth century (1922–26) had that index risen for more than two years in a row. For the first time in memory, the French economy had compiled a record of reliable, consistent progress.[14]

Productivity increased correspondingly. It rose 177.2 percent in the 1949–62 period.[15] As a result, purchasing power gained about 200 percent from 1946 to 1962.[16] Furthermore, France's relative position in Western Europe improved. It rose from twelfth to tenth in per capita gross domestic product, passing its two closest neighbors, West Germany and Belgium.[17]

The new prosperity was converted rapidly into a higher standard of living. For instance, the percentage of the population housed in "overcrowded" dwellings fell from 45.3 in 1946 to 27.6 in 1962. The percentages of homes with gas increased from 34.6 to 89.6, with electricity from 89.1 to 99.1, with running water from 36.9 to 80.9, with bath or shower from 5.6 to 30.5, and with flush toilet from 43.5 to 69.2.[18] The consumption of energy increased fifteenfold, from 1.36 million calories per capita in 1946 to 21.3 million in 1962.[19] The rate of automobile ownership rose from one vehicle for every 47.1 persons in 1946 to one for 7.6 persons in 1962, so that 37.9 percent of French households owned at least one automobile in 1962—a fourfold increase since 1946.[20] Per capita meat consumption rose from 43.4 kilograms in 1950 to 59.1 in 1960, while cereals consumption fell from 139.8 to 119.1 kilograms. The per capita consumption of "luxury" foods increased during the same period at the rate of 3 to 6 percent per year for prepared foods, 7 percent for ice cream, 5 percent for pastry, and 4 percent for cheese.[21]

The increasing size of the economic pie and the uses made of it helped to reduce social tension. The stagnation of the prewar period had meant that individuals and social groups could improve their lot only at the expense of others. Politics was the principal weapon employed in that struggle. That led to a great deal of political divisiveness and conflict. The rapid expansion of the economy meant that individuals and groups could rise economically by devouring the increments rather than their neighbors' shares. Political divisions and conflicts were reduced correspondingly.

Religion

Another change in French society that had especially significant implications for government was the decline in the political divisiveness of religion. At least since 1789, the intensity of religious and anti-religious feelings had been disruptive politically. Frenchmen who agreed on everything else but disagreed on the Church–State question usually wound up in opposing political camps, contributing thereby to the fragmentation of the political landscape. Those quarrels continued unabated through the Occupation and Liberation periods. Church and State had been closely associated in the wartime Vichy regime. The Church had endorsed openly a political party (the MRP) in the parliamentary elections of 1945 and 1946 and the Communists responded with virulent hostility. Those classical representatives of the clerical quarrel were the two largest parties during that period. Not surprisingly, then, the Church–State conflict (focused on the question of State subsidies to Church schools) was the critical policy issue of those years, the one most likely to disrupt electoral, parliamentary, and governmental coalitions.

By 1962, the clerical quarrel was greatly attenuated. The Marie and Barangé laws of 1951 and the Debré law of 1959 ensured the survival of church schools. Public opinion surveys showed that support for that policy had climbed from 23 percent in 1946 to 46 percent in 1951.[22] At the same time, enrollment in private (mainly Catholic) schools declined from 50.8 percent of the secondary students in 1946 to 25.0 percent in 1962 and from 16.3 percent of the elementary students to 15.7 percent,[23] seeming to confirm the waning of particularist feeling.

Religious practice declined somewhat less precipitously. Although statistics on religious affiliation are not very firm, they suggest that about 85 percent of Frenchmen regarded themselves as Catholic and 3 percent identified themselves with other religions throughout the period in question. However, the percentage who said they attended mass regularly fell from the 36 to 50 range in the early postwar period to 26 in 1961.[24]

Consequent upon that decline in the social manifestations of religious feeling was its depoliticization. The only significant overtly clerical party fell from 28.2 percent of the vote in the June 1946 parliamentary elections to 8.2 percent in 1962 and from a membership of 200,000 in 1946 to perhaps 40,000 in 1962, despite its gradual secularization throughout the period.[25] The Catholic trade union organization (the CFTC) followed a somewhat similar course. It declined from 26.4 percent of the vote in social security representation elections in 1947 to 20.9 percent in 1962[26] and, in 1964, abandoned its clerical stance and dropped the word "Christian" from its name.[27] Those changes coincided with convergent evolutions in the attitudes of the Church and the Communist Party, both becoming more conciliatory toward the other. The net result was a very significant decline in the political and social divisiveness of attitudes toward religion.

The Press

Another indicator of the decline in social and political tensions was the depoliticization process that transformed the daily press between 1946 and 1962. The press had been deeply involved in partisan politics at the Liberation. The early postwar governments had suppressed 172 newspapers because of alleged collaboration with the German occupiers or publication during the Occupation[28] and had licensed newspapers, largely on the basis of political acceptability. At least partly as a result, daily newspapers affiliated with government parties controlled 52.9 percent of the circulation, conservatives and Radical-Socialists controlled 24.0 percent, and 19.8 percent of the circulation was nonpartisan.[29]

By 1962, the situation had been reversed completely. Nonpartisan newspapers controlled 93.1 percent of the circulation of national dailies. The only remaining official political party daily in Paris was the Communist *Humanité*, although *Libération* survived only by subsidies from the Communists. The situation was the same in the provinces. Even those rare partisan dailies that survived toned down their politics considerably to escape extinction.

That transformation was both effect and cause. Partisan newspapers declined because partisan sentiment had fallen. Yet partisan sentiment was eroded further because it lacked the reinforcement of partisan newspapers. Either way, the phenomenon accords with the perception of a less divided French society.

Social Communication

Most forms of social communication grew significantly during the 1946-62 period, weaving France into a much tighter web of cohesion. The number of telephone communications annually per capita rose from 36 to 110, greatly offsetting a decline in mail communications from 96 per capita to 86.[30] The number of radios per 1,000 inhabitants increased from 140 to 244 and of television sets from zero to 74. The per capita annual expenditures for all forms of theatrical entertainment jumped from 16.8 francs of 1938 value to 638.8, a thirty-eight-fold increase. On the other hand, newspaper circulation fell from 323 per 1,000 inhabitants to 252.[31]

A similar phenomenon occurred in transportation. The most important single development was, of course, the sixfold increase in the ownership of private automobiles, mentioned above. In addition, the rate of usage of French airlines rose from 8.58 passenger/kilometers per capita per year in 1946 to 136.72, a sixteen-fold increase.[32]

Education was another medium that increased the amount of social communication in the 1946–62 period. Besides the greater homogenization along a secular axis mentioned in the section on religion above, a broader sector of the French population was sharing extended education. The rate of secondary school enrollment increased fourfold, from 1.5 to 5.9 percent of the population, and that of higher education doubled, from 0.3 to 0.6 percent.[33] The social-class character of students changed also. In 1946, 1.7 percent of French university students came from working-class homes, compared to 4.8 percent from farm families, 21.4 percent from business-owning families, and 55.8 percent from white-collar and professional families. By 1962, those percentages had changed to 7.9, 6.5, 16.6, and 60.0.[34] Taking into account changes in the distribution of the labor force, the proportion of working-class students increased from one per 2,997 workers to one per 313.8 and farming-class students increased from one per 1,139 farmers to one per 164.6. Secondary and university student bodies had hardly become microcosms of working society, but large strides had been made in that direction, with corresponding improvement in social communication.

Each communication was a social bond. Therefore, their mere increase suggests greater social cohesion. Moreover, the communications of the less affluent members of society probably increased at a disproportionately higher rate. Certainly, that was true for education. Thus, the different social groups became more similar in those respects. That greater similarity made deep and numerous political divisions less likely.

CONCLUSION

The changes described above produced a society that was much more cohesive in politically salient terms. The primary sector of the economy was reduced in size and distinctiveness so much that it no longer stymied the modernization process in politics and government. Conflicts arising from rural versus urban interests, poverty, religion, newspaper partisanship, and inadequate social communication were attenuated greatly.

The social changes had significant political, governmental, and constitutional implications. The fragmented and ideological political party system of the Third and Fourth Republics no longer reflected social reality. Neither did the fractionated omnipotent Parliament nor the weak, unstable Executive. The more harmonious and cohesive society could be represented faithfully in Parliament by broader, less antagonistic parties and alliances. It could serve as a sound foundation for an institution that, by its essential character, is the logical representation of the unity of society—that is, an autonomous, political chief executive, a president.

The final chapter of this book provides some theoretical and comparative ruminations to describe and explain the apparent connections between society, politics, constitutions, and governmental practice.

8

Elements for a Constitutional Theory

"A constitution is an envelope," de Gaulle once said; "what is inside can be changed." [1]

Perhaps the founder of the Fifth Republic had in mind that a parliamentary system could be made to evolve toward presidentialism. In particular, he believed that Great Men might effect such changes.

"A man of history is leaven, a seed. A chestnut tree does not resemble a chestnut."

The preceding study has agreed with de Gaulle's implication that the original contents of the Fifth Republic's constitutional envelope were parliamentary and that, in general, the presidential practices of the regime were not the result of specific provisions of the 1958 text. However, it has developed a different explanation for the evolution. It has described the evolution of French society, 1946–1962, and argued that the more cohesive France of 1962 provided a congenial foundation for a more presidential system.

This final chapter elaborates on that argument hypothetically and by using comparative materials. It bases that elaboration on an assumption that democratic governmental systems form their character largely in response to the needs and, thus, the character of society. It traces that relationship along an analytical path through hypothetical models of political and governmental institutions. Finally, it fits the democratic regimes of Great Britain, Germany, and France and the societies they have ruled into that system of models. In the process, it examines the proposition that the French political system under the Gaullists acquired and retained its presidential characteristics largely in response to changes that had occurred in French society after 1946. The generalizations that are developed in this argument should be useful in considering the broader meaning of the French case, but should not be read as immutable, universal laws.

FRAMEWORK OF ANALYSIS

Overview

This interpretation of the dynamic formation of the French constitutional system rests largely on the assumption that democratic political systems survive and thrive in symbiotic relationship with the societies they rule. That is, government is a service institution for society. It responds constructively to the needs of society. It changes in order to do so, or it gives way to another regime. In other words, in a free society with a democratic government, the main features of the constitutional system must be compatible with the principal characteristics of political salience in that society or the system will fail.

This assumption does not exclude de Gaulle's "chestnut theory" entirely. Great leaders may, indeed, inspire and catalyze, but, like the sower in the Biblical parable, they labor in vain if they cast their institutional seeds on barren soil—as happened to de Gaulle himself in 1944–46. Of course, institutions rarely spring forth spontaneously either, and this study does not mean to imply that they do. Someone must cast the seeds. They do not sow themselves. However, this study focuses on seeds and soil, rather than on the sower.

Nor is the effect of constitutions denied. They may render more concrete, clear, and tangible the institutional creations of great leaders. They may bring greater respectability to the institutions, making them seem more legal, legitimate, even proper, and, hence, giving them greater security and stability. However, constitutions lack vitality. They are too inert to override the daily dynamics of interest and convenience that arise from the character of the societies they rule.

To understand why those dynamics arise, in part, from the degree of cohesion of a society requires interpretation of the nature of government. The characteristic that is most distinctive in government is its authority and capacity to compel the obedience of its members. Other social institutions may influence; none but the State may command.

However, the State is an institutional fiction. It can compel only when commanded to do so. Those orders come from the human beings who control it. In a democracy, this means the most numerous part of society. Thus, government is the instrument by which the preponderant part of society imposes its will on the whole of that society or on selected parts of it. In Engels' words, the State is the executive committee of the ruling class.

Moreover, the effectiveness with which any instrument functions depends partly on the type of material it works. In the case of the State, the governed may be subject to its compulsion, but they are not thereby deprived of all will to accept or resist. Resistance is most likely to spring from a perception that the commands of the State are contrary to the resister's interest. Thus, the more broadly an interest of the preponderant element is shared in society, the narrower—and weaker—will be any resistance to governmental policy. The more cohesive the society, the more likely will be such breadth. Thus the government's will is imposed with difficulty and onerousness that varies according to the cohesiveness of society. The more cohesive the society, the more its various parts share perceptions and interests and, therefore, the more easily a preponderant will emerges and the more readily it may be imposed. Conversely, the less the social cohesion, the less the parts of society share perceptions and interests and, therefore, the less easily a preponderant will emerges and is imposed.

Differences in the degree of difficulty required to produce a preponderant will affect differentially the various aspects and institutions of politics and government. Political and governmental institutions tend to function differently in a cohesive, homogeneous society than they do in a fragmented one. The value of their services to society tends to vary by the type of society. This results in parallel variations in the structure and strength of those institutions. The character and significance of those differences may be seen by following the analytical path traced below.

Analytical Path

The following pages trace the flow of politics through successive institutions to suggest the differential effects of social environment. This section portrays a conceptual scheme rather than actual systems. Therefore, it uses hypothetical models of diametrically opposite types of societies and related institutions.[2]

One model will be labeled "Cohesive Society" and will exemplify the ideal social situation in which individuals and groups have perfectly harmonious, similar, or identical perspectives and interests in all matters of public concern. This ideal society occupies territory that lies entirely within one climatic zone on a single type of terrain. Its economy is integrated so tightly and oriented so uniformly that all social elements benefit or suffer together. It contains no cultural, linguistic, ethnic, or religious minorities of political consequence.

"Fragmented Society" is the ideal, hypothetical opposite. Its territory is infinitely diverse in climate, terrain, and orientation. Its economy contains many disparate elements of roughly equal size and importance with sharply conflicting interests and persepctives. Its population includes many large and antagonistic ethnic, cultural, linguistic and religious groups.

Political opinion crystallizes in patterns corresponding to the variations in society. In Cohesive Society, it forms a single block that varies only subtly in shade and texture. Its major elements differ in detail and emphasis, but agree on fundamentals and on the major matters that receive significant governmental attention. In contrast, political opinion in Fragmented Society is shattered. Its many abrasive pieces tumble about in perpetual conflict, unable to merge into broad, harmonious units. Their distemperate excretions form impermeable ideological incrustations. Their basic premises, patterns of thought, even vocabularies diverge so widely that they can scarcely communicate. They discourse in what the French call a "dialogue of the deaf."

The *political organizations* in society tend to reflect those patterns of political opinion. The politically active elements in society give practical effect to their opinions through organizational forms that are compatible with the nature of society and with the public opinion structure. In all democratic societies, regardless of their places on the Cohesive–Fragmented spectrum, interest communities and associations—under whatever label—convert opinion into policy proposals and work to change the proposals into policies. Similarly, they all use political parties and free elections to manage the selection of policy-makers and implementers. However, the communities, associations, parties, and electoral systems vary greatly among the types of society in the structure and functioning of the individual units and of the systems they form.

Interest communities in Cohesive Society tend to be few and broad. A pervasive sense of common or harmonious interest fuses neighboring communities or sets them tingling in sympathetic vibration. Even the least congenial components respect the good will and legitimacy of their compatriots and tolerate their expression of opinion and the efforts in its behalf. In Fragmented Society, on the other hand, the communities tend to be numerous and small. Their presence and activity work to perpetuate and exacerbate the disintegration of society in a crucible of political conflict. Even close neighbors are hostile and antagonistic. The rot of social discord poisons the minds of the people against all those whose social coordinates are not identical with their own.

Interest associations in Cohesive Society tend to form strong, unitary structures. Generally, a single "peak" association represents each interest community and the greater preponderance of the joiners of each community are to be found within that association. The associations work mainly through official channels in legally regulated, orderly, cooperative ways. They collaborate with rivals, with government, and with other types of groups in search of mutually beneficial solutions to problems. They even assume some of the responsibilities of statecraft through integral involvement in the official policy-making process. In Fragmented Society, each interest community is represented through several small associations that compete with each other, usually along ideological lines, as well as with their counterparts in other interest communities. The resulting conflicts may be exceptionally acrid in a typically internecine way. Their lack of a sense of common interest and their mutual suspicion leads these interest associations into illegal, even violent and destructive actions in striving to prevail over those whom they regard as their—perhaps mortal—enemies. Of course, such behavior reinforces the mutual antipathy among the associations and the communities they represent.

Political parties in Cohesive Society tend to be few and broadly based. There may be only two major parties or a greater number that are so congenial that they can cooperate closely in two genuinely collaborative coalitions. Because of the high level of political consensus and the good will among the interest communities, the parties draw supporters broadly across the social spectrum, solidifying the cohesion further. They tend to frame their appeals in pragmatic and managerial terms, competing for office like amateur athletes, sportsmanlike and with good fellowship. Their arguments stress performance, personal and institutional character, experience, and competence. Fragmented Society has many political parties that view each other with hostility and disdain. They only form coalitions with those they dislike less in order to spite or thwart those they dislike more. Because the society is so riven, each party tends to draw its supporters from a narrow range of the interest-community spectrum. Party appeals are largely ideological. They are aimed at their "natural" clients in those interest communities and emphasize gains at the expense of other communities and group loyalty, identity, and interests. They compete most fiercely with their nearest ideological neighbors because they are appealing to the same segment of the population. That ferocity tends to accentuate further the social fragmentation.

Electoral systems reflect and immortalize the respective party systems because they are made, revised, and retained mainly through the efforts of political leaders who have stakes in the partisan *status quo*. Thus, in Cohesive Society the plurality electoral system is preferred, because it tends to pay a premium to broad, managerial parties. The efficient, effective conduct of government has a higher priority than the clear expression of ideological views. In Fragmented Society, the proportional representation or the majority (two-round) electoral system is favored as being more compatible with narrow, ideological parties. Ideological expression is valued over governmental effectiveness.

Legislatures are deeply affected by partisan politics. The structures of party systems tend to be projected into Parliaments. In Cohesive Society, the broad, managerial parties organize Parliament into disciplined, effective alternatives. Because of the breadth of the parties, legislative memberships tend to form bimodal configurations and homogeneous majorities are normal. On the other side of the Chamber at any moment sits a broad opposition trying very hard to behave like an alternative majority. Thus, both sides strive for moderation and reasonableness in discourse and decision. Each protagonist does unto the other as it would be done unto when the roles are reversed. That attitude is reinforced by the realization that a managerially minded electorate has one eye on their conduct in office and the other on the next election. In Fragmented Society, the legislature contains many ideological parties. None holds a majority of the seats or even approaches it. Thus, coalitions are inevitable. However, the reciprocal hostility evident in the extraparliamentary parties penetrates the legislatures. Parliamentary alliances are kaleidoscopic, multicolored, and shifting frequently. The parties have difficulty collaborating loyally and constructively with their chief election rivals, past and future. Their natural legislative allies are their natural electoral foes. Partnership is necessarily circumstantial, opportunistic, and fleeting.

Executives follow the same patterns. In Cohesive Society, the Executive reflects the unity and stability of that social foundation by manifesting the same qualities. This tends to give it strength and independence. It speaks and acts for a unified national will—firmly, decisively, and independently of the legislature. Long, fixed terms in office are the norm. A single chief executive controls the government. In Fragmented Society, the strength and independence of the Executive is undermined by the social, political, and institutional divisions. The absence of clear national will denies it voice and muscle. The chief executive tends to be merely the first among equals in a collective body. That group is divided, unstable, and indecisive. As in Hobbes' state of nature, they exist in "continual fear, and danger of violent death" their lives being "poore, nasty, brutish, and short."

Once again, the sets of institutions outlined above represent ideal types at the extreme ends of an imaginary constitutional spectrum. No real institutions or societies, past or present, fit those descriptions. They form a theoretical construct designed to suggest the logic that might lead to the conclusion that the changes in the French political system since 1958 reflect the evolution of France from a fragmented toward a cohesive society.

Distribution of Power

The analytical path described above may lead to an explanation of the effect of variations in social cohesion on the distribution of power among the types of institutions. Those variations may have impact throughout all political systems, but so general a scheme need not be presented here. This study is concerned with the executive–legislative relationship and its theoretical exposition shall rest there.

Variations in degree of social cohesion can be related logically to variations in the distribution of power between the executive and legislative branches in political systems. The explanation flows from identification of the peculiarly distinctive qualities of those two types of institutions. They differ strikingly in possessing qualities of *unity* and *fragmentation*.

Unity is the essence of the Executive. The executive branch, almost by its nature, has *unity of constituent base*. It issues from a single, unified electorate after a unitary competition in which the same candidates participate throughout the constituency and a single decision is made by the voters. Also, the Executive has *unity of hierarchy*. A pyramidal authority structure rises to a solitary chief, either an institutionally singular collective cabinet or a personally single officer of whatever title. It has *unity of accountability*. It reports to the polity as a whole rather than to its parts separately. It has *unity in representational responsibility*, being expected to act on behalf of the polity as a single unit. It speaks for the people to the extent that, and in those respects that, they have a single will, or at least a high level of consensus. It has *unity of perspective*, in that its vision is presumed to extend the length and breadth of the land, encompassing all the people with the gaze of an institutionally single set of eyes.

In contrast, legislatures are characterized by the distinctive quality of *fragmentation*. They have *fragmented constituent bases*. Their members issue from a multitude of separate electorates, all having different electoral contests among different sets of candidates, resulting in separate decisions. Legislatures have *fragmented hierarchies*. Unlike the executive hierarchy, that of the legislature is composed of all Indians and no chiefs. None of its members can command the others the way the chief executive can command the rest of the executive structure. Unlike the Executive, all members of the legislature have coordinate claims to democratic legitimacy. The legislature has *fragmented accountability*, its members reporting separately to a multitude of components of the polity. It has *fragmented representational responsibility*, its members being expected to speak with as many different voices as are heard from the people. It has a *fragmented perspective* in that its members are expected to regard matters from many diverse viewpoints, each set of eyes attentive to a different set of matters and seeing things differently.

Those contrasting fundamental qualities affect the relative abilities with which those two principal political organs of government perform the various tasks that societies expect of the State.

Obviously, a 250-pound man is naturally better suited for the shot put than for riding in thoroughbred horse races, and the performance capabilities of his 100-pound brother are the reverse. Similarly, executive branches are suited better to deal with certain problems of society and legislatures have contrasting capabilities.

Because the Executive is peculiarly characterized by the quality of unity, it is suited better than the legislature to deal with those problems for the solution of which *action* is the most important and difficult governmental task. Those are problems for which popular consensus exists on the policy and the main task of government is not to formulate and win approval of that policy but to implement it as efficiently, expeditiously, and effectively as possible. An example of such a problem might be a popular all-out war. Consensus agrees on a policy of mustering maximum effort and directing it as effectively as possible toward the goal of total victory. The main task of government with respect to that problem is to give effect to that policy: *to act*. Because of the unity of its constituent base, of its accountability, of its representational responsibility, and of its perspective, the Executive is peculiarly well suited to recognize, catalyze, and proclaim the existence of that consensus. Because of the unity of its hierarchy and its position at the apex of the administrative and military structure, that same institution can marshal and apply the necessary and appropriate State resources to an extent and in ways not possible for the legislature.

Conversely, the legislature is suited better to solve those problems that require the *accommodation* of divergent and conflicting interests as the main governmental task. Those are problems where consensus on policy is absent.

The vital interests of the communities concerned with that problem must be identified and policies worked out to solve the problem while respecting those vital interests. An example might be the confluence of high rates of inflation and unemployment in an economy. The interests of various communities in the society may conflict on the choice of policies to solve those problems. Once the major interests agree on policy, its implementation is relatively easy. Because the constituent base of the legislature is fragmented, each of its members wins election with support by one or more of the principal interest communities in the polity. This makes them, in effect, accountable to their respective supporting communities, gives them representational responsibility for those communities, and imposes on them their perspectives. Because of the legislatures' fragmented hierarchy, its members can act, free of higher authority within the institution, to serve their constituents' interests. Thus, the legislature, by its nature, has the character of an assemblage of emissaries negotiating on behalf of the major communities of the polity. Thus, for those purposes, it has authority, sensitivity, and legitimacy not possessed by the Executive. Indeed, the Executive can use very little independent discretion in implementing the compromises painfully elaborated in the legislature, lest they come unglued—and perhaps the polity with them.

Because of their contrasting distinctions, Executives and legislatures differ in their general value to different types of societies. By its nature, Cohesive Society has less need for *accommodation* than does Fragmented Society. Fewer conflicts require resolution by authoritative negotiation. On the other hand, it tends to have a greater need for action, because its level of consensus tends to be higher in more policy areas than in Fragmented Society. The reverse of those propositions is true for Fragmented Society. The services that can be performed better by the Executive are more valuable to Cohesive Society and those that can be rendered better by the legislature are worth more to Fragmented Society.

Because power follows value and performance, the Executive tends to be the more powerful branch of government in Cohesive Society and the legislature the more powerful in Fragmented Society. However, in neither situation is the relative strength of the respective branches uniform across all policy areas. Although the Executive may be the stronger, in general, in a given society, some policy areas may be so divisive, even in that society, that the legislature has the more important role to perform—and the greater power. The reverse may be true in other societies where the legislature is generally the stronger branch.

If the nature of a society remains essentially the same over a fairly long period of time, the connection of the institutions to their constituent bases may be affected. For example, if a society remains stable near the cohesive end of the spectrum for some decades and the Executive dominates, the legislature tends to become dependent upon it electorally and its own direct connection loses viability. That is, the members of the legislature are elected, not on the basis of their own political merits, but on the basis of the voters' expectations of the effect those decisions will have on tenancy in the Executive. In effect, the MPs become "grand electors," acting in a nondiscretionary way to place and keep in office the people's choice for executive. Similarly, in a stable Fragmented Society with a long-time dominant legislature, the Executive depends on the legislature for its electoral connection. The voters are unable to express a clear preference in the choice of the chief executive, either directly or through a nondiscretionary electoral college of some sort. Instead, the Executive emerges from a coalition-building process in the legislature and may have no independent standing with the voters at all. In societies that fall in the intermediate range of the spectrum, neither institution establishes long-term dominance. Power shifts between them depending on short-term changes in the character of the society and on the types of problems that are current at the moment. Neither branch becomes dependent electorally on the other. Each maintains a viable electoral connection and its democratic legitimacy.

COMPARATIVE APPLICATION

The conceptual framework outlined above has been designed to support the argument that political systems vary between legislative and executive predominance as the societies they govern vary between fragmentation and cohesion. This is an alternative to the assumption that political systems work as they do because of the prescriptions of constitutional texts. The pages following apply that framework to three major European countries: Great Britain since 1918; the Weimar and Bonn Republics of Germany; and the Third, Fourth, and Fifth Republics of France. The relevant constitutional texts are reviewed to ascertain whether they were presidential or parliamentary. Then, the societies governed under those constitutions are described briefly and characterized as Cohesive or Fragmented. Finally, the political systems in operation are analyzed and categorized as tending toward presidential or parliamentary practice. Of course, none of these real examples fits the ideal, hypothetical models described above. Thus, the characterizations are necessarily somewhat arbitrary and approximate. Nevertheless, the distinctions seem sufficiently clear to be tenable.

Great Britain

Constitution

The British constitution is somewhat amorphous, because of not being a single, discrete document. However, the present system evolved gradually from The Settlement in the years after 1688 and became democratic with the introduction of virtually universal adult suffrage in 1918 (except women under 30). The constitution as it existed in 1918 was clearly parliamentary. Since 1841, "the principle of the dependence of a ministry on a majority in the House of Commons" has been unquestioned.[3] However, the presidentialist requirement that a government resign between electoral defeat and parliamentary meeting had not yet become fixed,[4] largely because single-party majorities in the House of Commons had not yet become usual.[5] Thus, the constitution did not regard the House of Commons as a nondiscretionary electoral college for the Executive and, consequently, it remained parliamentary.

Society

British society since 1918 has passed through three fairly distinct phases. Until the dust had settled from Irish Home Rule of 1922 and the General Strike of 1926, its basic cohesiveness was troubled by the rebellious presence of the Irish and by serious economic dislocations. Thereafter, until after World War II, British society was highly cohesive. Finally, since World War II, that cohesion has been weakened somewhat by various factors, but has remained quite high. The following discussion focuses on the long middle period, when it typified the cohesive society.

Geographically, Britain's small territory, semi-isolated from the European continent, fosters cohesion. Climatic and topographic variations are slight. It lies entirely in the North Sea climatic zone and has no broad plains nor rugged mountain ranges. By the twentieth century, proximity to Europe had brought it all the great movements of European history (Christianity, Renaissance, Reformation, capitalism, Enlightenment, socialism, etc.), but its maritime separation had spared it most of the accompanying turmoil. Few foreign armies had reached its soil to sow the social bitterness and division they had inflicted on continental countries so often.

Britain's inescapably maritime location had forced it to turn outward on the world. Social tensions that might have caused internal conflict otherwise were splayed out into the world at large. That maritime orientation had been beneficial economically, also. It facilitated Britain's development as the world's leading international commercial and shipping power, thereby producing the first modern industrial economy. Until after World War II, the modern sectors (manufacturing and service) dominated its economy much more overwhelmingly than in any other country. This left the primary sector (especially agriculture) too weak to inflect politics or be significantly devisive.

A further economic result was Britain's relatively high level of prosperity. She was second only to the United States in per capita gross national product as late as World War II. That was conducive to social cohesion, because the large economic pie deflected from politics some of the remaining economic tensions.

Ethnically, linguistically, and religiously, British society was quite cohesive during that period. All parts of Britain had Celtic roots, although substantial other ethnic populations had immigrated in the distant past, especially to England. The English were overwhelmingly dominant and the Scots, who were next, constituted less than 10 percent of the population. Ethnic particularity seemed to be in deep decline until well after World War II, as evidenced by the miniscule fraction of the people who could not speak English. Protestantism had about the same dominance religiously as did the English ethnically. Such ethnic and religious diversity as existed had little importance politically until the 1950s, because it found little distinctive expression. All significant elements seemed to have found comfortable homes in the major political currents of the British mainstream.

Changes in British society after World War II diluted its homogeneity and cohesion somewhat. For the first time, democratic Britain received substantial numbers of non-British immigrants. Also, the ethnic consciousness of the minority nationalities increased, producing the violence of Ulster, the nationalist political parties of Scotland and Wales, and the urban riots of the early 1980s. Even more significantly, the British economy declined substantially. It fell far behind other countries in international commerce and shipping and in per capita GNP. Although the primary sector of its economy remained smaller than in any other country, its lead was so reduced that it lost its advantage of relative modernity. Those changes left the basic character of British society intact, but weakened its cohesion somewhat.

Political System

The British political system has passed through three phases since 1918, also, each beginning several years after the corresponding social changes. Until about 1931, it had all the earmarks of a classical parliamentary regime with legislative dominance. From then until about 1964, the parliamentary form remained, but the executive branch was more dominant than dependent. Since 1964, it has taken some small steps back toward being a traditional parliamentary system again.

The political system of 1918–31 was characterized by ideological politics, frequent elections, multiparty Parliaments, backbench strength, coalition governments, and weak leadership. In 1918, the Labour Party took its most ideological position with the adoption of the socialist Clause 4 of its statutes. Elections were held at average intervals of 31 months. Parliaments lacked single-party majorities and coalition governments ruled more than half of the time. Conservative backbenchers forced out Austen Chamberlain and the 1916–1922 coalition government. Their Labour counterparts ousted MacDonald from the party leadership and withdrew from his Lib-Lab coalition in 1931. Most leaders were either colorless (Chamberlain, Bonar Law, Adamson, Clynes) or survived only by grace of their electoral enemies (Lloyd Goerge, MacDonald).

In that situation, the Executive had no popular constitutent base. Governments were made and unmade by parliamentary politics. The ministries were responsible to the House of Commons in the traditional parliamentary way.

Politics were significantly different in the second period. They were less ideological. Election intervals were nearly twice as long (56.5 months). Parliaments always had single-party majorities. Backbench influence waned. The only coalition government (1940–45) was a symbol of wartime unity rather than a political necessity. For most of the period, leadership was vigorous (Churchill, Attlee, Gaitskell, Macmillan, Wilson), transforming "cabinet government" into the "prime-ministerial government" described by Crossman.[6]

Those political changes made the House of Commons, in effect, primarily an electoral college to record the people's choices for prime minister. The determining electoral decisions for most voters became the contests between the prime-ministerial candidates of the two major political parties, which they settled by choosing between rival slates of parliamentary candidates. The winners were, in effect, prime-ministerial electors. The Executive had appropriated Parliament's popular constituent base.

After 1964, the pendulum swung a bit back the other way. The ideological contents of politics rose again, as exemplified by the views of Margaret Thatcher, Michael Foot, and Tony Benn. Election intervals decreased again to a 35-month average, in 1964–1979. Parliaments lacked single-party working majorities nearly half of the time. Backbench dissidence and influence increased, especially on the European Community issue, culminating in the takeover of the Labour Party by ideological radicals in 1980 and the formation of the Social Democratic Party. The Labour government of 1974–79 required the support of a parliamentary coalition and collapsed with the first defeat on a motion of no-confidence since 1924. Wilson (except on Europe) and Thatcher gave vigorous leadership, but Home, Heath, and Callaghan were reminiscent of the 1918–31 model. Nevertheless, the Executive retained its popular constituent base. Despite some erosion of independence, it remained ascendant.

Weimar Germany

Constitution

The German constitution of 1919 combined elements of parliamentary and presidential government, but the latter predominated. The chancellor and government formed a parliamentary-type Executive. They were parliamentary in that they required "for the administration of their offices the confidence of the Reichstag" and had to resign "if the Reichstag by formal resolution withdraws its confidence" (Art. 54). They were executive in that "political authority in national affairs" was conferred on the government (Art. 5) and the "general course of policy" was to be "determined" by the chancellor (Art. 56). On the other hand, the presidency was a presidentialist Executive. The office was presidentialist in being filled through direct popular election by "the whole German people" (Art. 41). It was Executive in that it held broad diplomatic, appointment, and military authority to the extent that it could require, even "by force of arms" that the states perform their duties under the constitution and national laws (Arts. 45–53). That authority was qualified by the provision that "all orders and directions of the president, including those concerning the armed forces, require for their validity the countersignature of the chancellor or of the appropriate minister" (Art. 50).

The ambiguity of those contradictory elements seemed to be resolved by two presidentialist factors. First, the president had explicit authority to appoint and dismiss "the chancellor and, on his proposal, the ministers" (Art. 53). Second, as a result of its mode of election, the presidency had a more direct popular connection than the chancellor or ministry. This gave it greater democratic legitimacy and the authority that entails. For those reasons, the Weimar constitution may be called predominantly presidential.

Society

Weimar Germany was significantly more fragmented socially—except ethnically and linguistically—than Britain has been during most of its democratic history. Geographically, its territory was much larger, had a greater variety of terrain, and had both maritime (North and Baltic Seas) and continental orientations, with all the divisiveness those factors engender. Also, its location as an integral, even central, part of Europe had brought it heavy suffering from the frequent conflicts that had swept that strife-torn continent for centuries, at further cost to its cohesion. Indeed, perhaps no country illustrates more vividly the disastrous effects of such a location on national unity, for it had been fragmented into as many as 300 autonomous units and was the last European power to emerge as a Nation–State.

Economically, Weimar was much less important internationally, less prosperous, and less homogeneously modern than pre-1939 Britain. Its economy was more fragile, as was shown with devastating clarity by its greater vulnerability to inflation in the early 1920s and to depression a decade later. The least modern economic sector (agriculture) occupied about five times as large a share of its labor force as in Britain and had available about 50 percent more arable land.

Religiously, Weimar's minority was much larger than Britain's. The population split about 2/3–1/3 between Protestant and Roman Catholic. However, its Jewish community was smaller (0.9 percent to 1.2 percent). Also, ethnically (95 percent German) and, to a lesser extent, linguistically, Weimar was more homogeneous than Britain.

Political system

In practice, Parliament in the Weimar political system was even more dominant than in Britain in 1918–31. Politics were more ideological. Election intervals were shorter (21.2 months). Parliaments never even came close to having single-party majorities. All governments were unstable coalitions. Leadership was inevitably weak, as fifteen chancellors served in fourteen years and the president after 1925 (von Hindenburg) verged on senility. All governments were the products of parliamentary politics rather than popular electoral mandates. Despite its preponderantly presidential constitution, Weimar was almost the archetype of traditional parliamentarism run amok.

Bonn Germany

Constitution

The 1949 "basic law" of the Federal Republic of Germany was un-equivocally parliamentary. Although it retained the offices of president and chancellor, the presidency lost almost all political importance, leaving no doubt that the chancellor and government—both responsible only to Parliament—were the political Executive. The presidency's powers in diplomacy and appoint-ments were stated much the same as in the Weimar constitution, but it lost all military authority.[7] Also, its Weimar authority to compel obedience by the states was transferred to the federal government (Art. 37).

The decisive difference from the Weimar constitution, however, lay in its elimination of the principal reason, mentioned above, for Weimar's presidential preponderance. First, it circumscribed more closely the president's authority to nominate chancellors and withheld the authority to dismiss them (Art. 63). Second, it replaced direct, popular election of the president by the parliamen-tary arrangement of election by a "Federal Convention" composed of the Bundestag members and an equal number of representatives of the state Parliaments (Art. 54). Thus, the presidency lost its claim to greater democratic legitimacy than the chancellorship or government, ensuring the parliamentary character of the constitution.

Society

German society under Bonn is significantly more cohesive than it had been under Weimar. This was partly the result of the thirty-years' evolution after 1919. Also, World War II effected significant changes.

Geographically, Bonn rules only about half of Weimar's territory. It stretches only about one-third as far, east to west, and has only about one-third as much coastline. This divides it less between maritime and continental orien-tations and among different types of terrain and climate.

Economically, Bonn is much stronger than was Weimar. Its international trade is, proportionately, much greater and it has suffered no serious economic dislocations. In fact, its recovery from World War II was acclaimed universally as the "economic miracle" of the period. During most of its history, its per capita gross national product has exceeded Britain's and, of course, its comparative international rank is higher than was Weimar's. Finally, the homogeneity of its economic modernity has increased dramatically. Bonn's agriculture has only about one-fifth the share of the labor force that Weimar's had and less than Britain's in 1932. It has half as much arable land as Weimar and one-fourth less than Britain.

Religiously, Bonn is divided evenly between Protestants and Roman Catholics. However, this parity seems to have imposed a *modus vivendi*, because religion faded from political consciousness almost completely in the 1960s. Ethnically and linguistically, Bonn's permanent population is even purer (99 percent) than was Weimar's. Although that purity has been diluted superficially by the presence of about 4.0 million "guest workers" (6.5 percent), their political impact is minimal because they are only temporary residents.

Political System

Although Bonn's political system has functioned in the presidential mode, this was not at all clear at the outset. The 1949 Bundestag was remarkably similar to the 1919 Reichstag. The SPD espoused socialist ideology and the CDU was heavily infused with Catholicism. The largest Bundestag party had a smaller percentage of seats (CDU, 34.6) than had the largest Reichstag party (SPD, 38.7). Ten parties held seats, compared to eight in 1919. Konrad Adenauer became chancellor by a single vote—his own.

The system evolved very quickly. After Kurt Schumacher died in 1952, the SPD shed its ideology rapidly and the Church withdrew from involvement in the CDU. The percentage of Bundestag seats won by the largest party rose to 49.9 in 1953 and 54.3 in 1957 and has fluctuated between 45 and 50 since then, though a single-party majority existed in only one Parliament. The number of Bundestag parties fell to six in 1953 and four in 1957 and has been three since 1961. Election intervals have been long and regular. Only in 1972 was Parliament dissolved early. Although all governments have been coalitions, they have been remarkably stable. Only twice in a generation has the coalition changed. Leadership (especially Adenauer, Brandt, and Schmidt) has been strong and comparably stable. Only five chancellors will have served in 35 years if Schmidt survives the 1980 Parliament.

Much as the House of Commons had done in the early 1930s, the Bundestag became a nondiscretionary electoral college for the chancellorship after the 1949 Parliament. Except for Kurt Kiesinger in 1966, chancellors have reached or retained office through election, in effect, by popular vote or through succession as heirs-apparent upon the resignation of fellow partisans who had been so elected. That is, they have held office by popular mandate rather than parliamentary politics. Each parliamentary election has been dominated by a contest between the "chancellor-candidates" of the two major parties. Much as in Britain after 1931, the political Executive took over Parliament's popular connection and the strength that brings.

Third Republic France

Constitution

The three laws of 1875 that established the Third French Republic were parliamentary, despite the presidentialism of the Monarchist chamber that enacted them. The Monarchists could not agree on a monarch, so they wanted a presidency on the American model that could be converted into a throne when they had resolved their dynastic squabbles.[8] They had given the presidency the authority to appoint and dismiss ministers under an earlier law that remained in effect.[9] Also, it was not responsible politically to Parliament and was elective for the long term of seven years. However, those presidentialist provisions were outweighed easily by the parliamentarist requirements that the president be elective by the two Chambers meeting together and that all its acts be counter-signed by ministers who were responsible to Parliament, individually and collectively.[10]

Society

Socially, Third Republic France was much more similar to Weimar Germany than to Britain or Bonn Germany, more fragmented than cohesive. Geographically, by location, size, terrain, and coastline (North Sea, Atlantic, Mediterranean), it had the same dual orientation and immersion in the European cauldron. Although its economy was less fragile, it resembled Weimar's in level of prosperity and international trade and in the lingering importance of its least modern sector.

Religiously, the main French cleavage lay between clericals and anti-clericals rather than between Catholics and Protestants, but their quarrels were even more bitter and divisive than religious disputes elsewhere. Ethnically, France was much more fragmented than either of the other countries.[11] Minority ethnic groups comprised some 35 to 40 percent of her population during the Third Republic. The Occitans made up the largest but least self-conscious group; Occitans inhabited most of the territory south of the Loire Valley and numbered 10 to 12 million persons. Other major groups were Bretons (2.5 million in Brittany and 300,000 elsewhere), Germans of Alsace and Lorraine after World War I (1.6 million), Flemish (perhaps 1.0 million), Corsicans (some 300,000), Catalans (250,000), Basques (100,000), and Italians in Nice and Savoy. Furthermore, by the end of World War I, nearly 1.6 million foreigners resided in France.[12] Linguistic minorities were less numerous, as a result of systematic governmental efforts to suppress their languages. For instance, only about one-fourth of the inhabitants of French Flanders spoke Flemish.

Political System

Despite sporadic early attempts to implement the presidentialist intentions of the framers of the 1875 constitution (MacMahon in 1877–79 and Boulanger in 1887–89), the Third Republic was squarely parliamentarist no later than 1879. It had a multiparty system in which the larger, more cohesive parties were highly ideological. No cohesive party ever won as many as one-fourth of the seats in the Chamber. All governments were unstable coalitions. After Mac-Mahon, presidents were ceremonial only and premiers were weak and transient. Nearly 100 ministries were formed in 65 years. All were the products of par-liamentary politics; none issued from popular mandates. The political

Executive never acquired a democratic constituent base and remained dependent on the Chamber in a very conventional parliamentarist way.

Fourth Republic France

Constitution

The French constitution of 1946 was explicitly and decisively parliamentary, despite attempts to avoid its predecessor's "abuses." It continued the offices of president and premier, but left no doubt that the latter was ascendant. The constitutional position of the presidents was similar to that of 1875, except that their power to nominate premiers was constricted and they could no longer dismiss them. Also, their acts now required the countersignatures of both the premier and the appropriate minister. The premier's status was bolstered by formal recognition in the text (unlike 1875) and by the elimination of individual responsibility of ministers to the Chamber. No whisper of presidential government issued from either the text or its framers' expressed intentions.

Society

French society during the Fourth Republic was discussed in detail in the preceding chapter. Suffice it to say here that, especially at the outset, the Fourth Republic was a fragmented society, much like Weimar and like the Third Republic that had ended only six years earlier. Most of the conflicts and divisions of the Third Republic remained and others appeared.

Political System

In practice, the Fourth Republic resembled its parliamentary predecessor closely. Ideological politics predominated throughout, although they were somewhat less strident in the later years. The multiparty system continued, but was simplified a bit, with six major parliamentary parties, none of which ever won more than 30.5 percent of the seats (PCF, 1946). Nevertheless, the three general elections occurred at precise four-and-a-half-year intervals. All the governments were unstable coalitions, whose lifespans averaged about six months. Leadership was weak and colorless. All governments were the products of parliamentary politics; none had electoral mandates. The regime remained squarely parliamentary.

Fifth Republic France

One of the main points of the preceding chapters of this book has been to fit the Fifth French Republic into this conceptual scheme. It need not be elaborated here. In brief, the 1958 constitution was parliamentary. French society had become much more cohesive by 1962 than it had been when the Fourth Republic was founded, and practice in the regime was heavily presidentialist.

SUMMARY

The comparative outline presented above can be summarized diagrammatically. (See Diagram 8.1.) The horizontal dimension distinguishes types of constitutions. The vertical dimension distinguishes types of societies. The regimes sketched above have been placed in appropriate quadrants, according to practice. Britain 1918–31 had a parliamentary constitution and a moderately fragmented society. Britain since 1931 has been parliamentary and cohesive. So has been Bonn Germany. Third and Fourth Republic France was parliamentary and fragmented. Fifth Republic France is parliamentary and cohesive. Weimar Germany was presidential and fragmented. The political systems with presidentialist regimes in practice (Britain since 1931, Bonn, and Fifth Republic France) are indicated by italics in the diagram.

DIAGRAM 8.1

Type of   Type of Constitution
Society

	Parliamentary	Presidential
Fragmented	France III France IV Britain 1918	Weimar
Cohesive	*Britain 1960* *France V* *Bonn* *Britain 1931*	

The point of the diagram is that the type of political system correlates more with the type of society than with the type of constitution. The four systems with presidentialist Executives had parliamentary constitutions. So did three of the four with parliamentarist Executives. The only system with a presidential constitution had a parliamentarist Executive in practice. Not much correlation there! On the other hand, all of the parliamentarist Executives governed fragmented societies and all of the presidentialist executives ruled cohesive societies.

This conceptual scheme does not, of course, pretend to scientific exactness. Like most complex matters in the social sciences, it does not partake of perfection. For instance, what seems to work for the major democracies of Western Europe may not apply elsewhere. However, it may enhance our understanding of the key institutional relationship in modern government by calling attention to some suggestive correlations between it and some aspects of social character, in France and elsewhere, and by noting the frailty of relevant provisions of the 1958 constitution. For one thing, it may help to explain why the contents of de Gaulle's "envelope" turned out so much more satisfactorily after 1958 than they had after 1945.

Conclusion

The foregoing study has two main aspects. First, it presents the results of an extensive amount of research on selected aspects of executive–legislative relations in Gaullist France. Second, it seeks to explain that relationship in terms of the character of French society.

The research for this study has been used to support separate but related arguments in the chapters. Chapter 1 shows that the original 1958 constitution was parliamentarist and was intended to be. Chapters 2 and 3 study key aspects of the structure of the political Executive. The former shows that the collective executive institutions developed in practice along presidentialist lines, despite the letter of the constitution and early efforts of Prime Minister Debré. The latter of those chapters contends that the key staff members in the political Executive were more presidentialist in type during the early crisis years of the regime than during the later period of more routine politics, the former situation requiring *action*, the peculiar contribution of the Executive, and the latter requiring more *accommodation*, the function for which legislatures are especially well suited. Chapters 4 through 6 examine law making under the Gaullists. The first of them shows that the explicit delineation of the domains of law and regulation in the 1958 constitution effected very little change in practice, contrary to the intentions and expectations of its framers. The second shows that the use of executive law-making authority varied predictably by the situation, but also that it never had substantial importance and became virtually defunct in a few years. Chapter 6 reports much the same result for the "reformed parliamentarism" provisions of the 1958 constitution. The constitutional devices intended to increase executive control over the parliamentary law-making process had little practical effect. The message of those three chapters is that the independent Executive under the Gaullists did not arise from those provisions of the constitution that were designed to regulate executive-legislative relations in law making.

Whence, then, did it come? One answer lies in the final two chapters of this book. The latter of those chapters presents and illustrates comparatively the argument that the character of political and governmental institutions reflects the degree of cohesion in the societies they rule and that the power relationship between legislatures and Executives tends to vary according to that factor, also, regardless of the form of the constitution. The political Executive tends to be dependent upon the legislature in a parliamentarist sense in fragmented societies and tends to be strong and independent in cohesive societies. Applying that interpretation comparatively, that chapter noted that in Great Britain and Bonn Germany the Executive had established its independence by pre-empting the popular constituent base of the legislature. Both the House of Commons and the Bundestag became nondiscretionary electoral colleges for the political Executive. The prime consideration of the voters in the parliamentary elections was the choice between the rival chief executive candidates of the two major political parties. Somewhat the same thing happened in France in 1958 and 1962, although there the choice lay not between two candidates, but between positive and negative responses to the incumbent—a sort of plebiscite. In each case, a popular referendum on a constitutional issue was followed closely by a parliamentary election. The basic issue in both elections was the same as it had been in the preceding referendum: whether de Gaulle should remain in office. Parliamentary candidates were chosen, not on their abilities to represent particular interests in the classic parliamentarist way, but on the basis of the stands they took on the incumbent chief executive. Thus, the MPs became, in effect, members of a nondiscretionary electoral college for the presidency.

The crucial moment in that process came in 1962. In the referendum and elections of that year, the French voters confronted the issue of the form of the regime—explicitly in the former, implicitly in the latter. If they had forced de Gaulle out, either by rejecting the constitutional amendment or by electing a non-Gaullist Assembly majority, France certainly would have reverted to its traditional parliamentarism.

By changing the constitution from parliamentary to presidential and by confirming the Assembly as a presidential electoral college, the French were doing more than tinkering with institutions. They were announcing their belief that their society had evolved to the point that its cohesion was sufficiently great that a coordinate branch of government was needed to represent its unity. They were saying that their social harmony had become great enough that they could trust it to a strong Executive. Chapter 7 shows how much, in fact, French society had increased in cohesion between 1946 (when the Fourth Republic was founded) and 1962.

However, the strong executive system that had developed was not the same, in principle, as the American presidential system. As in Britain and Bonn, the chief executive in the Fifth Republic has pre-empted the popular connection of the legislature. Even after 1962, when distinctly separate elections were held for president and Parliament, the Gaullist president converted the parliamentary elections into presidential plebiscites by threatening to resign if their supporters lost control of Parliament. In the United States, on the other hand, the presidency and Congress have preserved separate popular connections; neither is politically dependent on the other. This suggests that the long debate over the character of the Fifth Republic under the Gaullists may have been misdirected. The regime may have been neither a classical parliamentary system with the Executive dependent on the legislature nor a presidential system of the American type with the two branches having independent constituent bases. This does not mean, as some of its partisans claim, that it was unique with respect to the dependency of the branches. Rather, it seems to have been strikingly similar in the basic power relationship to "prime-ministerial" Britain and "chancellor-democracy" Bonn. However, this similarity went unnoticed because its title and mode of election seemed to throw the French chief executive into the same bag as the American president.

The Fifth Republic was distinctive in another respect. Unlike Britain and Bonn, it had formally separate popular electoral processes for legislature and Executive. Initially, they were fused only by its first president's threats to resign and the electorate's uncertainty of the consequences of split control of the branches. In 1981, its fourth president used a similar tactic to obtain a Socialist parliamentary majority. In the absence of such menaces, the Fifth Republic might evolve from its Gaullist shape into a genuinely presidential system.

If it does, it seems likely that it will be responding—as did the 1958 system—to French sociopolitical dynamics. The contents of the "envelope" will be changed again, but not by de Gaulle's "man of history." As before, they will be changed by the French people, inspired by leadership, perhaps, but responding at a more fundamental level to the needs of their society.

Appendix A

The Domain of Law in the Constitution
(Parentheses indicate originators of provisions)

Art. 3 . . . All French nationals of age, or both sexes, who are in full possession of their civil and political rights shall be electors in conditions determined by law (Debré).

Art. 6 . . . In the Overseas Territories of the Republic, the elected representatives of the Councils of the Administrative collectivities shall be part of the electoral college [for the presidency of the Republic] in conditions that shall be determined by an organic law (Council of State).

. . . The means of implementing the present article shall be set by an organic law (Interministerial Committee).

Art. 13 . . . An organic law shall determine the other offices to which appointments are to be made in the Council of Ministers (Interministerial Committee) as well as the conditions in which the power of nomination of the president of the Republic may be delegated by him to be exercised in his name (CCC).

Art. 23 . . . An organic law shall set the conditions in which replacement shall be provided for the holders of such offices [parliamentary seats, etc., by members of the government] (team of experts).

Also, it shall set the conditions in which persons shall be elected, in case of vacancies, to replace deputies or senators (Interministerial Committee).

Art. 25 . . . An organic law shall set the length of duration of each Parliament (Debré), the number of its members, their compensation, the conditions of eligibility, the system of ineligibilities and of incompatibilities (team of experts). Also, it shall set the conditions in which persons shall be elected, in case of vacancies, to replace deputies or senators (Interministerial Committee).

Art. 27 ... The organic law may authorize proxy voting exceptionally (Inter-ministerial Committee).

Art. 34 ... Laws shall be enacted by Parliament.

Laws shall set the rules concerning:

—The civic rights and the fundamental guarantees accorded to citizens for the exercise of public liberties; the obligations imposed by National Defense on the persons (Interministerial Committee) and goods (Council of State) of citizens

—The nationality (Interministerial Committee); the status (team of experts), and the capacity (CCC) of persons; matrimonial (CCC), inheritance (Inter-ministerial Committee), and charity (Council of State) systems

—The determination of crimes (Debré) and offenses (Council of State) as well as the penalties that apply to them; the penal procedure; amnesty (Debré); the creation of new orders of jurisdiction (Interministerial Committee) and the status of magistrates (team of experts)

—The distribution, the rates, and the means of collection as well as, when occasion requires, the assignment of all types of taxes imposed on the taxpayers; the system of issuing money (Council of State)

Laws also shall set the rules concerning:

—The electoral system of the parliamentary and local assemblies (CCC)

—The creation of categories of public establishments (Interministerial Committee)

—The fundamental guarantees accorded to the civil and military functionaries of the State (Council of State)

—The nationalization of enterprises (Interministerial Committee) and the transfers of the property of enterprises from the public sector to the private sector (CCC)

Laws shall determine the fundamental principles concerning:

—The general organization of national defense (CCC, made "general" by In-terministerial Committee)

—The free administration of the local collectivities (Interministerial Commit-tee), their authority (Interministerial Committee), and their resources (Council of State)

—Education (Interministerial Committee)

—The system of property (Council of State), real estate rights (Council of State), and civil and commercial obligations (Cabinet)

—Labor Law [*droit*] (Interministerial Committee), trade union law (CCC), and social security (Interministerial Committee)

Finance laws shall determine the resources and the burdens of the State in the conditions and with the reservations laid down by an organic law (team of experts).

Program laws shall determine the objectives of the economic and social action of the State (CCC and Debré).

The provisions of the present law can be made more precise and elaborated by an organic law (Council of State and Debré).

Art. 35 ... Declarations of war shall be authorized by the Parliament (Debré).

Art. 36 ... States of siege shall be decreed in the Council of Ministers. Their prolongation (team of experts) beyond twelve days (Council of State) can be authorized only by the Parliament.

Art. 37. Matters other than those which are in the domain of law have a regulatory character (Interministerial Committee).

Texts in legislative form intervening in these matters may be modified by decrees (Interministerial Committee) made with the advice of the Council of State (CCC). Any such texts as take effect after the present constitution comes into force can be modified by decree only if the Constitutional Council has declared that they have a regulatory character by virtue of the preceding clause (CCC and Debré).

Art. 41. If it shall appear in the course of the legislative procedure that a bill or an amendment is not in the domain of law . . ., the government may declare it to be out of order.

In case of disagreement between the government and the president of the appropriate Assembly, the Constitutional Council, at the request of one or the other, shall rule within one week (Debré).

Art. 53. Peace treaties (Debré), commercial treaties (CCC), treaties or agreements relative to international organizations (Debré), those that commit the State financially (Interministerial Committee), those which modify provisions of a legislative nature (Interministerial Committee), those which relate to the status of persons (Interministerial Committee), those which provide for the cession, exchange, or addition of territory (Debré) can be ratified or approved only by law.

Art. 57. The functions of member of the Constitutional Council shall be incompatible with those of minister or of member of Parliament. The other incompatibilities shall be set by an organic law (Interministerial Committee).

Art. 63. An organic law shall determine the rules of organization and of operation which shall be followed by the Constitutional Council, the procedure which shall be followed before it and especially the deadlines set for appeals to it (Council of State).

Art. 65. The High Council of the Magistracy ... shall be composed ... of nine members designated by the president of the Republic under conditions set by an organic law (Cabinet).

... It shall give advice under conditions set by an organic law on proposal of the minister of justice relative to nominations to judicial seats (Interministerial Committee). It shall be consulted on pardons under conditions set by an organic law (Council of Ministers).

Art. 66. No one shall be detained arbitrarily.

The judicial authorities ... shall ensure respect for that principle under conditions laid down by law (Cabinet).

Art. 67. An organic law shall set the composition of the High Court [of Justice], the rules of its functioning as well as the procedure to be followed before it (Interministerial Committee).

Art. 71. The composition of the Economic and Social Council (Interministerial Committee) and its rules of operation shall be set by an organic law (Council of State).

Art. 72 ... All other [types of] territorial collectivity shall be created by law (Interministerial Committee).

These collectivities administer themselves freely through elected councils under conditions laid down by law (Interministerial Committee).

Art. 73 ... The legislative system and the administrative organization of the overseas departments may be the objects of measures of adaptation necessitated by their particular situations (Cabinet; measures includes laws and regulations).

Art. 74 ... [The] organization [of the overseas territories] shall be defined and modified by law after consultation with the appropriate territorial Assembly (Cabinet).

Notes

1. THE 1958 CONSTITUTION

1. Nicholas Wahl, "The French Constitution of 1958: II. The Initial Draft and Its Origins," *American Political Science Review*, June 1959, p. 372.
2. "Discours de M. Debré devant le Conseil d'Etat," in *Documents d'études. Droit constitutionnel et institutions politiques*, supplement to *Notes et Etudes Documentaires*, February 1970, pp. 18–25; English trans. in William G. Andrews, ed., *European Political Institutions*, 2nd ed. (Princeton, N.J.: Van Nostrand, 1966), p. 55.
3. "Discours de la Place de la République," in supplement to *Notes et Etudes Documentaires*, February 1970, pp. 29–30; English trans. in Andrews, ed., *European Political Institutions*, pp. 41–42.
4. *Journal Officiel, Débats parlementaires, Assemblée nationale*, sitting of June 1, 1958, p. 2576.
5. Maurice Duverger, "Réformer le régime," *Le Monde*, April 12, 13, 1956; Georges Vedel, "Pour un éxécutif élu par la nation," in *Revue politique des idées et des institutions*, November 30, 1956, pp. 577–607; François Goguel, "Vers une nouvelle orientation de la révision constitutionnelle," in *Revue française de science politique*, July–September 1956, pp. 493–507; Gilbert-Jules, "Le Problème de la révision de la Constitution," in *Revue politique des idées et des institutions*, December 15, 1957, pp. 585–97.
6. That influence can be traced in detail in Jean-Louis Debré, *La Constitution de la Vᵉ République* (Paris: PUF, 1975). Also, see Wahl, "The French Constitution of 1958."
7. Guichard, at symposium on de Gaulle, New York University, November 14, 1980.
8. Le Troquer, *La Parole est à André Le Troquer* (Paris: La Table Ronde, 1962), p. 194; J. R. Tournoux, *Carnets secrets de la politique* (Paris: Plon, 1958), pp. 71–73; Paul-Marie de la Gorce, *Apogée et mort de la IVᵉ République* (Paris: Grasset, 1979),

pp. 544, 548; J. R. Tournoux, *Secrets d'Etat* (Paris: Presses Pocket, 1960), pp. 333–36, 373; Raymond Tournoux. *Le Tourment et la fatalité* (Paris: Plon, 1974), pp. 11–17; Jean Ferniot, *De Gaulle et le 13 Mai* (Paris: Plon, 1965), pp. 148–50.

9. Jules Moch, *Rencontres avec de Gaulle* (Paris: Plon, 1971), p. 297; André Passeron, *De Gaulle Parle* (Paris: Plon, 1962), p. 13. Raymond Janot had persuaded him to omit that commitment, Guy Mollet, "Les Institutions à l'épreuve des élections," *Revue politique et parlementaire*, January 1973, p. 4.

10. Tournoux, *Secrets d'Etat*, p. 385.

11. Moch, *Rencontres avec de Gaulle*, p. 300.

12. According to *Le Monde*, June 1/2, 1958, the following MPs attended: Réoyo, Poujadist; Pinay, Rogier, Duchet, Independents; Monichon, Rural and Social Action; Antier, Peasants; Triboulet, Michelet, and Debré, Social Republicans; Teitgen, Moisan, de Menditte, MRP; Queuille, Gaborit, Borgeaud, Democratic Left; Daladier, Radical; Edgar Faure, J. P. David, R.G.R.; Duveau, Houphouët-Boigny, Mitterrand, Perrin, UDSR-RDA; Maga, Félix-Tchicaya, PRA; Mollet, Ramadier, Courrière, SFIO.

13. Michel Debré, "L'Elaboration de la Constitution de 1958," pp 18–23 in *Espoir: Revue de l'Institut Charles de Gaulle* no. 3 (1973): 18; Wahl, "The French Constitution of 1958," p. 365; *JO. AN.*, 1st sitting of June 1, 1958, p. 2591; Ferniot, *De Gaulle et le 13 Mai*, p. 475; *Le Monde*, July 6/7, 1958, quoting René Pleven.

14. The initial members of the government were de Gaulle; Mollet, Pflimlin, Jacquinot, and Houphouët-Boigny, ministers of state; Debré, Social Rep., Justice and Keeper of the Seals; Maurice Couve de Murville, high civil servant, Foreign Affairs; Emile Pelletier, high civil servant, Interior; Pierre Guillaumat, high civil servant, Armed Forces; Pinay, Indep., Finance; Jean-Marie Berthoin, Rad.-Soc., National Education; Paul Bacon, MRP, Labor and Social Security; Bernard Cornut-Gentille, high civil servant, Max Lejeune, SFIO, and André Malraux, man of letters, unspecified assignments initially; Edouard Ramonet, Diss. Rad., Secretary of State for Industry and Commerce. Auriol and Ramadier, SFIO; Bidault, MRP; René Billères, Rad.-Soc.; François Bloch-Lainé, high civil servant; and Etienne Hirsch, high civil servant, were consulted but not appointed. Also, de Gaulle had courtesy consultations with Albert Sarraut, president of the Assembly of the French Union, and Emile Roche, president of the Economic Council. In addition to the sources cited above, the following references were consulted for the pre-parliamentary phase: Jean Ferniot, *De Gaulle et le 13 Mai*; Wahl, "The French Constitution of 1958," p. 365; *Le Monde*, May 24, 29, 31/June 1, 2, 3, 1958; *Combat*, May 31/June 1, 2, 1958; *Paris-Presse l'Intransigeant*, July 9, 1958; de Gaulle, *Mémoires d'Espoir* I, p. 33.

15. *JO. AN.*, 1st sitting of June 1, 1958, p. 2576.

16. *JO. AN.*, 1st sitting of June 1, 1958. Pierre Mendès-France, p. 2579; Jean Masson, p. 2580; Jacques Duclos, p. 2582; Pierre Courant, p. 2583; and Pierre-Henri Teitgen, p. 2591.

17. Mendès-France: "Parliamentary institutions, when they function well and correctly, assure this salutary confrontation" of views on public policy. Masson: "Parliament . . . remains the only expression of the national will."

18. Mendès-France and Duclos voted "no"; Masson, Courant, and Teitgen voted "yes." The Assembly had ample opportunity to impose parliamentarist conditions

and undoubtedly had a parliamentarist majority, given its past record, but seems to have been too overwhelmed by the crisis situation to insist at that moment. The deputies who spoke in the investiture debate, but did not address the constitutional issue of parliamentarism, were Jacques Isorni, Right; Pierre Clostermann, Rad.; Maurice Deixonne, SFIO; Georges Bonnet, RGR; François Tanguy-Prigent, SFIO; François Mitterrand, UDSR; Pierre Cot, Prog.; Patrice Brocas, Rad.; Jean Le Bail, SFIO; Rosan Girard, PCF; Luis Réoyo, Poujadist; François de Menthon, MRP; and Marcel Bouyer, Poujadist.

19. *Le Monde*, June 3, 1958.
20. *JO. AN.* 2nd sitting of June 2, 1958, p. 2623. The committee members were: PCF—Ballanger, Billat, Demusois, Duclos, Judge, Kriegel-Valrimont André Mercier, Perche, Yves Peron, Ramette, Girard; Indep.—Barrachin, Bruyneel, Delachenal, Giscard d'Estaing, Mignot, Tremolet de Villers, Fourcade; Rad.—Bourgès-Maunoury, Giacobbi, Gaillard, Ramonet, Degoutte; MRP—Bouxom, Paul Coste-Floret, Teitgen, Mme. Lefebvre, Moisan, Raymond-Laurent; RGR—David; SFIO—René Dejean, chairman, Lussy, Mazuez, Minjoz, Verdier, Juvenal, Alduy; diss. Rad.—de Bailliencourt; overseas Ind.—Dia; Poujadist—Juliard, Bône, Teulé, Vaugelade; Gaullists—Triboulet, Tirolien; UDSR—Guissou; RDA—Konaté; PRA—Tsiranana, *Le Monde*, June 3, 4, 1958; *JO. AN.*, 2nd sitting of June 1, 1958, p. 2594, and 2nd sitting of June 2, 1958, pp. 2617, 2618; *JO. AN.*, *Documents*, 1957–58 session, annexes 7233, 7238, 7239, pp. 1829–31.
21. The others were Guy Jarrosson, Indep.; Edgar Faure, RGR; Duclos, PCF; Jean Minjoz, SFIO; Paul Coste-Floret, MRP; Ramadier, SFIO; Teitgen, MRP; Maurice Kriegel-Valrimont, PCF; Robert Ballanger, PCF; Mollet, SFIO; François Mitterrand, UDSR; Christian Pineau, SFIO. *JO. AN.* 2nd sitting of June 2, 1958, pp. 2617–27; *JO. AN.*, *Documents*, 1957–1958 session, annex 7238, p. 1830.
22. *JO. AN.* 2nd sitting of June 2, 1958, p. 2624.
23. P. 2576, Ibid.
24. The members of the Universal Suffrage Committee at the time were: SFIO—Antoine Courrière, Jean Nayrou, Marcel Champeix, Paul-Emile Descomps, Alex Roubert, Ludovic Tron; GD—Paul Baratgin, Henri Borgeaud, Charles Brune, Antoine Colonna, André Cornu, Yvon Delbos, Joseph Raybaud; PCF—Jean Chaintron; ARS, René Blondelle; Indep.—Chamaulte, Henri Cordier, Pierre Marcilhacy, Quenum-Possy-Berry, Rivierez, Rochereau; Gaullists—Michel Debré, Geoffroy de Montalembert, chairman, Etienne Rabouin, Henri Torrès; MRP—Jacques de Menditte; RDA—Zéle, Zinsou. *Journal Officiel Débats parlementaires. Conseil de la République (JO. CR.)*, sitting of June 3, 1958, pp. 956–57; *Le Monde*, June 4, 1958.
25. Ferniot, *De Gaulle et le 13 Mai*, p. 446.
26. Michel Debré, *Une certaine idée de la France* (Paris: Fayard, 1972), p. 71.
27. Ferniot, *De Gaulle et le 13 Mai*, p. 446.
28. *France-Référendum*, September 28, 1958.
29. Each of the ministers of state nominated a staff member. Pflimlin named Erwin Guldner and Mollet picked André Chandernagor, both members of the Council of State who were on their ministerial staffs already. Jacquinot, Berthoin, and Houphouët-Boigny designated François Luchaire, Jean Portemer, and Jean Foyer, respectively; all were *agrégés en droit*. Foyer had served on René Capitant's min-

isterial staff in 1944–45 when Capitant was heavily engaged in de Gaulle's constitutional projects.

30. Wahl, "The French Constitution of 1958," p. 362.

31. They were Michel Aurillac, Roger Belin, Louis Bertrand, Jacques Boitreaud, François Duléry, Georges Galichon, Yves Guéna, Michel Guillaume, André Jacomet, Lucien Paoli, Alain Plantey, and Max Querrien. All of them were members of the Council of State. Debré, *La Constitution de la V e République*, p. 21. Wahl, in "The French Constitution of 1958," p. 359, includes Christian de la Malène, Debré's personal assistant, in the group. Pierre Avril lists only eighteen members, omitting Duléry, Foyer, Jacomet, Portemer, and Solal-Celigny, but adding Charles-André Massa, colonial inspector and associate of Houphouët-Boigny; and Michel Massenet of the Council of State, a close political associate of Soustelle. *Le régime politique de la V e république* (Paris: LGDJ, 1967), p. 8. Also, see Pierre Viansson-Ponté, *Histoire de la république gaullienne* (Paris: Fayard, 1970), I: 62; and François Luchaire, "Introduction," in François Luchaire and Gérard Conac, eds., *La Constitution de la république française*, 2 vols. (Paris: Economica, 1979), I: p. 11.

32. Goguel, "L'Elaboration de la Constitution," p. 74; Wahl, "The French Constitution of 1958," pp. 361–62, 371; Debré, "L'Elaboration de la Constitution," p. 19; *Le Monde*, July 13/14, 1958; *France-Référendum*, September 28, 1958; Antoine Azar, *Génèse de la Constitution du 4 Octobre 1958* (Paris: LGDJ, 1961), pp. 205, 205n.; Debré, *Une certaine idée*, p. 72; Mollet, *Quinze ans après: 1958–1973* (Paris: Michel, 1973), p. 13.

33. Wahl, "The French Constitution of 1958," pp. 361–62.

34. Leon Noël, *Comprendre de Gaulle*, (Paris: Plon, 1972), pp. 133–34; Michel Debré and Jean-Louis Debré, *Le Pouvoir politique* (Paris: Seghers, 1977), p. 27.

35. Luchaire, "La Responsabilité du Gouvernement devant le Parlement," *Notes et Etudes Documentaires 781, no. 2*, (May 22, 1961): 15; Mollet, *Quinze ans*, pp. 23, 76; Pflimlin, in René Rémond *et al.*, *La Démocratie à Refaire* (Paris: Les éditions ouvrières, 1963), p. 121.

36. Debré, "L'Elaboration de la Constitution, pp. 18–19; Debré, *Une certaine idée*, p. 72, Tournoux, *Secrets d'Etat*, p. 407.

37. Wahl, "The French Constitution of 1958," p. 371, says that "Debré presided over cabinet committee meetings when de Gaulle was absent." Other sources say that de Gaulle presided over all of its meetings.

38. Debré, "L'Elaboration de la Constitution, p. 19, and *Une certaine idée*, pp. 72, 73, 156; Debré, *La constitution de la V e République*, p. 18; Wahl, "The French Constitution," p. 362; Mollet, *Quinze ans*, p. 22; Mollet, *13 Mai 1958 13 Mai 1962* (Paris: Plon), p. 17, and *JO. AN.*, sitting of October 4, 1962, pp. 3210, 3213; Pompidou, *JO. AN.*, sitting of October 4, 1962, p. 3221; Goguel, "L'Elaboration de la Constitution," p. 75. Soustelle, who was a member of the government but not of the IMC, lists Mollet, Pflimlin, Debré, Pinay, and Berthoin. *Vingt-huit ans de Gaullisme* (Paris: Ed. J'ai lu, 1971), p. 169. Wahl says that the representatives of the four ministers of state attended this meeting. Mollet, in "Les institutions à l'épreuve," p. 3, said later that neither Pompidou nor Belin took part in the IMC discussions.

39. Wahl, "The French Constitution of 1958," p. 362; Debré, *La Constitution de la V e République*, p. 16; Mollet, "Les institutions à l'épreuve," p. 3, Jean-Louis Quermonne, in *Le gouvernement de la France sous la V e République* (Paris: Dalloz,

1980), p. 47n, notes that this was a singular IMC in that it included both ministers and high civil servants.

40. *L'Information*, June 14, 1958. Its meetings were held after dinner. Oliver Guichard, *Mon Général* (Paris: Grasset, 1980), p. 365.

41. *Le Monde, Combat*, June 24; *Combat*, June 27, July 1, 8, 19, 21; *Paris-Presse l'Intransigeant*, July 5, *Le Monde*, July 12, 13/14, 16, 20/21, 1958; Wahl, "The French Constitution," and Goguel, "L'Elaboration," *in passim*; Mollet, *13 Mai 1958–13 Mai 1962*, pp. 17–22, and *Quinze ans*, pp. 17, 22–23; Debré, *Une certaine idée*, pp. 72–73.

42. Mollet, *Quinze ans*, p. 17.

43. The minutes of the first two meetings appear in Debré, *La Constitution*, pp. 43–52, and Mollet, *Quinze ans*, pp. 50–63.

44. Mollet, *Quinze ans*, p. 69.

45. Debré, *La Constitution*, pp. 79–95. Mollet, *Quinze ans*, pp. 114–15, refers to "*textes*" prepared by the task force that had been distributed to the IMC members beginning with the third meeting (June 26), but the passages he quotes seem to come from the Celle-St. Cloud draft. On July 16, Debré presented the Celle-St. Cloud draft to the IMC.

46. Debré, *La Constitution*, pp. 97–108.

47. *Combat*, July 8, 1958; *Le Monde*, July 13/14, 1958.

48. Debré, *Une certaine idée*, pp. 72–73.

49. Mollet's descriptions of the deliberations, in *Quinze ans*, p. 117, documents this and he calls some of the meetings, "lively." Also, see Pflimlin's remarks in René Rémond et al., *La démocratie à refaire* (Paris: Les éditions ouvrières, 1963), p. 120; the remarks of Pflimlin's MRP colleagues in *Forces nouvelles MRP* August 2, September 13, 1958; and Debré, *La Constitution*, pp. 16–19.

50. *Combat*, June 27, July 8, 1958.

51. Debré, *Une certaine idée*, p. 73.

52. *JO. AN.*, 2nd sitting of May 20, 1967, pp. 1188–89.

53. Mollet, *Quinze ans*, p. 55; Debré, *Une certaine idée*, pp. 73–74, 156–57; Luchaire, "La responsabilité," p. 5; Wahl, "The French Constitution," p. 368. Quermonne, gives Janot the credit for proposing the delineation of "domains."

54. Debré, *La Constitution*, p. 18. Pompidou was a silent observer and does not seem to have contributed any ideas to the constitution at this stage. Guy Mollet, in "Les institutions à l'épreuve des élections," *Revue politique et parlementaire* no. 838 (1973): 3, cited by Françoise Decaumont, *La Présidence de Georges Pompidou: Essai sur le régime présidentialiste français* (Paris: Economica, 1979), p. 3n.

55. Debré, *Une certaine idée*, pp. 156–57.

56. *Combat*, September 8, 1958.

57. *Ibid.*, September 15, 1958.

58. *JO. AN.*, sitting of May 5, 1960, p. 674.

59. Debré, *La Constitution*, p. 18.

60. By this time, the composition of the government had been modified somewhat from its form as given above. Cornut-Gentille had been assigned the portfolio for Overseas France, Malraux for Cultural Affairs after a brief tenure at Information, and Lejeune for the Sahara. Other appointments had been made: Edmond Michelet, MRP, Veterans' Affairs; Roger Houdet, Indep., Agriculture; Robert Buron, MRP, Public Works, Transportation, and Tourism; Eugène Thomas, SFIO, Posts, Telephones, and Telegraphs; Pierre Sudreau, high civil servant, Construc-

tion; Bernard Chenot, high civil servant, Public Health and Population; André Boulloche, high civil servant and SFIO activist, Minister-Delegate to the Premiership; Jacques Soustelle, Gaullist, Information.

61. Debré, in *La Constitution*, pp. 109–32, publishes notes on the discussion in those meetings.
62. Soustelle, *Vingt-huit ans*, p. 169.
63. Debré, *La Constitution*, pp. 113–14; Soustelle, *Vingt-huit ans*, p. 170.
64. *L'Espérance Trahie* (Paris: Ed. de l'Alma, 1962), at pp. 60–61; Soustelle, *Vingt-huit ans*, pp. 168, 169, 171. Jacques Soustelle, "Institutions of the Fifth Republic," in Milorad M. Drachkovitch, ed., *French Fifth Republic*, (Berkeley: University of California, 1960), p. 111.
65. *L'Information* and *Combat*, July 24, 1958; *Le Monde*, July 25, 29, 1958; *La Croix*, July 27/28, 1958; Debré, "L'Elaboration," p. 20.
66. Raymond Tournoux, *Le Feu et la cendre* (Paris: Plon, 1979), p. 210.
67. *Journal Officiel. Débats parlementaires. Sénat, (JO. S.).* Sitting of October 9, 1962, p. 1306.
68. *Le Figaro*, June 13, 1958; *L'Information*, June 14, 1958; *Le Monde*, July 11, 1958; *Combat*, July 11, 1958.
69. *Combat*, July 2, 19, 1958; *Forces nouvelles* MRP, July 5, 1958, Mollet, *13 Mai 1958*, pp. 5–16. Very likely, they and the other IMC members consulted more widely than that but did not report it publicly.
70. *Le Monde*, July 8, 1958.
71. *Combat*, August 2, 6, 9, 11, 25, 1958; *Le Monde*, August 6, 7, 10/11, 20, 28, 1958; *France-Observateur*, August 14, 1958. For a long interview with Debré, published during this period, see *Revue de Défense nationale*, August/September, 1958, pp. 1277–89.
72. No. 58–599 of July 16, *Travaux préparatoires de la constitution. Avis et débats du comité consultatif constitutionnel* (Paris: La documentation française, 1960), p. 17. This source must be used with caution. Several members of the CCC have pointed out that it is "analytical" rather than stenographic and have complained that it distorted as it summarized. Marcel Waline, "Note pratique sur la publication des *Travaux préparatoires de la Constitution*," *Revue du Droit public et de la science politique*, January/February 1960, pp. 83–84. Robert Bruyneel, *JO. AN.*, sitting of 17 July 1962, p. 964 col. 2, called the *Travaux préparatoires*, "very much sweetened not to say sometimes inaccurate." Jean Nayrou, also JO. AN., agreed. See also articles in the press in mid-1959 by Nayrou and by François Valentin (June 18) as cited by Antoine Courrière, JO. S., sitting of 30 June 1959, pp. 353–54. However, all these critics imply that the distortions tended in the direction of supporting the government's allegedly later, more presidentialist, interpretation. Furthermore, the *Travaux préparatoires* were frequently cited by other members of the CCC in parliamentary debates and elsewhere. Nowhere does anyone suggest that more presidentialist sentiments by the government or anyone else were suppressed or distorted. Certainly, neither Debré nor de Gaulle expressed dissatisfaction with the accuracy with which their words were reported, and the *Travaux préparatoires* was published under Debré's direction. Debré, "L'Elaboration" and *Une certaine idée*; de Gaulle, *Mémoires d'Espoir* I: 35. Waline, "Note pratique sur la publication des *Travaux préparatoires*," alleges that the members of the CCC had no opportunity to check the account for accuracy before publication, but several months earlier Debré had announced in response to a parliamentary question that a "600-page

stenographic" manuscript of the "analytical account" had been prepared and was available to be consulted by anyone who wished. *JO. S.*, sitting of 30 June 1959, p. 353 col. 2. Also, see Luchaire and Conac, *La Constitution de la République Française*, p. 11.

73. The deputies were René Dejean, SFIO, the committee chairman; Albert de Bailliencourt, Rad.; Robert Bruyneel, Ind.; Jacques Fourcade, Ind.; Gabriel Lisette, RDA/UDSR; Léopold-Sédar Senghor, PRA; Pierre-Henri Teitgen, MRP; Paul Coste-Floret, MRP; Lucien Degoutte, Rad.; Raymond Triboulet, Gaullist; Philibert Tsirinana, SFIO; André Mignot, Ind.; Paul Alduy, SFIO; André Gayrard, Poujadist; Edmond Barrachin, Ind.; and Jean-Paul David, diss. Rad. The senators were Geoffrey de Montalembert, Gaullist, the committee chairman; François Valentin, Ind.; Marcel Champeix, SFIO; Jean Gilbert-Jules, Rad.; Pierre Marcilhacy, unaffiliated; Pierre-Max Monidion, Ind.; Jean Nayrou, SFIO; Lamine Gueye, PRA; Jacques de Menditte, MRP; and Joseph Raybaud, Rad.
74. *Le Monde*, July 28, 1958; *La Croix*, July 29, 1958.
75. *Travaux préparatoires*, pp. 19, 33; Wahl, "The French Constitution," p. 365.
76. *Le Monde*, August 8, 1958; *Travaux préparatoires*, pp. 33, 35, 118, 120.
77. *Le Monde*, August 6, 8, 1958.
78. *Travaux préparatoires*, sessions 1, 2, 7, 11, 16, and 17.
79. *Le Monde*, August 2, 9, 1958; *Combat*, August 7, 8, 1958; *Travaux préparatoires*, pp. 60, 63, 94.
80. *Travaux préparatoires* published 159 columns on those topics in a total of 304.
81. *Travaux préparatoires*—Reynaud, pp. 47, 57, 85, 90; Coste-Floret, pp. 49, 57, 58, 82, 90, 123, 182; de Bailliencourt, pp. 50, 87; Waline, pp. 51, 84, 89, 126; Barrachin, pp. 51, 52, 91, 195, 196; Lauriol, p. 52; Van Graefschepe, p. 52; Valentin, pp. 53, 88, 124; Gilbert-Jules, pp. 59, 88, 181; Teitgen, pp. 82, 83, 87, 123, 127, 181; Dejean, pp. 82, 87, 88, 112, 125, 126, 184; Montalembert, pp. 82, 89; Malterre, pp. 88, 89; Bruyneel, pp. 88, 124; Pré, pp. 89, 125; Gayrard, pp. 89, 184; Marcilhacy, p. 90; Blocq-Mascart, pp. 90, 125; David, p. 91. I have not included discussions of details of the mechanical controls on parliament.
82. Ibid., p. 58.
83. Ibid., p. 49.
84. Ibid., pp. 51, 196.
85. Ibid., p. 85.
86. Ibid., p. 181.
87. Ibid., p. 118.
88. Ibid., p. 118.
89. Ibid., p. 181.
90. Ibid., p. 183.
91. Ibid., pp. 44–45, 54, 109.
92. Jacques Fauvet, *Le Monde*, August 17/18, 1958.
93. Ibid.
94. *Le Monde*, August 20, 1958; André Passeron, *De Gaulle Parle . . .* (Paris: Plon, 1962), pp. 29–30; *The Times* (London), August 21, 1958; *La Croix*, August 19, 1958; *Combat*, August 18, 1958.
95. Merry Bromberger, *Le destin secret de Georges Pompidou* (Paris: Fayard, 1965), pp. 158, 161.
96. *Travaux préparatoires*, p. 126.
97. Debré, *La constitution*, p. 282.

98. Ibid. Subsequent editing softened the language, but the substance survived.
99. Debré, "Discours devant le conseil d'Etat"; *Le Monde*, August 29, 1958; *Combat*, August 18, 23, 1958; *L'Information, L'Aurore*, August 28, 1958; *France-Référendum*, September 28, 1958.
100. *Le Monde*, August 30, 1958; Debré, *La Constitution*, p. 193.
101. "Organization of the armed forces" in the CCC revision.
102. That is, "The establishment of jurisdictions," government; "the establishment and competence of jurisdictions," CCC; "the rules concerning the creation of new categories of jurisdictions," Council of State.
103. Luchaire says that this article was drafted so hastily (in less than 48 hours) that the framers were "perfectly well aware of the weakness of this point in their constitution" and added the elastic clause to permit later rectifications. *Le parlementarisme peut-il être limité sans être annihilé* (Paris: Association française de science politique, 1965), pp. 19–20.
104. The text appears in Debré, *La Constitution*, pp. 180–219.
105. *Le Monde*, September, 2, 3, 4, 5, 1958; *L'Information*, September 2, 1958; Passeron, *De Gaulle Parle*, p. 30.
106. Debré, *La Constitution*, 179 ff.; Mollet in "Les institutions à l'épreuve," p. 8.
107. De Gaulle, "Discours de la Place de la République," p. 30.
108. *Discours et messages*, vol. III, *Avec le renouveau* (Paris: Plon, 1970), pp. 77, 261.
109. Ibid., p. 301.
110. Tournoux, *La Tragédie, du général* (Paris: Plon, 1967), p. 632.
111. *Discours et messages*, vol. IV, *Pour l'Effort, August 1962–December 1965* (Paris: Plon, 1970), p. 21. He used this formula, also, in his radio–television addresses of October 4, 18, and 26. Ibid., pp. 31, 35, 40.
112. Ibid., pp. 22–23, 31 (October 4). Also, see de Gaulle, *Mémoires d'Espoir* II: 17–20.
113. *Mémoires d'Espoir* I: 35–37.
114. André Passeron, *De Gaulle 1958–1969* (Paris: Bordas, 1972), pp. 313–14.
115. January 31, 1964, press conference, *Discours et Messages* IV: 168.
116. Interview of Debré, *Revue de Défense nationale*, p. 1281.
117. Nicholas Wahl, "Aux origines de la Nouvelle Constitution," in *Revue française de science politique*, March 1959, pp. 34, 39n.
118. Debré "Construire enfin un régime parlementaire," speech at Legueil, August 17, 1958, in Debré, *Refaire un démocratie, un état, un pouvoir* (Paris: Plon, 1958), pp. 15–35.
119. "Renoncer à l'anarchie pour éviter la dictature," Chateau-la-Vallière, August 24, 1958, in Debré, *Refaire un démocratie*, pp. 36–50.
120. Ibid., pp. 73–75.
121. *Combat*, September 6/7, 1958.
122. *Courrier de la nation*, September 11, 1958.
123. *Le Monde*, September 17, 1958.
124. *JO. AN.*, 1st sitting of 15 January 1959, p. 27, 1st sitting of 16 January 1959, p. 77.
125. "Commentaires sur la constitution du 4 Octobre 1958," *Notes et études documentaires*, April 11, 1959, Sécrétariat générale du gouvernment esp. pp. 7, 8, 9, 10, 11, and 12.
126. *JO. S.*, sitting of June 2, 1959, p. 148.
127. *JO. AN.*, sitting of May 26, 1959, p. 557.
128. *Entreprise*, September 12, 1959, pp. 10–11.

129. "L'Autorité gouvernementale," in *Jeune Patron*, May 1965, notes from a speech to "Horizons" dinner, November 19, 1964, pp. 35–40.

130. Debré, "*L'Elaboration*, p. 21.

131. The third was a majority electoral system. See "The Constitution of 1958, Its Raison d'Etre and How It Evolved," in William G Andrews and Stanley Hoffmann, eds., *The Fifth Republic at Twenty* (Albany, N.Y.: SUNY Press, 1981), pp. 11–24.

132. Ibid., p. 21. Also, see Debré's comments in "L'Elaboration," pp. 497–512.

133. *Combat*, September 15, *Le Monde*, September 16, 1958.

134. Mollet, "Une revision constitutionnelle," p. 10.

135. Mollet, *Les Chances du socialisme. Réponse à la société industrielle* (Paris: Fayard, 1968), p. 44.

136. Mollet, *Quinze ans*, p. 23.

137. Ibid., p. 38, see also p. 114.

138. Ibid., p. 41.

139. Ibid., p. 43.

140. Ibid., p. 149.

141. *Combat*, September 8, October 21, 1958; *Forces nouvelles MRP*, November 1, 1958.

142. *JO. AN.*, 1st sitting of December 13, 1962, p. 53.

143. Rémond *et al.*, *La démocratie à refaire*, pp. 120–22; *JO. AN.*, 1st sitting of December 13, 1962, p. 53.

144. *JO. AN.*, April 26, 1962, p. 750.

145. Soustelle, *L'Espérance*, pp. 60–61; Soustelle, *Vingt-huit*, pp. 168, 169, 171, 172.

146. Sudreau, *L'Enchainement* (Paris: Plon, 1967), pp. 213–16, 236. The latter reference was reprinted from *Le Monde*, May 18, 1967. See also Buron, *Le plus beau des métiers* (Paris: Plon, 1963), p. 165.

147. Luchaire, "La Responsabilité. p. 3.

148. Ibid., p. 5.

149. Tournoux, *La Tragédie*, pp. 633–34.

150. *JO. AN.* sitting of 2 June 1959, p. 712; also, see his comments in *JO. AN.*, sitting of May 5, 1960, pp. 661–62; 2nd sitting of October 19, 1961, pp. 2642–43.

151. Chandernagor, "La Constitution trahie," pp. 339–47 in April 1960, p. 340.

152. Rémond *et al.*, *La démocratie à refaire*, pp. 127–28.

153. Chandernagor, *Un parlement: pour quoi faire?* (Paris: Gallimard, 1967), p. 38.

154. *Le Monde*, November 21, 1958.

155. Pierre Marcilhacy, "De l'enfantement d'une Constitution," *Revue politique des Idées et des Institutions*, September 1958, p. 423.

156. Mignot, *La nouvelle constitution* pp. 9, 21, 23, 29.

157. *Combat*, September 13/14, 26, 1958; *Force nouvelles MRP*, September 13, 1958.

158. Marcilhacy, *Les Chouans de la liberté* (Paris: Nouvelles éditions latines, 1963), pp. 103–04.

159. *Le Figaro*, February 12, 1960.

160. Marcilhacy, "Pour oeuvrer durablement, adoptons d'abord les institutions," in *Revue politique et parlementaire*, February 1964, p. 11.

161. *JO. AN.*, sitting of January 21, 1959, p. 150; 2nd sitting of April 29, 1959, p. 317; and 1st sitting of December 10, 1959.

162. Coste-Floret, "Réflexions sur le contrôle parlementaire," in *Revue politique des Idées et des Institutions*, March 30, 1959, p. 161; he made similar observations in "Le future Constitution: Du choix des ministres," in *Revue politique des Idées et des*

Institutions, June 15, 1958, p. 298; "Quoi après de Gaulle?", *Entreprise*, April 16, 1960, pp. 18–19; JO.AN., sitting of November 22, 1960. pp. 2957–58, and 2nd sitting of January 15, 1959, p. 49.

163. Paul Reynaud, "La Malaise constitutionnelle," in *Revue de Paris*, June 1960, pp. 12, 13; also, *JO. AN.*, 2nd sitting of April 26, 1962, p. 768; Reynaud, *Et après* (Paris: Plon, 1964), p. 56.

164. Barrachin, "Institutions un vrai régime présidentiel," in *Revue politique et parlementaire*, Janurary 1964, p. 3.

165. *JO.AN.*, 1st sitting of October 14, 1959, pp. 1758–59. Also see David's remarks in *JO.AN.*, sitting of May 5, 1960, p. 633; and 2nd sitting of April 26, 1962, p. 755.

166. Tournoux, *La Tragédie*, p. 641.

167. *JO.AN.*, sitting of July 17, 1962, p. 964.

168. Léon Noël, "Ministres et députés," in *Revue française de science politique*, April 1968, pp. 213–29.

169. *JO.AN.*, 2nd sitting of January 20, 1959, p. 115.

170. Tournoux, *La Tragédie*, p. 298. Also, see Léon Noël, *L'Avenir du Gaullisme* (Paris: Plon, 1973), p. 109.

171. Deixonne, *Le Populaire de Paris*, September 19, 1958.

172. Paul Ramadier, "Refléxions sur le project constitutionnel," *Points de vues et controverses*, suppl. to August 1958.

173. *Le Figaro, Le Monde*, September 13, 1958.

174. *JO. S.*, sitting of July 17, 1962, p. 949.

175. *JO. AN.*, sitting of April 24, 1962, p. 947.

176. Michelet, *La querelle de la fidelité*, (Paris: Fayard, 1971), p. 176.

177. *JO. S.*, sitting of July 27, 1962, p. 1307.

178. *JO. AN.*, 1st sitting of October 15, 1959, p. 1805.

179. *JO. AN.*, 1st sitting of May 27, 1959, pp. 605–606; *Le Figaro*, September 13, 1958.

180. *Le Figaro*, February 12, 1960.

181. *JO. AN.*, sitting of May 5, 1960, p. 667.

182. Typical of the initial commentaries on this point are Jean Chatelain, *La Nouvelle constitution et le régime politique de la France* (Paris: Berger-Levrault, 1959), pp. 70–71; Marcel Prélot, *La Nouvelle constitution* (Paris: Le Centurion, 1958), pp. 43ff; Raymond Aron, *France—The New Republic* (New York: Oceana, 1960), pp. 22ff; Stanley H. Hoffmann, "The French Constitution of 1958: The Final Text and its Prospects," *American Political Science Review*, June 1959, pp. 332–57; Georges Burdeau, "La conception du pouvoir selon la Constitution du 4 Octobre 1958," *Revue française de science politique*, March 1959, pp. 87–100; Maurice Duverger, "Les institutions de la cinquième République," *Revue française de science politique*, March 1959, pp. 101–34; Duverger, *La Cinquième République* (Paris: PUF, 1959), pp. 16–19; Ferdinand A. Hermens, *The Fifth Republic* (South Bend, Ind.: University of Notre Dame, 1960), pp. 28–44; Roy C. Macridis and Bernard E. Brown, *The De Gaulle Republic: Quest for Unity* (Homewood, Ill.: Dorsey, 1960), pp. 176–78; Henry W. Ehrmann, "Constitutional Developments in the French Fifth Republic," in Milorad Drachkovitch, ed., *French Fifth Republic* (Berkeley, Cal.: University of California Press, 1960), p. 18; Nicholas Wahl, *The Fifth Republic* (New York: Random House, 1959), p. 26; Philip M. Williams and Martin Harrison, *De Gaulle's Republic* (New York: Longmans, 1960), pp. 121–31.

183. For a discussion of the original presidential electoral college in terms of democratic

legitimacy, see William G. Andrews, "Three Electoral Colleges," *Parliamentary Affairs*, Spring 1961, pp. 178–88.

184. Jean Massot, *La Présidence de la République en France* (Paris: La Documentation française, 1977), pp. 60–61. The list below totals 76,400. In fact, the returns show only 76,359 registered electors, leaving 41 vacancies. In addition, the colleges for the overseas, Algerian, and Saharan departments and the overseas territories had 1,762 electors and 3,643 electors were members of the colleges for the member states of the Community, who voted for the same candidates for president of the Community but not for president of the Republic. *L'Année politique 1958* (Paris: PUF, 1959), pp. 654–55. The details of the composition of the electoral college were specified in Ordinance 58-1064 of November 7, 1958.

185. *L'Année politique 1959* (Paris: PUF, 1960), p. 11. If the original presidential electoral system had operated after the new Senate was installed, the range of popular connections would have extended over an even longer span of time, for the new senators had terms of nine years, rather than six. Thus, it would have been possible for the electoral college to include some senators who had been elected nine years earlier by muncipal councilors who had been elected by popular vote six years before that.

186. *L'Année politique 1958*, pp. 653–54. If this analysis is carried to the level of the commune, the disparity in the presidential electoral college is even greater, the most rural communes having 33 percent of the population and 51 percent of the votes. Duverger, *La Cinquième République*, p. 30. Comparable data for the National Assembly are not available. These ratios have more than theoretical significance. The more rural departments were less Gaullist in 1958 in the National Assembly and more so in the presidential elections. Thirty-five percent of their deputies bore the UNR label, compared to 43.6 percent for the rest of France and 83.1 percent of their electors voted for de Gaulle, compared to 73.7 percent in the more urban France. The 1958 presidential elections were too lopsided for that distortion to have been decisive, but it would have determined the outcome in elections as close as those of 1965, 1969, and 1974.

187. De Gaulle attempted to strengthen the democratic legitimacy of the presidency by converting the referendums of the Constitutional Law of June 3, 1958, and of Art. 11 of the constitution into plebiscites. However, that action was extraconstitutional—if not unconstitutional—and cannot be considered an indication of the type of regime established by the constitution.

2. EXECUTIVE COUNCILS AND COMMITTEES

1. Laws of August 31, 1871, Art. 2, and February 25, 1875, Art. 6.
2. Documents d'études, no. 9, October 1970 (*La IIIe République*); Andrée Martin-Pannetier, *Institutions et vie Politique Françaises de 1789 à nos jours* (Paris: L.G.D.J., 1971), p. 52. However, as late as 1913, President of the Republic Raymond Poincaré said that the "Council of Ministers deals with the more important business, the Cabinet Council with current questions of internal politics, the former meeting about twice as much as the latter," Raymond Poincaré, *How France Is Governed* (London: T. Fisher Unwin, 1913), p. 197.
3. Serge Arné, *Le Président du conseil des ministres sous la IVe République* (Paris: Pichon and Durand-Auzias, 1962), p. 91; Marcel Martin, ed., *Les Institutions*

Politiques de la France (Paris: La Documentation française, 1959), pp. 234–35; Philip M. Williams, *Crisis and Compromise* (London: Longmans, 1964), pp. 196n., 204.

4. Interview with Michel Debré, July 10, 1978.
5. See, for instance, his speech to the Council of State, August 27, 1958, in William G. Andrews, ed., *European Political Institutions*, 2nd. ed. (Princeton, N.J.: Van Nostrand, 1966), pp. 43–55.
6. *Le Monde*, January 11/12, 1959.
7. Interview with Michel Debré, July 10, 1978.
8. *Le Monde*, March 20, 1959.
9. For accounts of other 1959 meetings, see *Le Monde*, January 29, February 3, April 19/20, May 15, August 26, October 6, December 4, 8, 1959; *Combat*, June 18, 1959. Other meetings may have been held, but not reported in the press.
10. *Le Monde*, February 24, 1960.
11. *Le Monde*, March 2, 1960.
12. *Le Monde*, March 22, April 24, July 14, November 10, 1960, January 25, August 29, 1961; *Combat*, April 6, 7, 1960, April 17, 1962; *Le Figaro*, April 18, May 16, 1961; Pierre Avril, *Le Régime politique de la V ͤ République*, 2nd. ed. (Paris: L.G.D.J., 1967), p. 245. Etienne Burin des Roziers in Gilbert Pilleul, ed., *"l'Entourage" et de Gaulle* (Paris: Plon, 1979), p. 173. These accounts conflict with the recollections, twenty years later, of François Goguel and Couve de Murville, in *ibid.*, pp. 176–77. However, Pompidou did hold business luncheons to which all members of the government were invited. Claude Dulong, *A L'Elysée au Temps de Charles de Gaulle* (Paris: Hachette, 1974), p. 142n.
13. *Le Monde*, April 29, May 16, June 20, 21, 1969; Jean-Louis Quermonne, *Le Gouvernement de la France sous la V ͤ République* (Paris: Dalloz, 1980), p. 214.
14. *Le Monde*, December 4, 8, 1959.
15. *Le Monde*, August 25, 26, 1959; *La Croix*, August 27, 1959.
16. *Le Monde*, April 29, 1960.
17. *Le Monde*, February 24, March 2, 1960.
18. Patrice Verrier, *Les Services de la présidence de la république* (Paris: PUF, 1971), p. 45.
19. Charles de Gaulle, *Memoirs of Hope: Renewal and Endeavor* (New York: Simon & Schuster, 1971), p. 272. That decision may have been motivated partly by lingering resentment over his exclusion from the Reynaud government's Council of Ministers when he was an undersecretary of state in 1940. Michel Debré and Jean-Louis Debré, *Le Pouvoir politique* (Paris: Seghers 1976), p. 66.
20. J. L. Bodiguel, M.-Ch. Kessler, M. Sineau, "Cent ans de Sécretariats d'état," in Institut français des Sciences administratives, *Les Superstructures des administrations centrales* (Paris: Ed. Cujas, 1973), p. 54; Claude Dulong, *A L'Elysée au temps de Charles de Gaulle; Le Figaro*, June 26, 1969; Victor Silvera, "La Structure du septième gouvernement de le Vème République," in *Revue administrative*, July/August 1969, p. 445.
21. Silvera, "La Structure du septième gouvernement," p. 445.
22. Bodiguel et al., "Cent ans de Sécretariats d'état," p. 55, Françoise Decaumont, *La Présidence de Georges Pompidou* (Paris: Economica, 1979), p. 177n. For instance, no meeting was held in the first five months of 1971.
23. Victor Silvera, *"La Structure du huitième gouvernement de la Véme République,"* in *Revue administrative*, September/October 1972, p. 491.

24. *Le Monde*, March 3/4, 1974, In fact, the Council of Ministers membership under Messmer III was seventeen and would have been thirty with the secretaries of state.

25. Jean Massot, *La Présidence de la République en France* (Paris: La documentation française, 1977), p. 33.

26. Dulong, *A L'Elysée au temps de Charles de Gaulle*, pp. 121–22; Pierre Viansson-Ponté, "Les Pouvoirs Parallèles," in *L'Evénement*, March 1966, p. 30; Marceau Long, "Le Sécretariat Général du Gouvernement," 1978 lecture at the University of Aix-Marseilles, mimeograph, p. 17.

27. On April 22, 1964, when de Gaulle underwent surgery; on September 30, 1964, during his South American trip; on May 17, 1968, during his Rumanian trip, and on Febraury 14, 1973, when Pompidou was "suffering from the flu." Verrier, "Les services de la présidence," p. 45n; *Le Monde*, May 18, 1968, February 15, 1973.

28. *Le Figaro*, March 11, 1974.

29. *Combat*, January 22, 1964.

30. *Combat* and *Information*. February 5, 1959.

31. *Le Monde*, February 28 and August 30, 1969; *Articles et documents* (La documentation française), Nos. 1,947 and 1,973.

32. *Le Monde*, July 14/15, 1968.

33. *Le Monde*, October 8, 1959; *Combat*, August 13, 1959; *Chronique des jours moroses 1969–1970* (Paris: Presses de la Cité, 1971), p. 31; Dulong, *L'Elysée au temps de Charles de Gaulle* p. 119.

34. *Combat*, June 26, 1969; Jean-Pierre Farkas, "Comment l'Elysée gouverne," in *Paris-Match*, January 19, 1974, p. 33; *Le Monde*, June 25, 1969.

35. *Le Monde*, August 19, 25, 1959; January 13, 1966.

36. *Combat*, June 3, 1968; *L'Aurore*, January 4, 1973.

37. *Chronique des jours moroses*, pp. 280–81.

38. Official communiqué, May 21, 1968, La documentation française.

39. *Le Monde*, June 16, 1959, November 26, 1968, August 30, 1969, January 20/21, 1974; Raymond Tournoux, *Journal secret: Une année pas comme les autres* (Paris: Plon, 1975), pp. 27–28.

40. Only two ministers ever chose to resign—Boulloche in 1959 on state aid to private schools and Sudreau on the October 1962 referendum.

41. For the texts of the ministers' remarks on this issue, see J. R. Tournoux, *La Tragédie du général* (Paris: Plon, 1967), pp. 631–47.

42. Gérard Belorgey, *Le Gouvernement et l'administration de la France* (Paris: Colin, 1967), p. 111; Edgard Pisani, *Le Général indivis*, (Paris: Albin Michel, 1974), p. 128; Dulong, *L'Elysée au temps de Charles de Gaulle* pp. 119–20; Massot, *La Présidence*, pp. 174–75; Jean Massot, *Le Chef du gouvernement in France* (Paris: La Documentation française, 1979), p. 189; Long, "Le Sécretariat Générale," pp. 13–15.

43. Massot, *La Présidence*, p. 175; Buron, *Le plus beau des métiers* (Paris: Plon, 1963), p. 219; Belorgey, *Le gouvernement et l'administration*, p. 111.

44. *Le Monde*, October 1, 1964, May 18, 1968.

45. *Le Monde*, February 16, 18/19, 1973.

46. The hand-shaking ritual was omitted at three meetings when Pompidou was too ill for the effort. *Le Monde*, April 9, 1974.

47. Pierre Galante, *The General!* (New York: Random House, 1968), p. 206.

48. *Chronique des jours moroses*, pp. 174, 217; Robert Buron, *Le plus beau des métiers*

pp. 218–19; Dulong, *L'Elysée au temps de Charles de Gaulle* pp. 120–21; *Le Figaro*, October 8, 1973.

49. Long, *Le Sécretariat Général*, pp. 14–15.

50. *Le Figaro*, October 8, 1973; *L'Organisation du Travail gouvernemental et les services du premier ministre* (Paris: La documentation française, September 1972); Massot, *La Présidence*, p. 117; Long, *Le Sécretariat Général*, pp. 16–17; Decaumont, *La Présidence de Georges Pompidou*, pp. 174–75.

51. Pisani, *Le Général indivs*, p. 131; Jacques Soustelle, *Vingt ans de gaullisme*, (Paris: Ed. J'ai lu, 1971), p. 181; Jacques Soustelle, *L'espérance trahie* (Paris: Ed. de l'Alma, 1962), p. 94; Buron, *Le plus beau des métiers* p. 220; *Chronique des jours moroses*, p. 217. Pierre Viansson-Ponté, *Les Gaullistes: Rituel et Annuaire* (Paris: Seuil, 1963), pp. 44–46. For exceptions to these generalizations, see below [ms. pp. 93–95].

52. Soustelle, *Vingt-huit ans de gaullisme*, p. 181.

53. Pierre Viansson-Ponté. *Histoire de la république gaullienne*, 2 vols. (Paris: Gallimard, 1970), I: 167, 206.

54. Bernard Chenot, *Etre ministre*, (Paris: Plon, 1967), p. 66.

55. Pisani, *Le Général indivis*, p. 128; Buron, *Le plus beau des métiers*, p. 223.

56. Pisani, *Le Général indivis*, p. 128.

57. *Le Figaro*, October 8, 1973.

58. Charles Debbasch, *La France de Pompidou* (Paris: PUF, 1974), p. 40.

59. Pisani, *Le Général indivis*, pp. 129–30.

60. Ibid., pp. 130–31.

61. Ibid., p. 129.

62. *Le Figaro*, October 8, 1973.

63. Viansson-Ponté, *Histoire de la république gaullienne*, I: 206.

64. Jack Hayward, *The One and Indivisible French Republic* (New York: Norton, 1973), p. 96; *Chronique des jours moroses*, p. 31; Merry Bromberger, *Le Destin Secret de Georges Pompidou* (Paris: Fayard, 1965), p. 299.

65. *Le Figaro*, October 8, 1973.

66. An allusion to de Gaulle's purge trials of Vichy ministers.

67. Tournoux, *La Tragédie du général*, pp. 315–20. A variation of this incident is related in Galante, *The General!*, p. 208. Raymond Tournoux, *Le feu et la cendre* (Paris: Plon, 1979), p. 229.

68. Tournoux, *La Tragédie*, p. 221; Philippe Alexandre, *Le Duel de Gaulle Pompidou* (Paris: Grasset, 1970), p. 217.

69. *Le Monde*, November 26, 1968; Anne and Pierre Rouanet, *Les Trois derniers chagrins du général de Gaulle* (Paris: Grasset, 1980), pp. 426–30; Jean-Marcel Jeanneney in Pilleul, *"l'Entourage" et de Gaulle*, pp. 326–29.

70. Philippe Alexandre, *Exécution d'un homme politique* (Paris: Grasset, 1973), P. 279.

71. Pisani, *Le Général indivis*, p. 133.

72. Debbasch, *La France de Pompidou*, p. 40.

73. Williams, *Crisis and Compromise*, p. 198.

74. Ibid., p. 294; Arné, *Le Président du conseil*, p. 79n.

75. Arné, *Le Président du conseil*, p. 305.

76. Ibid., p. 199; Dulong, *L'Elysée au temps de Charles de Gaulle*, p. 146; Vincent Auriol, *Journal du Septennat, 1953–1954* (Paris: Colin, 1970), I: lvi, 36, 60, 153, 172–73, 517.

77. Auriol, *Journal du Septennat*, I: 56.

78. Dulong, *L'Elysée au temps de Charles de Gaulle*, p. 146.
79. Auriol, *Journal du Septennat*, p. 239.
80. Martin, *Les Institutions Politiques*, p. 239.
81. Verrier, *Les Services de la Présidence*, p. 16.
82. Martin, *Les Institutions Politiques*, pp. 239–40; William G. Andrews, "Swan Song of the Fourth Republic", in *Parliamentary Affairs*, Autumn 1962, pp. 485–499.
83. De Gaulle press conference, September 9, 1965; *Année politique 1965*, p. 441; Dulong, *L'Elysée au temps de Charles de Gaulle*, p. 139. Decaumont, *La Présidence de Georges Pompidou*, p. 165, says forty-five in the last forty-one months of Pompidou's presidency, but fifty in the first eighteen. Massot, *Le Chef du gouvernement*, p. 164, says fifty-eight meetings in fifty-nine months. Viansson-Ponté, *Les Gaullistes*, pp. 43–44. The terms of designation applied to these committees is a matter of some confusion. The leading French scholar on this topic says that *"conseil"* was used for those that the president chaired and *"comité"* for those that the prime minister chaired. Also, he says that the qualifier *"interministériel"* distinguished standing committees and *"restreint"* ad hoc committees. The use of *"réunion"* or *"entretien"* implied less formal meetings. André G. Delion, "Les conseils et comités interministériels," *A.J.D.A.*, June 1975, p. 268. Prime Minister Pompidou said in 1964 that "we have acquired the habit of reserving the term of *'conseil'* to the meetings organized under the presidence of the Chief of State, and the term of *'comité'* to the meetings organized at the Hotel Matignon." *JO. AN.*, April 24, 1964, p. 949, However, Marceau Long, general secretary of the government, informed this writer by letter of February 1, 1980, obtained with the assistance of Professor Léo Hamon, that a review of the secretariat's archives disclosed that prime-ministerial committees were designated as follows:
    1. From the first semester of 1958 until end of 1963—*"conseil restreint"*
    2. From the end of 1963 until June 1964—*"conseil restreint"* or *"comité interministériel,"* "though the exact reason for the choice of one term or the other cannot be determined"
    3. From June 1964 to February 1965—*"comité interministériel"*
    4. Since February 1965—*"comités restreints"*
    5. Throughout the entire time—all prime-ministerial committees created by decree were designated *"comité interministériel"*
    Also, Alain Prate, technical counselor to President de Gaulle, has reported that the presidential committees were called *"réunions tenues sous la présidence du général de Gaulle"* until about 1963, when they became *"conseils restreints."* Pilleul, *"l'Entourage" et de Gaulle*, p. 172.
84. Ord. 59-147 of January 9, 1959; D-59-942 of July 31, 1959.
85. Dulong, *L'Elysée au temps de Charles de Gaulle*, p. 143. In practice the Defense Committee came to be called the Defense Council, in keeping with the practice of using "council" when the president chaired; Massot, *La Présidence*, p. 178; Verrier, *Les Services de la présidence*, p. 48.
86. Avril, *Le Régime politique*, p. 229.
87. Ibid., p. 229; Jean Baillou and Pierre Pelletier, *Les Affaires Etrangères* (Paris: PUF, 1962), p. 29; Herbert Tint, *French Foreign Policy Since the Second World War* (London: Weidenfeld and Nicolson, 1972), p. 240; Verrier *Les Services de la présidence*, p. 48; Bernard Tricot, "Rapport introductif: Les conseils restreints à l'Elysée du temps du général de Gaulle," in Pilleul, *"l'Entourage" et de Gaulle*, p. 165.
88. D. 60-1455 of November 1960 and D. 62-808 and 809 of July 18, 1962.

89. Its official title was *"Comité des affaires algériennes;"* D. 60-120 of February 13, 1960.
90. Tricot, "Rapport introductif," p. 166.
91. Bernard Tricot, *Les Sentiers de la Paix*, (Paris: Plon, 1972), p. 142.
92. Dulong, in *"l'Entourage" et de Gaulle*, p. 147.
93. D. 62-344 of March 26, 1962.
94. Tricot, "Rapport introductif," p. 167.
95. Tricot, *Les Sentiers de la Paix*, p. 142. Also, see Tricot, "Rapport introductif," pp. 166–67.
96. De Gaulle, *Memoirs of Hope*, p. 85; Tricot, *Les Sentiers de la Paix*, p. 142; William G. Andrews, *French Politics and Algeria* (New York: Appleton-Century-Crofts, 1962), p. 120.
97. D. 61-491 of May 18, 1961.
98. Raymond Barillon *et. al.*, *Dictionnaire de la Constitution* (Paris: Ed. Cujas, 1976), p. 45.
99. *Arreté* of May 16, 1961.
100. D. 61-491 of May 18, 1961.
101. Dulong, *l'Elysée au temps de Charles de Gaulle*, p. 149; Francis de Baecque, *l'Administration centrale de la France* (Paris: Colin, 1973), p. 109.
102. *Le Monde*, March 10, 1960.
103. Baillou and Pelletier, *Les Affaires Etrangères*, p. 29; Maurice Couve de Murville, *Une politique étrangère, 1958-1969* (Paris: Plon, 1971); de Baecque, *L'Administration centrale*, p. 108.
104. J. A. Laponce, *The Government of the Fifth Republic* (Berkeley and Los Angeles: University of California Press, 1961), pp. 295–96.
105. The importance of this power is indicated by the fact that about 2,000 appeals for presidential grace are made each year and fifty persons received death sentences under criminal law, 1959–77, of whom thirty were reprieved. Debré and Debré *Le Pouvoir politique*, p. 42.
106. The High Council of the Magistracy is not discussed here because it is not, strictly speaking, a committee of the executive, even though the president of the Republic chairs some of its meetings.
107. Dulong, pp. 50–51, 140; Verrier, *Les Services de la présidence*, p. 50; Burin des Roziers in Pilleul, *"l'Entourage et de Gaulle"*, p. 174; Decaumont, *La présidence de Georges Pompidou*, p. 164.
108. Tricot, "Rapport introductif," p. 170.
109. Bromberger, *Le Destin Secret*, p. 318.; Tricot, "Rapport introductif," p. 171.
110. Interview with Michael Debré, July 10, 1978.
111. Dulong, *L'Elysée au temps de Charles de Gaulle*, p. 140. For a list of the "themes" of the *ad hoc* councils, see Tricot, "Rapport introductif," p. 168. Decaumont, *La Présidence de Georges Pompidou*, p. 165.
112. Decaumont, *La Présidence*, p. 162.
113. Debré and Debré, *La Pouvoir politique*, p. 60; Dulong, *L'Elysée au temps de Charles de Gaulle*, p. 139; Massot, *Le Chef du gouvernement*, p. 164. Ezra N. Suleiman, "Presidential Government in France," in Richard Rose and Ezra N. Suleiman, eds., *Presidents and Prime Ministers* (Washington D.C.: American Enterprise Institute, 1980), pp. 115–16.
114. *Repertoire permanent de l'administration française* 1968 (Paris: La Documentation française, 1968), pp. 6–9; *Repertoire permanent de l'administration française 1974*, .pp. 9–13.

115. Ordinances of November 23, 1944.
116. Delion, "Les conseils et comités interministériels", p. 274.
117. Interview with M. Michel Debré, July 10, 1978.
118. Delion, "Les conseils et comités interministériels", p. 274; *Le Monde, in passim; Fondation nationale de sciences politiques* clipping file.
119. Robert Langlois-Meurinne, *Le Premier ministre dans l'Administration française* (Paris: Faculty of Law Thesis, 1965), p. 142.
120. *Le Monde*, March 1, 1960.
121. D. 62-555 of May 10, 1962.
122. D. 53-455 of May 19, 1953.
123. *Combat*, March 3, 1966.
124. D. 60-106 of February 2, 1960; D. 61-1187 of October 31, 1961.
125. D. 60-1219 of November 19, 1960; D. 61-728 of July 6, 1961.
126. D. 63-114 of February 14, 1963.
127. D. 60-1219 of November 19, 1960. *JO. LD.*, November 20, 1960, p. 1063.
128. Pierre Rouanet, *Pompidou* (Paris: Grasset, 1969), pp. 105–106.; D. 63-114 of February 14, 1963.
129. Olivier Guichard, *Amenager la France*, (Paris: Laffont, 1964), p. 216.
130. Massot, *Le Chef du gouvernement*, pp. 216–17.
131. Decree of July 25, 1935.
132. D. 59-766 of June 19, 1959.
133. D. 62-1530 of December 22, 1962; Massot, *Le Chef du gouvernement*, p. 220n.
134. D. 48-1029 of June 25, 1948, D. 52-1016 of September 3, 1952, and D. 58-344 of April 3, 1958; Massot, *Le Chef du gouvernement*, pp. 197–98.
135. *Repertoire permanent de l'administration française 1965*; Massot, *Le Chef du gouvernement*, p. 198.
136. D. 58-1144 of November 28, 1958; Massot, *Le Chef du gouvernement*, pp. 216–17; Francis de Baecque, *L'Administration centrale de la France* (Paris: Colin, 1973, pp. 119–20; J. R. Frears, *France in the Giscard Presidency* (London: Allen & Unwin, 1981), p. 121.
137. Frears, *France in The Giscard Presidency*, p. 221, Decrees of July 30, 1970; D. 71-94 of January 7, 1971; February 2, 1971.
138. D. 60-309 of March 18, 1960; D. 61-362 of April 8, 1961, D. 64-182 of February 26, 1964, D. 70-728 of August 5, 1970; Law of December 3, 1966; Decree of May 12, 1970; Decree of April 12, 1945; D. 64-628 of June 25, 1964; Ord. 45-2563 of October 18, 1945; D. 45-2572 of October 18, 1945; Decree of February 2, 1971; *Figaro*, January 28, 1971; Decree of August 11, 1971; Decree of December 17, 1971; Decree of July 5, 1972; *Nation*, June 29, 1972.
139. Interview with Michel Debré, July 10, 1978.
140. Dulong, *L'Elysée au temps de Charles de Gaulle*, p. 142.
141. Bromberger, *Le Destin Secret*, pp. 318–19.

3. EXECUTIVE PERSONNEL

1. 58-1254 of December 19, 1958.
2. Patrice Verrier, *Les Services de la présidence de la république* (Paris: PUF, 1971), pp. 71, 85, 87–89, 92; Victor Silvera, "Vie de la Présidence et des Ministères du 16 juin au

15 août 1969," in *Revue administrative*, July/August 1969, p. 475; Jean Massot, *La Présidence de la République en France* (Paris: La Documentation française, 1977), pp. 164–72.

3. Claude Dulong, *La Vie Quotidienne à l'Elysée au temps de Charles de Gaulle* (Paris: Hachette, 1974), p. 91. The roles of the other two services are self-explanatory and, in any case, they are not major concerns of this chapter.
4. Pompidou's presidential staff listed in Françoise Decaumont, *La Présidence de Georges Pompidou* (Paris: Economica, 1979), pp. 275–80.
5. These data on the size of the Elysée staff do not take into account occasional personnel assigned there unofficially. They are said to equal in number the official staff. Pierre Viansson-Ponté, "Les Pouvoirs Parallèles," in *L'Evénement*, March 1966, p. 31. Nor does it count nonpolitical staff such as household, clerical, maintenance, and security personnel. One estimate places the size of the total Elysée staff at 500 persons. Jean-Pierre Farkas, "Comment l'Elysée Gouverne," in *Paris-Match*, January 19, 1974, p. 32.
6. This may be compared to de Gaulle's staff while he was premier, 1958–59, when nine of nineteen members had been active in the RPF. Olivier Guichard, *Mon Général* (Paris: Grasset, 1980), p. 359.
7. Charles de Gaulle, *War Memoirs: The Call to Honor. 1940–1942* (New York: Viking, 1955), pp. 56, 72, 80, 100, 277. Unless indicated otherwise, all biographical data were drawn from *Who's Who in France* and Société Générale de la Presse.
8. Pierre Viansson-Ponté, *Les Gaullistes: Rituel et Annuaire* (Paris: Seuil, 1963), pp. 96–97.
9. Ibid., pp. 77–78.
10. Nicholas A. Wahl, "The French Constitution of 1958: The Initial Draft and its Origins," in *American Political Science Review*, June 1959, p. 361.
11. Paul Gillet, "Jacques Foccart," in *Les Héritiers du général* (Paris: Denoel, 1969), p. 52.
12. Dulong, *L'Elysée au Temps de Charles de Gaulle*, p. 112.
13. Gillet, "Jacques Foccart," pp. 49–53. Viansson-Ponté, *Les Gaullistes*, pp. 116–18; Viansson-Ponté, "Les pouvoirs parallèles," p. 30.
14. Verrier, *Les Services de la présidence*, p. 27; *Le Monde*, October 26, 1967.
15. *Le Monde*, May 11, 1973.
16. The other three original special assistants in the presidential office appear to have had no previous professional appointments under de Gaulle. They were Luc-René Boissonis, Gérard de la Villèsbrunne, and Jacques Narbonne.
17. René Backman, "Olivier Guichard," in *Les Héritiers du général*, p. 94; Olivier Guichard, *Un chemin tranquille* (Paris: Flammarion, 1975), Olivier Guichard, *Mon Général* (Paris: Grasset, 1980).
18. Viansson-Ponté, *Les Gaullistes*, pp. 71–72.
19. Bernard Tricot, *Les Sentiers de la Paix: Algérie 1958/1962* (Paris: Plon, 1972).
20. André de Lattre and Pierre Lelong; Jean Méo, Gérard Ducher, Paul Antoine Henry, Henry-Jean Manière.
21. For the reminiscences of several of de Gaulle's staff members, see Gilbert Pilleul, ed., *"L'Entourage" et De Gaulle* (Paris: Plon, 1979).
22. Michel Jobert, general secretary; Mme. Marie-Anne Dupuy, head of the office staff; Edouard Balladur, deputy-general secretary.
23. Mme. Marie-France Garaud, Georges Gaucher, Mme. Simonne Servais, Bernard, Michel Woimant, but not François Lavondes.

24. Except in cases of promotions.
25. Ducher, Court of Accounts; Henry, Manière, de la Villèsbrunne, diplomacy; Méo, engineer; Boissonnis, financial administration; Narbonne, university teacher.
26. In 1945, without his knowledge or consent he had been nominated and elected mayor of his home village to succeed his grandfather, who had served in that office for fifty-eight years, and had been re-elected each time thereafter.
27. The subsequent political careers are traced only through the Gaullist period.
28. About 10,000 French families bear such names, one in 5,000. Only 174 Frenchmen bear the title of "count," about one in 400,000. Four of them served on de Gaulle's staff.
29. Also, a quasi-professional rank, "press attaché," appeared sometimes, though it is not included in this study.
30. Dominique Venner, *Guide de la politique* (Paris: Balland, 1972), pp. 190–91.
31. Ibid., pp. 255–56.
32. Full career information is not available on 9 of the 151.
33. Also, three went to former members of de Gaulle's presidential staff.
34. Guèna, Mazeaud, Guichard, Ortoli, Chirac, Lelong, Roulland, Lecat, Chasseguet, and Couvert-Castera. Roulland had been a deputy earlier also.
35. Guèna, Mazeaud, Guichard, Jobert, Ortoli, Chirac, and Lecat.
36. Perrilliat, Galy-Dejean, Sabouret, and Roulland.
37. Sams, Martin de Beaucé, Sabouret, Chirac, Lecat, and Perrilliat.
38. The seventeen civil servant fathers included two councilors of state, a *maître des réquêtes* at the Court of Accounts, three magistrates, and a finance inspector.
39. In the twelve years of the Fourth Republic, only two persons served in the government without having won seats in Parliament, the exceptions being very brief and for quite peculiar reasons.
40. However, it had been filled by politicians Edmond Michelet and Jacques Duhamel in the Chaban-Delmas and first Messmer governments.
41. Pierre Viansson-Ponté, *Histoire de la République Gaullienne*, (Paris: Fayard, 1971), II: 300–301, 577.
42. Lunet de la Malène, Giscard d'Estaing, Drion de Reyniac, Dechartre (pseudonym of Duprat-Geneau), Cornut-Gentille, Couve de Murville.
43. Missoffe to a de Mitry, Chirac to a niece of Geoffroy Chodron de Courcel, Palewski to a Duchess de Talleyrand Périgord, Galley to a daughter of Marshal Leclerc de Hautecloque, Malaud to a Gorguette d'Argoeuves, Inchaupsè to a d'Iribarne, Herzog to a Countess de Cosse Brissac, Chalandon to a Princess Salomé Murat, and Guèna to an Oriane de la Bourdonnaye.
44. *Le Monde*, May 21, 1974.
45. Jean Petot, *Les Grandes étapes du régime républican français (1792–1969)* (Paris: Cujas, 1970), p. 551.
46. However, this information is not available for nearly one-fourth (79) of the ministers.

4. DOMAIN OF LAW

1. CE, February 19, 1904, *Chamber syndicale des fabricants-constructeurs de matériel pour chemins de fer et tramway, Recueil Dalloz*, 1905, III: 58.
2. CE, May 4, 1906, *Babin, Recueil Dalloz*, 1908, III: 7.

3. For instance, laws of September 20, 1947, Organic Statute for Algeria, *Journal officiel, Lois et decrêts* (cited hereafter as *JO. LD.*), September 21, 1947, pp. 9470–74; Economic and Financial Recovery, *JO. LD.*, August 17, August 18, 1948, pp. 8082-84; Economic and Financial Recovery, *JO. LD.*, July 11, 1953, pp. 6143-48; State of Emergency in Algeria, *JO. LD.* April 3, April 7, 1955, pp. 3479–80. See also Jean Groux, "Les Domaines respectifs de la loi et du réglement d'après la constitution de 1958," *Notes et Etudes documentaires*, July 28, 1962, pp. 12–13.
4. For a discussion of this law, see Georges Galichon, "Aspects de la procédure législative en France," in François Goguel, ed., *Le Travail Parlementaire* (Paris: PUF, 1955), p. 128; Jacques Soubeyrol, *Les Décrêts-Lois sous la Quatriéme République* (Bordeaux: University of Bordeaux, 1955), pp. 79–90, and the sources he cites.
5. *JO. LD.*, July 11, 1953, p. 6144 (Art. 5).
6. A 1955 list of the contents of the domains appears in Galichon, "Aspects de la Procédure Législative," pp. 129–31.
7. Nicholas Wahl, "Aux origines de la Nouvelle Constitution," *RFSP*, March 1959, pp. 30–66, and sources he cites.
8. Jacquier Brière (pseudo. for M. Debré and Emmanuel Monick), *Refaire la France* (Paris: Plon, 1945), pp. 153–54.
9. Jean-Louis Debré, *La Constitution de la Vᵉ République* (Paris: PUF, 1975), pp. 26–27, 29.
10. Ibid., pp. 32–37.
11. *JO. AN.* 1st sitting of June 1, 1958, p. 2576; *Le Monde*, June 4, 1958.
12. J.-L. Debré, *La Constitution de la Vᵉ République*, p. 44; Guy Mollet, *Quinze ans aprés* (Paris: Michel, 1973), p. 52.
13. Ibid., p. 55.
14. Ibid., p. 107.
15. J.-L. Debré, *La Constitution*, pp. 39–40, 49–52.
16. Ibid., p. 57.
17. Ibid., pp. 55, 58–59.
18. Ibid., pp. 56–58. The "Constitutional Commission" is not mentioned elsewhere in the draft.
19. Mollet, *Quinze ans aprés*, p. 107.
20. The successive drafts of the 1958 constitution are published in J.-L. Debré, *La Constitution*.
21. The text of the draft submitted to the CCC is published in *Travaux préparatoires de la constitution du 4 octobre 1958: Avis et débats du comité consultatif constitutionnel* (cited hereafter as *Travaux préparatoires*), (Paris: La documentation française, 1960), pp. 23–30.
22. J.-L. Debré, *La Constitution*, p. 136.
23. *Travaux préparatoires*, p. 104.
24. Ibid., p. 45.
25. Ibid., pp. 100–108, 192.
26. Ibid., p. 204.
27. Ibid., pp. 211–12.
28. Ibid., pp. 206, 215, 218, 219.
29. Ibid., pp. 104, 106, 206, 208, 209, 223.
30. Ibid., p. 212.
31. Ibid., pp. 114–15.

32. J.-L. Debré, *La Constitution*, pp. 180–219.
33. Mollet, *Quinze ans après*, p. 107.
34. M. Debré, "The New Constitution" in William G. Andrews, *European Political Institutions*, 2nd ed. (Princeton, N.J.: Van Nostrand, 1966), p. 46.
35. J.-L. Debré, *La Constitution*, pp. 180–219.
36. Ibid.
37. Ibid., pp. 221–44.
38. Jean-Louis Quermonne, *Le Gouvernement de la France sous la Ve République* (Paris: Dalloz, 1980), pp. 353–56.
39. For a contemporary discussion of the scope of Article 34, see Jean L'Huillier, "La délimitation des domaines de la loi et du réglement dans la constitution du 4 octobre 1958," *Recueil Dalloz. Chronique*, 1959, pp. 173–78.
40. These statistics were compiled from the annual *Tables Chronologiques* of the *Journal officiel*. These dates span the legislative sessions of Parliament from the founding of the Fourth Republic until Pompidou's death.
41. Numbered decrees, ordinances, and referendal laws.
42. Even if the first two years of the Fourth Republic are excluded as having been exceptional, its rate drops only to 220 laws and 1,286 decrees per year. Also, see Jean Massot, *Le Chef du Gouvernement en France* (Paris: La Documentation française, 1979), pp. 157–58, for a similar comparison.
43. Article 72 (territorial collectivities) is counted twice, because it has two provisions for law making.
44. L. 68-458 of May 23, 1968, *JO. LD.*, May 24, 1968, p. 5178.
45. L. 63-807 of December 1, 1963, *JO. LD.*, December 2, 1963; p. 10662.
46. L. 67-4.
47. L. 63-579.
48. L. 63-807.
49. L. 64-699.
50. L. 68-946.
51. L. 71-498.
52. L. 66-482, L. 68-1175, L, 70-8, L, 71-385, L. 72-628.
53. L. 68-1180.
54. L. 60-760.
55. L. 61-1262.
56. L. 63-883.
57. L. 63-645.
58. L. 66-297.
59. L. 71-552.
60. L. 64-1265, L. 65-1001, L. 70-588, L. 71-567. On this question, see Pierre Delvolve, "Le Plan et la procédure parlementaire," in Delvolve and Henri Lesguillons, *Le Contrôle parlementaire sur la politique économique et budgetaire* (Paris: PUF, 1964), pp. 51–53.
61. L. 59-899, L. 60-776, L. 60-1305, L. 61-530, L. 61-1409, L. 62-880, L. 64-1270, and L. 70-1058.
62. The Constitutional Law 74-904 of October 29, 1974 lengthened that list to include sixty senators or sixty deputies.
63. The texts of the decisions are published in *JO. LD.* and in the annual *Recueil des décisions* of the Constitutional Council. A selection of thirty leading opinions and some useful information on the Council are published in Louis Favoreau and Loïc

Philip, *Les Grandes Décisions du Conseil Constitutionnel* (Paris: Sirey, 1975).

64. CC 59-1 FNR of November 27, 1959; CC 61-2 FNR of June 30, 1961; CC 61-3 FNR of September 8, 1961; CC 61-4 of October 18, 1961; CC 64-6 FNR of May 22, 1964; and CC 66-7 FNR of December 21, 1966.

65. CC 68-8 FNR of November 27, 1968.

66. CC 63-5 FNR of June 11, 1963.

67. CC 60-8 DC of August 11, 1960 and CC 64-27 of December 18, 1964.

68. CC 68-35 DC of January 30, 1968.

69. Another decision, CC 60-11DC of January 20, 1961, also brought by the prime minister, is listed in the *Recueil* as being concerned with the question of domains, but does not, in fact, address that matter. Rather, it concerns Art. 40: "Bills and amendments shall be out of order when their adoption would have the effect either of reducing public revenues or creating or increasing a public expenditure (*charge*)."

70. CC 61-3 FNR of September 8, 1961 and CC 61-4 FNR of October 18, 1961.

71. *Journal officiel, Assemblée nationale. Débats parlementaires.* (cited hereafter as *JO. AN.* April 27, 1960), p. 468 (2nd sitting of April 26).

72. CC 61-12L of February 17, 1961; 64-29L of May 12, 1964; 65-35L of July 2, 1965; 67-48L of December 12, 1967; Léo Hamon, "Note," *Recueil Dalloz-Sirey, Jurisprudence*, 1967, pp. 445–47.

73. CC-1 of November 27, 1959; 60-9L of October 14, 1960; 61-14L of July 18, 1961; 61-16L of October 18, 1961; 64-6 FNR of May 22, 1964; 64-27L of March 17, 19, 1964; 64-28L of March 17, 1964; 64-29L of May 12, 1964; 64-30L of September 17, 1964; 64-31L and 64-32L of December 21, 1964; 65-33L of February 9, 1965; 66-7 FNR of December 21, 1966; 66-37L of March 10, 1966; 66-39L and 66-40L of July 8, 1966; 67-44L of February 27, 1967; 67-45L of May 9, 1967; 67-46L of July 12, 1967; 67-47L of December 12, 1967; 69-52L and 69-53L of February 27, 1969; 69-54L of June 10, 1969; 69-56L of July 9, 1969; 69-58L of October 24, 1969; 70-59L and 70-60L of February 23, 1970; 70-62L of May 21, 1970; 70-63L of July 9, 1970; 70-64L of November 13, 1970; 70-65L of December 17, 1970; 71-68L and 71-69L of April 1, 1971; 71-70L ⁿf April 23, 1971; first and third decisions of February 29, 1972; decisions of December 2, 1972; February 20, 1973; July 11, 1973, November 7, 1973, and November 28, 1973. See also Hamon, "Note," *Recueil Dalloz-Sirey, Jurisprudence*, 1966, pp. 17–20, *Recueil Dalloz, Jurisprudence, 1960*, pp. 518–19.

74. CC 60-2L of January 29, 1960; 60-4L and 60-5L of April 7, 1960; 60-6L and 60-7L of July 8, 1960; 60-8L of October 14, 1960; 60-10L of December 20, 1960; 61-2 FNR of June 30, 1961; 61-3 FNR of September 8, 1961; 61-4 FNR of October 18, 1961; 61-11L of January 20, 1961; 61-17L of December 22, 1961; 62-18L of January 16, 1962; 62-19L of April 3, 1962; 62-20L of December 4, 1962; 63-5 FNR of June 11, 1963; 63-23L of February 19, 1963; 63-25L and 63-26L of July 30, 1963; 64-27DC of December 18, 1964; 64-29L of May 12, 1964; 65-34L of July 2, 1965; 66-38L of March 10, 1966; 68-8 FNR of November 27, 1968; 68-51L of April 4, 1968; 70-66L of December 17, 1970; second decision of February 29, 1972, decision of November 8, 1972. See also Hamon, "Note," *Recueil Dalloz, Jurisprudence*, 1964, pp. 331–32.

75. CC 59-1 FNR of November 27, 1959; see also Hamon, "Note," *Recueil Dalloz, Jurisprudence*, 1960, pp. 533–35.

76. CC 63-25L of July 30, 1963; see also Hamon, "Note," *Recueil Dalloz-Sirey, Jurisprudence*, 1964, pp. 455–⁵⁻

77. CC 66–42L of November 17, 1966 and CC 71–67L of April 1, 1971.
78. CC 63-22L of February 19, 1963; see also Hamon, "Note," *Recueil Dalloz, Jurisprudence*, 1964, pp. 92–93. *Contraventions*, the lowest category of criminal penalty—unlike *peines* and *délits*—were not included in Article 34.
79. CC 65–34L of July 2, 1965; see also Hamon, "Note," *Recueil Dalloz-Sirey, Jurisprudence*, 1967, pp. 615–17.
80. CC 61-14L of July 18, 1961; CC 64-31L of December 21, 1964; and CC 65-33L of February 9, 1965.
81. CC 60–3L of January 29, 1960; Hamon, "Les domaines de la loi et du réglement à la recherche d'une frontière," in *Recueil Dalloz, Chroniques*, 1960, p. 255.
82. *Fédération nationale des syndicats de police*, November 24, 1961, *Recueil des décisions du Conseil d'Etat, (CE)*, p. 658; see also, Barry Nicholas, "Loi, Réglement, and Judicial Review in the Fifth Republic," in *Public Law* (Autumn 1970), pp. 263–64, and the sources he cites.
83. Hamon, "Note," *Recueil Dalloz-Sirey, Jurisprudence*, 1970, pp. 695-96.
84. This list has been compiled from tables published annually in the *Recueil des décisions du Conseil Constitutionnel* and the texts of the decisions in CE.
85. It refused to rule on an Article 16 decision on the ground that it was legislative and, therefore, beyond its purview.
86. Germain Warlin, "Le Domaine législatif et le domaine réglementaire dans la coûtume constitutionnelle française," in *Annals de la Faculté de Droit* (Istanbul, 1970), and "Le domaine législatif et le domaine réglementaire dans la jurisprudence actuelle," in *Annals de la Faculté de Droit*, 1969, pp. 1ff.; François Vincent, "De l'inutilité de l'article 34 dans la constitution du 4 October 1958," in *Actualité juridique*, November 1965, pp. 546–76.
87. *Union nationale des associations familiales*, November 27, 1964, *CE*, p.
88. *Sieur Landy*, June 4, 1965, *CE*, p. 336.
89. *CGT, Union de Fédérations syndicales professionnelles*, July 8, 1966, *CE*, p. 456.
90. *Fédération hospitalière de France et al.*, December 2, 1966, *CE*, p. 634.
91. *Demoiselle Husson et al.*, June 11, 1969, *CE*, p. 298.
92. *Sieur Karle*, May 18, 1960, *CE*, p. 333.
93. *Société Eky*, February 12, 1960, *CE*, p. 101; *Sieur Najean de Bévère*, February 4, 1970, *CE* 79.
94. *Sieur Rhiem c/ORTF*, December 7, 1970, *CE*, p. 895.
95. *Ordre des avocats . . . de Paris et al.*, July 4, 1969, *CE*, p. 358; *S.A. Librairie François Maspéro*, October 8, 1971, *CE*, p. 589.
96. *Association républicaine des anciens combattants*, January 29, 1965, *CE*, p. 58.
97. *Sieur Beausse*, February 2, 1962, *CE* 82.
98. *Sieur Ruben de Servens et al.*, March 2, 1962, *CE*, p. 143.
99. *Sieur Bellet*, June 18, 1965, *CE*, p. 370.
100. *Demoiselle Husson et al.*, June 11, 1969, *CE*, p. 298, Vincent, "De l'inutilité de l'article 34," pp. 566–67, 572–74.

5. EXECUTIVE LAW MAKING

1. Article 1 of the law of February 25, 1875, Relative to the Organization of the Institutions of Government. For a general study of this topic, see Otto

Kirchheimer, "Decree Powers and Constitutional Law in France Under the Third Republic," in *American Political Science Review*, 34, no. 6, (December 1940).

2. Alphonse Bertrand, *Les Origines de la Troisième République (1871–1876)* (Paris: Perrin, 1911), pp. 307 ff., 323.

3. A. Esmein and Henry Nézard, *Eléments de droit constitutionnel français et comparé*, 2 vols. (Paris: Sirey, 1921), II: 75 ff.; Louis Trotabas, *Constitution et gouvernement de la France* (Paris: Colin, 1930), pp. 64–68; Léon Duguit, *Manuel de droit constitutionnel* (Paris: Boccard, 1918), pp. 459–64, 500–25; Joseph Barthélemy and Paul Duez, *Traité de droit constitutionnel* (Paris: Dalloz, 1933 ed.), pp. 201–202.

4. Duguit, *Manuel de droit constitutionnel*, pp. 461–63; Clinton L. Rossiter, *Constitutional Dictatorship: Crisis Government in the Modern Democracies* (Princeton, N.J.: Princeton University Press, 1948), p. 82.

5. Esmein and Nézard, *Eléments de droit constitutionnel*, p. 97; also, see Jacques Soubeyrol, *Les Décrêts-Lois sous la Quatrième République* (University of Bordeaux, 1955), p. 22. Other sources list more and the count depends on the location of the line between rules and laws. See Duguit, *Manuel de droit constitutionnel*, pp. 500–17.

6. *JO.* August 3, 1919, p. 7083; Rossiter, *Constitutional Dictatorship*, pp. 91ff.

7. *JO.* August 3, 1919, p. 7077; *JO. CD.*, August 4, 1914, pp. 3109–20.

8. *JO. CD.*, December 22, 23, pp. 3121–28, 3131–43.

9. Ibid., February 4, 11, 25, March 4, 11, 25, 26, 1915, pp. 86–88, 108–14, 117, 218, 282, 288, 334–49, 442–45, 474–75, 491–92. The exception was a decree restricting trade with Germany and Austro-Hungary, an amendment to which was defeated, pp. 200–335.

10. Duguit, *Manuel de droit constitutionnel*, para. 117.

11. *JO. CD.*, *Documents*, regular session, 1916, no. 2783, p. 1785.

12. *JO. CD.*, December 13, 1916, p. 3638.

13. Ibid., p. 3639.

14. Ibid., December 15, 1916, p. 3691.

15. Duguit, *Manuel de droit constitutionnel*, para. 123; Rossiter, *Constitutional Dictatorship*, p. 111.

16. Soubeyrol, *Les Décrêts-Lois*, p. 24; Duguit, *Manuel de droit*, para. 123. However, the government did ban absinthe and new saloons by decree. Rossiter, *Constitutional Dictatorship*, p. 113.

17. Jean Filippi, *Rapport au nom de la Commission spéciale chargée d'examiner le projet de loi . . . autorisant le Gouvernment . . . à prendre des mésures d'ordre économique et social*, *JO. S. Documents*, 2nd regular session, 1966–67, annex 271, pp. 145–46; Soubeyrol, *Les Décrêts-Lois.*, pp. 24–27; Jean-Louis Quermonne, *Le Gouvernement de la France sous la Ve République*, (Paris: Dalloz, 1980), p. 34.

18. Filippi, *Rapport au nom de la Commission*, pp. 145–46; *JO.*, various issues in March and April 1938; *JO. LD.*, April 14, October 6, 1938, pp. 4426, 11666, March 20, 1939, p. 3646.

19. *JO. LD.*, December 10, 1939, p. 13834.

20. *JO. CD.*, November 30, 1938, pp. 2015–21; *JO. S.* December 1, 1939, pp. 685–88.

21. Rossiter, *Constitutional Dictatorship*, p. 126.

22. *JO. LD.*, August 11, 1940, pp. 4676–77.

23. *JO. LD.*, July 11, 1940, p. 4513.

24. *JO. ANC.*, August 22, 1946, p. 3183; September 3, 1946, pp. 3499–3500; September 28, 1946, pp. 4229–30; Soubeyrol, *Les Décrêts-Lois*, pp. 62–71.

25. Soubeyrol, *Les Décrêts-Lois*, pp. 69–70; Robert Pelloux, "La nouvelle Constitution de la France," *Recueil Dalloz. Chroniques*, 1946, p. 82.
26. Georges Vedel, *Manuel élémentaire de droit constitutionnel* (Paris: Sirey, 1949), p. 500.
27. For instance, *JO. AN.* August 8, 1948, pp. 5520 (Grimaud), 5522–25 (de Chambrun), 5526 (Marie), 5527 (Duclos), 5530 (Capitant), 5531 (Faure), 5532–34 (Pronteau), 5547 (Badie), August 9, pp. 5568–71 (Capitant).
28. Filippi, *Rapport au nom de la Commission*, p. 5; see also Serge Arné, *Le Président du conseil des ministres sous la IV e République* (Paris: LGDJ, 1962), p. 153, and Philip M. Williams, *Crisis and Compromise* (London: Longmans, 1964), p. 270.
29. Soubeyrol, *Les Décrêts-Lois*, pp. 46–61.
30. One each in 1949, 1952, 1954, 1955, and 1958; two each in 1947, 1951, 1953, and 1956; three in 1948; four in 1950; and five in 1957. Filippi, *Rapport au nom*, pp. 147–49; Pierre Ebrard, "L'Article 38 de la Constitution du 4 octobre 1958 et la V e République," in *Revue du droit publique* (*RDP*) March/April 1969, p. 262.
31. Filippi, *Rapport au nom*, p. 148.
32. Ibid., pp. 148–49; *JO. AN.* May 18, 1967, p. 1064 (Pompidou); Soubeyrol, *Les Décrêts-Lois*, pp. 100, 124–30; de Gaulle press conference, May 16, 1967.
33. *JO. LD.*, August 18, 1948, pp. 8082–83. The Council of State agreed. *RDP*, January/March 1953, pp. 170–71.
34. M. Malleville, "L'Application de la loi du 17 août 1948", *Etudes et documents*, No. 8, 1954.
35. Soubeyrol, *Les Décrêts-Lois*, pp. 117–31; C.E. Freedman, *The Conseil d'Etat in Modern France* (New York: Columbia University Press, 1961), p. 90.
36. Jean Charpentier, "Les Lois-Cadres et la fonction gouvernementale," in *RDP*, March/April 1958, pp. 229–30.
37. *JO. AN.*, *Documents*, March 16, 1956, annex 1242, p. 824.
38. Law 56-619, *JO. LD.*, June 24, 1956.
39. Charpentier, *Les Lois-Cadres*, pp. 233, 235, 262–63.
40. Law 57-908, *JO. LD.*, August 10, 1957, pp. 7906–15.
41. Jean Meynaud and Alain Lancelot, "Groupes de Pression et Politique du Logement," *Revue française de science politique (RFSP)*, December 1958, pp. 845–46; Jean-Marie Cotteret, *Le pouvoir législatif en France* (Paris: LGDJ, 1962), pp. 67–68; Williams, *Crisis and Compromise*, p. 273.
42. Ord. 58-711, *JO. LD.*, August 10, 1958, p. 7537; D. 58-712 and D. 58-713. *JO. LD.* August 10, 1958, pp. 7537–38.
43. Law 58-95, *JO. LD.*, February 6, 1958, pp. 1379–83.
44. *JO. AN.*, *Documents*, March 12, 1958, annexes 6880–91, pp. 1531–39.
45. *JO. AN.*, March 27, 1958, pp. 2046–64; *JO. CR.*, March 28, 1958, pp. 798–806; William G. Andrews, *French Politics and Algeria* (New York: Appleton-Century-Crofts, 1962), pp. 135–62.
46. Arné, *Le Président du Conseil*, p. 159; Jean-Louis Quermonne, "La Réforme de structure des territoires d'outre-mer et des territories associés selon la loi-cadre du 23 juin 1956," *Recueil Dalloz, Chroniques*, 1957, pp. 5–12; Liet-Vaux, Georges, "La Loi-Cadre sur la construction et les principes démocratiques", *Gazzette du Palais*, 1957, p. 1; M.M., "Differentes conceptions de la notion de loi-cadre," *Revue pratique de droit administrative. Actualité*, September 1957.
47. Law 55-385, *JO. LD.*, April 7, 1955, pp. 3479–80; Arné, *Le Président du Conseil*, pp. 157–58.

48. D. 55-386, D. 55-444, D. 55-1147, *JO. LD.*, April 7, 1955, p. 3481, May 20, 1955, p. 5005, August 29/30, 1955, p. 8640.

49. Law 55-1080, *JO. LD.*, August 14, 1955, pp. 8170–71.

50. D. 55-440, D. 55-780, D. 55-1120, D. 55-1274, and D. 55-1478, *JO. LD.*, April 24, 1955, p. 4166, June 12, 1955, p. 5915, August 21, 1955, p. 8411, October 1, 1955, p. 9646, November 14/15, 1955, p. 11118; Roland Drago, "L'Etat d'Urgence . . . et les libertés publiques," in *RDP*, July/September 1955, pp. 670–705.

51. Law 58-487, *JO. LD.*, May 17, 1958, p. 4734.

52. D. 58-489, D. 58-490, 58-491, *JO. LD.*, May 17, 1958, pp. 4736–37; Arné, *Le Président du Conseil*, p. 158; Andrews, *French Politics and Algeria*, pp. 72-73.

53. *JO. AN.*, May 13, 1958, p. 2253 (Pflimlin); *JO. AN.*, *Documents*, May 23, 1958, annex 7188, p. 1810.

54. *JO. AN.*, May 27, 1958, p. 2542; *Le Monde*, May 29, 1958; *JO. CR.*, May 28, 1958, p. 929.

55. *JO.*, *Tables, Travaux parlementaires*, 1958, p. 33.

56. Law 57-1263, *JO. LD.*, December 14, 1957, pp. 11346–47.

57. *JO. AN.*, June 1, 1958, p. 2576, 2592–93.

58. *JO. AN.*, June 2, 1958, pp. 2604–10; *JO. CR.*, June 2, 1958, pp. 937–40, 951–52.

59. *JO. LD.*, June 4, 1958, p. 5327; March 17, 1956, p. 2591.

60. Ord. 58-915, *JO. LD.*, October 8, 1958, p. 9214.

61. *JO. AN.*, *Documents*, June 1, 2, 1958, annexes 7232, 7235, 7236, 7237, pp. 1828–30.

62. *JO. AN.*, June 2, 1958, pp. 2611–16, 2632–34.

63. *JO. CR.*, June 2, 1958, pp. 941–48, 952–53.

64. *JO. AN.*, *Documents*, June 1, 1958, annex 7233, p. 1829.

65. For a fuller discussion of this action, see Chapter 1.

66. D. 58-545, D. 58-547, D. 58-550, D. 58-557, D. 58-558, D. 58-559, and D. 58-560, *JO. LD.*, June 25, 1958, p. 5877; June 26, 1958, p. 5928; June 28, 1958, p. 5992; June 29, 1958, pp. 6069–73.

67. *JO. LD.*, January 10, 1959, p. 695; January 31, 1959, p. 1475.

68. *JO. LD.*, December 9, 1958, pp. 11023–24.

69. Marcel Gabilly, "La Saison de grands commis," in *Revue de Paris*, February 1959, p. 131 n.

70. *JO.*, *Table chronologique, 1958* and *1959*.

71. Gabilly, "La Saison de grands commis," p. 129.

72. This list is drawn from *JO. LD.* See also "Aperçus sur les principales réformes . . . du 1ᵉ juin 1958 au 5 février 1959," *Notes et documents* 2515, February 26, 1959; "Bilan de pouvoirs spéciaux," *Entreprise*, February 28, 1959, pp. 22–25; "De Gaulle législateur," *Nouvelle critique*, February 1959, pp. 7–16; D.L., "Les Nouvelles Réformes," *Banque*, February 1959, pp. 75–80; and Gabilly, "La Saison de grands commis,".

73. Gabilly, "La Saison de grands commis," p. 136.

74. Charles Debbasch, "Les Ordonnances de l'Article 38 dans la constitution du 4 octobre 1958," *Semaine juridique*, May 30, 1962, no. 1701, 8 pp.

75. D. 59-194 of January 30, 1959, *JO. AN.*, *Documents*, February 2, 1960, p. 1.

76. Ord. 59-149, *JO. LD.*, January 10, 1959, pp. 694–95.

77. Ord. 58-1171, *JO. LD.*, December 9, 1958, pp. 11022–24. The new Assembly convened on December 9.

78. "When the institutions of the Republic, the independence of the nation, the integrity of the territory, or the execution of its international commitments are

endangered in a grave and immediate manner and the regular functioning of the constitutional institutions of government is interrupted, the president of the Republic shall take the measures required by the circumstances after official consultation with the prime minister, the presidents of the Assemblies as well as the Constitutional Council.

"He shall inform the nation about them by a message.

"These measures must be inspired by a will to ensure to the constitutional institutions of government, in the least delay, the means to accomplish their mission. The Consititutional Council shall be consulted about them.

"Parliament shall convene by right.

"The National Assembly cannot be dissolved during the exercise of exceptional powers."

79. Jean-Louis Debré, *Les Idées constitutionnelles du général de Gaulle* (Paris: LGDJ, 1974), pp. 186–92; Jean-Louis Debré, *La Constitution de la Ve République* (Paris: PUF, 1975), pp. 287–95.

80. *Travaux préparatoires à la constitution du 4 octobre 1958* (Paris: La documentation française, 1960), pp. 118–19; Michèle Voisset *L'Article 16 de la Constitution du 4 octobre 1958* (Paris: LGDJ, 1969), p. 413; "L'Article 16 de la Constitution de 1958," *Notes et études documentaires*, suppl. to March 1970, p. 4.

81. *Travaux préparatoires*, p. 45.

82. Ibid., p. 118.

83. Michel Debré, "La nouvelle constitution," in *Revue française de science politique* (*RFSP*), March 1959, p. 23.

84. Jean-Louis Debré, *La Constitution de la Ve République*, p. 291; *Travaux préparatoires*, p. 24.

85. *Travaux préparatoires*, pp. 49, 57, 129–30.

86. Voisset, *L'Article 16*, p. 413.

87. Jean-Louis Debré, *Les Idées constitutionelles*, p. 230; *Travaux préparatoires*, pp. 45, 48, 49, 56, 112–13, 194.

88. "The government may, for the execution of its program, ask Parliament for authorization to take, by ordinances, during a limited period, measures which normally are in the domain of law.

"The ordinances shall be taken in the Council of Ministers after consultation with the Council of State. They shall take effect from publication but shall become null and void if the ratification bill is not submitted to Parliament before the date set by the enabling act.

"Upon the expiration of the period mentioned in the first paragraph of this article, the ordinances can no longer be modified except by law for those matters which lie in the legislative domain."

89. *Travaux préparatoires*, p. 194.

90. Georges Burdeau, ed., "Les Articles, 34, 37, et 38 de la constitution de 1958," *Note et études documentaires*, suppl. to April 1970, pp. 29–32.

91. *JO. LD.*, March 18, 1972, p. 2849.

92. P. Montané de la Roque, "L'Article 38 de la Constitution du 4 octobre 1958 et la loi de pouvoirs spéciaux du 4 fevrier 1960," in *Mélanges offerts à Jacques Maury* (Paris: Dalloz & Sirey,) II: 209–10.

93. "Article 11. The president of the Republic, on proposal of the government during the sessions or on joint proposal of the two assemblies, published in the *Journal officiel*, may submit to referendum any bill concerning the organization of the

institutions of government, providing for the ratification of a Community agreement or tending to authorize ratification of a treaty that, without being contrary to
the constitution, would have an effect on the functioning of the institutions. . . ."
94. Jean-Louis Debré, *La Constitution*, pp. 283–86.
95. *Travaux préparatoires*, pp. 126–28.
96. Ord. 60-372, *JO. LD.*, April 17, 1960, p. 3584. That ordinance was issued under
   authority of the enabling act of February 4, 1960.
97. Laws 67-1114, 67-1121, 68-1248, 69-1161, 70-1199, 71-1061, and 72-1121, according
   to the records of the *Service de la séance* of the National Assembly. It kept no
   records of this matter for the first two legislatures.
98. Jacques Fauvet and Jean Planchais, *La Fronde des Généraux* (Paris: Arthaud,
   1961); *Le Monde*, April 23/24, 28, 1961.
99. D. 61-395, *JO. LD.*, April 23, 1961, p. 3843.
100. *Le Monde*, April 25, 1961. *JO. LD.*, April 24, 1961, pp. 3876–77.
101. *JO. LD.*, April 24, 1961, pp. 3874–75.
102. *JO. AN.*, April 25, 1961, p. 510; *JO. S.*, April 25, 1961, p. 88.
103. *JO. LD.*, April 24, 1961, p. 3876; April 26, 1961, p. 3907; April 27, 1961, p. 3930;
   April 28, 1961, p. 3947; May 4, 1961, pp. 4115–16; May 5, 1961, p. 4147; June 8,
   1961, pp. 5194–95; June 9, 1961, p. 5227; June 18, 1961, p. 5483; September 9, 1961,
   p. 8410; September 30, 1961, p. 8963.
104. *JO. LD.*, April 24, 1961, p. 3876.
105. Voisset, *L'Article 16*, p. 174.
106. Ibid., pp. 155, 187. Martin Harrison, "The French Experience of Exceptional
   Powers: 1961," in *Journal of Politics*, February 1963, p. 143n., gives a total of 1,081
   military and 156 national police officers and over 3,000 local police.
107. *JO. AN.*, April 25, 1961, p. 510.
108. *Le Monde*, April 27, 1961.
109. *JO. AN.*, April 27, May 16 and May 18, 1961, pp. 535, 773–74, 842–43; Jean-Luc
   Parodi, *Les Rapports entre le législatif et l'exécutif sous la Ve République*, 2nd. ed.
   (Paris: Colin, 1972), p. 56.
110. *JO. AN.*, June 1, 1961, p. 930; June 28, 1961, p. 1182; July 4, 1961, p. 1436; *JO. S.*,
   June 28, 1961, p. 575, August 31, 1961, p. 1037.
111. *Le Monde*, May 12, 1960.
112. William Pickles, "Special Powers in France: Article 16 in Practice," in *Public Law*
   (London), Spring 1963, p. 41.
113. *JO. AN.*, *Documents*, issues of March 2, 9, 1963, pp. 150, 213–16, 222–23, annexes
   1193, 1237, 1248, 1249; *JO. AN.*, June 20, 21, 1961, pp. 1168–77, 1196–98; Pickles,
   "Special Powers in France," p. 41.
114. *JO. AN.*, June 28, 1961, pp. 1326–28; June 29, 1961, pp. 1341 87; *JO. S.* June 28,
   1961, pp. 570–73; July 5, 1961, pp. 680–704.
115. *Le Monde*, August 1, 2, 3, 4, 5, 9, 10, 30, 31, 1961; Parodi, *Les Rapports*, pp. 281–82.
116. *JO. LD.*, September 30, 1961, p. 8963.
117. *JO. AN.*, *Documents*, October 13, 1961, p. 565.
118. *Le Monde*, January 25 through February 3, 1960; Quermonne, *Le Gouvernement de
   la France*, pp. 359–60.
119. *JO. AN.*, *Documents*, February 2, 1960, annex 532, p. 5.
120. Ibid., pp. 5–6.
121. *JO. AN.*, February 2, 1960, pp. 115–29, 147–48.
122. *JO. S.*, February 3, 1960, pp. 24–41, 43–44.

123. Ibid., p. 40 (Defferre).

124. Ebrard, "L'Article 38," p. 264; Philip M. Williams, *The French Parliament 1958–1967* (London: Allen & Unwin, 1968), p. 73.

125. Ord. 60-563, *JO. LD.*, June 16, 1960, p. 5418.

126. Ord. 61-101, *JO. LD.*, February 1, 1960, p. 1203.

127. Ord. 60-1101, *JO. LD.*, October 18, 1960, p. 9483; J. M. Becet, "La Pratique des ordonnances de l'article 38," in *Revue administrative*, November/December 1968, p. 707.

128. *JO. AN.*, *Documents*, April 25, 1961, annex 1103, p. 9.

129. *JO. AN.*, June 23, 1964, pp. 2110–11; October 10, 1972, pp. 4004–05; *JO. S.*, November 9, 1972, p. 2000.

130. *JO. AN.*, *Documents*, annex 875, p. 477; May 6, 1964, annex 933, pp. 545–47; June 16, 1964, annex 981, pp. 619–20; *JO. AN.*, June 3, 1964, pp. 1588–95; June 23, 1964, pp. 2110–11, 2115; *JO. S.* June 11, 1964, p. 548; June 25, 1964, p. 810.

131. *JO. AN.*, October 10, 1972, pp. 3998–4006; *JO. S.*, November 9, 1972, 1995–2001.

132. Williams, *French Parliament*, pp. 85–89, is a case study of this bill.

133. *JO. AN.*, *Documents*, July 6, 1960, annex 734, p. 346.

134. *JO. AN.*, July 18, 1960, pp. 1957–83, 2010–11.

135. *JO. S.*, July 21, 1960, pp. 1035–47, 1067.

136. *JO. AN.*, July 22, 1960, pp. 2162–63. Law 60-733, *JO. LD.*, August 2, 1960, p. 7130.

137. Ord. 60-907, *JO. LD.*, August 31, 1960, p. 8039, Ords. 60-1253, 60-1254, 60-1255, 60-1256. November 30, pp. 10708–12; *Le Monde*, December 5, 1973.

138. Ords. 60-1245 and 60-1246, *JO. LD.*, November 27, 1960, pp. 10603–08.

139. *JO. AN.*, December 14, 1960, p. 4646.

140. Ibid., p. 4651.

141. Ibid., December 15, 1960, p. 4654.

142. Ibid.

143. *JO. AN.*, July 18, 1961, pp. 1737–38.

144. *JO. AN.*, *Documents*, May 18, 1961, annex 1197, pp. 151–56; *JO. AN.*, July 18, 1961, p. 1739.

145. *JO. AN.*, *Documents*, May 18, 1961, annex 1197, p. 156.

146. *JO. AN.*, July 18, 1961, pp. 1738–39, 1754–55.

147. Ibid., November 23, 1961, pp. 5014, 5047–49; Williams, *French Parliament*, p. 88.

148. Williams, *French Parliament*, pp. 88–89.

149. *JO. LD.*, August 25, 1961, p. 7987.

150. *JO. S.*, *Documents*, 1st regular session 1961-62, I, no. 1, *Projet de loi rélatif a l'accueil et à la réinstallation des Français d'outre mer.*

151. *JO. S.*, *Documents*, 1st regular session 1961-62, I, no. 4, *Rapport au nom de la Commission des Lois constitutionnelles . . .*; I, no. 7, *Avis presenté au nom de la commission des Affaires étrangers . . .*; I, no. 19, *Avis presenté au nom de la Commission des Affairs economiques . . .*; I, no. 6, *Avis presenté au nom de la Commission des Finances. . . .*

152. *JO. S.*, October 12, 1961, p. 1147.

153. *JO. S.*, October 24, 1961, p. 1218.

154. Ibid., pp. 1219, 1222–24.

155. Ibid., pp. 1224–29.

156. Ibid., pp. 1245–51; October 25, 1961, pp. 1256–82.

157. *JO. AN.*, November 21, 1961, p. 4934; *JO. AN.*, *Documents*, November 16, 1961, annex 1543, pp. 734–37.

158. *JO. AN.*, November 23, 1961, p. 5014.

159. *JO. AN.*, November 21, 1961, pp. 4936–37.

160. Ibid., pp. 4937–43; November 22, 1961, pp. 4955–77, 4980–85.

161. Ibid., pp. 4985–92; November 23, 1961, pp. 5004–20.

162. Ibid., November 29, 1961, pp. 5122–27, 5141–42.

163. Ibid., December 14, p. 5631; *JO. S.*, December 14, 1961, p. 2592.

164 Law 61-1439. *JO. LD.*, December 28, 1961, pp. 11996–97.

165. Ords. 62-91, 62-168, 62-169, 62-400, 62-401, 62-525, *JO. LD.*, January 28, 1962, p. 965; February 15, 1965, pp. 1605–06, April 12, 1965, p. 3786, April 22, 1965, p. 4224.

166. *JO. AN.*, *Documents*, June 6, 1962, annex 1748, p. 311.

167. *Rapport d'ensemble sur les diverses aspects des problèmes soulevès par l'application de la loi no. 61-1439 du 26 décembre 1961* . . ., October 2, 1965; *Le Monde*, October 5, 1965.

168. Article 24 of Law 62-933, *JO. LD.*, August 10, 1962, p. 7967.

169. *JO. AN.*, *Documents*, July 4, 1962, annex 1825, p. 479.

170. Ibid., July 16, annex 1852, pp. 539–54.

171. *JO. AN.*, July 19, 1962, pp. 2680–81.

172. *JO. S.*, *Documents*, 1962, Annex 316, pp. 73–75.

173. *JO. S.*, July 24, 1962, pp. 1131–36; July 25, 1962, pp. 1205–1208.

174. *JO. AN.*, *Documents*, June 5, 1964, annex 949, p. 566.

175. Ibid., November 12, 1964, annex 1165, pp. 130–31.

176. André Chandernagor and Jean Foyer, both of whom had served on the task force of experts that had helped to draft the 1958 constitution.

177. *JO. AN.*, November 17, 1964, pp. 5416–19.

178. *JO. S.*, *Documents*, 1964, annex 43.

179. *JO. S.*, December 2, 1964, pp. 2068–72; Law 64-1231, *JO. LD.*, December 15, 1964, p. 11146.

180. *JO. AN.*, *Documents*, May 11, 1966, annex 1817, p. 1037.

181. Ibid., June 3, 1966, annex 1896, p. 1229.

182. *JO. AN.*, June 7, 1966, p. 1737.

183. *JO. S.*, *Documents*, 1966, annex 241; *JO. S.*, June 24, 1966, p. 1010; Law 66-481, *JO. LD.*, July 7, 1966, 5781.

184. *JO. AN.*, *Documents*, annex 864, pp. 923–24.

185. Ibid., annex 897, pp. 955–58.

186. *JO. AN.*, November 29, 1969, pp. 4345–46.

187. *JO. S.*, December 16, 1969, pp. 1793–97; Law 69-1169, *JO. LD.*, December 28, 1969, p. 12670.

188. Ebrard, "L'Article 38," p. 264; *JO. AN.*, May 20, 1967, pp. 1175, 1199.

189. Ords. 68-1082, 69-394, 69-815, 69-819, 69-1176, *JO. LD.*, December 4, 1968, p. 11399; April 27, 1969, pp. 4262–63; September 5, 1969, pp. 8927–28, 8941; December 28, 1969, pp. 12679–80.

190. Ords. 72-447 and 72-1242, *JO. LD.*, June 2, 1972, pp. 5543–44; December 30, 1972, pp. 13829–30.

191. *JO. AN.*, June 27, 1973, p. 2575.

192. *JO. LD.*, March 29, 1973, p. 3494.

193. *JO. S.*, June 14, 1973, pp. 731–33.

194. *JO. AN.*, June 27, 1973, pp. 2575–76.

195. Law 73-628, *JO. LD.*, July 11, 1973, p. 7488.

196. *Année politique 1966*, pp. 70, 73–74.

197. *JO. AN.*, *Documents*, November 3, 1966, annex 2118, p. 810.
198. Ibid., November 30, 1966, annex 2199, pp. 1005–08; *JO. AN.*, December 2, 1966, pp. 5222–23.
199. Ibid., pp. 5250–51.
200. *JO. S.*, *Documents*, 1966, annex 108.
201. *JO. S.*, December 14, 1966, pp. 2455–71; Law 66-949, *JO. LD.*, December 23, 1966, p. 11304.
202. *L'Express*, September 4–10, 1967.
203. Press conference, *Le Monde*, May 19, 1967.
204. *JO. AN.*, *Documents*, May 9, 1967, annex 174, p. 1479.
205. *Le Monde*, May 9, 11, 12, 13, 1967; *L'Express*, May 1–7, 1967, p. 44.
206. *Le Monde*, May 12, 13, 14/15, 19, 1967.
207. *JO. AN.*, May 18, 1967, p. 1067.
208. Ibid., May 19, 1967, p. 1109.
209. Ibid., pp. 1109–36; May 21, 1967, pp. 1171–1211.
210. *Le Monde*, May 27, 1967; Filippi, *Rapport au nom de la Commission*, pp. 136, 137, 141.
211. *Le Monde*, May 28/29, 1967.
212. *JO. S.*, June 1 and 2, 1967, pp. 518–51, 558–74, 576–77.
213. *JO. AN.*, *Documents*, June 7, 1967, annex 276, p. 1636; *JO. S.*, *Documents*, June 8, 1967, annex 286.
214. *JO. AN.*, June 7, 1967, pp. 1651–52.
215. Ibid., June 8, 1967, p. 1703.
216. Ibid., June 9, 1967, pp. 1728–32.
217. Ibid., June 13, 1967, pp. 644–45.
218. *JO. AN.*, June 14, 1967, p. 1808; June 15, 1967, pp. 1844, 1906–09, 1941.
219. Law 67-482, *JO. LD.*, June 23, 1967, p. 6211.
220. *JO. AN.*, May 26, 1967, pp. 1348–72.
221. Ibid., June 29 and 30, 1967, pp. 2378–97, 2399–2415, 2455–74.
222. Ords. 67-578, 67-579, 67-580, 67-581, 67-693, 67-694, 67-695, 67-706, 67-707, 67-708, 67-709, 67-768, 67-808, 67-809, 67-810, 67-811, 67-812, 67-813, 67-816, 67-820, 67-821, 67-824, 67-825, 67-827, 67-828, 67-829, 67-830, 67-832, 67-833, 67-834, 67-835, 67-836, 67-837, 67-838, 67-839, *JO. LD.*, July 13, 1967, pp. 7238–41; August 17, 1967, pp. 8288–91; August 21, 1967, pp. 8403–14; September 12, 1967, p. 9168; September 22, 1967, pp. 9501–06; September 23, 1967, pp. 9532–57; September 26, 1967, p. 9507; September 27, 1967, p. 9557; September 28, 1967, pp. 9588–99.
223. "La participation des salariés aux fruits de l'expansion des entreprises," "La Réforme de la securité sociale," "Les Ordonnances économiques de 1967." *Notes et études documentaires*, February 5 (no. 3460), January 5 (no. 3452), March 26, 1968 (no. 3475); Ebrard, "L'Article 38," Becet, "La Pratique des ordonnances," G. Adam, "Quelles leçons tirer des ordonnances?", *Recherche sociale*, November/December 1967, pp. 1–7; "Les Ordonnances de la loi du 22 juin 1967," *Chambre d'agriculture*, October 15, 1967, November 1, 1967, and December 15, 1967; S. Dickschat, "L'Article 38 de la Constitution et la loi d'habitation du 22 juin 1967," in *RDP*, July 1968, pp. 837–71.
224. Ord. 67-812; Filippi, *Rapport au nom*, p. 137.
225. Articles 23-27 of Ord. 67-813; *JO. AN.*, November 8, 1967, p. 4657.
226. Ibid., October 3, 1967, p. 3399.

227. Ibid., October 10, 1967, pp. 3431–45, 3447–68.

228. Ibid., October 12, 1967, pp. 3573–74, 3613–14.

229. Ibid., October 25, November 4, 8, 10, December 5, 1967, pp. 4097, 4101, 4103–4108, 4473, 4657, 4667–68, 4670–71, 4699–4700, 4717, 4923, 5540; *JO. S.*, November 22, 24, 1967, pp. 1611–15, 1618–19, 1626, 1628, 1631, 1737.

230. *JO. AN.*, December 8, 1967, pp. 5724–32; May 17, 1968, pp. 1939–43, 1945–53.

231. *JO. S.*, October 31, 1967, pp. 1038–39, 1043–51, April 23, 1968, pp. 145–55.

232. *JO. AN.*, *Questions écrites*, 1967, Numbers 102, 1372, 1700, 2504, 3069, 3197, 3403, 3480, 3734, 3835, (misprinted as 3855), 4150, 5324, 4453, 4663, 4688, 4755, 4860, 4905, 4995, 5201, 5230, 5662; 1968, 6064, 6281, 6316, 6711, 7323, 7858, 7861, 8487, 8707, 8943, 8999, 9026. Two other oral questions without debate in the Assembly were submitted but never scheduled: 1967, 1107, and 4202.

233. *JO. AN.*, *Documents*, April 2, 1968, annex 640, pp. 1037–38; *JO. AN.*, July 22, 1968, p. 2401; *JO. S.*, July 23, 1968, p. 546.

234. *JO. AN.*, *Documents*, 1968, annex 6, p. 1363.

235. *Le Monde*, July 20, 1968.

236. *JO. AN.*, *Documents*, July 19, 1968, annex 198, pp. 1489–98.

237. *JO. AN.*, July 22, 1968, pp. 2413–55; *Le Monde*, July 24, 1968.

238. *JO. S.*, July 23, 24, 1968, pp. 547, 552–55, 562–75, 577–78.

239. Ibid., July 24, 1968, p. 575; *JO. AN.*, July 25, 1968, p. 2570.

240. Ibid., p. 2593.

241. *JO. S.*, July 25, 1968, pp. 623–27, 630, 638–39.

242. *JO. AN.*, July 25, 1968, pp. 2612–15; *JO. S.*, July 25, 1968, pp. 630–35, 640.

243. Law 68-698, *JO. LD.*, August 2, 1968, p. 7522.

244. *JO. AN.*, December 11, 19, 1969, pp. 4851–60, 5097; *JO. S.*, December 17, 19, 1969, pp. 1848–54, 1935–36; Law 70-13, *JO. LD.*, January 6, 1970, p. 196.

245. *JO. LD.*, March 20, 1962, p. 3019–32.

246. D. 62-310, *JO. LD.*, March 21, 1962, p. 3075.

247. *JO. AN.*, March 20, 21, 1962, pp. 457–92, 510–24; *JO. S.*, March 20, 21, 1962, pp. 71–78, 88–114.

248. Filippi, *Rapport au nom . . .*, pp. 163–64, lists thirty-five. Another seventeen also list that law as their authority.

249. *JO. AN.*, April 26, 27, 1962, pp. 748–51, 753–73, 776–802, 823–30.

250. Ibid., May 30, June 5, 1962, pp. 1397–1410, 1426–56, 1458–81, 1504.

251. Ibid., July 24, 25, 1962, pp. 2838–41, 2865.

252. Ord. 62-618, *JO. LD.*, June 2, 1962, p. 5316.

253. Jerome B. King, "France: The Canal Affair and the OAS Cases," in Ronald F. Bunn and William G. Andrews, eds., *Politics and Civil Liberties in Europe* (Princeton, N.J.: Van Nostrand, 1967), pp. 37–92; Pierre Stillmunkes, "La classification les actes ayant force de loi en droit public français, pp. 261–292, in *Revue de droit public*, March/April 1964, pp. 284–285; *Recueil des décisions du Conseil d'état*, October 19, 1962, pp. 552–53.

254. *JO. AN.*, *Documents*, December 19, 1962, annexes 46, 47, pp. 97–102.

255. *Le Monde*, December 29, 30/31, 1962, January 4, 1963; *JO. AN.*, *Documents*, January 3, 1963, annexes 58 and 59, pp. 110–20.

256. *JO. AN.*, January 4, 1963, pp. 308–11.

257. *Le Monde*, January 4, 1963.

258. *JO. S.*, *Documents*, 1963, Special session annexes 33, and 34.

259. *JO. S.*, January 9, 1963, pp. 3–43, 49–52.

260. *Le Monde*, January 11, 1963.
261. *JO. AN.*, *Documents*, January 11, 1963, annexes 100 and 101, pp. 154–56; *Le Monde*, January 12, 13, 1963.
262. *JO. AN.*, January 11, 1963, pp. 654–62, 688–90; *JO. S.*, January 11, 1963, pp. 58–65.
263. *JO. S.*, January 9, 1963, p. 41.
264. Ord. 63-776, *JO. LD.*, August 2, 1963, p. 7155; *JO. AN.*, July 24, 1963, p. 4453; *JO. S.*, January 11, 1963, pp. 58–65.
265. *JO. AN.*, *Documents*, February 2, 1960, annex 528, pp. 1–2; April 25, 1961, annex 1099, pp. 6–7; March 20, 1962, annex 1663, p. 2; January 17, 1963, annex 117, p. 14.
266. For a more general discussion of this concept, see William G. Andrews, "The Presidency, Congress, and Constitutional Theory," presented to the 1971 APSA meeting and reprinted in pp. 13–33 of Norman C. Thomas, ed., *The Presidency in Contemporary Context* (New York: Dodd, Mead, 1975), and Aaron Wildavsky, ed., *The President* (Boston: Little, Brown, 1975), pp. 24–45.

6. PARLIAMENTARY LAW MAKING

1. Michel Debré, "La Nouvelle Constitution," in *Revue française de science politique* (*RFSP*), March 1959, p. 17; English translation as "The New Constitution," in William G. Andrews, ed., *European Political Institutions*, 2nd. ed., (Princeton, N.J.: Van Nostrand, 1966), p. 50.
2. *JO. AN.*, *Débats*, June 2, 1958, p. 2576; June 3, 1958, pp. 2617–19, 2623–26.
3. Jean-Louis Debré, *La Constitution de la Vᵉ République*, (Paris: PUF, 1975), pp. 26, 27, 29.
4. Ibid., p. 43–49.
5. Ibid., p. 47.
6. M. Debré, "The New Constitution," p. 47.
7. *Loi constitutionnelle du 16 Juillet 1875*, Art. 2.
8. Raymond Poincaré, *How France is Governed* (London: Unwin, 1913), p. 179; Walter Rice Sharp, *The Government of the French Republic* (New York: Van Nostrand, 1938), pp. 106–107; Edward M. Sait, *Government and Politics of France* (New York: World, 1920), p. 178.
9. Philip M. Williams, *Crisis and Compromise* (London: Longmans, 1964), p. 212; D. W. S. Lidderdale, *The Parliament of France* (London: Hansard, 1951), p. 53.
10. J.-L. Debré, *La Constitution*, p. 71.
11. Ibid., p. 117.
12. *Travaux préparatoires de la constitution du 4 octobre 1958* (Paris: La documentation française, 1960), pp. 99–100, 169, 210.
13. J.-L. Debré, *La Constitution*, p. 192.
14. Ibid., pp. 192, 228.
15. Ibid., p. 64.
16. Ibid., p. 150.
17. *Travaux préparatoires*, pp. 129–30, 208.
18. J.-L. Debré, *La Constitution*, pp. 188, 226.
19. Ibid., pp. 66, 77, 80, 86, 99, 112, 149; *Travaux préparatoires*, pp. 132, 193, 207.
20. J.-L. Debré *La Constitution*, p. 225.
21. 1959, 2; 1960, 1; 1962, 3; 1965, 1968, 1969, 1974, 1 each.

22. Unless indicated otherwise, the statistics in this section were supplied by Mr. Robert Marquis, Service de la séance, National Assembly. Beginning in 1967, they were published in annual booklets, first (1967–72) as *Assemblée nationale. Statistiques*, then (1972–) as a special issue of *Bulletin de l'Assemblée nationale*.

23. Fall 1962 (50 hours) and Spring 1968 (100 hours) were abbreviated by dissolutions.

24. L.69-1557 of December 31, 1959.

25. L.62-933 of August 8, 1962.

26. L.63-22 and L.63-23 of January 15, and L.63-69 of January 30, L.53-156 of February 23, L.63-215 of March 1, L.63-222 of March 5, L.63-233 of March 7, and L.63-254 of March 15.

27. L.63-138 of February 20 and L.63-214 of March 1.

28. *JO. AN.*, February 6, 1963, p. 2039 (sitting of February 5).

29. L.66-10 of January 6, 1966.

30. On the above six sessions, see Philip M. Williams, *The French Parliament 1958–1967* (London: Allen & Unwin, 1968), pp. 43–44.

31. L.68-877 of October 9, 1968, L.68-878 of October 9, 1968, and L.68-978 of November 13, 1968.

32. For instance, those sessions in 1973 through 1976 averaged 392 hours.

33. L.68-671 of July 25, L.68-678 of July 26, L.68-687 of July 30, and L.68-688, L.68-689, L.68-690, L.68-691, L.68-695, L.68-696, L.68-697, L.68-698, and L.68-703.

34. Lidderdale, *The Parliament of France*, pp. 109–10.

35. *Loi constitutionnelle du 16 juillet 1875*, Art. 5.

36. Lidderdale, *Parliament of France*, p. 110.

37. Ibid.

38. Jean Petot, *Les Grandes étapes du régime républicain français (1792-1969)* (Paris: Cujas, 1970), pp. 472, 523–33.

39. Debré, *La Constitution*, pp. 71, 83, 102, 118, 154, 193, 229, 253; *Travaux préparatoires*, p. 100.

40. Sharp, *The Government of the French Republic*, p. 117; W. L. Middleton, *The French Political System* (New York: Dutton, 1933), 160–61.

41. Herman Finer, *The Theory and Practice of Modern Government* (New York: Dial, 1934), pp. 455–56.

42. Georges Galichon, "Aspects de la Procédure Législative en France," in François Goguel, ed., *Le Travail Parlementaire* (Paris: PUF, 1955), p. 151. The other members were the president and vice presidents of the Chamber and the chairmen of the standing committees and parliamentary groups.

43. In the 1924 legislature, 432 agendas were adopted without discussion and 152 were the object of interpellation debates. Finer, *The Theory and Practice*, p. 559n.

44. James Bryce, *Modern Democracies*, 2 vols. (London: Macmillan, 1921), I: 287–89; R. K. Gooch, "The Government and Politics of France," in James T. Shotwell, ed., *Governments of Continental Europe* (New York: Macmillan, 1940), pp. 167–68; Lidderdale, *The Parliament of France*, pp. 113–16; Serge Arné, *Le Président du conseil des ministres sous la IVᵉ République* (Paris: LGDJ, 1962), pp. 180–82; Williams, *Crisis and Compromise*, pp. 220, 223–25; Marcel Martin, ed., *Les Institutions politiques de la France* (Paris: Documentation française, 1959), p. 132.

45. Williams, *Crisis and Compromise*, p. 258; Arné, *Le Président*, pp. 184–85.

46. Debré, *La Constitution*, p. 35.

47. Ibid., pp. 39–42.

48. Ibid., p. 73.

49. Ibid., p. 86.
50. Ibid., p. 122.
51. Ibid.
52. Ibid., p. 162; *Travaux préparatoires*, p. 116.
53. *Travaux préparatoires*, pp. 102, 234.
54. This section draws heavily on Jean Grangé, "La Fixation de l'ordre du jour des Assemblées parlementaires," in E. Guichard-Ayoub, C. Roig, and Jean Grangé, *Etudes sur le Parlement de la V*ᵉ *République* (Paris: PUF, 1965), for agenda making in the first legislature.
55. Grangé, "La Fixation," p. 194; *JO. AN., Débats*, May 13, 1960, pp. 785–86 (1st sitting of May 12), June 2, 1960, p. 1116 (1st sitting of June 1); December 6, 1960, p. 4270 (1st sitting of December 5).
56. *JO. AN., Débats*, July 27, 1963, pp. 4577–80 (1st sitting of July 26).
57. That right is, of course, restricted by other provisions of the constitution that forbid amendments that would increase expenditures, reduce revenues, trespass in the domain of regulation, etc.
58. Alain Brouillet, *Le Droit d'amendement dans la Constitution de la V*ᵉ *République* (Paris: PUF, 1973).
59. Originally, Article 151, later Article 154.
60. Except that the president was elected only at the beginning of a legislature or when a vacancy occurred.
61. They were not listed for 1959–61. Also, two were double-listed in 1973.
62. This list does not include the occasional government bills that appeared on the complementary agenda.
63. M. Debré, "The New Constitution," p. 47.
64. Williams, *The French Parliament*, p. 50.
65. M. Ameller, *Les questions, instrument de contrôle parlementaire* (Paris: LGDJ, 1964); Williams, *The French Parliament*, pp. 46–51.
66. 12 in 1962 and 14 in 1969.
67. 1959, 392; 1960, 274; 1961, 108.
68. *Questions d'actualité*. Another type, "written questions," are freely used but do not absorb agenda time. In the later years of the Gaullist period, the number of written questions and answers were: 1967—5, 481 and 3,506; 1968—5,780 and 4,606; 1969—6, 805 and 5,222; 1970—7,547 and 5,565; 1971—7,282 and 5,467, 1972—7,575 and 5,285; 1973—6,666 and 4,413.
69. *JO. AN., Tables*, for 1959–66; Service de la séance for 1967–72; *AN. Statistiques* for 1973.
70. Williams, *The French Parliament*, p. 50; Pierre Avril, *Les Français et leur Parlement* (Paris: Casterman, 1972), p. 90.
71. Besides the organized question periods, MPs can, of course, put questions to ministers during debates, especially in support of amendments to bills—and often get faster answers. Brouillet, *Le Droit d'amendement*, pp. 101–105.
72. Grangé, "La Fixation," p. 241, is referring to the first legislature only, but his observation seems to hold for the others as well.
73. 133 days compared to 431. Data are available only for 1969–73, *Service de la séance* and *Statistiques*.
74. *Loi constitutionnelle du 16 juillet 1875*, Art. 6.
75. Sait, *Government and Politics of France*, p. 56; Williams, *Crisis and Compromise*, p. 202.
76. *JO. AN.*, May 30, 1958, p. 2556 (sitting of May 29).

77. January 14, 1946 and June 18, 1948. Debré, *La Constitution*, pp. 29, 33.
78. Ibid., p. 54.
79. Ibid., pp. 64, 67, 78, 81, 99, 114, 188, 226; *Travaux préparatoires*, p. 131.
80. *Loi constitutionnelle du 16 juillet 1875*, Art. 6; Art. 53 in 1946.
81. Marcel Sibert, *La Constitution de la France du 4 Septembre 1879 au 9 Août 1955* (Paris: Pedone, 1946), pp. 140–60, Sharp, *The Government of the French Republic*, pp. 107, 147.
82. Eugene P. Chase et al., *Democratic Governments of Europe* (New York: Nelson, 1937), p. 321.
83. Joseph Barthélémy, *Essai sur le travail parlementaires et le système des commissions* (Paris: Delagrave, 1934), p. 219.
84. Galichon, "Aspects de la procédure . . .," p. 145.
85. J.-L. Debré, *La Constitution*, pp. 7, 86, 117, 192, 229; *Travaux préparatoires*, p. 100.
86. J.-L. Debré, *La Constitution*, pp. 68, 84, 102–103, 119, 122, 162, 202, 234; *Travaux préparatoires*, pp. 180–85.
87. *Le Monde*, April 25, 1961; *JO. LD.*, April 24, 1961, pp. 3876–77.
88. *JO. AN.*, January 16, 1959, p. 24 (1st sitting of January 15); December 12, 1962, pp. 23–24 (sitting of December 11); April 4, 1973, pp. 748–49 (sitting of April 3); June 26, 1969, p. 1719 (sitting of June 25).
89. *JO. AN.*, December 8, 1960, pp. 4370–73 (1st sitting of December 7); March 21, 1962, p. 452 (1st sitting of March 20); October 3, 1962, pp. 3191–92 (sitting of October 2); April 3, 1969, p. 812 (sitting of April 2); April 5, 1972, pp. 799–800 (sitting of April 4).
90. 1959–71, 1,787 total. 1972 and 1973 not available. Compiled from *JO. AN., Tables*. Responses to oral questions and formal declarations are not included.
91. I–107; II–156; III–143; IV–137.
92. For a statistical tabulation of participation in debates by subject categories, see Herbert Maisl, "Les Groupes parlementaires a l'Assemblée nationale: Bilan des deux premières années de la quatriéme législature (juillet 1968–decembre 1969)," in *Revue de droit publique*, July–August 1970, pp. 1020–22.
93. François Platone, "Le Contenu des débats parlementaires sous la cinquième ré-publique," in *RFSP*, February 1970, p. 99. Although his research covers only the first two legislatures, the level established in the second legislature seems to have held fairly constant thereafter.
94. Information on committees supplied by Mr. Guy Flaujac, Services des commissions, services législatifs, of the Assembly, and compiled from the *Bulletin des commissions. Table des matières*, 1959–72, and *AN. Statistiques*, 1967–73.
95. *Loi constitutionnelle du 16 juillet 1875*, Art. 3.
96. For instance, in 1928–29, 1,078 private members bills and 475 government bills were introduced in the Chamber, but the majority of the important bills enacted had been introduced by the government. F. A. Ogg, *European Governments and Politics* (New York: Macmillan, 1939), p. 521. In another selection of four years (1913, 1925, 1926, 1927), government bills represented 45.2 percent of all bills introduced, but 76.6 percent of those enacted; 54.5 percent of all government bills and 13.7 percent of all private members bills were enacted. Finer, *Theory and Practice of Modern Government*, p. 456n.
97. Jean-Marie Cotteret, *Le Pouvoir législatif en France* (Paris: LGDJ, 1962) p.
98. J.-L. Debré, *La Constitution*, pp. 29, 32–36.
99. Ibid., p. 42.
100. Ibid., p. 58.

101. Ibid., p. 72.
102. Ibid., pp. 75–78.
103. Ibid., p. 84, 102.
104. Ibid., p. 119.
105. *Travaux préparatoires*, pp. 109–10.
106. J.-L. Debré, *La Constitution*, pp. 196–97, 231.
107. *AN. Statistiques* for 1973. For 1959–72, the percentage was 32.3, but in 1973, private members submitted 622 bills, more than three times the average of the previous fourteen years.
108. Geneviève Bastid-Burdeau, *La Génèse de l'initiative législative: Un cas: l'Agriculture 1958–1968* (Paris: PUF, 1973), p. 12.
109. That is, 1.84 columns to 0.52 columns per bill, using as a sample the 200 bills (29 government, 171 private members) published in *JO. AN.*, *Documents*, 2nd regular session, 1966–67, pp. 1337–1588. Also, in 1973, government bills were 4.1 times as long and in 1973–76, 2.7 times as long as their private counterparts. *AN. Statistiques*, 1973–76.
110. Bastid-Burdeau, *La Génèse*, p. 63.
111. Brouillet, *Le Droit d'amendement*, pp. 43–44.
112. William E. Rappard, *Source Book on European Governments* (New York: Van Nostrand, 1937), pp. II, 72–73; Lidderdale, *The Parliament of France*, pp. 221–22.
113. Williams, *Crisis and Compromise*, p. 263.
114. J.-L. Debré, *La Constitution*, pp. 58, 72, 85, 103, 119, 157, 195, 231.
115. The discrepancies between this table and the previous one result from slightly different ways in which the statistical services of the Assembly count bills.
116. Sharp, *Government of the French Republic*, pp. 112–16, 301–303; Sait, *Government and Politics of France*, pp. 204–12; Chase, *Democratic Governments*, pp. 414–15.
117. Lidderdale, *Parliament of France*, pp. 170–71; Williams, *Crisis and Compromise*, p. 223.
118. J.-L. Debré, *La Constitution*, p. 31, 35, 42, 73, 120, 194, 232; *Travaux préparatoires*, p. 115.
119. Dimitri-Georges Lavoff, "Les Commissions de l'Assemblée nationale sous la Cinquième République," in *Revue du droit publique*, November–December 1971, p. 1439.
120. Information from M. Flaujac.
121. Gaston Rimareix and Yves Tavernier, "L'Elaboration et le vote de la Loi complémentaire à la Loi d'Orientation Agricole," in *RFSP*, 1963, no. 2, pp. 389–425.
122. J.-L. Debré, *La Constitution*, pp. 42, 73, 85, 103, 120, 158, 196, 231.
123. *Travaux préparatoires*, p. 115.
124. Lidderdale, *Parliament of France*, p. 188; Galichon, "Aspects de la Procédure Législative", p. 162.
125. Except that final reviews in the government changed "dispose of" to "have," Debré, *La Constitution*, pp. 74, 86, 103, 121, 159, 196, 232; *Travaux préparatoires*, p. 116.
126. Detailed statistics on the origin of amendments are not available before 1967. The total number of amendments submitted before 1967 was 12,355. The total number submitted, 1967–73, was 13,346, of which 1,635 or 12.3 percent, were government. The same percentage of the 1959–66 total would have meant 1,514 government amendments.
127. The Assembly adopted 1,377 government amendments, 1967–73.
128. Total, 6,172, 1967–73.

129. Committees submitted 5,490 amendments, so their adoption rate was 67.7 percent and they contributed 60.2 percent of the successful total.
130. Of 6,210 submitted, an 18.3 percent adoption rate and 18.4 percent of the successful total.
131. Brouillet, *Le Droit d'Amendement*, pp. 98–99.
132. Jean-Pierre Dussaife, "Le Parlement face à la réforme des taxes sur le chiffre d'affaires," in *RFSP*, June 1966, p. 530.
133. *JO. AN.*, July 18, 1957, p. 3718 (2nd sitting of July 17). Pierre Avril, "Le Vote Bloqué," in *Revue du droit publique*, May–June, 1965, pp. 399–457.
134. *JO. AN.*, December 20, 1957, p. 5515 (sitting of December 19).
135. J.-L. Debré, *La Constitution*, pp. 196, 232.
136. Ibid.
137. Using the official count, rather than the one in Avril, "Le Vote Bloqué" which is less.
138. Data are not availabe on three of the four blocked votes in 1971. The dependence of the blocked vote success on a homogeneous majority is indicated, also, by its many failures in the Senate, where the Gaullists never held a majority. In 1959–70, the government was defeated on 83 of 128 blocked votes (64.9 percent), Avril, "Le Vote Bloqué."
139. The Somalia referendum bill. Léo Hamon and Jacques Vaudiaux, "Vie et droit parlementaire," in *Revue du droit publique*, September–October 1967, p. 903.
140. Lidderdale, *The Parliament of France*, p. 221.
141. Rappard, et al., *Source Book on European Government*, p. II 65.
142. Ibid., p. ii 73.
143. Williams, *Crisis and Compromise*, p. 263.
144. R. K. Gooch, *The French Parliamentary Committee System* (Archon Books, n.p., 1969, reprint of 1935 ed.), p. 175.
145. Debré, *La Constitution*, pp. 35, 58, 72, 84, 85, 103, 119, and 121.
146. *Travaux préparatoires*, pp. 113–16; Debré, *La Constitution*, pp. 159, 194, 196.
147. Earlier data not available.
148. In fact, the chair did rule against the government on a few occasions and it withdrew its declarations, rather than delay the legislative process by appealing to the CC. Nicholas Dénis. "L'Application des Nouvelles Régles de la Procédure Parlementaires Etablies par la Constitution de 1958," in *RFSP*, December 1960, p. 908. In addition to the case cited by Dénis, the government withdrew declarations twice in 1972. The government never appealed such a ruling.
149. Lidderdale, *The Parliament of France*, pp. 192–200; Williams, *Crisis and Compromise*, p. 259 and n.; Gooch, *The French Parliamentary Committee System*, p. 33.
150. Debré, *La Constitution*, pp. 34, 73, 85, 103, 121, 159, 197, 232; *Travaux préparatoires*, pp. 174–76, 190–91.
151. Data for 1973 were not available.
152. Information in this paragraph was supplied by M. Marquis.
153. *Commission mixte paritaire*.
154. Gooch, *The French Parliamentary Committee System*, pp. 143, 177.
155. J.-L. Debré, *La Constitution*, pp. 35, 73, 85, 121.
156. *Travaux préparatoires*, pp. 174–78, 190–91. For instance, it wanted either assembly as well as the government to be able to refer a bill to a JCC.
157. J.-L. Debré, *La Constitution*, pp. 159–60, 197, 232.

158. Henri Trnka, "Evolution de la procédure de la Commission Mixte Paritaire au cours de la second législature de la Cinquiéme République," in *Revue du droit publique*, July–August 1967, at pp. 755, 759, 760; Trnka, "La Commission Mixte Paritaire," in ibid., May–June 1963, pp. 477-534; Léo Hamon and co-authors, "Vie et droit parlementaires," various issues of ibid., esp. March-April 1963, pp. 264ff., and January–February 1965, pp. 39ff.
159. Information from M. Flaujac.
160. The JCC cannot be used for international agreements.
161. Monnerville, *JO. S.*, 1966, p. 1169, as cited by Pierre Avril, *Le Régime politique de la V e République* (Paris: LGDJ, 1967), p. 385n.
162. *Travaux préparatoires*, p. 184; Debré, *La Constitution*, pp. 319-27.
163. Probably the nuclear striking force would have had three censure motions also, except that the summer vacation was nibbling away at the Opposition forces. Parodi, *Les rapports entre le législatifs et l'exécutif sous la cinquième république*, (Paris: Colin, 1972), pp. 33–34; Philip M. Williams and Martin Harrison, *Politics and Society in de Gaulle's Republic* (Garden City, N.Y.: Anchor, 1973), p. 268; Williams, *The French Parliament*, p. 54. The special powers motion fell short 8, 8, and 9 votes; 1960 budget 168; program law, 70, 63, 62; Pierrelatte, 35.
164. Henry Lesguillons, "L'Intervention du pouvoir exécutif dans la procédure de décision budgetaire en France," in Pierre Delvolve and Lesguillons, *Le Contrôle Parlementaire sur la politique économique et budgétaire* (Paris: PUF, 1964), pp. 232-33.
165. Williams, *Crisis and Compromise*, p. 268.
166. Debré, *La Constitution*, pp. 58, 73, 85, 104, 122, 161, 198–99, 233; *Travaux préparatoires*, pp. 178–80, 186.
167. The *new* deliberation should not be confused with the *second* deliberation under Art. 101 of the Assembly rules, which has no express basis in the constitution. *Second* deliberation is reconsideration requested before the vote explanations (which immediately precede the vote as a whole) in the Assembly. A request by the government cannot be refused. *New* deliberation takes place only after the bill has been passed finally by both chambers and sent to the president.
168. *Loi constitutionnelle du 16 juillet 1875*, Art. 7.
169. Art. 36.
170. Gooch, "The Government and Politics of France", p. 113.
171. Williams, *Crisis and Compromise*, p. 200n.
172. Debré, *La Constitution*, pp. 62, 66, 76, 80–81, 98, 112, 148, 185, 224; *Travaux préparatoires*, p. 126.
173. Constitutional law 74-904 of October 29, 1974 extended that list to include sixty deputies or sixty senators.
174. Williams, *Crisis and Compromise*, pp. 305–306; Lidderdale, *The Parliament of France*, p. 264.
175. Debré, *La Constitution*, pp. 88, 94, 106, 126, 165, 204, 236.
176. Conseil constitutionnel, *Recueil des décisions*, 1961, pp. 24–25 and 293, decisions no. 60-11DC of June 20, 1961, and no. 61-16DC of December 22, 1961; *1963*, pp. 23-24, decision no. 63-21DC of March 12, 1963; *1970*, pp. 29-30, decision no. 70-41DC of December 30, 1970.
177. *Loi constitutionnelle du 25 Janvier 1875*, Arts. 3 and 5.
178. Gooch, "The Government and Politics of France", pp. 233–34.
179. Debré, *La Constitution*, pp. 30, 36, 40, 47, 54, 63, 66, 77, 80, 99, 112, 149, 184, 225.

180. In 1962, the issue was constitutional amendment; in 1968, it was restoration of public order.
181. CC 59-2 DC of June 17, 18, and 24, 1959.
182. CC 69-37 of November 20, 1969.
183. CC 73-49 DC of May 17, 1973.
184. CC 59-2 DC of June 17, 18, and 24, 1959; CC 59-3 DC of June 24 and 25, 1959.
185. CC 59-3 DC of June 24 and 25, 1959.
186. CC 69-37 DC of November 20, 1969.
187. CC 59-3 of June 24 and 25, 1959.
188. Ibid.
189. Ibid.
190. CC 59-5 DC of January 15, 1960.
191. CC 73-49 DC of May 17, 1973.

7. THE TRANSFORMATION OF FRENCH SOCIETY, 1946-1962

1. Stanley Hoffmann, "Paradoxes of the French Political Community," in Hoffmann et al., *In Search of France* (Cambrige, Mass.: Harvard University Press, 1963).
2. "L'Espace économique française," *Etudes et conjoncture*, special number 1951, p. 35.
3. "Evolution de la population active en France depuis cent and d'après les dé-nombrements quinquennaux," *Etudes et conjoncture*, May/June 1953, p. 250; "L'Espace économique," p. 35, with the 1946 figure adjusted to allow for the 5.5 percent residue of persons with irregular or unknown employment; Henri Mendras, *Sociologie de la campagne française* (Paris: PUF, 1971), p. 18. Another source gives the "agricultural population" in 1851 as 40.01 percent, indicating no perceptible decline in a century. Henri Calvet, *La Société française contemporaine* (Paris: Fernand Nathan, 1956), p. 75. Also, see François Caron, *An Economic History of Modern France*, Columbia U.P., N.Y., 1979, 384 pp., p. 33.
4. "Une nouvelle série d'enquête sur l'emploi: L'enquête d'octobre 1962," *Etudes et conjoncture*, April 1965, pp. 40–42.
5. Mendras, *Sociologie de la campagne française*, p. 55; "Premiers résultats de l'enquête au 1/10ᵉ sur les structures agricoles en 1963," *Etudes et conjoncture*, June 1965, p. 109.
6. René Cercler, *Problèmes agricoles* (Paris: ed. Internationales, 1948), pp. 119, 121; *Annuaire statistique 1957*, pp. 82–83, and *1963*, p. 107; "L'Evolution du remembrement rural en France, ses résultats actuels," *Revue du Ministère de l'Agriculture*, March 1956.
7. Mendras, *Sociologie de la campagne*, p. 16; Georges Dupeux, *La Société française 1789-1960* 3rd ed. (Paris: Colin, 1964), p. 242.
8. "Les Comptes de la nation de l'année 1962," *Etudes et conjuncture*, August/September 1963, p. 630.
9. From 1 million T. in 1950 to 3.5 million T. 1968. Pierre Le Roy, *L'Avenir de l'Agriculture française* (Paris: PUF, 1972), p. 34.
10. Jean Fourastié and Jean-Paul Courtheoux, *L'Economie française dans le monde* (Paris: PUF, 1967), p. 38.
11. Pierre Maillet, *La Croissance économique* (Paris: PUF, 1972), p. 37; Claude Quinn, "L'Appareil français en 1960," in *Consommation*, April–June 1962, p. 15; *Le Monde*, October 3, 1973.

12. "L'Espace économique," p. 24; *Récensement de 1962. Villes et agglomérations urbaines* (Paris: INSEE, 1964), p. 17; *Résultats statistiques du recensement générale de la population effectué le 10 mars 1946* (Paris: PUF, 1948), I: 3, 53, 62, 86; *Recensement générale de la population de 1962. Résultats du dépouillement exhaustif* (Paris: Imprimérie nationale, 1967), pp. 6, 16–18, 62–65; *Recensement générale de la population de 1962. Villes et agglomérations urbaines*, p. 214.

13. "Les Comptes nationaux dans le monde," *Economie et statistique*, no. 27 (1971), p. 69. Arthur S. Banks, ed., *Cross-Polity Time-Series Data* (Cambridge: MIT Press, 1971), p. 259.

14. *Annuaire statistique rétrospectif 1966* (Paris: INSEE, 1966), p. 556.

15. "La Productivitié nationale et le mouvement cyclique en France de 1949 à 1963," *Etudes et conjoncture*, September 1964, p. 52.

16. Données statistiques sur l'évolution des rémunérations salariales en France de 1938 à 1963," *Etudes et conjoncture*, August 1965, p. 113, extrapolating from the 182 percent increase of 1949 to 1962.

17. Banks, *Cross-Polity Time-Series Data*, pp. 255–68.

18. "Evolution des conditions de logement en France depuis cent ans," *Etudes et conjoncture*, October/November 1957, pp. 1170, 1213, 1222–23; "L'Equipement des ménages en décembre 1962," *Etudes et conjoncture*, October 1965, pp. 15, 18.

19. "Industrie," *Etudes et conjoncture, Union française*, August/September 1946, p. 58; Fourastié and Courtheoux, *L'Economie français*, pp. 45, 106.

20. "Inventaire des ressources de l'économie française," *Etudes et conjoncture. Union française*, September/November 1947, p. 69; "L'équipement des ménages en véhicules automobiles à la fin de l'année 1962," *Etudes et conjoncture*, September 1964, p. 52; "L'équipement des ménages en décembre 1962," p. 28. "Fourfold" is an estimate based on data in Christiane Thomas, "Quinze millions d'automobiles en 1975," *Economie et statistiques*, no. 16 (1970), p. 48, and André Villeneuve, "L'accoutumance à l'automobile," *Economie et statistiques*, no. 23 (1971), p. 3.

21. J. Dumard, "Evolution de la consommation alimentaire des français de 1950 à 1960," in *Paysans*, October/November 1962, pp. 44–45; Jacqueline Beaujeu-Garnier, *La Population française* (Paris: Colin, 1969), p. 237.

22. Harry W. Paul, *The Second Ralliement: The Rapprochement between Church and State in France in the Twentieth Century* (Washington: Catholic University Press, 1967), p. 185.

23. *Annuaire statistique 1946* (Paris: INSEE, 1947), pp. 31–33, 37–39; *Annuaire statistique de la France 1964. Résultats de 1963* (Paris: INSEE, 1965), p. 89.

24. Fernand Boulard, *Premiers itinéraires en sociologie réligieuses* (Paris: Les editions ouvrières Economie et humanisme, 1954), pp. 24, 25 n.; *La France est-elle encore catholique?* (Paris: Les Presses d'aujourd'hui, n.d. (1954?)), pp. 7, 14, 19; Alain Hervé, "Comment va l'église en France?", in *Réalités*, August 1961, pp. 66, 67; "Les Attitudes réligieuses de la jeunesse," *Sondages* 3 1959, p. 11.

25. Claude Leleu, *Géographie des élections françaises depuis 1936* (Paris: PUF, 1971), pp. 31, 47, 61, 69, 79, 97, 125; Philip M. Williams, *Crisis and Compromise*, (London: Longmans, 1964), p. 198; Philip M. Williams and Martin Harrison, *Politics and Society in de Gaulle's Republic* (Garden City, N.Y.: Anchor, 1973), p. 126; Jean Charlot, *Répertoire des publications des partis politiques français 1944–67* (Paris: Colin, 1970), pp. 176–77.

26. Jean-Daniel Reynaud, *Les syndicats en France* (Paris: Colin, 1963), p. 136.

27. R. E. M. Irving, *Christian Democracy in France* (London: Allen & Unwin, 1973), p. 81.

28. Jean Mottin, *Histoire politique de la presse 1944–1949* (Paris: Ed. Bilans Hebdomadaires, 1949), *in passim*; Williams, *Crisis and Compromise*, p. 392 n.

29. Mottin, *Histoire politique*, pp. 43–46. ·

30. *Annuaire statistique 1951*, pp. 161, 164; *Annuaire statistique 1963*, pp. 291–92.

31. "Une enquête par sondage sur l'écoute radiophonique en France," *Etudes et conjoncture*, October 1963, p. 925; "L'équipement des ménages en décembre 1962," October 1965, p. 26; *Annuaire statistique 1946*, pp. 120, 243; *Annuaire statistique 1963*, pp. 302, 306, 307; Mottin, *Histoire politique*, pp. 43–46.

32. René Dubreule and Jean Courtassol, eds., *La France Blessée et renaissante* (Tourcoing: Temps que passe, n.d.), p. 183. *Bulletin mensuel de statistique*, April 1963, p. 19. However, rail traffic fell slightly, from 781.17 passenger/kilometers per capita per year to 768.7. *Bulletin de la statistique générale de la France*, May/June 1947, p. 350; *Bulletin mensuel de statistique*, April 1963, p. 17.

33. Calculated from data in *Annuaire statistique 1946*, pp. 31–33, 37–39; and *Annuaire statistique de la France 1964. Résultats de 1963*, p. 89.

34. *Coût et développement de l'enseignement en France* (Paris: INSEE, 1958), p. 22; *Annuaire statistique 1965*, p. 99; Calvet, *La Société française*, p. 75.

8. ELEMENTS FOR A CONSTITUTIONAL THEORY

1. André Malraux, *Felled Oaks* (New York: Holt, Rinehard & Winston, 1971), p. 105.

2. This description of flow is, of course, schematic, for all of these relationships are much more complex than can (or need) be described here.

3. Cecil S. Emden, *The People and the Constitution*, 2nd. ed. (London: Oxford University Press, 1956), pp. 157–59.

4. Ibid., p. 165.

5. No such majority had existed during 24 of the 33 years immediately preceding 1918.

6. Richard H. S. Crossman, *The Myths of Cabinet Government* (Cambridge, Mass.: Harvard University Press, 1972), and *The Diaries of a Cabinet Minister* (New York: Holt, Rinehard & Winston, 1976–78), 3 vol.

7. Initially, of course, Germany was not supposed to have military forces at all and, when this was changed in 1956, the Minister of Defense and the chancellor were given that authority (Art. 65a).

8. David Thomson, *Democracy in France Since 1870*, 4th. ed. (New York: Oxford University Press, 1964), pp. 91–93.

9. Law of February 25, 1875.

10. Law of August 31, 1871.

11. The French government has suppressed statistical data on those matters systematically, apparently from fear of their centrifugal effect. Thus, the information presented here is based mainly on unofficial estimates. See, for instance, Paul Serant, *La France des Minorités* (Paris: Laffont, 1965); and Charles R. Foster, ed., *Nations Without a State* (New York: Praeger, 1980).

12. Lathrop, Stoddard, *Racial Realities in Europe* (New York: Scribner's, 1924), p. 85.

Bibliography

ARTICLES AND BOOK CHAPTERS

Adam, G., "Quelles leçons tirer des ordonnances?," *Recherche sociale*, November/December 1967, 1–7.

Andrews, William G., "The Presidency, Congress, and Constitutional Theory", in Norman C. Thomas, ed., *The Presidency in Contemporary Context*, Dodd, Mead, N. Y., 1975, and Aaron Wildavsky, ed., *The President*, Little, Brown, Boston, 1975.

Andrews, William G., "Swan Song of the Fourth Republic", *Parliamentary Affairs*, Autumn 1962, pp. 485–499.

Andrews, William G., "Three Electoral Colleges," *Parliamentary Affairs*, Spring 1961, pp. 178–88.

"Aperçus sur les principales réformes ... du le juin 1958 au 5 février 1959," *Notes et documents* 2515, February 26, 1959.

"L'Article 16 de la Constitution de 1958," *Notes et études documentaires*, suppl. to March 1970, 16 pp.

Avril, Pierre, "Le Vote Bloqué," *Revue du droit public*, May-June 1965, 399–457.

Barrachin, Raymond, "Institutons un vrai régime présidentiel," *Revue politique et parlementaire*, January 1964, pp. 3–8.

Becet, J.M., "La Pratique des ordonnances de l'article 38," *Revue administrative*, November /December 1968, 704–715.

"Bilan de pouvoirs spéciaux," *Enterprise*, February 28, 1959, pp. 22–25.

Burdeau, Georges, "La conception du pouvoir selon la Constitution du 4 Octobre 1958," *Revue française de science politique*, March 1959, pp. 87–100.

Burdeau, Georges, ed. "Les Articles 34, 37 et 38 de la constitution de 1958," *Notes et Etudes documentaires*, suppl. to April 1970, 32 pp.

Charpentier, Jean, "Les Lois-Cadres et la fonction gouvernementale," *Revue du droit public*, March/April 1958, 821–860.

Coste-Floret, Paul, "Le future Constitution: Du choix des ministres," *Revue politique des Idées et des Institutions*, June 15, 1958, p. 298.

Coste-Floret, Paul, "Refléxions sur le contrôle parlementaire," *Revue politique des idées et des Institutions*, March 30, 1959, 161–169.

D.L., "Les Nouvelles Reformes," *Banque*, February 1959. pp. 75–80.

"De Gaulle legislateur," *Nouvelle critique*, February 1959, pp. 7–16.

Debbasch, Charles, "Les Ordonnances de l'Article 38 dans la constitution du 4 octobre 1958," *Semaine juridique*, May 30, 1962, no. 1701, 8 pp.

Debré, Michel, "L'Autorité gouvernementale," *Jeune Patron*, May 1965, pp. 35–40.
Debré, Michel, "The Constitution of 1958, Its Raison d'Etre and How It Evolved," pp. 11–24, in William G. Andrews and Stanley Hoffmann, eds., *The Fifth Republic at Twenty*, SUNY Press, Albany, N.Y., 1981, 521 pp.
Debré, Michel, "L'Elaboration de la Constitution de 1958," *Espoir: Revue de l'Institut Charles de Gaulle*, no. 3, 1973, pp. 18–23.
Debré, Michel, "La nouvelle constitution," *Revue française de science politique*, March 1959, 7–29.
Delion, André G., "Les conseils et comités interrministériels," *A.J.D.A.*, June 1975, 268–276.
Dénis, Nicholas, "L'Application des Nouvelles Règles de la Procédure Parlementaire Establies par la Constitution de 1958," *Revue française de science politique*, December 1960, 899–911.
Dickschat, Siegfried, "L'Article 38 de la Constitution et la loi d'habitation du 22 juin 1967," *Revue du droit public*, July 1968, pp. 837–71.
Drago, Roland, "L'Etat d'urgence . . . et les libertés publiques," *Revue du droit public*, July/September 1955, 670–705.
Dumard, J., "Evolution de la consommation alimentaire des français de 1950 à 1960," *Paysans*, October/November 1962, 27–46.
Dussaife, Jean-Pierre, "Le Parlement face à la reforme des taxes sur le chiffre d'affaires," *Revue française de science politique*, June 1966, 521–531.
Duverger, Maurice, "Réformer le régime," *Le Monde*, April 12, 13, 1956.
Duverger, Maurice, "Les institutions de la cinquième République," *Revue française de science politique*, March 1959, 101–134.
Ebrard, Pierre, "L'Article 38 de la Constitution du 4 octobre 1958 et la Ve République," *Revue du droit public*, March/April 1969, 259–304.
Farkas, Jean-Pierre, "Comment l'Elysée gouverne," *Paris-Match*, January 19, 1974, 31–34, 75.
Gabilly, Marcel, "La Saison des grands commis," *Revue de Paris*, February 1959, 128–136.
Gilbert-Jules, Jean, "Le Problème de la révision de la Constitution," *Revue politique des idées et des institutions*, December 15, 1957, 585–597.
Goguel, François, "Vers une nouvelle orientation de la révision constitutionnelle," *Revue française de science politique*, July-September 1956, 493–507.
Gonod, Michel, "Le petit monde de l'Elysée", *Le Spectacle du monde*, August 1965, 22–25.
Gooch, R.K., "The Government and Politics of France," in James Shotwell, ed., *Governments of Continental Europe*, Macmillan, New York, 1940, 1092 pp.
Grangé, Jean, "La Fixation de l'ordre du jour des Assemblées parlementaires," in R.E. Guichard-Ayoub, C. Roig, and Jean Grangé, *Etudes sur le Parlement de la Ve République*, PUF, Paris, 1965, 294 pp.
Groux, Jean, "Les Domaines réspectifs de la loi et du règlement d'après la constitution de 1958," *Notes et Etudes documentaires*, July 28, 1962, 50 pp.
Hamon, Léo and Jacques Vaudiaux, "Vie et droit parlementaire," *Revue du droit public*, September-October 1967, 893–948.
Hamon, Léo, "Les domaines de la loi et du règlement á la récherche d'une frontière," *Recueil Dalloz, Chroniques*, 1960, 253–260.
Harrison, Martin, "The French Experience of Exceptional Powers: 1961," *Journal of Politics*, February 1963, 139–158.
Hervé, Alain, "Comment va l'église en France?" *Realités*, August 1961, 66–75.
Hoffmann, Stanley H., "The French Constitution of 1958: The Final Text and its Prospects," *American Political Science Review*, June 1959, pp. 332–57.
Homont, André, "Les services centraux auprès de la Présidence de la République," *Jurisclasseur administratif*, fasc. 115 para. 5, 1964.

King, Jerome B., "France: The Canal Affair and the OAS Cases," in Ronald F. Bunn, and William G. Andrews, eds., *Politics and Civil Liberties in Europe*, Van Nostrand, Princeton, N.J., 1967, 222 pp.

Kirchheimer, Otto, "Decree Powers and Constitutional Law in France Under the Third Republic," *American Political Science Review*, 34, no. 6, December 1940, 1104-1123.

Lavoff, Dimitri-Georges, "Les Commissions de l'Assemblée nationale sous la Cinquième République," *Revue du droit public*, November/December 1971, 1429-1465.

L'Huillier, Jean L., "La Délimitation des domaines de la loi et du réglement dans la constitution du 4 octobre 1958," *Recueil Dalloz. Chronqiue*, 1959, 173-178.

Liet-Vaux Georges, "La Loi-Cadre sur la construction et les principes démocratiques," *Gazette du Palais*, 1957.

M.M., "Differentes conceptions de la notion loi-cadre," *Revue pratique de droit administratif. Actualité*, September 1957.

Maisl, Herbert, "Les Groupes parlementaires à l'Assemblée nationale: Bilan des deux premières années de la quatrième législature juillet 1968-decembre 1969," *Revue du droit public*, July/August 1970, 1005-1033.

Malleville, M., "L'Application de la loi du 17 août 1948", *Etudes et documents*, No. 8, 1954.

Marcilhacy, Pierre, "De l'enfantement d'une Constitution," *Revue politique des idées et des Institutions*, September 1958, 421-425.

Marcilhacy, Pierre, "Pour oeuvrer durablement, adoptons d'abord les institutions," *Revue politique et parlementaire*, February 1964, 7-11.

Meynaud, Jean and Alain Lancelot, "Groupes de pression et politique du logement," *Revue française de science politique*, December 1958, pp. 821-860.

Mollet, Guy, "Les institutions a l'épreuve des élections," *Revue politique et Parlementaire* no. 838, 1973.

Montané de la Roque, P., "L'Article 38 de la Constitution du 4 octobre 1958 et la loi des pouvoirs speciaux du 4 février 1960," *Mélanges offerts à Jacques Maury*, Dalloz & Sirey, Paris, II: 209-10.

Nicholas, Barry, "*Loi, Règlement*, and Judicial Review in the Fifth Republic," *Public Law*, Autumn 1970, 251-276.

Noël, Léon, "Ministres et deputés," *Revue française de science politique*, April 1968, 213-29.

"Les Ordonnances de la loi du 22 juin 1967," *Chambre d'agriculture*, October 15, 1967, 48 pp., November 1, 1967, 36 pp., and December 15, 1967, 56 pp.

Passeron, André, "La Maison civile du président de la République", *Le Monde*, October 25, 1967.

Pelloux, Robert, "La nouvelle Constitution de la France," *Recueil Dalloz, Chroniques*, 1946.

Pickles, William, "Special Powers in France: Article 16 in Practice," *Public Law*, London, Spring 1963, 23-50.

Platone, François, "Le Conténu des débats parlementaires sous la cinquième République." *Revue française de science politique*, February, 1970, 93-104.

Quermonne, Jean-Louis, "La Réforme de structure des territoires d'outre-mer et des territories associés selon la loi-cadre du 23 juin 1956," *Recueil Dalloz, Chroniques*, 1957, 5-12.

Ramadier, Paul, "Refléxions sur le project constitutionnel," *Points de vues et controverses*, suppl. to August 1958.

Reynaud, Paul, "La Malaise constitutionnelle," *Revue de Paris*, June 1960, 5-13.

Silvera, Victor, "De quelques refléxions sur certains aspects de la stabilité gouvernementale et de l'exercice de l'action administrative sous la Ve République", *Actualité juridique (Droit administratif)*, Feb., 1967, no. 2, 78-82.

Silvera, Victor, "La Structure du huitième gouvernement de la Vème République," *Revue administrative*, September/October 1972, 484-492.

Silvera, Victor, "La Structure du septième gouvernement de la Vème République," *Revue administrative*, July/August 1969, 444-452.

Silvera, Victor, "Vie de la Présidence et des Ministères du 16 juin au 15 août 1969," *Revue administrative*, July/August 1969, 474-477.

Stillmunkes, Pierre, "La classification les actes ayant force de loi en droit public français," *Revue du droit public*, March/April 1964, 261-292.

Suleiman, Ezra N., "Presidential Government in France," pp. 94-138, in Richard Rose and Ezra N. Suleiman, eds., *Presidents and Prime ministers*, American Enterprise Institute, Washington, D.C., 1980, 347 pp.

Tavernier, Yves and Gaston Rimareix, "L'Elaboration et la vote de la Loi complementaire à la Loi d'Orientation Agricole," *Revue française de science politique*, 1963, no. 2, 389-425.

Trnka, Henri, "La Commission Mixte Paritaire," *Revue du droit public*, May-June 1963, 477-534.

Trnka, Henri, "Evolution de la procédure de la Commission Mixte Paritaire au cours de la second législature de la Cinquiéme République," *Revue du droit public*, July-August 1967, 739-770.

Vedel, Georges, "Pour un éxécutif élu par la nation," *Revue politique des idées et des institutions*, November 30, 1956, 577-607.

Viansson-Ponté, Pierre, "Les Pouvoirs Paralléles," *L'Evénement*, March 1966, 25-31.

Vincent, François, "De l'inutilité de l'article 34 dans la constitution du 4 octobre 1958," *Actualité juridique*, November 1965, 546-76.

Wahl, Nicholas, "Aux origines de la Nouvelle Constitution." *Revue française de science politique*, March 1959, 30-66.

Wahl, Nicholas, "The French Constitution of 1958: II. The Initial Draft and Its Origins," *American Political Science Review*, June 1959, 358-382.

Waline, Marcel, "Note pratique sur la publication des travaux préparatoiries de la Constitution," *Revue du droit public*, January/February 1960, 83-84.

Warlin, Germain, "Le Domaine législatif et la domaine règlementaire dans la coûtume constitutionnelle française," *Annals de la Faculté de Droit* (Istanbul) 1970, 51-87.

Warlin, Germain, "Le domaine législatif et le domaine règlementaire dans la jurisprudence actuelle," *Annals de la Faculté de Droit* (Istanbul) 1969, 1ff., 11-20.

Books and Pamphlets

Alexandre, Philippe, *Le Duel de Gaulle Pompidou*, Grasset, Paris, 1970, 420 pp.

Alexandre, Phlippe, *Exécution d'un homme politique*, Grasset, Paris, 1973, 298 pp.

Ameller, M., *Les questions, instrument de contrôle parlementaire*, LGDJ, Paris, 1964, 227 pp.

Andrews, William G., *French Politics and Algeria*, Appleton-Century-Crofts, New York, 1962, 217 pp.

Arné, Serge, *Le Président du conseil des ministres sous la IVe République*, Pichon and Durand-Auzias, Paris, 1962, 462 pp.

Aron, Raymond, *France-The New Republic*, Oceana, New York, 1960, 114 pp.

Auriol, Vincent, *Journal du Septennat, 1953-1954*, Colin, Paris, 1970, 2 vols.

Avril, Pierre, *Les Français et leur Parlement*, Casterman, Paris, 1972, 145 pp.

Avril, Pierre, *Le Régime politique de la Ve République*, 2nd. ed., LGDJ, Paris, 1967, 437 pp.

Avril, Pierre, *Le régime politique de la Ve république*, LGDJ, Paris, 1967, 398 pp.

Azar, Antoine, *Génèse de la Constitution du 4 Octobre 1958*, LGDJ, Paris, 1961, 284 pp.

Baecque, Francis de, *L'Administration centrale de la France*, Colin, Paris, 1973, 39 pp.
Baillou, Jean and Pierre Pelletier, *Les Affaires Etrangères*, PUF, Paris, 1962, 378 pp.
Barthelémy, Joseph, and Paul Duez, *Traité de droit constitutionnel*, Dalloz, Paris, 1933 ed., 955 pp.
Barthelémy, Joseph, *Essai sur le travail parlementaire et le système des commissions*, Delagrave, Paris, 1934, 373 pp.
Bastid-Burdeau, Génevière, *La Génése de l'initiative législative: Un cas: l'Agriculture 1958–1968*, PUF, Paris, 1973, 107 pp.
Beaujeu-Garnier, Jacqueline, *La Population française*, Colin, Paris, 1969, 248 pp.
Belorgey, Gérard, *Le Gouvernement et l'administration de la France*, Colin, Paris, 1967, 451 pp.
Bertrand, Alphonse, *Les Origines de la Troisième République (1871–1876)*, Perrin, Paris, 1911, 377 pp.
Boulard, Fernand, *Premiers itinéraires en sociologie réligieuses*, Les editions ouvrières Economie et Humanisme, Paris, 1954, 156 pp.
Bromberger, Merry, *Le destin secret de Georges Pompidou*, Fayard, Paris, 1965, 349 pp.
Brouillet, Alain, *Le Droit d'amendement dans la Constitution de la Ve République*, PUF, Paris, 1973, 159 pp.
Bryce, James, *Modern Democracies*, Macmillan, London, 1921, 2 vols.
Buron, Robert, *Le plus beau des métiers*, Plon, Paris, 1963, 253 pp.
Calvet, Henri, *La Société française contemporaine*, Fernand, Paris, 1956, 380 pp.
Caron, François, *An Economic History of Modern France*, Columbia U.P., New York, 1979, 384 pp.
Cercler, René, *Problèmes agricoles*, Ed. Internationales, Paris, 1948, 238 pp.
Chandernagor, André, *Un parlement: pour quoi faire?* Gallimard, Paris, 1967, 186 pp.
Charlot, Jean, *Repertoire des publications des partis politiques français 1944–67*, Colin, Paris, 1970, 245 pp.
Chase, Eugene P., *et al.*, *Democratic Governments of Europe*, Nelson, New York, 1937, 520 pp.
Chatelain, Jean, *La Nouvelle constitution et le régime politique de la France*, Berger-Levrault, Paris, 1958, 482 pp.
Chenot, Bernard, *Etre ministre*, Plon, Paris, 1967, 173 pp.
Chronique des jours moroses 1967–1970, Presses de la Cité, 1971.
Claude, Henri, *Gaullisme et grand capital*, Eds. sociales, Paris, 1960, 224 pp.
Cotteret, Jean-Marie, *Le pouvoir législatif en France*, LGDJ, Paris, 1962, 191 pp.
Couve de Murville, Maurice, *Une politique étrangère, 1958–1969*, Plon, Paris, 1971, 499 pp.
Crossman, Richard H.S., *The Diaries of a Cabinet Minister*, Holt, Rinehart & Winston, New York, 1976–78, 3 vols.
Crossman, Richard H. S., *The Myths of Cabinet Government*, Harvard University Press, Cambridge, Mass., 1972, 126 pp.
Debbasch, Charles, *La France de Pompidou*, PUF, Paris, 1974, 324 pp.
Debré, Jean-Louis, *Les Idées constitutionnelles du général de Gaulle*, LGDJ, Paris, 1974, 461 pp.
Debré Michel, *Refaire une démocratie, un état, un pouvoir*, Plon, Paris, 1958, 79 pp.
Debré, Michel, *Une certaine idée de la France*, Fayard, Paris, 1972, 307 pp.
Debré, Michel, and Emmanuel Monnick, *Refaire la France*, Plon, Paris, 1945, 176 pp., (under pseudo. Jacquier Brière.).
Debré, Michel, and Jean-Louis Debré, *Le Pouvoir politique*, Seghers, Paris, 1977, 159 pp.
Debré, Jean-Louis, *La Constitution de la Ve République*, PUF, Paris, 1975, 340 pp.
Decaumont, Françoise, *La Présidence de Georges Pompidou: Essai sur le régime présidentialiste Français*, Economica, Paris, 1979, 302 pp.
Delvolve, Pierre, and Henri Leguilons, *Le Contrôle parlementaire sur la politique économique et budgétaire*, PUF, Paris, 1964, 250 pp.
Drachkovitch, Milorad M., ed., *French Fifth Republic*, University of California, Berkeley, 1960, 127 pp.

Dubreule, René and Jean Courtassol, eds., *La France Blessée et renaissante*, Temps que passe, n.d., Tourcoing.

Duguit, Léon, *Manuel de droit constitutionnel*, Boccard, Paris, 1918, 589 pp.

Dulong, Claude, *L'Elysée au Temps de Charles de Gaulle*, Hachette, Paris, 265 pp.

Dupeux, Georges, *La Société française 1789–1960*, Colin, Paris, 3rd ed., 1964, 295 pp.

Duverger, Maurice, *La Cinquième République*, PUF, Paris, 1959, 323 pp.

Emden, Cecil S., *The People and the Constitution*, 2nd ed., Oxford University Press, London, 1956, 339 pp.

Esmein, A., and Henry Nezard, *Elements de droit constitutionnel française et comparé*, Sirey, Paris, 1921, 2 vols. 600 and 677 pp.

Fauvet, Jacques, and Jean Planchais, *La Fronde des Généraux*, Arthaud, Paris, 1961, 274 pp.

Favoreu, Louis, and Loïc Philip, *Les Grandes Décisions du Conseil Constitutionnel*, Sirey, Paris, 1975, 442 pp.

Ferniot, Jean, *De Gaulle et le 13 Mai*, Plon, Paris, 1965, 492 pp.

Finer, Herman, *The Theory and Practice of Modern Government*, Dial, New York, 1934, 918 pp.

Foster, Charles R., ed., *Nations Without a State*, Praeger, New York, 1980, 215 pp.

Fourastié, Jean, and Jean-Paul Courthéoux, *L'Economie française dans le monde*, PUF, Paris, 1967, 128 pp.

La France est-elle encore catholique?, Les Presses d'aujourd'hui, Paris, 1954, 56 pp.

Frears, J.R., *France in the Giscard Presidency*, Allen & Unwin, London, 1981, 224 pp.

Freedman, C.E., *The Conseil d'Etat in Modern France*, Columbia University Press, New York, 1961, 205 pp.

Galante, Pierre, *The General!*, Random House, New York, 1968, 242 pp.

Gaulle, Charles de, *Discours et messages*, Plon, Paris, 1970, 5 vols.

Gaulle, Charles de, *War Memoirs*, Viking, New York, 1955–1960, 3 vols.

Goguel, Francois, *Le Travail Parlementaire*, PUF, Paris, 1955, 200 pp.

Gooch, R.K., *The French Parliamentary Committee System*, Archon Books. n.p., 1969 (reprint of 1935 ed.,), 259 pp.

Gorce, Paul-Marie de la, *Apogée et mort de la IVe République*, Grasset, Paris, 1979, 616 pp.

Guichard, Olivier, *Amenager la France*, Laffont, Paris, 1964.

Guichard, Olivier, *Mon Général*, Grasset, Paris, 1980, 464 pp.

Guichard, Olivier, Un chemin tranquille, Flammarion, Paris, 1975, 214 pp.

Hayward, Jack, *The One and Indivisible French Republic*, Norton, New York, 1973, 306 pp.

Les Héritiers du général, Denoël, Paris, 1969, 235 pp.

Hermens, Ferdinand A., *The Fifth Republic*, University of Notre Dame, South Bend, Ind., 1960, 87 pp.

Hoffmann, Stanley, *et al.*, *In Search of France*, Harvard University Press, Cambridge, Mass., 1963, 443 pp.

Institut français des Sciences administratives, *Les Superstructures des administrations centrales*, Ed. Cujas, Paris, 1973, 367 pp.

Irving, R.E.M., *Christian Democracy in France*, Allen & Unwin, London, 1973, 308 pp.

Langlois-Meurinne, Robert, *Le Premier ministre dans l'administration française*, Faculty of Law Thesis, Paris 1965.

Laponce, J.A., *The Government of the Fifth Republic*, University of California Press, Berkeley and Los Angeles, 1961, 415 pp.

Le Roy, Pierre, *L'Avenir de l'agriculture française*, PUF, Paris, 1972, 126 pp.

Le Troquer, André, *La Parole est à André Le Troquer*, La Table Ronde, Paris, 1962, 246 pp.

Leleu, Claude, *Géographie des élections françaises depuis 1936*, PUF, Paris, 1971, 353 pp.

Lidderdale, W.S., *The Parliament of France*, Hansard, London, 1951, 296 pp.

Luchaire, François, and Gérard Conac, eds., *La Constitution de la république française*, Economica, Paris, 1979, 2 vols.

Luchaire, François, "La Responsabilité du Gouvernement devant le Parlement," *Notes et Etudes Documentaires*, 781, no. 2, May 22, 1961, 159 pp.

Marcridis, Roy C., Bernard E. Brown, *The De Gaulle Republic: Quest for Unity*, Dorsey, Homewood, Ill., 1960, 400 pp.

Maillet, Pierre, *La Croissance économique*, PUF, Paris, 1972, 128 pp.

Marcilhacy, Pierre, *Les Chouans de la liberté*, Nouvelles editions latines, Paris, 1963, 179 pp.

Martin-Pannetier, Andrée, *Institutions et vie Politique Françaises de 1789 à nos jours*, LGDJ, Paris, 1971, 226 pp.

Martin, Marcel, ed., *Les Institutions Politiques de la France*, La Documentation française, Paris, 1959, 532 pp.

Massot, Jean, *La Présidence de la République en France*, La Documentation française, Paris, 1977, 234 pp.

Mendras, Henri, *Sociologie de la campagne française*, PUF, Paris, 1971, 124 pp.

Michelet, Edmond, *La querelle de la fidelité*, Fayard, Paris, 1971, 189 pp.

Middleton,W.L., *The French Political System*, Dutton, New York, 1933, 296 pp.

Moch, Jules, *Rencontres avec de Gaulle*, Plon, Paris, 1971, 406 pp.

Mollet Guy, *Les Chances du socialisme. Réponse à la société industrielle*, Fayard, Paris, 1968, 138 pp.

Mollet, Guy, *Quinze ans après: 1958-1973*, Michel, Paris, 1973, 168 pp.

Mollet, Guy, *13 Mai 1958-13 Mai 1962*, Plon, Paris, 244 pp.

Mottin, Jean, *Histoire politique de la presse 1944-1949*, Ed. Bilans Hebdomadaires, Paris, 1949, 189 pp.

Noël, Léon, *Comprendre de Gaulle*, Plon, Paris, 1972, 296 pp.

Noël, Léon, *L'Avenir du Gaullisme*, Plon, Paris, 1973, 110 pp.

Ogg, F. A., *European Governments and Politics*, Macmillan, New York, 1939, 936 pp.

L'Organisation du Travail du gouvernement et les services du premier ministre, La documentation française, Paris, September 1972, n.p.

Pado, Dominique, *Les 50 jours d'Alain Poher*, Denoël, Paris, 1969, 305 pp.

Parodi, Jean-Luc, *Les Rapports entre le législatif et l'éxéctuif sous la Ve République*, 2nd. ed., Colin, Paris, 1972, 325 pp.

Le parlementarisme peut-il être limité sans être annihilé, Association française de science politique, Paris, 1965, 37 pp.

Passeron, André, *De Gaulle 1958-1969*, Bordas, Paris, 1972, 319 pp.

Passeron, André, *De Gaulle Parle*, Plon, Paris, 1962, 1966, 2 vols.

Paul, Harry W., *The Second Ralliement: The Rapprochement between Church and State in France in the Twentieth Century*, Catholic University Press, Washington, 1967, 234 pp.

Petot, Jean, *Les Grandes étapes du régime républicain français 1792-1969*, Cujas, Paris, 1970, 842 pp.

Pilleul, Gilbert, ed., *"l'Entourage" et de Gaulle*, Plon, Paris, 1979, 385 pp.

Pisani, Edgard, *Le Général indivis*, Albin Michel, Paris, 1974, 320 pp.

Poincaré, Raymond, *How France is Governed*, T. Fisher Unwin, London, 1913, 375 pp.

Prélot, Marcel, *La Nouvelle constitution*, Le Centurion, Paris, 1958, 191 pp.

Quermonne, Jean-Louis, *Le gouvernement de la France sous la Ve République*, Dalloz, Paris, 1980, 682 pp.

Rappard, Wiliam E., *Source Book on European Governments*, Van Nostrand, New York, 1937, 832 pp.

Rémond, René, *et al. La Démocratie à Refaire*, Les editions ouvrières, Paris, 1963, 288 pp.

Reynaud, Jean-Daniel, *Les syndicats en France*, Colin, Paris, 1963, 290 pp.

Reynaud, Paul, *Et après*, Plon, Paris, 1964, 205 pp.

Rossiter, Clinton L., *Constitutional Dictatorship: Crisis Government in the Modern Democracies*, Princeton University Press, Princeton, N.J., 1948, 322 pp.

Rouanet, Anne and Pierre, *Les Trois derniers chargrins du général de Gaulle*, Grasset, Paris, 1980, 487 pp.

Rouanet, Pierre, *Pompidou*, Grasset, Paris, 1969, 315 pp.

Sait, Edward M., *Government and Politics of France*, World, New York, 1920, 478 pp.

Serant, Paul, *La France des Minorités*, Laffont, Paris, 1965, 411 pp.

Sharp, Walter Rice, *The Government of the French Republic*, Van Nostrand, New York, 1938, 373 pp.

Sibert, Marcel, *La Constitution de la France du 4 septembre 1879 au 9 Août 1955*, Pedone, Paris, 1946, 472 pp.

Soustelle, Jacques, *L'Espérance Trahie*, Ed. de l'Alma, Paris, 1962, 328 pp.

Soubeyrol, Jacques, *Les Décrets-Lois sous la Quatrième République*, University of Bordeaux, Bordeaux, 1955, 232 pp.

Soustelle, Jacques, *Vingt-huit ans de Gaullisme*, Ed. J'ai lu, Paris, 1971, 433 pp.

Sudreau, Pierre, *L-Enchainement*, Plon, Paris, 1967, 310 pp.

Thomson, David, *Democracy in France Since 1870*, 4th ed., Oxford University Press, New York, 1964, 346 pp.

Tint, Herbert, *French Foreign Policy Since the Second World War*, Weidenfeld and Nicolson, London, 1972, 273 pp.

Tournoux, J.R., *Secrets d'Etat*, Press Pocket, Paris, 1960, 447 pp.

Tournoux, J.R., *Carnets secrets de la politique*, Plon, Paris, 1958, 177 pp.

Tournoux, J.R., *La Tragédie du général*, Plon, Paris, 1967, 697 pp.

Tournoux, Raymond, *Le Feu et la cendre*, Plon, Paris, 1979, 379 pp.

Tournoux, Raymond, *Journal secret: Une année pas comme les autres*, Plon, Paris, 1975, 342 pp.

Tournoux, Raymond, *Le Tourment et la fatalité*, Plon, Paris, 1974, 474 pp.

Tricot, Bernard, *Les Sentiers de la Paix*, Plon, Paris, 1972, 443 pp.

Trotabas, Louis, *Constitution et gouvernment de la France*, Colin, Paris, 1930, 213 pp.

Vedel, Georges, *Manuel élémentaire de droit constitutionnel*, Sirey, Paris, 1949, 616 pp.

Venner, Dominique, *Guide de la politique*, Balland, Paris, 1972, 447 pp.

Verrier, Patrice, *Les Services de la présidence de la république*, PUF, Paris, 1971, 96 pp.

Viansson-Ponté, Pierre, *Après de Gaulle Qui?* Seuil, Paris, 1968, 284 pp.

Viansson-Ponté, Pierre, *Les Gaullistes: Rituel et Annuaire*, Seuil, Paris, 1963, 190 pp.

Viansson-Ponté, Pierre, *Histoire de la république gaullienne*, Fayard, Paris, 1970, 2 vols.

Viansson-Ponté, Pierre, *Les Politiques*, Calmann-Levy, Paris, 1967, 276 pp.

Voisset, Michèle, *L'Article 16 de la Constitution du 4 octobre 1958*, LGDJ, Paris, 1969, 437 pp.

Wahl, Nicholas, *The Fifth Republic*, Random House, New York, 1959, 130 pp.

Williams, Philip M., *Crisis and Compromise*, Longmans, London, 1964, 546 pp.

Williams, Philip M., *The French Parliament 1958-1967*, Allen & Unwin, London, 1968, 136 pp.

Williams, Philip M., and Martin Harrison, *De Gaulle's Republic*, Longmans, New York, 1960, 279 pp.

Index

289

Bruyneel, Robert, 31, 241, 244–245; constitutional views, 31
Bryce, James, 272
Budget, Secretary of State for, 63; constitutional provisions for State, 10, 13, 27, 48; enactment by ordinance of 192–193, 197
Budgets, 42, 110, 130–131, 139, 141–143, 148, 150, 154, 159, 162, 166, 171, 179, 185–186, 189–190, 192, 194, 196, 236, 273, 277
Bundestag, 224–225, 232
Bunn, Ronald, F., 270
Burdeau, Georges, 248, 265
Burin des Roziers, Etienne, 75, 79, 250, 254
Buron, Robert, 14, 30, 95, 243, 247, 251–252; constitutional views, 30
CCC (Consultative Constitutional Commission), 4, 7–9, 11, 15–24, 106–108, 110–111, 115, 133–134, 160–161, 164–165, 172–173, 177, 179, 181–183, 185, 187–189, 192–193, 195–196, 235–236, 244, 247, 258; formation of, 16–17; members of, constitutional views, 31; work of, 16–20
CD (Democratic Center), PDM (Progress and Modern Democracy), 148–149, 187
CDU (Christian Democratic Union) (Germany), 225
CFTC (French Confederation of Christian Workers), 15–16, 207
CGC (General Confederation of White Collar Workers), 17
CGPME (General Confederation of Small and Medium-Sized Enterprises), 15
CNPF (National Council of French Management), 96
Cabinet (staff), 70
Cabinet Council, Cabinet, 1, 3, 5, 10–11, 14, 20–21, 23, 25, 28, 30, 39–43, 48, 55–56, 66, 106, 111, 123, 159, 161, 165, 172–173, 179, 181, 191–192, 236–237, 242, 249; before 1958, 39–40; constitutional status of, 40; constitutional work of 1958 of, 11; meetings of, contents of, 42; schedule of, 41; style and form of, 36, 42
Callaghan, James, 222
Calvet, Henri, 278, 280
Cameroons, 130
Campenon-Bernard, 96
Capitant, René, 147, 241–242, 263
Carnot, Sidi, 89
Caron, François, 278
Carrère, Gilbert, 75
Cassin, René, 11–12, 21–22, 29, 104
Castex, Anne, 75

Catalans, 226
Catholic Church, 206–207, 225
Catroux, Diomède, 3–4
Catroux, General Georges, 115
Censure, motions of, 18, 27, 37, 110, 138–139, 147–150, 154, 160, 163, 166–167, 171, 174, 191–192, 227
Centrists, *see* CD
Cercler, René, 278
Chaban-Delmas, Jacques, 41, 43, 45, 54, 61, 77–78, 80–81, 83–86, 88, 91–93, 116, 162, 173, 257
Chadeau, André, 85
Chaintron, Jean, 241
Chalandon, Albin, 54, 96, 257
Chamaulte, 241
Chamber of Deputies, 91–22, 95, 122–123, 163–164, 172, 179–180, 194, 227, 262; Budget Committee of, 122; Conference of Presidents of, 164; President of, 122
Chamberlain, Austen, 221
Chamberlain, Neville, 221
Chambrun, Charles Pineton de, 95, 97, 263
Champeix, Marcel, 241, 245
Chancellor (German), 222–225, 233, 280
Chandernagor, André, 17, 30, 145, 241, 247, 268; constitutional views, 30
Charbonnel, Jean, 94
Charlot, Jean, 279
Charpentier, Jean, 263
Chase, Eugene P., 274–275
Chasseguet, Gérard, 79, 81, 257
Chateau de la Celle-St. Cloud, 10–12, 243
Chatelain, Jean, 248
Châtenet, Pierre, 95
Chazelle, René, 17
Chenot, Bernard, 21, 244, 252
Chief of State, 13, 18, 22, 25–29, 42, 50, 253
Chiefs of staff, military, 57–58, 70–72
Chirac, Jacques, 54, 257
Christen, Xavier de, 88
Church schools, State aid to, 162
Churchill, Winston, 222
Civil rights, public liberties, 103–107, 109, 114, 117, 128, 130, 139, 235–236
Civil service, 130, 139–140, 144
Civil Service, Minister of State for, 63
Clemenceau, Georges, 133
Clerical quarrel attenuated, 205–206
Clermont-Tonnerre, Antoine de, 88
Clostermann, Pierre, 241
Clynes, J. R., 221
Cohesive Society, 208, 213–216, 218–219, 227–228, 232

Index of References to Articles of 1958 Constitution